camus and sartre

camus & sartre

the story of a friendship and the quarrel that ended it

ronald aronson

the university of chicago press
chicago and london

The University of Chicago Press, Chicago 60637
The University of Chicago Press, Ltd., London

Paperback edition 2005
Printed in the United States of America
13 12 11 10 09 08 07 06 05 3 4 5
ISBN: 0-226-02796-1 (cloth)
ISBN: 0-226-00024-9 (paperback)

Library of Congress Cataloging-in-Publication Data

Aronson, Ronald, 1938–
Camus & Sartre : the story of a friendship and the quarrel that ended it / Ronald Aronson.
p. cm.
Includes bibliographical references and index.
ISBN 0-226-02796-1 (alk. paper)
1. Sartre, Jean Paul, 1905– . 2. Camus, Albert, 1913–1960.
I. Title: Camus and Sartre. II. Title.
B2430.S34 A83 2003
194—dc21 2003012780

♾ The paper used in this publication meets the minimum requirements of the American National Standard for Information Sciences—Permanence of Paper for Printed Library Materials, ANSI Z39.48–1992.

for phyllis

contents

acknowledgments

I thank Steve Golin and Geri Thoma for seeing the possibilities within my earlier drafts, reading them critically and sympathetically, and helping me to realize this book. Francis Jeanson and I discussed his role as "the third man in the story" during three intense days in July 2001, in Claouey, France. I am indebted to him for his generosity and for the hospitality he and his wife Christiane Phillip showed to Phyllis and me. Michel Rybalka read the entire manuscript with unmatched attention to both the large picture and the small. With his usual good cheer and energy, Adrian van den Hoven checked my translations, corrected many infelicities of thought and language, and shared his ideas about the book's concluding section.

Jean-Pierre Boulé, Milt Tambor, and Linda Lieberman also read the manuscript and made many useful suggestions. Ira Konigsberg was there when I needed him, reading key chapters and talking through important last-minute questions with me. Other people who read all or part of the book and who made useful suggestions or encouraged the project, or both, include Judith Ellis, David Drake, David Schweickart, Anson Rabinbach, and Richard Gull. I had helpful discussions with many people, including Ernst Benjamin, Walter Skakoon, Eric Bockstael, and Pamela Aronson. Robert Deneweth, Frank Koscielski, Karen McDevitt, and Charles Rooney read the proofs with me. At key moments Carole Keller worked tirelessly with me to prepare the manuscript. Two talented young members of the excellent staff at the University of Chicago Press deserve special mention. As this project moved from manuscript to book, manuscript editor Russell Harper was an inexhaustible resource, guide, and problem solver. Editorial associate Elizabeth Branch Dyson frequently lent her sure literary sense and sound advice. I am grateful to all these people for making this book possible.

I also would like to thank the History Seminar at the University of Natal, Durban, and the Humanities Center at Wayne State University, as well as the Sartre Society of North America, to all of whom I presented parts of this book. In the course of working on this book I was pleased to be able to present some of my conclusions in the *Times Literary Supplement*, and some of the materials I discovered in *Dissent* and *Sartre Studies International.*

Wayne State University helped in other ways, locating and obtaining materials and granting me sabbatical leaves and travel support. It also provided an ideal setting in which to teach about the topics that eventually grew into this book, in 1992 in a graduate seminar, and in 1994 in a National Endowment for the Humanities Summer Seminar for School Teachers.

Phyllis Aronson lived with this project for over six years, sharing it as only a life partner can. From beginning to end she read drafts of every chapter, talked with me about all the issues, whether major or minor, and commented with a sure touch on the style, the language, the pace, and the tone. She deserves special thanks.

prologue

"To the Editor of *Les Temps modernes*. . . ."

"My Dear Camus: Our friendship was not easy, but I will miss it. If you end it today, that doubtless means that it had to end. Many things drew us together, few divided us. But these few were still too many. . . ."

"To the Editor": but everyone knew that this was one good friend talking to the other. "If you end it": the celebrated philosopher of freedom, placing responsibility on his friend before subjecting him to the stream of violent abuse that did in fact end the friendship.

These unforgettable words, so personal and yet so public, so authentic and yet so saturated with bad faith, signaled two simultaneous turning points, that of a personal relationship and that of a historical era. The friendship between Albert Camus and Jean-Paul Sartre was at its peak immediately after the liberation of France. Both the men and the friendship reflected the initially boundless postwar optimism. For several years and despite growing differences, their friendship weathered the postwar purges, France's colonial wars, the domestic return to politics as usual, and, above all, the growing influence of the Cold War, with its pressure to take sides. But as the Soviet-American conflict intensified, leading to the war in Korea, the middle ground, which both men had occupied together, disappeared. In the end Camus and Sartre split not only because they took opposing sides but because each became his own side's moral and intellectual leader.

In a philosophically intense and personally brutal argument, the two main voices of postwar French intellectual life publicly destroyed almost ten years of friendship. At first reluctantly and hesitantly, and then with a rush that seemed uncontrollable, Sartre and Camus also shattered their political milieu and any traces of what was once their common project of creating an independent Left.

Unlikely terrain for a major historical drama: a few densely printed articles in a Paris journal with a circulation of a little more than 10,000. The August 1952 issue of *Les Temps modernes* sold out immediately, was reprinted, and sold out again. Meanwhile, the exchange was presented in a two-page insert in the daily newspaper Camus had once edited, *Combat.* The forerunner of today's *Le Nouvel Observateur* also ran extensive excerpts from their letters. The rupture became the talk of Paris, discussed in no less than a dozen newspaper or magazine articles. Headlines included "The Sartre-Camus break is consummated" in *Samedi-Soir* and "Sartre against Camus" in *France-Illustration.* The protagonists as well as their supporters agreed that the falling-out encapsulated what Francis Jeanson, in his review of Camus's *The Rebel*, called "the burning issues of our time." As Sartre's old schoolfriend Raymond Aron pointed out, the differences contained in these articles "immediately assumed the character of a national dispute." After Camus answered Jeanson with an attack on him and Sartre, followed by Sartre's violent and Jeanson's interminable replies to Camus, Camus and Sartre never spoke to each other again.

: : :

The Sartre-Camus relationship began on Camus's side in 1938 and on Sartre's in 1942 with their enthusiastic discovery of each other's early books, followed by immediate friendship in 1943 when the two first met. Philosophically and politically akin, they talked of various collaborations and shared similar ambitions. They were often paired at the Liberation, becoming France's most celebrated writers as existentialism became a postwar cultural craze. Struggling to avoid being seen as Sartre's acolyte, Camus disavowed the label again and again, while his friend took him as the exemplar of his new theory of commitment. The two were activist-intellectuals following parallel paths—Camus as editor of *Combat*, the Resistance newspaper that had become a Paris daily; Sartre as creator and director of what immediately became France's foremost political and cultural journal, *Les Temps modernes*.

As they continued to socialize, their non-Communist leftism was strained by the beginnings of East-West polarization. The division marked by Churchill's "Iron Curtain" speech in early 1946 was brought into their circle by the arrival in Paris that fall of fiercely anti-Communist Arthur Koestler, following the French publication of his *Darkness at Noon* and *The Yogi and the Commissar*. Koestler's person and ideas placed a demand on all of them—to choose for or against Communism.

Such pressures were intensified by the events of the next few years, and marked Sartre's and Camus's writing and their evolving political positions. As earlier, a dialogue between Sartre and Camus can be discerned in their writings, neither mentioning the other by name but each formulating his thoughts in relation to the other. Still friends, though often pulled in opposing directions, they continued to work for an independent "third force" for as long as possible—which is to say, almost until the Cold War became hot and, along with their own development, finally forced a choice for or against Communism. Their friendship persisted until the very moment of the explosion. Then, estranged, they continued to argue with each other until Camus's death.

It is a riveting story. Why hasn't it been told in full before now? One or two brief accounts have been written, a handful of writers have explored the issues between Camus and Sartre, but no one has recounted the detailed story of the relationship and its end. Why is such a book still necessary today, almost fifty years after the events it describes?

One reason is that it has only recently become possible. Materials are now available—biographies, scholarly editions of texts, considered readings of various writings, detailed investigations of dozens of biographical questions and writings—that permit us to understand much more of what happened between the two men. It is now possible to turn to *this* question, of their relationship, in retrospect, and to explore beneath the veil that they, and most of their biographers, have placed over it. We will see how drawn to each other they were at first; how close and cross-fertilizing were their original paths; how they interacted with each other *on paper,* including direct and indirect comments on each other's works; how their writings treated common questions; how their political, literary, and intellectual projects overlapped; and then how the two writers began to explicitly oppose each other. Indeed, how even after their break they continued to wrestle with, respond to, and challenge each other.

But the story's telling has waited not only on the accumulation of materials. We were kept from seeing what happened between them for a more essential reason: the Cold War itself. Its demand that everyone take sides in a pitched struggle of good against evil—to which Sartre and Camus fell victim in their distinctive ways—converted their conflict into a mere morality play. If one was right, then the other had to be wrong, and the resulting story lacked nuance. No wonder no one has felt impelled to tell it in full.

As an integral part of the history of the Cold War, the Sartre-Camus relationship demanded to be seen through partisan eyes. Thus Sartre's lifelong companion, Simone de Beauvoir, writing well after the breakup, could scarcely describe Camus without judging him. A "petty tyrant" at *Combat,* this was a man given to "abstract rages" and "moralism." "Unable to compromise," he became "a more and more resolute champion of bourgeois values." Obsessed by anti-Communism, Camus had become a devotee of questionable "great principles." If Sartre's choices were right and Camus's wrong, then (as in Beauvoir's telling) the good side won and the bad side was defeated. This version prevailed throughout Sartre's and Beauvoir's lifetime. Another view surfaced with the post–Cold War reversal of opinion. According to a Camus partisan, "Sartre . . . proclaimed his alliance with the Stalinists no matter what, Camus refuse[d] to join the radical chic crowd that trucked with murderers; for this he was mocked and humiliated by the Sartreans and nearly everyone was a Sartrean then." In this rereading Communism's fall now allows us to reverse history's verdict, setting the record straight about Camus, who "had 20/20 political vision."

The problem is that living and seeing history as a morality play rules out living and seeing its ambiguities and tragedies. The term *tragedy* conveys the sense of a profound loss, and we will see that the story of Camus and Sartre ends badly both personally and historically. This is not to deny that Sartre seemed unfazed by the broken friendship at the time, or that he later made light of the relationship and the rupture. Yet in one of his most revealing later interviews, Sartre says of Camus, "He was my last good friend." This is not surprising, considering how close were some of their starting points, how parallel were their postwar missions, how easily they once seemed to negotiate their sharp differences in class background and temperament, not to mention the good times they had together. Nevertheless, lacking any other direct testimony by

Sartre, we are left to speculate what the conflict might have cost him. But there is no doubt that it powerfully affected Camus. It silenced him. It was a cloud that hovered over him during his last years. He showed pain, a sense of betrayal, and even shame at what he experienced as a public humiliation. And he returned to it hauntingly in what Sartre described, in his eulogy after Camus was killed in an automobile accident in 1960, as "perhaps the most beautiful and the least understood" of Camus's books, *The Fall.*

In using the term *tragedy* I mean to get beyond the Cold War partisanship that has colored, along with so much else, the perception of the Sartre-Camus conflict. I intend to describe both adversaries with understanding and sympathy, as well as critically. This means appreciating the fundamental legitimacy of *both sides* of their conflict. Sartre and Camus were not driven apart by individual idiosyncrasy. They split because, in Sartre's later terminology, they came to "incarnate" the world-historical conflict between two of the century's major ideological antagonists. Although Camus was never a partisan of capitalism and Sartre was never a Communist, these two antagonists wound up representing far larger forces than themselves. Each one struggled against the looming split for several years and at the same time continued to develop and respond to events in ways that made that split more likely. A historical logic animated the controversy as Sartre and Camus, eschewing the clichés of Communism and capitalism in all their sterile and self-interested bad faith, were driven to articulate the fundamental reasons why thoughtful people, intellectuals committed to the broadest possible freedom and social justice, would support or oppose Communism.

After their split a dispiriting "either/or" would prevail on the Left: supporting revolutionary movements and governments meant agreeing to ride roughshod over freedom; defending freedom meant opposing the only significant project challenging capitalism. In a deep sense, we are talking about the Left's defeat in the twentieth century, its splintering of hope. The hopes of a generation to advance toward socialism *and* freedom were to be frustrated. People were forced to make an impossible choice: between Sartre's grim dialectical realism (Communism as the only path to qualitative change, and the ugly face of such a change) and Camus's principled leftist rejection of Communism (which left him unable to identify with any significant force struggling for change). Sartre and Camus articulated the half-rights and half-wrongs, the half-truths and half-lies of what became the tragedy of the Left—not only in France but across the world—for at least the next generation.

Camus and Sartre came to insist that there were only two alternatives, reflected in their plays *The Just Assassins* and *The Devil and the Good Lord*, Camus's rebel and Sartre's revolutionary. But in choosing capitalist freedom *or* Communist socialism, they in effect chose not only against each other but against themselves. In making their choice, however they affirmed themselves and whatever the arguments, Sartre and Camus, along with their generation, also betrayed themselves and their highest values.

: : :

After their split, and to the end of their lives, each saw the other in the simplistic terms of his own chosen morality play: the only betrayal each one recognized was by his former friend. For Camus, the explosion confirmed that Sartre had never been his friend, and that politically Sartre and those around him had a taste for servitude. For Sartre, Camus stopped growing and betrayed the vital connection with his historical world that had made him so attractive during and after the war. After their spectacular break, as sometimes happens with a painful divorce, each one seemed bent on eliminating the other from his life. Camus until his death in 1960, and Sartre until his in 1980, cooperated as if in a conspiracy to erase the traces of their friendship.

Biographers and scholars of Sartre and Camus have been their accomplices. Some have drawn their relationship as brief and insignificant, looking at it primarily to anticipate its ending. After all, didn't their philosophies, temperaments, literary styles, and social origins all demonstrate that the rupture was essential, the friendship accidental? This stance seems to correspond to the law of "analysis after the event" described by Doris Lessing. Since it resulted in a break, we are tempted to focus from the start on "the laws of dissolution" of the relationship. As with a broken marriage, we fixate on the logic of the breakup, as if the two were bound to fall out and that is all that matters. Moreover, both Sartre and Camus put their whole being into the choice that broke them apart. Each man's total stake in being right fed his inability to see in their relationship anything other than the seeds of the split. This was only intensified by the stark judgments of right and wrong immediately imposed by the Cold War, and then by the disposition of writers devoted to one or the other to side with their man. Thus other biographers and scholars have been unable to look at the Sartre-Camus relationship without seeing either Sartre or Camus as being in the wrong from the start. Their early critical notes toward each other, it is said, or their paths of political commitment, or their first important writings already indicated their true colors.

Were they fated to break apart? However they came to see their friendship later, both Sartre and Camus at their best would have rejected the notion that any relationship was destined to end from the moment it began. In fact Sartre developed an extended argument against such fatalism, calling it bad faith. Both men's writings and lives demand that we read their story as each of them must have lived it—with openness toward what might happen. To appreciate the relationship in their own spirit, we must approach it with their shared sense of unpredictability, choice, freedom, and absurdity.

Doing otherwise has meant ignoring the full, rich drama of the relationship. It has left us instead with a highly skewed short story, according to which Camus and Sartre had good times briefly but not much of a friendship; they didn't influence each other; their connection was superficial and didn't last very long; and their breakup was inevitable. Even Beauvoir's account, which is as close as we can come to an "official" story—from one side at least—conforms to this pattern, indeed, sets the pattern. But searching out and trying to piece together the real story in its fascinating and painful detail means putting the relationship in the center. Once given its due, it takes on a whole set of new and different meanings. Sartre and Camus were strongly attracted to each other, affected each other deeply, were involved in and had conflicts over each other's intimate life, and remained entangled with each other long after their breakup. It was not mere rhetoric when Sartre, in his eulogy for his estranged friend, said that "being apart is just another way of being together."

: : :

Paradoxically, this Camus-Sartre biography is already a "revisionist" history simply by virtue of my attempt to tell the full story, and to do so without taking sides. My argument—first that their relationship was an important and powerful one, and second that the Cold War deformed it as it did so much else—is based on firm evidence. To understand the two men and their time required searching the archives of Camus's newspaper *Combat*, of the Communist weekly *Action*, and of the former Resistance and fellow-traveling *Les Lettres françaises*, as well as those of *l'Humanité* and *Le Monde.* There are now seven biographies, and they are essential for learning about the two men. They give us much material on the two writers' lives and interaction, including the many new personal details about Camus amassed by Olivier Todd, the privileged interviews with Sartre by John Gerassi, and Annie Cohen-Solal's insight into the Camus-Sartre sense of kinship. For all her inevitable partisanship, Beauvoir also is indispensable in her official story developed over two volumes of her memoirs, in the interviews and other information presented in Deirdre Bair's biography, and in her letters to Nelson Algren. Then, too, Beauvoir wrote a major novel about the postwar period, *The Mandarins*; collected many of Sartre's and her own letters, and gave us the 1973–75 interviews with Sartre. Sartre's 1975 interview with Michel Contat is also illuminating, and the thousands of details about Sartre assembled by Contat and Michel Rybalka are essential. I have made much use of Camus's materials faithfully assembled in Roger Quilliot's two *Pléiade* volumes, as well as Camus's three notebooks, and his letters to his teacher, Jean Grenier.

Indispensable as all these materials are, they do not give us the key to the story. My stress on the two men's importance to each other does not come from what Camus and Sartre said about their relationship in these various places, or from Beauvoir, but rather from a little-noticed primary source, one free of retrospective bias: the published writings of Sartre and Camus themselves. I don't mean only the twenty or so times they mention each other by name but also the many places where they engage with each other without naming each other, discussing major issues in the process.

Sartre and Camus lived in their writings, and their writings are the main source of the story of their relationship. From 1938 to 1960 they wrote to each other, about each other, and in response to each other. Their written interactions form some of the key moments in each man's development. Often they referred to each other directly: at first Camus reviewed Sartre's *Nausea* and *The Wall*; then Sartre analyzed *The Stranger* and *The Myth of Sisyphus*. Sometimes they spoke in code, especially after their break. Often they referred to each other in ways that require us to tease the references out of specific situations. Camus frequently argued against pro-Communist leftist intellectuals, whose leader after 1952 he considered to be Sartre. After 1952, Sartre argued against believers in nonviolence, and he took Camus as their spokesperson. Read properly, twenty years of such interactions, first in friendship and then in antagonism, tell us much about the relationship between the two. Although many other sources help narrate the Camus-Sartre biography, it is through their writings that two of the twentieth century's greatest intellectuals tell their story. It is time for us to listen.

1

first encounters

Jean-Paul Sartre and Albert Camus first met in June 1943, at the opening of Sartre's play *The Flies.* When Sartre was standing in the lobby, according to Simone de Beauvoir, "a dark-skinned young man came up and introduced himself: it was Albert Camus." His novel *The Stranger,* published a year earlier, was a literary sensation, and his philosophical essay *The Myth of Sisyphus* had appeared six months previously. The young man from Algiers was marooned in France by the war. While convalescing from an exacerbation of his chronic tuberculosis in Le Panelier, near Chambon, Camus had been cut off from his wife by the Allied conquest of French North Africa and the resulting German invasion of unoccupied France in November 1942. He wanted to meet the increasingly well-known novelist and philosopher—and now playwright—whose fiction he had reviewed years earlier and who had just published a long article on Camus's own books. It was a brief encounter. "I'm Camus," he said. Sartre immediately "found him a most likeable personality."

In November, Camus moved to Paris to start working as a reader for his (and Sartre's) publisher, Gallimard, and their friendship began in earnest. At their first get-together at the Café Flore—where Sartre and Beauvoir worked, kept warm, ate, and socialized—the three started off awkwardly. Then they started talking shop, Camus and Sartre sharing their regard for the surrealist poet Francis Ponge's *Le Parti pris des choses.* What "led to the ice being broken" between them, according to Beauvoir, was Camus's passion for the theater. Camus had led an amateur political theater troupe in Algiers. "Sartre talked of his new play [*No Exit*] and the conditions that would govern its production. Then he suggested that Camus should play the lead and stage it. Camus hesitated at first, but when Sartre pressed the point he agreed." They held a few rehearsals in Beauvoir's hotel room for what was to be a low-budget touring production. "The readiness with which Camus flung himself into this venture endeared him to us; it also hinted that he had plentiful time at his disposal. He had only recently come to Paris; he was married, but his wife had stayed behind in North Africa." Sartre was pleased with Camus's work in the role of Garcin, but his financial backer withdrew; this man's wife, who was to be showcased in *No Exit,* was arrested for suspected Resistance activity. Sartre was then offered the chance to present the play in a professional production on the Paris stage, and Camus obligingly backed out. But the friendship was cemented. "His youth and independence created bonds between us: we were all solitaries, who had developed without the aid of any 'school'; we belonged to no group or clique."

If the friendship seemed so easy at the beginning, one reason was that Sartre and Camus had already gotten to know each other in ways more important than a handshake. Avid readers, each absorbed in shaping his own ideas and styles, the young writers had read each other's books well before they met. Their reviews of each other's early writings are still among the most interesting and enthusiastic commentaries. Although not uncritical, Sartre's and Camus's first responses to each other express the literary and philosophical kinship that underlay their relationship. They also introduce us to one of the most important sites of their interaction for over twenty years—their sometimes direct, sometimes veiled, references to each other. From their first meeting to the last words they exchanged, we will find some of their most vital and charged encounters on paper.

Camus discovered Sartre in October 1938 when he read and reviewed *Nausea.* The young *pied-noir* (a Frenchman born in Algeria), was a fledgling reporter and author of a column entitled "The Reading Room" for an Algiers left-wing daily. He had published locally two small books of essays, *The Wrong Side and the Right Side* and *Nuptials,* and after abandoning a first novel had begun writing *The Stranger.* Though only in his mid-twenties, the would-be novelist wrote remarkably self-assured responses in his literary column to the new fiction being published in Paris, including Gide's *The Counterfeiters,* Nizan's *The Conspiracy,* Silone's *Bread and Wine,* Huxley's *Those Barren Leaves,* Amado's *Bahia*, and Sartre's *Nausea* and *The Wall.*

Camus's review of *Nausea* was demanding and appreciative. He was no dazzled provincial, light-years from Paris's sophistication, but a peer who deeply shared Sartre's purposes and cheered him on, only to be disappointed by what he saw at this early period as Sartre's ultimate failure. *Nausea* recounts the breakdown of the reassuring daily life of Antoine Roquentin, who is staying in a northern port city and working on a biography of a Revolution-era marquis. Roquentin feels nauseated as he experiences the absurdity normally hidden by his routines, and the truth of that absurdity appears ever more sharply as his life slowly gives way around him. It is a dazzling thought-experiment, containing some marvelous characterizations and descriptions. As Camus had told a friend several months before he wrote the review, he had "thought a lot about" the book, and it was "very close to a part of me." He led off his review by asserting that "a novel is nothing but philosophy expressed in images." In a good novel, however, the philosophy becomes one with the images. Camus gave no indication of knowing that the novelist was also a philosopher who had already published a book on the imagination in 1936 and a long article entitled "The Transcendence of the Ego" the following year. He himself had earned the *diplôme d'études supérieures* (the equivalent of a master's degree) in philosophy with a thesis on Saint Augustine and Plotinus. Sartre, he insisted, broke the balance between his novel's theories and its life. As a result, its author's "remarkable fictional gifts and the play of the toughest and most lucid mind are at the same time both lavished and squandered." Lavished: each of the book's chapters, taken by itself, "reaches a kind of perfection in bitterness and truth." Daily life in Bouville "is depicted with a sureness of touch whose lucidity leaves no room for hope." And each of Sartre's reflections on time effectively illustrated the thinking of philosophers from Kierkegaard to Heidegger. Squandered: the descriptive and the philosophical aspects of the novel "don't add up to a work of art: the passage from one to the other is too rapid, too unmotivated, to evoke in the reader the deep conviction that makes art of the novel."

Camus went on to praise Sartre's descriptions of absurdity, the sense of anguish that arises as the ordinary structures imposed on existence collapse in Antoine Roquentin's life, and his resulting nausea. Sartre's deft handling of this strange and banal subject moves with a "vigor and certainty" reminiscent of Kafka. But—and here Sartre differs from Kafka—"some indefinable obstacle prevents the reader from participating and holds him back when he is on the very threshold of consent." By this, Camus meant not only the imbalance between ideas and images but also Sartre's negativity. Sartre dwells on the repugnant features of humankind "instead of basing his reasons for despair on certain of man's signs of greatness." And the reviewer was also bothered by the "comic" inadequacy of Roquentin's final attempt to find hope in art, considering how "trivial" art is when compared with some of life's redeeming moments.

Though strongly critical, Camus appreciated Sartre's ideas and enjoyed his honesty and his capacity to break new ground. The review's closing words stress his admiration:

> This is the first novel from a writer from whom everything may be expected. So natural a suppleness in staying on the far boundaries of conscious thought, so painful a lucidity, are indications of limitless gifts. These are grounds for welcoming *Nausea* as the first summons of an original and vigorous mind whose lessons and works to come we are impatient to see.

Was this merely a reviewer's posture, a way of balancing criticism with just enough praise so as to not sound peevish? The impatient critic did not have long to wait. Less than six months later, Sartre's next book fully satisfied him. In February 1939, in reviewing Sartre's collection of stories *The Wall*, Camus enthusiastically hailed Sartre's lucidity, his portrayal of the absurdity of existence, and his depiction of characters whose freedom was useless to them. Their negativity—if anything, stronger in *The Wall* than in *Nausea*—now troubled him less. Overwhelmed by their freedom, these people could not overcome absurdity as they bumped up against their own lives. They had "no attachments, no principles, no Ariadne's thread," because they were unable to act. "From this stems both the immense interest and the absolute mastery of Sartre's stories." The reader does not know what the characters will do from one moment to the next; their author's "art lies in the detail with which he depicts his absurd creatures, the way he observes their monotonous behavior."

Camus confessed to being unable to put these stories down. They gave their reader "that higher, absurd freedom which leads the characters to their own ends." It was a useless freedom, which "explains the often overwhelming emotional impact of these pages as well as their cruel pathos." Sartre described an absurd human condition, but he refused to flinch before it. The philosophy and the images were now in balance. Camus's conclusion indicated not only his enthusiasm for the author but his sense of common purpose with a writer who,

> in his two books, has been able to get straight to the essential problem and bring it to life through his obsessive characters. A great writer always introduces his own world and its message. Sartre's brings us to nothingness, but also to lucidity. And the image he perpetuates through his characters, of a man seated amid the ruins of his life, is a good illustration of the greatness and truth of his work.

"Greatness and truth"—"*la grandeur et la vérité.*" Might Sartre have seen this tribute? On his side, all we know for certain is a literary encounter that took place in fall 1942. Discovering Camus only weeks after sending off the completed manuscript of *Being and Nothingness,* he was moved to devote a generous, detailed, 6,000-word essay to *The Stranger.* In this striking article, Sartre reads that book alongside *The Myth of Sisyphus,* the fiction in relation to the philosophy. As he writes, let us listen to the different voices:

> The absurd . . . resides neither in man nor in the world if you consider each separately. But since man's dominant characteristic is "being-in-the-world," the absurd is, in the end, an inseparable part of the human condition. Thus, the absurd is not, to begin with, *the object of a mere idea; it is revealed to us in a doleful illumination.* "Getting up, tram, four hours of work, meal, sleep, and Monday, Tuesday, Wednesday, Thursday, Friday, Saturday, in the same routine . . . ," and then, suddenly, "the seeing collapses," and we find ourselves in a state of hopeless lucidity.

Here Sartre is approvingly summarizing and quoting from a passage near the beginning of *The Myth of Sisyphus,* where Camus lays out his basic ideas. Surprisingly, the quoted passage sounds like Camus's paraphrase of none other than Roquentin's experience in *Nausea.* Sartre continues, in apparent agreement with Camus: "If we are able to refuse the misleading aid of religion or existential philosophies, we then possess certain basic, obvious facts: the world is chaos, a 'divine equivalence born of anarchy'; tomorrow does not exist, since we all die. 'In a universe suddenly divested of illusions and lights, man feels an alien, a stranger.' "

Turning directly to the context in *The Myth of Sisyphus* where this sentence occurs, and reading from this point forward, we are reminded of *Nausea*: "At any streetcorner the feeling of absurdity can strike a man in the face." And on the next page of *The Myth of Sisyphus* is the Sartre-like passage about daily routine collapsing, which Sartre quotes in his review. As we turn the page, Sartre's novel is mentioned explicitly: "This nausea, as a writer of today calls it, is also the absurd." Whose voice, then, is heard in the original quotation above? In a stunning reflection of kinship, Sartre enthusiastically quoted Camus—whose analysis drew upon Sartre. It is *both of their voices at one and the same time.*

Beyond this kinship, Sartre compared Camus with Kafka and Hemingway, whom he admired, and praised *The Stranger* for its "skillful construction."

> There is not a single unnecessary detail, nor one that is not returned to later on, and used in the argument. And when we close the book, we realize that it could not have had any other ending. In this world that has been stripped of its causality and presented as absurd, the smallest incident has weight. There is no single one which does not help to lead the hero to crime and capital punishment. *The Stranger* is a classical work, an orderly work, composed about the absurd and against the absurd.

The author of *Nausea* obviously admired the imaginative power of *The Stranger*. The stark simplicity of Camus's language, his ability to evoke the physical, the unforgettable descriptions of the funeral vigil, the next morning's procession, and Meursault's daily routines combine with more disturbing aspects—Meursault's lack of normal human emotion, his mindless murder of the Arab, the prosecutor's outrage at the young man's indifference toward his mother's death, his own defiance of the jury and its sense of propriety, as well as the improbability of a death sentence for a white man who has killed an Arab in Algeria—to create the great novel of French Algeria. But how did the author of *Being and Nothingness* respond to *The Myth of Sisyphus*? Having just completed one of the most original and profound philosophical constructions of the twentieth century, Sartre showed respect for the philosophical essayist who, "by virtue of the cool style of *The Myth of Sisyphus*" as well as its subject, "takes his place in the great tradition of those French moralists" regarded as Nietzsche's forerunners. "The turn of his reasoning, the clarity of his ideas, the cut of his expository style and a certain kind of solar, ceremonious and sad sombreness, all indicate a classic temperament."

Just as Sartre must have noticed that *The Stranger* came alive as fiction in ways that his own *Nausea* did not—as Camus had astutely pointed out four years earlier—so also he must have seen that for all its appeal as popular philosophizing *The Myth of Sisyphus* was the work of a dabbler in philosophy and not a systematic builder of ideas. Camus briefly dismissed existentialists such as Jaspers, Heidegger, and Kierkegaard en route to insisting that nothing could overcome life's absurdity. Sartre, on the other hand, had spent years working through the phenomenology of Heidegger and Husserl until he synthesized them in *Being and Nothingness* into a work that sought to penetrate the very nature of being. Starting with Cartesian individual consciousness, Sartre carefully described basic structures of existence, fundamental human projects, and characteristic patterns of behavior such as bad faith. By the end of the book he was poised to follow his philosophy's implications, as he did over the next several years, into virtually every aspect of existence—from daily life and politics to ethics, artistic creation, and the nature of knowledge. In *The Myth of Sisyphus,* on the other hand, starting from the premise that "the meaning of life is the most urgent of questions," Camus stayed on the terrain of experience and its frustrations rather than pursuing "the learned and classical dialectic." Thus both *The Myth of Sisyphus* and *Being and Nothingness* began with the absurd and exuded the same zeitgeist; yet they were vastly different.

Just how different is conveyed joltingly in a single, nasty "by the way": "Camus shows off a bit by quoting passages from Jaspers, Heidegger, and Kierkegaard, whom, by the way, he does not always seem to have quite understood." The philosopher, *agrégé* from the Ecole Normale Supérieure, puts down the philosophizer, *diplôme d'études supérieure* from the University of Algiers.

Perhaps this is why Camus was not thrilled by Sartre's article. In a letter to his teacher Jean Grenier, who published his own review of *The Stranger* in the very same issue of *Cahiers du Sud,* Camus reacted to Sartre on Camus:

> Sartre's article is a model of "taking apart." Of course, every creation has an instinctive element which [he] does not envision, and intelligence does not play such an important role. But in criticism this is the rule of the game, which is fine because on several points he enlightened me about what I wanted to do. I also see that most of his criticisms are fair, but why that acid tone?

Acid dissolves, after all, takes things apart. Perhaps the remark about tone means no more than Camus's discomfort at seeing his work being taken apart and explained. Clearly uneasy with being put under Sartre's microscope, Camus defends himself by opposing his instinctive creativity to Sartre's critical acuity, even while conceding that the latter requires more intelligence.

Sartre's put-down may well have been repayment for a slight the reader will have noticed in a passage from *The Myth of Sisyphus* quoted above: "this nausea, as a writer of today calls it, is also the absurd." Three years earlier Camus had referred to Sartre the author of novels and short stories as a great writer. Now, relying on the ideas of *Nausea,* and having mentioned Nietzsche, Schopenhauer, and Jaspers by name, Camus gives his peer only the most oblique mention. The anonymous "writer of today," thereby placed on a lower level than the named great thinkers, in turn demonstrates his own ability not only to analyze and even cuff a young upstart but also to take the opposite tack, devoting considerable space in his article to generously showing how Camus fits into the aristocracy of literature and ideas.

In addition to revealing a potential for prickliness toward each other, these remarks remind us that the two men's kinship was not sameness. In addition to their mutual praise and sense of discovery, these texts suggest many differences between Sartre and Camus. Sartre had a more negative and Camus a more positive view of both nature and human reality. Merely to open *The Stranger* alongside *Nausea* is to be struck by the contrast between Meursault/Camus's dazzling physicality and Roquentin/Sartre's famous disgust for the physical. Camus reveled in the sensuous world of North Africa, as in *Nuptials*, and his reader can hardly ignore its intensity and its pleasures. Sartre's writing never embraced the physical world or the body in the direct, unquestioning, and often joyous way so natural to Camus. Indeed, one of the most striking contrasts in modern fiction, as Camus himself knew, is that between the gray, ugly Bouville—"Mudville"—of *Nausea* and *The Stranger*'s bright, shimmering port city, its beach, and its surrounding countryside, Le Havre and Algiers.

Their reviews of each other point up another key difference. Although both wrote important works of philosophy and fiction and successfully tackled a number of other genres, by temperament the one was primarily a philosopher, absorbed with theories and general ideas, the other primarily a novelist, most comfortably capturing concrete situations—Camus's distinction between "intelligence" and the "instinctive element." The brilliant young philosopher took absurdity as his starting point and slowly, in the five years between *Nausea* and *Being and Nothingness*, explored how human activity constitutes a meaningful world from brute, meaningless existence. The philosophizing novelist built an entire worldview on the sense that absurdity is an unsurpassable given of human experience.

Despite these differences, the two writers' initial admiration for each other sprang from the closeness of their starting points and the similarity of their projects. Each was trying to make his mark in fields kept quite distinct in French education and culture. Each one immediately noticed that the other was writing both philosophy and literature. And each immediately saw how much they shared. Their writing, with its unconventional plots and seemingly unmotivated characters, stressed that existence was absurd. They faced this absurdity honestly and lucidly, and they agreed that most people (including philosophers) did not do so. They prized living authentically.

: : :

How strong was their personal attraction? Thirty years after they met, Sartre remembered Camus as "amusing: extremely coarse, but often very amusing. . . . What we found engaging was his Algerian side. He had an accent like that of the South of France and he had Spanish friendships, friendships that went back to his contacts with the Spaniards and Algerians." And Beauvoir added: "He was the one in whose company we enjoyed ourselves most and had most fun. We saw a very great deal of one another—we exchanged innumerable stories." We perceive from these memories how, after their break, the two played down their relationship. But they were clearly drawn to each other. There was an undeniable chemistry between opposites who were also so similar. Camus was, Sartre said, "my absolute opposite: handsome, elegant, a rationalist."

In the squat, wall-eyed, voluble, genial little man, Camus saw a mind of astonishing virtuosity, power, depth, and creativity. Yet Sartre was friendly and unpretentious, and knew how to have a good time. Sartre and Beauvoir, as children of professional families, possessed far greater sophistication—and higher social standing—than the son of a washerwoman from the mixed Arab and European Belcourt quarter of Algiers. And, as Sartre and Beauvoir's social circle expanded during the last months of the war to include a number of well-known people, Camus was part of it. He could not fail to ignore Sartre's appreciation of him.

Sartre was far less conventional than Camus. And Sartre loved to theorize about anything and everything—the irritating opposite of Camus. However, although Sartre loved to talk and, as we will see, freely admitted his mistakes, he paradoxically exposed his deepest vulnerabilities far less than Camus, whose own vulnerabilities always seemed on the very surface of his skin, in his moods, and in his eyes. In such differences each one momentarily complemented and in some sense completed each other.

In *The Prime of Life* Beauvoir has provided a compelling record of the spirit of those wartime days when, together with Camus and other new acquaintances, famous or soon to be famous, including Pablo Picasso, Michel Leiris, Georges Bataille, and Raymond Queneau, they held fiestas or presented plays or just got drunk. "Prematurely, and despite all the threats that still hung over so many of us, we were celebrating victory." Food was scarce, but Beauvoir sometimes would get hold of some meat and have friends over. She spoke of offering "my guests bowls of green beans and heaped dishes of beef stew, and I always took care to have plenty of wine. 'The quality's not exactly brilliant,' Camus used to say, 'but the quantity is just right.' "

In spring 1944, Camus directed a reading of a play by Picasso before a group of friends. Brassaï, one of the players, took a photograph, the only one showing Sartre and Camus together. After the other guests had left, ahead of curfew, the performers and a handful of close friends kept the party going until five in the morning. Another time, in Beauvoir's words,

> we constituted a sort of carnival, with its mountebanks, its confidence-men, its clowns, and its parades. Dora Maar used to mime a bullfighting act; Sartre conducted an orchestra from the bottom of a cupboard; Limbour carved up a ham as though he were a cannibal; Queneau and Bataille fought a duel with bottles instead of swords; Camus and Lemarchand played military marches on saucepan lids, while those who knew how to sing, sang. So did those who didn't. We had pantomimes, comedies, diatribes, parodies, monologues, and confessions: the flow of improvisations never dried up, and they were always greeted with enthusiastic applause. We put on records and danced; some of us, such as Olga, Wanda, and Camus, very well; others less expertly.

The intensity of their pleasures reflect the tensions of wartime, its many deprivations, and the fact that they could all sense the German occupation drawing to a close.

Looking back at those days, Beauvoir portrayed Camus as the young provincial come to Paris in pursuit of success, as in Balzac's *Lost Illusions*.

> He relished success and fame, and made no secret of the fact; to carry it off with a blasé air would have been something less than natural. Occasionally he allowed a touch of the original Rastignac to peep out, but he didn't seem to take himself too seriously. He was a simple, cheerful soul. In a good mood he was not above somewhat facile jokes; there was a waiter at the

> Flore called Pascal, whom he insisted on referring to as Descartes. But he could afford to allow himself such indulgences; his great charm, the product of nonchalance and enthusiasm in just the right proportions, insured him against any risk of vulgarity. What I liked most about him was his capacity for detached amusement at people and things even while he was intensely occupied with his personal activities, pleasures, and friendships.

These reminiscences, published in 1963, are carefully constructed, as were the interviews between Beauvoir and Sartre published after Sartre's death twenty years later. Beauvoir tried to convey an intensely enjoyable but nonetheless casual friendship with an easygoing and uncomplicated provincial. One problem with this picture is that she mentioned Camus too often in her memoirs and seemed too concerned with his opinions and his political and personal evolution to treat him casually. Another is that in her reminiscences, as in real life, Camus was anything but simple.

Had she tried to tell the full story, she would have said that Camus presented her and Sartre with a façade of simple cheer that masked the complexities of his personality and his life. These were revealed in, but hidden by, his occasional sharply ironic remarks. Later on she mistook his self-confidence, which itself was subject to periodic bouts of profound self-doubt, for arrogance. Complicating her own feelings was the fact that Beauvoir offered herself to Camus as a lover, but he rebuffed her. This reminds us that Beauvoir was not simply an observer of the Sartre-Camus relationship but was deeply involved in it—a third force, with her own independent feelings about Camus. She later complained that he was rude and impatient with her, perhaps, she surmised, because he was a Mediterranean ladies' man who found her unattractive and could not accept her as an intellectual equal. She didn't know that Camus had commented sneeringly to Arthur Koestler, "Imagine what she would be saying on the pillow afterwards. How awful—such a chatterbox, a total bluestocking, unbearable." Still, Camus and Beauvoir had many exchanges about important matters, sometimes in Sartre's presence and sometimes alone. Late one night when they were alone, he opened up to her about the enormous pain of his love life.

Beauvoir's memoirs are invaluable but inevitably biased by her own partisanship and disappointments. They are driven by the three goals that dominated much of her life: to preserve her relationship with Sartre, to present a positive image of it, and to protect Sartre. Since her memoirs have until recently provided us with much of what we know about the Camus-Sartre relationship, we must listen to them carefully but also, wherever possible, compare them to what she wrote and said elsewhere or to the testimony of others.

In describing these early days, at least two major strands must be added to what Beauvoir saw fit to put in her memoirs. First, Sartre was strongly attracted to the handsome young man. Camus's role in Sartre and Beauvoir's life at the time was enormous. With his Bogartesque virility, he seemed tough and self-contained, yet vulnerable. This vulnerability came in part from the tuberculosis that controlled his day-to-day life—he coughed up blood, was often exhausted, needed treatment and rest cures, was declared unfit for the teaching profession and military service. Looming over these trials and humiliations was the constant threat of dying early. Yet he did not voice this fear to his new friends: around them, Camus was given to irony and pained looks but not to soul-searching or self-revelation.

Later in life, when both men were gone, Beauvoir said a number of things that brought her story into question. Already in mid-1943 she had overheard people comparing the two newly famous writers with each other, and much later she admitted originally seeing Camus as Sartre's literary rival, someone with "such flash, such dazzle," that she feared he would tower over the short, ugly genius. She also described herself and Camus as being in competition for Sartre in the early days: "We were like two dogs circling a bone. The bone was Sartre, and we both wanted it." In her old age, Beauvoir admitted being frightened by the intensity with which Sartre fell for Camus when they first met. He spoke of him in language he might have used of a woman he was after. Since Sartre was "the strongest heterosexual" Beauvoir knew and had "without a doubt not one trace of homosexuality in his disposition," she was disturbed and worried about his "infatuation" with Camus.

Another noteworthy feature of the two men's relationship was that Camus, eight years Sartre's junior and introduced by him to the Parisian intellectual world, insisted on remaining independent of Sartre and Beauvoir and on leading a full life of his own. Since the mid-1930s, Sartre and Beauvoir had attracted talented and attractive young men and women, usually their former students. These became *la famille*, with whom they were connected not only amorously but also philosophically and politically, as well as supporting these young people financially. They naturally assumed that this young man would become the latest satellite in the Sartre-Beauvoir family. Instead, Camus remained independent, to the point of bristling whenever he was linked publicly with Sartre. Reminiscing with Sartre thirty years later, Beauvoir said, "I think it irritated him very much when people thought he was more or less your disciple, he being very young, and you being better known." No wonder, as we shall see, Camus after the Liberation was at pains to distinguish himself from "existentialism."

Missing from Beauvoir's picture is that the two great intellectuals did not talk much about ideas. But they certainly talked about women, though probably not about the actress Maria Casarès, who would become the great love of Camus's life and the one woman to whom, in a sense, he would remain loyal. Nor would they have talked about Beauvoir, for obvious reasons. Sartre and Beauvoir theorized their various relationships into "contingent" loves that remained subsidiary to their "necessary" love for each other; Camus, forever torn between Maria and his wife Francine, as well as being involved with countless others, was unable to resolve his life's central frustration. So much of both men's energy was devoted to seducing women and negotiating the complications of endless relationships that this inevitably became a topic between the two men.

Were they in competition with each other? We have seen that their early encounters with each other's writings afforded each man opportunities for rivalry. Yet Camus's reviews, even when critical, betrayed no note of competitiveness. And when Sartre analyzed *The Stranger* in relation to *The Myth of Sisyphus*—a situation made to order for rivalry—Camus stepped aside, accepting that he and Sartre had different strengths. On his side, Sartre generously integrated Camus into the body of French literature. But gatekeeping is the function of the one who has arrived first, the senior colleague. And Sartre did use his superiority as a philosopher to take a swipe at Camus. Still, Sartre was pleased when Camus invited him to join the jury for Gallimard's new Prix de la Pléiade, although Beauvoir, speaking about it forty years later, remained irritated that a nobody like Camus would be the one to ask "a writer of distinction" like Sartre.

Beauvoir later spoke of Sartre being "a bit jealous" of Camus, but not as a writer; Camus's good looks gave him an advantage that Sartre resented. Later, Sartre mentioned Camus's affair with *famille* member Wanda Kosakiewicz as one of the four or five actions on Camus's part that caused the friendship to go sour. During the early months of the friendship, in the winter of 1944, Sartre wrote to Beauvoir, who was away on vacation: "What was [Wanda] thinking about to go running after Camus? What did she want from him? Wasn't I so much better? And so nice? She should watch out." Sartre later mentioned as a major cause of the break a "complicated story" which disturbed Camus, between him and an unnamed woman in Camus's life.

Although each had begun by evaluating the other, their philosophical-literary kinship and personal attraction tended to forestall competition between the self-made scholarship student and the privileged genius. And when they were becoming friends in 1943–44, their self-evident differences similarly prevented clashes. Once, when drunk, Sartre said to Camus: "I'm more intelligent than you, huh? More intelligent!" Camus agreed. Another time Camus saw

Sartre showing off to a pretty girl and asked him, "Why are you going to so much trouble?" Sartre replied, "Have you taken a look at my mug?"

: : :

Sartre had considerably more social power than Camus and was already becoming a celebrity before they met. His discussion of Camus's first books was an important step in Camus's career. In the realm of writing and ideas, Sartre was a full step ahead, at ease in the Parisian world of letters and culture and also in his self-confident project of greatness. If his article on Camus showed how comfortably Sartre moved among the great names, Camus offered something that Sartre found more compelling than membership in the Pantheon. There was, after all, a war on, and an Occupation, and a Resistance. Sartre was taking a long time to become involved in the world. He and Beauvoir had remained apolitical throughout the tumultuous 1930s, watching from the sidelines during the great Popular Front demonstration of July 4, 1935, and refusing to vote in the elections that would bring it to power. In his earliest published writings, Sartre depicted freedom and spontaneity as having nothing to do with the real world. In his novel-in-progress, *Roads to Freedom,* the character Mathieu was free to act, but his freedom was useless. As expressed in the climactic line of *Being and Nothingness,* "man is a useless passion." Sartre was a stranger to effective action.

Camus, on the other hand, so much more comfortable in his own skin, was able to commit himself and run risks in the real world. He became seriously involved in one of the main Resistance movements shortly after their friendship began. "Like us," said Beauvoir, "he had moved from individualism to a committed attitude; we knew, though he never mentioned the fact, that he had important and responsible duties in the Combat movement." "Like us" was false: Camus was a giant step ahead of Sartre. The Occupation, the Resistance, and the Liberation, we will now see, affected both of them decisively and added a political dimension to their personal attraction and literary-philosophical kinship. Politics would drive them apart in 1952 only after bringing them together in 1944.

2

occupation, resistance, liberation

The day before Sartre and Camus met at the opening of *The Flies,* a German officer was assassinated about a mile away. The Resistance was stepping up its activities and consolidating. In the previous week, on May 27, the first meeting of the National Committee of Resistance had been held in Paris. As the friendship between Camus and Sartre entered the spring and summer of 1944, the struggle against the German occupier became a central focus. In these months the relationship sketched in chapter 1 was reversed: Camus, veteran of more than one political war, led the near-novice, Sartre.

On August 21, 1944, in the midst of the insurrection against the Germans, the underground newspaper *Combat* surfaced in Paris, with Albert Camus as its editor. During these heady days Beauvoir and Sartre visited Camus at the plant commandeered by the Resistance for *Combat* as well as two other underground papers that had likewise come out into the open before the Germans left. Beauvoir remembered "Camus and his young friends, working with guns at the ready, all the iron doors closed, a little scared because at any moment German soldiers could come and it would have been a bad mess." And she also recalled: "The whole building was a hive of tremendous chaos and tremendous gaiety, from top to bottom. Camus was exultant. He asked Sartre to write a descriptive report of the Liberation period." Camus offered Sartre the opportunity of a lifetime. With the resulting articles the thirty-nine-year-old philosopher and writer who had not known how to engage himself directly in the world could now participate—by going into the streets and observing events, and then by describing them to a mass audience.

Under his name there appeared a series of eyewitness articles on the insurrection that liberated Paris: "Walking around Paris during the uprising"—"*Un Promeneur dans Paris insurgé*." The first article, published on August 28, described public reactions to the insurrection: "In this time of intoxication and joy, everybody feels the need to plunge back into the collective life." And the last one, seven days later, described the Liberation parade in which resistance fighters of the underground marched with de Gaulle's Free French Army: "Never before have civilian fighters—armed for guerilla warfare and ambushes, for rebellion and the barricades' unequal struggle—and impeccable soldiers and their leaders been seen parading to the same approving cheers." Beyond the celebration, the crowd sensed that after the Germans' departure it was time to begin "a tougher and more patient struggle to establish a new order."

Sartre was the first writer to be honored with a byline as *Combat* emerged from clandestinity. His name was placed in bold letters running across the top of the front page of each issue. Beauvoir, however, wrote to Nelson Algren three years later that "we wrote reports about what was happening and brought them to Camus, with a certain enjoyable sense of danger in the streets where from time to time bullets were fired." Her "we" meant, according to one of Sartre's bibliographers, that *she* wrote the articles under Sartre's supervision. After Sartre's death, Beauvoir confided to her biographer that it was she, not the two of them and certainly not Sartre, who had written the famous *Combat* articles about the insurrection. She wrote them because "he was too busy." It is no small point. These articles appeared to show Sartre coming down to earth in a new and decisive way, at a defining historical moment, and they have long been regarded as the best eyewitness account of those days.

The second story has the editor of *Combat* visiting his friend at the Comédie-Française during the insurrection. Sartre was assigned with members of the Resistance theater group, the Comité National du Théâtre (CNT), to protect the Comédie-Française from German sabotage. Exhausted from his walk across the city, Sartre had fallen asleep in one of the seats. Camus woke him with the words, "You have turned your theater seat in the direction of history!" Sartre had probably confided to his friend his desire to take part in real-world events, and Camus was poking fun at his dozing at such a time. This remark, uttered with Camus's affectionate irony, would be central in their later falling-out. As we will see, Camus recalled it during the controversy, with a sharp edge, and Sartre repaid him a thousandfold.

These two anecdotes say much about Camus and Sartre during this period, and about their relationship. The precedence later accorded to Sartre as a political animal belied their true standing in relation to each other. Camus was the captain of the boat that Sartre, it seems, kept missing. In the first anecdote, Camus presented his friend to the widest possible public, but, we learn much later, Sartre's achievement in these famous articles was questionable. And in the second anecdote, Camus poked fun at a friend who had talked about a rendezvous with history that he seemed unable to pull off. The Comédie-Française story, along with Beauvoir's striking claim to have authored his first famous piece of journalism, suggests how difficult it must have been for Sartre to negotiate the process of commitment that Camus so effortlessly assumed.

Political activity came much more naturally to Camus. He had been a member of the Communist Party for two years, from the fall of 1935 until the summer or fall of 1937. He was an active member; he was well known as organizer of an Algiers theater company that performed avant-garde and political plays. Considering his reluctance in the 1950s to support the Algerian National Liberation Front—as well as the detachment of *The Stranger* concerning Meursault's inexplicable murder of the young Arab —Camus's exit from the Algerian branch of the French Communist Party (PCF) is noteworthy. He was expelled for refusing to follow the shift in the Party line that, under the colonial interpretation of the Popular Front, would soft-pedal previous PCF support for Arab nationalism. The idea was to create the widest possible anti-fascist front, including as many *pieds-noirs* as possible. Camus believed that the party's commitment to Algerian Arabs should have precedence over such strategic concerns. After leaving the PCF, Camus continued his theater activity, and from October 1938 until January 1940 he worked on *Alger républicain* and its sister paper and, later, successor, *Le Soir républicain.*

Under its editor, Pascal Pia, who would later help him publish *The Stranger* and would bring him into the Resistance, Camus learned newspaper work. He did book reviewing and layout as well as crime and court reporting. A crusading journalist, Camus played a role in winning acquittals for the defendants in more than one important case. Between June 5 and 15, 1939, he wrote a series of reports on famine and poverty in the mountainous coastal region of Kabylia. These were among the first detailed articles ever written by a European Algerian describing the wretched living conditions of the native population. Camus called upon the colonial administration to set a minimum wage, build schools, and distribute food, because "if colonial conquest could ever be justified, it is to the degree that it helps conquered peoples keep their personality. And if we have a duty to this land, it is to allow one of the proudest and most humane peoples in this world to remain faithful to themselves and their destiny."

By the start of World War II, Camus was second only to Pia at *Alger républicain* and soon took over as editor of *Le Soir républicain*. His early opposition to the war, and the spectacle of Camus and his friend and mentor Pia running their left-wing daily into the ground because they rejected the urgency of fighting Nazism, is one of the most striking but least commented-on moments of his life. His initial opposition to the war quickly led to conflicts and ruptures with friends.

"The reign of beasts has begun," he wrote in his notebook on September 7, 1939. His mid-September editorial in *Le Soir républicain* teetered on the edge of despair because the peace had been lost: "So many efforts for peace, so many hopes placed on man, so many years of struggle have resulted in this collapse and this new carnage." In a second editorial he advocated ending the war through negotiations with Hitler that would in part reverse the errors in the Treaty of Versailles. Although he rejected "a regime where human dignity counted for nothing and where freedom was sneered at," he presented the following formula for ending the war:

> Do not humiliate, try to understand, deprive Hitler of the basic reasons for his prestige, grant everything that is just while refusing what is unjust, revise Versailles while respecting Poland and Czechoslovakia, see clearly, reject training for hatred, establish human and European solidarity, adjust national policies to an economy that has become international: these are our positions.

Camus misunderstood Nazism. His principled advocacy of Algerian Muslims at the time of his earlier rejection of the Popular Front turns out to have been intertwined with a lack of urgency about combating fascism and Nazism. And now, as editor-in-chief of *Le Soir républicain* during the war's first few months, he guided the newspaper to its death in a hopeless battle against the military censors and even against its owners—insisting on antiwar principles that rejected the necessity of doing battle to defeat Nazism. Of course, his views were in keeping with a time-honored tradition of French pacifism, rejecting as they did the inevitable slaughter that war entailed. Camus did, in fact, report for military service out of solidarity with those young men, like his brother, who had become soldiers. And he was angered that his tuberculosis disqualified him. He intended to serve loyally and to advocate a negotiated peace in the barracks.

While Camus's editorship of *Le Soir républicain* calls into question his political judgment in 1939, when he was only twenty-six, it also draws attention to his remarkable political strength. He found it natural to take an unpopular stand even on this issue, with virtually his whole world against him, although it meant certain and swift government repression. An instinctive political being, Camus was both independent and courageous. He did not need to wait to find out what others thought, or to weigh the consequences, before making up his mind and acting. He was quite capable of being a party of one, if it came to that, and of going against all the trends of history—as long as he believed that he was in the right. These strengths would never flag.

Le Soir républicain ran out of paper, lost most of its advertisers, and was about to be throttled by its directors when the inevitable banning order was issued in the beginning of January 1940. Pia went off to Paris to work on *Paris-Soir*, and Camus soon followed. Camus remained in Paris during the German invasion of France and the beginning of the Occupation. In January 1941 he returned with his new wife Francine to Algeria, where he finished *The Stranger, The Myth of Sisyphus,* and *Caligula.* Pia helped him place the first two books with Gallimard. Because Kafka, as a Jew, was on the "List Otto" of prohibited authors, whose works French publishers had agreed not to publish and not even to allow to be discussed by other authors, Camus was faced with excising his chapter on Kafka from *The Myth of Sisyphus.* Although he briefly considered the possibility of publishing the full manuscript in Switzerland or Algeria to avoid censorship, he accepted the alteration and the book was passed by the censor in Paris.

The Stranger became the publishing event of an Occupation that sought, above all, to promote the illusion of normal life as one of the fruits of collaboration with the Germans. Remaining in Algiers until mid-1942, and then recuperating from illness in Le Panelier in the Massif Central, Camus kept on with the business of writing. According to one legend, he set up a Resistance group in

Oran (on the Algerian coast) before returning by sea to France in August 1942; according to another he was sent from Algeria to France by the Resistance. In reality, he worked on *The Plague* and became connected with France's major publishing house, saw his books acclaimed, entered into the intellectual world of occupied Paris, and was financially rewarded as a writer—all by the age of thirty. Returning to France not to fight but to recuperate from tuberculosis, he established himself in Paris before entering the Resistance.

: : :

As natural as politics seemed to Camus, to Sartre it was another world. To appreciate Sartre's activity during the war, as well as what Camus meant to him during the Occupation, we must go back well before 1939 to the time when Sartre's approach to the major questions of life was abstract and theoretical. Above all, he was searching for intellectual bearings, having rejected the idealism of his philosophical education while being uninterested in Marxism. Only one contemporary school of thought appealed to this young writer, budding philosopher, and novelist absorbed in understanding the nature of being itself, and that was phenomenology, because it started from the concrete individual's consciousness and yet promised to reach the real world. This German philosophy was both radical and self-confident, like Sartre, and it was intellectually congenial to someone schooled in Cartesian thought. Sartre first encountered it in the spring of 1933. Beauvoir delightfully captured the conversation that led to his philosophical turning point:

> Raymond Aron was spending a year at the French Institute in Berlin and studying Husserl simultaneously with preparing an historical thesis. When he came to Paris he spoke of Husserl to Sartre. We spent an evening together at the Bec de Gaz in the Rue Montparnasse. We ordered the specialty of the house, apricot cocktails; Aron said, pointing to his glass: "you see, my dear fellow, if you are a phenomenologist, you can talk about this cocktail and make philosophy out of it!" Sartre turned pale with emotion at this. Here was just the thing he had been longing to achieve for years—to describe objects just as he saw and touched them, and extract philosophy from the process. Aron convinced him that phenomenology exactly fitted in with his special preoccupations: bypassing the antithesis of idealism and realism, affirming simultaneously both the supremacy of reason and the reality of the visible world as it appears to our senses. On the Boulevard Saint-Michel Sartre purchased Levinas's book on Husserl, and was so

eager to inform himself on the subject that he leafed through the volume as he walked along, without even having cut the pages.

Sartre applied to succeed Aron at the French Institute in Berlin, and spent the 1933–34 academic year there reading Husserl. Nothing shows the young man's detachment more than the date and the place: he went to Nazi Germany in search of a philosophical way to encounter reality while many of the best German intellectuals were fleeing. He was reading Husserl, the proscribed Jew, and Heidegger, the Nazi chancellor of the University of Freiburg, while daily street scenes launched the catastrophe of Nazism.

Sartre had already studied the imagination's power to create an unreal world. Phenomenology now gave him a way to place consciousness *in* the world: consciousness is always consciousness of something outside of itself, never a world unto itself. It would take several years for the philosophical implications of Husserlian intentionality to develop into Sartre's existentialism. Only then, and only after the war had begun, would Sartre pose the goal of acting in the world.

: : :

History forced itself upon Sartre: the declaration of war, mobilization, a soldier's routine during the Phony War of 1939–40. For the first few months, Sartre was able to use military service to do even more reading, observing, and writing than he usually did in civilian life. In his notebook he announced that he was ready to take on the world. Then came the fall of France, and Sartre became a prisoner of war. For Christmas 1940, Sartre wrote *Bariona,* a play about the birth of Christ during the Roman occupation of Palestine. This play, which he also directed and acted in, sought to inspire his fellow prisoners not to cooperate with the Germans. In the camp he was a determined noncollaborator. Sartre also managed to lead a study group of priests in reading Heidegger's philosophy. Returning to Paris after his release from the camp in March 1941 for faked medical reasons, Sartre burned with a newfound political moralism. He refused to sign the loyalty oath demanded of teachers that included a statement that one was not a Jew or a Freemason. But this was a gesture without cost because, as he said, "the inspector-general of education was a secret Resistant and he gave me my job back at the Lycée Pasteur anyway."

Sartre was now determined to form a Resistance group. Socialisme et Liberté was created with Beauvoir, Maurice Merleau-Ponty, members of the Sartre-Beauvoir *famille*, and several current and former students. The members took risks in printing and distributing anti-German leaflets. But with the Soviet Union at peace with Nazi Germany, the Communist Party more or less acquiesced in the Occupation until June 21, 1941, and the Socialists were not yet ready to renounce the Vichy government, which most of their deputies had voted to empower. Thus Sartre's little group floundered for a number of reasons, including a lack of politically experienced leadership, its members' amateurishness, and the fact that the most experienced political activists had not yet begun to mobilize against the Germans and Vichy. Beauvoir told how "[Jacques-Laurent] Bost walked through the streets carrying a duplicating machine, and [Jean] Pouillon went around with his briefcase stuffed full of pamphlets." Typical of their dilettantism was the summer cycling trip Sartre and Beauvoir took to the unoccupied zone to convince writers such as André Gide, André Malraux, and Socialist leader Daniel Mayer to associate themselves with Socialisme et Liberté. Unsurprisingly, they all refused; not only did they consider it too early to be organizing resistance, but the group's function was never clear and Sartre's history of political passivity failed to inspire confidence. When the vacation was over, Sartre went back to Paris and dissolved the group.

Sartre now became amazingly productive: during the next three years he wrote *Being and Nothingness* and the plays *The Flies* and *No Exit*; put the finishing touches on the novel *The Age of Reason*; wrote its sequel, *Troubled Sleep*; and wrote several screenplays and major critical essays. He did much the same thing during the war as he had done before the war: he wrote. After the brief interlude of Socialisme et Liberté, he never again sought to directly resist the Germans, as did those who entered the *maquis* (the underground) or those who joined underground propaganda networks or carried clandestine documents. It is, of course, hard to imagine the half-blind, easily noticeable, and very talkative Sartre in either of these first or second rungs of Resistance activity. He tried to join such a group on at least one occasion, but as one of his contacts said afterwards, it wouldn't have been easy "to wear that face and those eyes underground." But he did explore action and commitment as one of his main philosophical and literary themes. As a published author who was both anti-Nazi and anti-Vichy, Sartre was invited early in 1943 into the Resistance writers' group, the Comité National des Ecrivains (CNE), by its PCF leaders, and he began writing in the CNE's clandestine *Les Lettres françaises.* He contributed a scathing article on Drieu la Rochelle, collaborator and editor of *La Nouvelle Revue française*, in April; and articles on literature and freedom and postwar films a year later, one attacking pro-Vichy playwright Marcel Aymé in July 1944. He also wrote a brief screenplay entitled "Résistance," which he hoped would be filmed after the Occupation was over. Although not one of the very few active rebels, Sartre certainly did what he could within his accustomed life. He remained in the third rung of the Resistance: he identified with it, associated with members more active than he, knew a bit about what was happening, and occasionally contributed his talents and participated in meetings. Above all, he continued to write, no matter what the circumstances:

> Our hotel rooms were not heated . . . so I always worked in cafés. During the war, Castor ["Beaver," Sartre's nickname for Beauvoir] and I worked on the first floor of the Flore, she at one end, I at the other, so we wouldn't be tempted to talk. We wrote from 9:00 to 1:00, went to Castor's room to eat whatever she had scrounged up the night before, or whatever our friends, who ate with us, brought along, then back to the Flore to write some more, from 4:00 to 8:00 or 9:00.

As a "writer who resisted and not a resistant who wrote," Sartre's major contribution was *The Flies*. First performed in mid-1943, *The Flies* counseled violent struggle against the usurpers, a rewriting of Aeschylus—under the eyes of the censors—which encouraged resistance. Orestes, returning home with his tutor, sees his city covered with flies, symbolizing guilt for having acquiesced in his father's murder. The people are manipulated by Agistheus (his father's murderer) and Zeus, to keep them from seeing that they are free. The play's most important anti-Vichy and anti-German message was Sartre's rejection of guilt and repentance as serving the usurpers, and his call to murder the murderers.

While taking direct aim at the regime of penitence preached by Vichy after the fall of France, Sartre was simultaneously exploring the obstacles to commitment. Orestes at first belongs nowhere, is "gloriously aloof," "light as gossamer and walk[s] on air." He kills Agistheus and Clytemnestra in order to avenge his father, but perhaps above all to become a real person among other people, to "take a burden on [his] shoulders." At the end, rather than remaining in Argos with his people, he melodramatically marches off, bearing their burden, the buzzing flies, as his own. Sartre was later criticized for having his play performed at the Théâtre de la Cité, renamed because its original namesake, Sarah Bernhardt, was Jewish; for submitting it to censorship; and for giving an interview about it to the pro-German *Comoedia*. But can anyone watch the play and ignore its theme of rebellion? Indeed, it was a feat in 1943 to have such an inflammatory play passed by the censors, even though some members of the Resistance scorned it for this reason. Immediately after the Liberation, the play was praised by the Communist newspaper *Action* as a "magnificent expression" of the drama being lived by the French people during the Occupation.

: : :

Shortly after meeting Sartre at the opening night of *The Flies*, Camus made his first wartime intervention, one that was typically more direct than anything Sartre did. In order "to make our battle more effective," he wrote the first of four "letters to a German friend" in July 1943. It was published clandestinely late that year; the second was written in December 1943 and published in early 1944. (The last two appeared after the Liberation.) In these articles Camus ostensibly explained to a German friend he had not seen for five years why the French were defeated; why they had slowly, painfully, taken up arms against their occupiers; and why they would win. In the process, he constructed a national myth.

The first letter reflected a major change in Camus and, as he described it, in France. Holding war at arm's length because of "the loathing we had for all war," the French people took "time to find out if we had the right to kill men, if we were allowed to add to the frightful misery of this world." Despising war, suspicious of heroism, committed to seeking truth, the French were defeated in 1940 because "we were concerned, while you [Germans] were falling upon us, to determine in our hearts whether right was on our side." We paid dearly for this detour—"with prison sentences and executions at dawn, with desertions and separations, with daily pangs of hunger, with emaciated children, and above all, with humiliation of our human dignity." Only when we were "at death's door," and "far behind" you Germans, did we understand the reasons for fighting, so that now we would struggle with a clear conscience and "clean hands." Our moral strength was rooted in the fact that we were fighting for justice, with spirit and the sword both on our side: accordingly, "your defeat is inevitable."

The subsequent letters continued to contrast the French with the Germans on moral grounds that were drawn directly from Camus's philosophy. If both adversaries began with a sense of the world's absurdity, Camus claimed that the French acknowledged and lived within this awareness, while the Germans sought to overcome it by dominating the world. The French, a fundamentally nonviolent people, would rouse themselves to fight only for family and justice, and if they did so with misgiving, they also acted with conviction. "We waited until we saw clearly, and, in poverty and suffering, we had the joy of fighting at the same time for all we loved. You, on the other hand, are fighting against everything in man that does not belong to the mother country."

Letters to a German Friend showed Camus the political moralist at work. He sought to promote Resistance morale by an interesting sleight of hand—rejecting nationalism while reaffirming French national superiority. Camus wrote in sophisticated moral tones, speaking with the internationalist voice of someone who, after all, had German friends and who hated to make war. He even turned the fall of France to his country's moral advantage: we lost because of our doubts about killing, which will now heighten our moral strength and give us clean hands for the battles to come. This bit of Resistance mythmaking contained Camus's self-justification for making, as he suggested the French had done, "a long detour" before going into action. "We had first to see people die and risk dying ourselves. We had to see a French worker walking toward the guillotine at dawn down the prison corridors and exhorting his comrades from cell to cell to be courageous." In other words, we had to experience the horrors of the Occupation before deciding to make war against the occupier.

But Camus's appeal to morality became moralizing. After all, what was he implying about all those who had not waited, who began the Resistance on the first day of the Occupation, many of them rallying to de Gaulle? And those who, like the Communists, were ready to resist violently and with great heroism as soon as the order was given? Camus suggested that all those resisters, as well as all those who fought on the battlefield before France fell, were premature or impure, that they came to violence too easily. They had dirty hands. Defeated France, nonviolent France, the France that was ambivalent about making war was now slowly rising, propelled by the right reasons. This France had never made a mistake—it was morally right when it refused to fight and was defeated; now it was morally right in its violent determination.

Unlike Sartre, who would criticize his own early passivity, Camus never admitted to having made a mistake. It was even more remarkable to find this nationalist fantasy and self-righteousness in a Frenchman from the colonies, a pied-noir who had grown up in a situation of built-in colonial violence deemed necessary to quell the natives, to appropriate their land, and to keep them in their place. Camus, in *The Stranger*, had captured flashes of this violence in Raymond's and Meursault's complicity in the beating of the Arab girlfriend; in their being stalked by, and in turn stalking, her brother and his friend; and in the book's turning point, Meursault's murder of the nameless Arab. But Camus never acknowledged that such violence was central either to his place in the world or to the society in which he was raised.

Letters to a German Friend suggests a second comparison between Camus and Sartre at this stage of each man's development. Sartre's Orestes embraces violence in his decision to kill Agistheus and Clytemnestra, in part as a way of becoming real, of gaining solidity and weight. For Sartre the path out of an imaginary, self-obsessed existence had to pass through violent action. In the *Letters*, Camus only reluctantly accepted violence, and for a specific function: to free France from the Germans. Although Meursault's gratuitous murder of the Arab in *The Stranger* has always shocked commentators, much of Camus's political life and work was a critical engagement with political violence. After the war he became more and more visible as an opponent of political violence, culminating in *The Rebel.* After the break with Sartre he wrote a powerful essay against the death penalty, and at the beginning of the Algerian War he campaigned against both sides' violence against civilians. Sartre, on the contrary, treated violence as a token of becoming real. If Camus worried increasingly about the harm it did to its victims and its negative moral effects, Sartre focused on its positive political and psychological effects on those who chose to practice it, especially the victims of oppression, when all other paths became blocked. In this sense violence became central to both Sartre's and Camus's politics and outlook, the one viscerally embracing it, the other equally powerfully repelling it. In occupied France, the child of privilege was dramatically comfortable with dirty hands at a time when the pied-noir from Algiers was determined to enter and leave the struggle with his hands clean.

: : :

By late 1943, Pascal Pia had become a major figure in the Combat movement. Camus arrived in Paris at a moment when his journalistic skills could be of use, and was catapulted almost by chance into an important role. In December 1943 or January 1944, he was first approached by Pia to edit a proposed political-cultural journal sponsored by the Combat movement. In March he was asked to take Pia's place as editor-in-chief of *Combat*, as Pia was given more important tasks. *Combat* was then being published monthly, in ever-larger editions of up to 150,000 copies. Working for Gallimard by day, Camus was also writing *The Plague.* The Combat organization gave him false papers, a sign of the risks he was running but also a badge of honor and importance. To his comrades he assumed the name of Beauchard—it was a security rule that no one in the same group should know the others' real names. Together they wrote, edited, and laid out each edition of *Combat,* and made sure that the plates got to the printers.

It was dangerous work. Claude Bourdet, the leader of Combat, who recalled bringing Camus into the movement in January, was arrested shortly afterwards and sent to Buchenwald; Jacqueline Bernard, who worked on *Combat* with Camus, was picked up by the Germans and sent to the concentration camp at Ravensbrück. Both survived. André Bollier, *Combat*'s printer in Lyon, did not. He committed suicide when about to be arrested by the Germans. Once, while waiting in line to be searched by French and German police with other men, Camus handed Maria Casarès the design for the masthead of *Combat*. Fearing that the women would also be searched, she swallowed it.

By the time Camus became involved, Combat, like the other Resistance organizations, had evolved to the point where its ideas, structures, and activities had taken shape. Camus's main contribution was his familiarity with newspaper production. He wrote at least two articles for clandestine *Combat*: one (already mentioned) that called for commitment to the struggle, published in March 1944; and another, dated May 1944, that described the German massacre of 86 men in the village of Ascq. During this period, Camus asked Sartre and Beauvoir to accompany him to a meeting of the team that put out the newspaper. Sartre later recalled, "I became a member of his Resistance group shortly before the Liberation; I met people I didn't know who together with Camus were seeing what the Resistance could do in this last stage of the war." "Became a member" is a considerable exaggeration. At the meeting, as Jacqueline Bernard recalls it, the little man offered his writing skills "even for stories about dogs run over in the street." Sartre was not yet serious about sustained political involvement, either as a writer or as an activist.

On August 21, 1944, in the midst of the insurrection in Paris against the German occupiers, the first open issue of *Combat* appeared, a single sheet with two unsigned editorials. The first editorial, later included by Camus in his collected political essays, began: "Today, August 21, as we appear in the open for the first time, the liberation of Paris has been achieved. After fifty months of occupation, of struggle and sacrifice, Paris is reborn to the sense of freedom despite the shots bursting out in the streets." The second, said to be "inspired" by Camus and later read by him on the air, bore as its title the slogan on the newspaper's masthead: "From Resistance to Revolution." It called for creating a "people's and workers' democracy" and a new constitution that would guarantee freedom, structural change, the end of trusts and of the rule of money, and a new foreign policy. "In the present state of affairs this is called a Revolution."

: : :

When the Liberation occurred, Camus was spokesman for one of the major Resistance movements at the moment of its victory. More, he had become the editor of a leading platform of the Resistance itself in time to interpret, evaluate, and, if possible, guide a national transformation. In what Bourdet called one of "those accidents which condition the life of individuals, if not societies," Pia's young friend had appeared precisely when needed—arriving in France just before it was cut off from Algeria, and in Paris just after publishing the books that made his reputation. Bourdet had found time to read both books before their meeting. While working at Gallimard and sharing fiestas with Sartre and Beauvoir, Camus gave much of his time to the Resistance during the last five months before the Liberation.

Camus's and Sartre's rapid rise in the literary world immediately after the war was facilitated by their comparative lack of competitors. Some of their potential rivals, such as Vladimir Jankélévich, had devoted themselves to the struggle against the Germans, many among them becoming prisoners or concentration camp inmates or being killed. Others had refused to publish on principle, while still others had compromised themselves by pro-German or pro-Vichy conduct during the Occupation. Meanwhile, Camus and Sartre were developing a significant body of writing that hungry readers would devour after Liberation. Put more sharply, their careers actually profited from the Occupation. Camus himself recalled that his friend René Leynaud wrote nothing during the Occupation because, having thrown himself wholly into the Resistance, "he had decided that he would write *afterwards.*" But "afterwards" never came for Leynaud, who was arrested by Vichy militiamen on May 16, 1944, and machine-gunned a month later, along with eighteen other prisoners, by German soldiers evacuating Lyon. Afterwards, the celebrated author of *The Stranger* wrote the preface to a posthumously published book of Leynaud's poems.

Other writers had given themselves wholly to the struggle from the beginning, rejecting censorship or losing jobs because of their hostility to Vichy or the Nazis. Some refused to publish with Gallimard because it accommodated itself to the Germans. Others either remained silent or gave their works to a handful of clandestine publishers such as Editions de Minuit. One of Camus's closest postwar friends, the poet René Char, wrote nothing once he became a full-time resistant. Camus's glowing Resistance reputation came from several months' work on *Combat* toward the end of the Occupation and a few articles. For this he received the Resistance Medal in 1946, which he said he "never asked for and will never wear. I did very little, and it hasn't yet been given to friends who died alongside me." He always showed the greatest respect for those who gave more, though he never corrected his friends as they spread the legend of Camus the resister. Yet because the legend was based on a period of genuine involvement, almost from the moment the Camus-Sartre friendship began Sartre's outstanding exemplar of commitment was none other than the tough, sensitive Algerian.

Later, Sartre remade the story on the basis of subsequent events and attitudes. In 1952 he labeled Camus as a man trying to escape commitment and history, a charge still being made long afterward. In interviews in the 1970s, Sartre made Camus a whipping boy of political detachment, whose ideas had been wrong from the moment they met. But when they actually met, Sartre felt rather differently, and for good reason. When the two were socializing in late 1943 and early 1944, Camus could in fact have shown his new friend his clandestine articles and told him about his underground activities. Camus was living the commitment that Sartre's fiction and plays would be exploring as their central problem for the next ten years.

In addition to their mutual kinship as writers and intellectuals, their complementary and contrasting ways, and their enjoyment in being together, the Camus-Sartre relationship acquired another aspect during the Occupation. Is it a coincidence that Sartre's short screenplay "Résistance," written as he and Camus were becoming close, focused on a young man who briefly edited an underground newspaper? On two later occasions, Sartre was explicit about what Camus meant to him during this period.

The more famous of these was, paradoxically, his 1952 letter breaking off the friendship. A tribute to the Camus of their early years appeared within his denunciation of the Camus of *The Rebel.* Sartre wrote that during the war "you gave yourself unreservedly to the Resistance. You lived through a fight which was austere, without glory or fanfare. Its dangers were hardly exalting; and worse, you took the risk of being degraded and vilified." Sartre acknowledged that Camus lived this history "more deeply and fully than many of us (myself included)." Camus became "the admirable conjunction of a person, an action, and a work." Sartre, like Camus, had written important works but obviously saw himself as being less developed. In 1944, said Sartre eight years later, he regarded his friend as a model human being fully integrated within himself and with his times.

Did he compliment Camus so as better to attack him? We have evidence of Sartre's admiration from shortly after the Liberation. In 1945, in a lecture before an American audience, he talked about Camus as the outstanding example of the politically engaged writers who emerged from the Resistance. In this talk on the "new" French writers, Sartre spent most of his time on "Albert Camus who is thirty years old," giving his audience a preview of his friend's novel-in-progress, *The Plague,* which Sartre had read in manuscript.

Camus's many assets inspired admiration and jealousy in others less famous and less successful with women than Sartre. One evening, a drunken young *Combat* film critic climbed onto the bar at a nightclub and proclaimed:

> I'm going to speak to you about an injustice worse than the one we denounce in column after column of our daily for the intellectual elite; this injustice is alive and is right here in front of us—it's Camus; he has everything it takes to seduce, to be happy, to be famous, and in addition he has the insolence to be not only talented but a genius. Against this injustice there's not a damn thing we can do!

To many, Camus was a man who had and did everything: a famous writer and a good-looking competitor for every beautiful woman, he was also a Resistance militant and now the editor of a major newspaper, and his editorials reached the entire country. No wonder Sartre, just before returning to the attack in his 1952 article, admitted, "How we loved you then."

: : :

It was understandable and even appropriate that Camus the editor would become a major postwar voice, but how could Sartre stake an equal claim to be heard? When he insisted right after the Liberation that "the best among us joined the Resistance in order to salvage the country," he spoke not as a member of the Resistance but as "a writer who resisted." How, then, did he manage to position himself, along with Camus, as one of the major interpreters of the Resistance?

A compilation published in the United States in 1947, entitled *The Republic of Silence*, indicated Sartre's success in doing so. The title itself came from Sartre's article on the Resistance in the first legal issue of *Les Lettres françaises*, in September 1944. A quotation from the article graced the book's title page. After introducing Sartre as having been "fearless and active in the underground," the editor included the full text of the article. Camus was also included in the collection, but anonymously, with his May 1944 piece on the massacre in Acsq. The anonymity of Camus's article reflected its character as a clandestine document of the struggle.

Sartre's place in this compilation and his visibility in the September 9 issue of *Les Lettres françaises* tell a remarkable story. He did not pretend to have been *in* the Resistance. He relied on doing what he could do best, namely *writing about* the Occupation and Resistance afterwards, and being their *interpreter*. Now, after the Liberation, in addition to the articles appearing under his name in *Combat,* Sartre wrote "The Republic of Silence" for *Les Lettres françaises,* voice of the Comité National des Ecrivains, and "Paris under the Occupation" for *La France Libre,* the Free French journal published in London by his friend

Raymond Aron. And a year later, to commemorate the Paris insurrection, he wrote, with a greater sense of authority, "The Liberation of Paris: An Apocalyptic Week." At the same time, he was still putting out an enormous body of new writing and was speaking out on all manner of issues.

In "The Republic of Silence," Sartre presented the Occupation through the prism of his ideas. He began challengingly, with words that would provoke people to recall their experience during the Occupation:

> Never were we more free than under the Germans. We had lost all our rights, first and foremost the right to speak; we were openly insulted daily, and we had to remain silent; we were deported en masse, because we were workers, because we were Jews, because we were political prisoners. Everywhere we looked—on the walls, in the newspapers, on the movie screens—we kept seeing that foul and insipid image that our oppressors wanted us to believe was the way we really were. Because of all this we were free. Since the Nazi poison was seeping into our very thoughts, each accurate thought was a victory; since an all-powerful police was trying to coerce us into silence, each word became as precious as a declaration of principle; since we were hunted, each gesture had the weight of a commitment. The often frightful circumstances of our struggle enabled us finally to live, undisguised and fully revealed, that awful, unbearable situation that we call the human condition.

This interpretation gained attention because what Sartre had to say was striking and original, and it resonated with many of his readers. He went on to connect those who did little, such as himself, with those who did a great deal. Without claiming too much for those who were fiercely anti-Nazi and anti-Vichy but remained mostly passive, he expressed their solidarity throughout the war with the real resisters. At the same time he insisted that the activists' own survival and effectiveness depended on that solidarity. In other words, "The Republic of Silence" directly links all those like him with "the elite among us who were active members of the Resistance Movement." Establishing this connection was the theme of his article.

> Each of us—and what Frenchman was not at some time or another during this period in this position?—who had some knowledge of the resistance operations was led to ask himself the agonizing question: "If they torture me, will I hold out?" . . . And we were alone, without a single helping hand anywhere. And yet, in the depths of that solitude, others were present, all

> the others, all the comrades of the Resistance Movement they were defending. A word was all it took for ten or a hundred arrests. Isn't that total responsibility, the revelation of our freedom in total solitude? Thus, in shadow and blood, a republic was formed, the strongest of republics. Each citizen knew he was dependent on everyone else as he also knew that he could count only on himself, freely and irremediably. By choosing himself in his freedom, he chose the truth of all. Each Frenchman had at every moment to conquer and affirm this republic—without institutions, army, or police—against Nazism. . . .

In a dazzling move, the article connects "each of us" among those who supported the Resistance passively with those who participated in some of its less dangerous and demanding activities, and with the heroes active in the underground sabotage, communication, and transportation networks and in the *maquis.* If the silent supporters—which he took to mean virtually everyone—had talked under interrogation, the militants would have been betrayed. And so the Resistance became redefined as a vast "Republic of Silence"—all of whose members contributed to it *in their own way.* Although only a few hundred thousand actively resisted, the myth that virtually the whole nation supported the Resistance became integral to postwar France's self-image. Sartre's mythmaking had a powerful double effect: he legitimized all those, including himself, who sided in any way with the Resistance, and at the same time he became this silent republic's spokesperson.

Despite his claim to articulate the spirit of life under Vichy and the Germans, another article published a few months later, "Paris under the Occupation," revealed a curious understanding of those who actively resisted. Under the Occupation, Sartre wrote, the dehumanization, the petrification of human beings

> was so intolerable that many people, in order to escape from it and to recover their future, threw themselves into the Resistance. Strange future, closed off by torture, prison or death but which we at least produced with our own hands. But the Resistance was only an individual solution and we always knew that: without it the English would have won the war, with its help they would have lost it anyway if they were supposed to lose it. In our eyes, it had above all a symbolic value; and that is why many resisters were filled with despair: they were always symbols. A symbolic rebellion in a symbolic city: only the torture was real.

From this point of view the Resistance was a moral gesture of little consequence to the war's outcome.

As wonderfully descriptive as this article was, Sartre's discussion of the Resistance as an "individual solution," as symbolic, reflected an odd detachment. Like Orestes' determination to act in order to become real in *The Flies,* Sartre did not see the Resistance as being primarily about having an effect on events. This point of view was probably not widely shared among those who risked their lives to defeat Germany and end the Occupation. In this key sense, Sartre misunderstood the Resistance, perhaps because his *political* grasp of commitment was undeveloped, as he himself acknowledged thirty years later.

One indication of his distance from real events, I suspect, was his handing off to Beauvoir the opportunity to do something of practical use when Camus asked him to write about the insurrection. As a study of his fundamental philosophical terms reveals, the imaginary remained his starting point and the sole Sartrean terrain for meaningful and satisfying human activity—at least until he began to reshape his key terms after the war. On the conceptual level his journey toward the real world was fraught with structural tensions leading to inevitable frustration. Given that these theoretical limitations complemented his personal starting points, it would be hard to imagine Sartre becoming any more than a strongly sympathetic observer and an occasional, tangential participant in the Resistance.

: : :

Although Camus took Sartre and Beauvoir to a meeting of the Combat group, they had neither the background nor the skills for working on a newspaper. Still, he considered them close enough friends to insist that they not stay at home when it briefly appeared that the group members' names had been betrayed to the Germans. For a moment at least, they shared a sense of risk.

Since they shared so much, it is not surprising that Camus and Sartre sketched common postwar projects. Having unlimited ambition, the two were the most prominent of the "new" men emerging from the years of defeat, occupation, and struggle. Camus and Sartre became friends at one of those unique moments marked by a profound divide with the previous generation. Although distinctly different, they shared a core outlook and literary sensibility and were part of the same intellectual, political, and publishing circle. They were becoming famous together. As they had done briefly in connection with *No Exit,* they now explored working together.

After the war, they said in conversations with Beauvoir, they would all start a journal together. And Camus, Sartre, and Maurice Merleau-Ponty discussed coauthoring the "ethics" section for the projected Gallimard encyclopedia of philosophy. Sartre wanted it to be "a team manifesto—a position paper on concrete morality adapted to the circumstances." They agreed on so much, they knew their ideas to be sufficiently fresh and distinct, and they were so congenial with one another that together they could dream of becoming postwar France's intellectual guides. Now that France could breathe and, more to the point, read freely, they would be at the center of things. As Beauvoir put it, "We were to provide the postwar era with its ideology." And so they did.

3

postwar commitments

For a blessed moment after the Liberation it seemed as if the "singing tomorrows" famously anticipated by martyred Gabriel Péri had arrived. Yes, hunger was pressing; millions were displaced or still in prison camps, concentration camps, or German work camps; there were severe shortages of everything; and energies were now turned to driving the last Germans out of France and winning the war. But for the movement that had just fought and won a civil war, and had begun to fight in regular formation alongside the Allies, these challenges belonged to a free people. As Camus put it, in one of the Resistance's first open newspaper editorials during the insurrection, "The liberation of Paris constitutes only one step toward the liberation of France, and here the word LIBERATION must be taken in its broadest sense." This meant, among other things, an end to "the privileges of money." The editorial struck the dominant chords of Resistance thought. The Liberation government, its military cadres, the social and political forces it reflected, and, indeed, the mood of France itself would tilt decisively to the left. How could ordinary people not take the making of history into their own hands and create radical changes when many of them had participated in a struggle that had swept away the whole rotten Vichy edifice? After all, they had defeated and disarmed the collaborators, and would now punish and wholly discredit them. And the struggles of de Gaulle and the Resistance had come together in a victory not only for the Allies but for a sovereign France.

The uniforms of the hated Germans and the despised Vichy militia were off the streets; the dreaded tensions of the Occupation were over. In another decisive sign of change, the whole collaboration press was abolished overnight, and heroic Resistance newspapers like *Combat* became the principal media of liberated France. A social, cultural, and political layer that had thrived by collaborating with the Germans now passed into the shadows, including much of the literary and journalistic establishment. And amid all the urgencies, revolutionary change was palpable, a mood of possibility, including a new attitude toward politics that claimed to differ not only from Vichy but also from the Third Republic, which had collapsed with the fall of France in June 1940.

In the climate of anticipation that coincided with the ascendancy of the Resistance, Camus and Sartre soon became the leading intellectuals of postwar France. Speaking with overtones of commitment in the face of danger, their words and works took on the aura of the struggle. Continuing on and off for another three years as editor and chief editorialist of the main non-Communist Left newspaper to emerge from the war, Camus self-consciously represented the moral spirit of the Resistance and its demand for radical change. Sartre began to speak about *engagement*—commitment—and developed it into the key theme of the postwar era by creating a journal as well as producing a flood of articles, books, and plays, all of which placed it at their center. Between the Liberation and the end of 1945, each man achieved a fame that reached across all audiences. The two were ubiquitous, writing philosophy, criticism, novels, plays, stories, and essays, and their journalism added to that body of work almost by the day.

Their celebrity clearly lay in their ability to voice the extraordinary experiences France had been living through. They provided students and young people, and the educated French in general, with new literary heroes. They took the place of writers like Gide and Malraux. Gide had written politically important books on Africa and the Soviet Union in the 1920s and 1930s, decades that in retrospect seemed to lead to the fall of France. Malraux, less than four years older than Sartre, was often treated as an elder at the Liberation. While his prewar books such as *Man's Hope* and *Man's Fate* still spoke to youth, the once-heroic spokesman for de Gaulle no longer did.

Sartre's and Camus's ideas gave focus to the postwar mood of the younger generation, especially among those who had lived through one extreme situation after another. Many in this generation were profoundly individualist and thus not likely to fall under the intellectual and political discipline of Communism. Given to struggle, and even sometimes to hope, they were leftist in temperament but in a way that was fiercely independent and skeptical. The experience of the last few years had made these young people receptive to outlooks based on a sense of the world's absurdity. Sartre and Camus attracted them not only because of the ideas they voiced but because they were determined to act on their ideas. That Sartre and Camus were opposed to capitalism went without saying. While never speaking about economics, they had a dozen other reasons for wanting to bring about a democratic socialist society.

Both men were natural egalitarians. A child of the working class, Camus never used his success to raise himself above others, especially those who had shared his childhood in Algiers. It was beyond question that the playing field should be leveled. Sartre's more privileged childhood engendered in him a deep hostility to privilege. Always unassuming toward others, he had a visceral hatred for those who believe that they have rights over others—and those institutions that embed such rights in their normal functioning. As both Camus and Sartre developed, the only social system they found acceptable was one in which all human beings would relate to each other with mutual respect. To be political was to promote socialism. Their most fundamental social values were nonconformist, democratic, individualist, and antiauthoritarian. Although from sharply contrasting worlds, they both regarded the well-being of the working class as the touchstone of social change. Each saw his political task as creating an independent presence that would steer between the Communists and the other existing leftist groups, voicing a new and militant politics that would avoid ineffectual idealism while insisting on building an alternative to bourgeois society.

Remarkably, the one edited the leading new leftist newspaper to emerge from the Resistance, the other the leading new left-wing journal. Each of these publications promoted the ideas and values of the Resistance. As editors, both Camus and Sartre sought to enlist its new voices in a coalition that would reach beyond previous antagonisms and take advantage of the widespread desire for new thinking and a moral and political renewal of French society. The two publications differed as sharply as any newspaper differs from an intellectual journal. Camus was invited to participate in *Les Temps modernes* and declined because of the press of work at *Combat;* his colleague Albert Ollivier took his place. But it is no easier to visualize Camus at the editorial meetings of *Les Temps modernes* than to imagine Sartre working with the staff of *Combat.* Camus's strengths and interests did not include the theoretical complexity, sophistication, and originality required on the board of *Les Temps modernes.* Sartre's more abstract and theoretical passion, on the other hand, would not have predisposed him to the tasks of running a newspaper.

As a committed journal, *Les Temps modernes* was intended to be, and for many was, the critical consciousness of the society; it wholly rejected anti-Communism and yet kept both the Communist Party and the Soviet Union at arm's length. It was an interdisciplinary journal that treated every significant question of the day, taking in not only philosophy and literature but all other fields as well. Prophetic and moral, it did battle on every front and aimed at creating a "synthetic anthropology." Showcasing a number of France's most important new writers—especially Sartre, Beauvoir, and Merleau-Ponty—it immediately drew others and soon became the dominant cultural journal in France, the model for every other serious journal.

Combat turned out to be a new kind of newspaper. Fiercely independent, it was determined to avoid pandering to mass tastes, succumbing to commercialism, or kowtowing to wealth and privilege. It offered employment and writing opportunities to many of the talented new men and women who emerged from the Resistance. When Beauvoir visited Portugal, she wrote reports for *Combat.* Jacques-Laurent Bost, an intimate of Beauvoir and Sartre, was hired by Camus as a war correspondent and given a contract for his book. He later sent reports to *Combat* from the United States. "Whenever you asked Camus for a favour," Beauvoir recalled, "he would do it so readily that you never hesitated to ask for another; and never in vain. Several of our young friends also wanted to work for *Combat;* he took them all in. Opening the paper in the morning was almost like opening our mail."

Camus wrote scores of editorials for *Combat.* His Algerian publisher Edmond Charlot, on arriving in Paris at the end of 1944, noticed that the newspaper was sold out as soon as it appeared on the stands and that the editorials were "the talk of Paris." Camus's *The Misunderstanding,* first staged before a sharply divided audience after the Allied landings in Normandy, was revived after the Liberation and was published along with his play *Caligula. Letters to a German Friend* was brought out as a small book; *The Myth of Sisyphus* was reprinted, as was *The Stranger*; and his collection of early Algerian essays, *Nuptials,* was reprinted twice. In May and June 1945, Camus wrote an important series of articles on Algeria. *Caligula* premiered in late September 1945. Although Camus was laboring slowly on *The Plague* at this time, and often lost confidence in his abilities, his public would never have guessed. Within a few months, Camus's readers were able to purchase no less than five books of his essays, plays, and fiction, and they read his editorials virtually every day.

Shortly after the Liberation, Sartre published *No Exit,* his pieces on the Occupation, and articles on the theater and in defense of existentialism, and he was interviewed more than once. In late November, the major newspapers were invited by the American government to send reporters to the United States: Beauvoir reports that she never saw "Sartre so elated as the day Camus offered him the job of representing *Combat.*" In the first few months of 1945 he traveled in the United States and published thirty-two articles in *Combat* and *Le Figaro,* ranging from discussions of the Tennessee Valley Authority, Hollywood, and American workers to explorations of the American psyche and the country's cities. Then, what Beauvoir described as the "existentialist offensive" began. In early fall 1945, within a span of a few weeks, Sartre's *The Age of Reason* and *The Reprieve* were published, as was Beauvoir's *The Blood of Others;* her play, *Les Bouches inutiles* opened; Beauvoir gave a public lecture on the novel and metaphysics; *Les Temps modernes* was launched; and Sartre gave his celebrated lecture "Existentialism Is a Humanism."

On the evening of October 29, 1945, Sartre traveled alone to the Centraux meeting hall to deliver this lecture, which had been advertised in *Combat, Le Monde, Le Figaro,* and *Libération* and via leaflets posted at several bookstores. The event's success shocked its organizers. The hall was filled to overflowing, and some of the crowd massed together outside; Sartre thought they were demonstrating against him as he approached. In the hall, chairs were broken, women fainted, and the aisles were so packed that Sartre himself took fifteen minutes just to get to the stage.

The lecture was widely reported. Maurice Nadeau's article in *Combat* appeared under the headline, "Too many attend Sartre lecture. Too hot, people fainting, police and ambulances. Lawrence of Arabia an existentialist." In the more than fifty years since it was first given, Sartre's lecture, often read in the United States under the misleading title *Existentialism and Human Emotions,* has served as the most common introduction to his philosophy. Its key theme, "existence precedes essence," means that humans are self-determining, creating rather than receiving their own identity. That is, we are fully responsible for what we become: "Man is nothing else but what he makes of himself." Arguing persuasively against essentialist and determinist thought, including religion and

Marxism, Sartre clearly and simply—too simply, he later thought—described freedom as inseparable from human existence.

Les Temps modernes had been launched two weeks earlier, on October 15, and suddenly "existentialism" was on everybody's lips. Beauvoir recalled:

> We were astonished by the furor we caused. Suddenly, in much the same way as one sees the picture in certain films breaking out of its frame and spreading to fill a wider screen, my life overflowed its old boundaries. I was pushed out into the limelight. My own baggage weighed very little, but Sartre was now hurled brutally into the arena of celebrity, and my name was associated with his. Not a week passed without the newspapers discussing us. *Combat* printed favourable comments on everything that came from our mouth or our pens. *Terre des hommes,* a weekly started by Pierre Herbart and destined to survive only a few months, devoted numerous friendly or bittersweet columns to us in every number. Gossip about us and our books appeared everywhere. In the streets, photographers fired away at us, and strangers rushed up to speak to us. At the Flore, people stared at us and whispered.

Existentialism became the first media craze of the postwar era, and was tailor-made for the post-Liberation press that had burgeoned to thirty-four new dailies in a year. Camus was included with Sartre and Beauvoir in discussions of existentialism. A major element of Sartre's and Camus's appeal was the sense of scandal surrounding their works. Both writers rejected religion and conventional niceties. Sartre depicted unsavory characters and extreme situations that shocked moderate temperaments—such as three people locked up forever in the hell of a Second Empire drawing-room. Camus portrayed an unmotivated murder by a man lacking normal feelings and rejecting decent opinion. Such writing by residents of the Left Bank was in turn linked by the conveniently outraged popular press with that neighborhood's postwar bohemians. In describing the nightclubs of the Left Bank, the mass-circulation *Samedi-Soir* characterized all their seedy patrons as existentialists. It even published an article explaining how Sartre had enticed a young woman to his room to smell a camembert cheese!

A full page in *France-Dimanche,* with a circulation of over a million, was devoted to "Sartre, that unappreciated man," who walked into the Café de Flore "with short steps, his head buried in the dirty wool of a shabby jacket, its pockets bursting with books and papers, a Balzac novel from the public library under the arm." Sartre was described as seating himself at a table, "gazing about him with emotion, while removing the scarves from his neck and . . . warmed by a few cognacs, the small pipe stuck in his sensual lips burning cheap tobacco . . . taking a two-bit pen from his briefcase . . . to scribble forty pages of manuscript." Then, with a small group of his disciples "gathered around him like a school of sardines," he went on his way to the nightclubs of Saint-Germain.

Such celebrity was not restricted to France. As Beauvoir said of the "inane glory" that befell Sartre immediately after the war, "a new fact, the advent of 'one world,' transformed him into an author of world fame; he had imagined that *Nausea* would not be translated for many years; as a result of modern techniques, the rapidity of communications, his works were already appearing in a dozen languages." Likewise, by 1947 Camus's *The Stranger* had appeared in English, Swedish, and Italian; *Caligula* and *The Misunderstanding* in Danish, Italian, and English; *The Myth of Sisyphus* in Italian and Swedish; and *Letters to a German Friend* had been published in Argentina, Switzerland, and Italy—all of which prepared the way for a worldwide reception for *The Plague,* translated into a dozen languages within a year of its publication in 1947. From then on, Camus began to be mentioned for the Nobel Prize.

How did Camus and Sartre respond to their sudden fame? As early as October 1945, Camus reflected in his journal: "At the age of thirty, almost overnight, I knew fame. I don't regret it. I might have had nightmares about it later on. Now I know what it is. It's not much." This lack of pleasure led, after the reception given to *Caligula,* to a tone of complaint: "Thirty articles. The reason for the praise is as bad as the reason for the criticism. Scarcely one or two authentic voices or voices moved to emotion. Fame! In the best of cases, a misunderstanding." Camus did not take his success well. He could be cold and irritable, and easily fell into pomposity and self-importance. Of course, the demands of renown were enormous, and even a full-time secretary at Gallimard could not handle all those who wanted to meet and interview him, to ask him for political support or personal advice. Years later he wrote a story about an artist so devoured by his celebrity that he dried up. Camus seemed to sour with fame. One of his biographers suggests that he was ruined by it.

Sartre, on the other hand, took to his celebrity easily, perhaps because he had always taken his genius for granted. He later recalled that his fame brought down attacks from both the Right and the Left: "Fame, for me, was hatred." But he also knew how to take advantage of it. He recalled, "[Since] I could see more or less what was happening, I conceived of the idea of a 'total public,' something earlier writers had never been able to do. The writer could have a total public if he told this public what it was thinking, though perhaps not with complete clarity."

: : :

Although he was not usually given to seeing male friends without Beauvoir, during the first year of their friendship Sartre had often met Camus in the morning at the Café des Deux Magots. His memories were inconsistent, however. Thirty years later, he reminisced, "For a year or two things went quite well," and he dwelled on how amusing Camus had been. But "in a certain way intimacy was lacking. It didn't lack in conversation, but it wasn't deep. One had the feeling that there might be a clash if we touched on certain things, and we didn't touch on them. We had a great liking for Camus, but we knew we shouldn't go too far." Still, the energy between the men was intense and deep enough that Sartre, at the time, considered Camus his closest friend.

Saint-Germain-des-Prés was an exciting place to live and work in. In the postwar years Sartre and Camus spent much time together and with others in bistros, cellars, and indoor and outdoor cafés. As we know from Beauvoir's memoirs, Camus was a major part of their lives, and they talked, ate, drank, and danced together. After finishing work at Gallimard, Camus and his secretary would sometimes join Sartre and Beauvoir at a café. After a drink they might go on to a bistro for dinner or meet other friends to watch Boris Vian and Juliette Gréco perform, and wind up the evening at an outdoor café for a final drink, becoming boisterous, staggering home.

Camus usually did not reveal his deepest concerns to Sartre and remained somewhat restrained with him. He was more likely to confide in Beauvoir. When Sartre was in New York at the end of 1945 she reported having seen Camus "quite often."

> Because I was a woman—and therefore, for he was quite feudal about such things, not quite an equal—he would end up telling me intimate secrets about himself; he gave me bits of his notebooks to read and told me about the difficulties in his private life. There was one theme that preoccupied him, and he often came back to it: some day he must write the truth! The fact is that in his case there was a much greater gap than for many others between his life and his work. When we went out together, drinking, laughing, chatting, late into the night, he was funny, cynical, rather coarse and often very bawdy in his conversation; he would admit his emotions, give way to

> his impulses; he was capable of sitting down in the snow on the edge of the sidewalk at two in the morning and meditating pathetically about love. "You have to choose. Love either lasts or it goes up in flames; the tragedy is that it can't last and go up in flames as well." I liked the "hungry ardour" with which he abandoned himself to life and pleasure.

Beauvoir's own detailed memories contrast strikingly with Sartre's generally vague and muffled recollections. She reported that their only clear political disagreements in 1945 were minor. Camus, imposed upon by a former collaborator playwright, Marcel Aymé, signed a petition requesting de Gaulle to grant clemency to the writer Robert Brasillach, a collaborator who had been sentenced to death. Beauvoir and Sartre held fast in their support for the death sentence. Then in November 1945, Camus defended de Gaulle against Communist leader Maurice Thorez. Beauvoir recalled:

> As I was leaving him he shouted through the car window: "At least General de Gaulle cuts a better figure than M. Jacques Duclos [second in the PCF hierarchy to Thorez]." Such an ill-tempered way of arguing surprised me, coming from him. At present his position was a long way from De Gaulle's, but even further from the Communists.

: : :

Sartre and Camus talked little about literature and philosophy except to make sweeping judgments about writers like Mauriac or Marcel, whom they didn't like, or Faulkner, whom they did. Sartre said much later that it "would be very complicated" to describe their postwar friendship. "We had curious relations and I think they did not quite tally with those he would have liked to have with others. In the same way ours with him were not the kind we liked having with people." What kind did Sartre like having? After his school comrade Paul Nizan's death at the front in 1940, and after his other school comrade Raymond Aron's wartime departure for London, Sartre made only one close friendship with a peer, and that was with Camus. Although cooperating both philosophically and politically with an intellectual equal such as Maurice Merleau-Ponty, or with an independent-minded junior such as Francis Jeanson, Sartre never became personally close with either man. And other young men who joined the Sartre-Beauvoir *famille* were always his satellites.

Beauvoir wrote that as Camus became famous, his opinions became more sweeping, his personal style more peremptory. But I believe he had a more specific reason for being touchy toward them. Camus had no taste for submitting to the kind of relationship they "liked having with people." Although Sartre respected this independence, Camus was at pains to avoid being seen as Sartre's satellite. But as the two were becoming the talk of Paris and of France, this perception grew, and Camus felt he had to define himself *in contrast* to Sartre. And this need for self-definition became even more urgent because Sartre was taking Camus *as a model* and making his friend's way of being into his own theory.

: : :

This development in their relationship turns on the word Sartre made famous that fall, *engagement*, commitment. Well before Sartre's famous introduction to *Les Temps modernes,* Camus had powerfully called for commitment to the Resistance in a March 1944 unsigned article in the clandestine *Combat*. He was grappling with the refrain "this doesn't concern me," often voiced by the uncommitted. In response, he insisted that each act of the enemy and each act of the Resistance concerns "all of us. For all French people today are linked by the enemy in such a way that one person's gesture creates the spirit of resistance in everyone else, and distraction or indifference in only one person leads to the death of ten others." Typically terse and avoiding broad appeals to theory or history, Camus's call to arms demonstrated the commitment that would occupy him until 1947 as editor of *Combat* and for the rest of his life as an activist intellectual.

The Plague, which he was working on during this time, was Camus's manual of commitment. It conveys the unheroic determination to do what must be done in the face of a total threat, without, as the narrator says, "attributing overimportance to praiseworthy actions." Those who participated in the novel's "sanitary squads" did so because "they knew it was the only thing to do, and the unthinkable thing would then have been not to have brought themselves to do it." The situation demanded it; that was all. At first the journalist Rambert, who like Camus has been parted from his wife and longs to join her, schemes to leave quarantined Oran. But eventually he decides to stay. He learns through experience that combating the pestilence is "the concern of all"; it can only be done in a collective act requiring unstinting teamwork, the willingness to submit oneself to the demands of the situation, and an acceptance of the risks inherent in the act.

There is a simplicity in this solidarity that is bracing and, occasionally, even exhilarating, as when Rieux and Tarrou swim together. This wonderful passage, describing not the struggle but the moment of release from it, is one of the high points of Camus's work.

> They undressed, and Rieux dived in first. After the first shock of cold had passed and he came back to the surface the water seemed tepid. When he had taken a few strokes he found that the sea was warm that night with the warmth of autumn seas that borrow from the shore the accumulated heat of the long days of summer. The movement of his feet left a foaming wake as he swam steadily ahead, and the water slipped along his arms to close in tightly on his legs. A loud splash told him that Tarrou had dived. Rieux lay on his back and stayed motionless, gazing up at the dome of sky lit by the stars and moon. He drew a deep breath. Then he heard a sound of beaten water, louder and louder, amazingly clear in the hollow silence of the night. Tarrou was coming up with him, he now could hear his breathing.
>
> Rieux turned and swam level with his friend, timing his stroke to Tarrou's. But Tarrou was the stronger swimmer and Rieux had to put on speed to keep up with him. For some minutes they swam side by side, with the same zest, in the same rhythm, isolated from the world, at last free of the town and of the plague. Rieux was the first to stop and they swam back slowly, except at one point, where unexpectedly they found themselves caught in an ice-cold current. Their energy whipped up by this trap the sea had sprung on them, both struck out more vigorously.
>
> They dressed and started back. Neither had said a word, but they were conscious of being perfectly at one, and the memory of this night would be cherished by them both. When they caught sight of the plague watchman, Rieux guessed that Tarrou, like himself, was thinking that the disease had given them a respite, and this was good, but now they must set their shoulders to the wheel again.

Neither spoke a word, which was precisely the point. This was a communion of combatants, who had no need to say how much they shared. Their silence captured Camus's sense of commitment.

Such writing, and their author's activity and personality, unquestionably inspired Sartre to become politically engaged. That process was difficult and lengthy, and one of the key steps along the way was Sartre's friendship with Camus. Sartre told what his friend meant to him in a lecture he gave in New York while reporting from the United States for Camus in early 1945. This revealing statement never appeared in French during his lifetime but only in English translation—in *Vogue* in July 1945. Since Sartre himself was one of the "new writers" he was talking about, with his own second and third novels in press as he spoke, the lecture was a masterpiece of self-promotion by means of celebrating his friend.

Sartre began by asserting that after the experiences of war, defeat, occupation, resistance, and liberation, the writing of an earlier generation seemed "slowed down, tired out, no longer pertinent." A new literature was arising, "the result of the Resistance and the war; its best representative is Albert Camus who is thirty years old." Today's new writers were profoundly marked by their experience of struggling against the Occupation.

> In publishing a great many clandestine articles, frequently under dangerous circumstances to fortify the people against the Germans or to keep up their courage, they became accustomed to thinking that writing is an act; and they have acquired the taste for action. Far from claiming that the writer is not responsible, they demand that he should at all times be able to pay for what he writes. In the clandestine press not a line could be written which did not risk the life of the author, or the printer, or the distributors of Resistance tracts; thus, after the inflation of the years between the wars when words seemed like paper-money which no one could pay for in gold, the written word has regained its power.

Direct participation in the Resistance taught these writers "that the freedom to write, like freedom itself, must be defended by arms under certain circumstances." But this obligation profoundly affected how they regarded literature, which was "no fancy activity carried on independent of politics." Younger writers like Camus sought to *commit* their readers—this is why *committed literature* (*littérature engagée*) was so widely discussed at that moment in France.

Sartre now focused on the books that had made Camus's reputation and through which he had encountered him, *The Stranger* and *The Myth of Sisyphus*, both of which had been conceived and largely written before the war, and recast them as wartime writings. Camus's books, he said, were "profoundly sombre" because France had lived through a tragic period. He connected Camus's sense of absurdity with the horrors of the war—for example, the concentration camps—insisting that Camus's pessimism was healthy and constructive. "It was when he lost all hope that man found himself, for he knew then that he could rely only upon himself. The constant presence of death, the perpetual threat of torture, made such writers as Camus measure the powers and the limits of man." Living in an extreme situation, where the question "Would I talk if I were tortured?" was concrete and ever present, Camus and other Resistance writers were concerned not only with man as a psychological or a social being but, Sartre said, "with the total, the metaphysical man," and they learned that "in extreme suffering there is still room for that which is human to reign." Unlike Malraux, certainly one of the heroic writers of our time, Camus had a sense of humility, the kind of patience learned during the Resistance. He understood how little one person can do, and that the human spirit always dwells in and has to deal with an absurd world.

Sartre now went on to discuss *The Plague,* which he had recently read in manuscript but whose completion and publication would take another two years. He summarized it for his American audience and drew important lessons from it. The doctor does his job "simply and without illusions, he defies Evil and the Universe, he affirms against all odds the rule of the human spirit." No wonder Camus moved into political journalism after the war, writing editorials that rejected realism in politics. "Realism destroys the very idea of humanity, for it is a submission to things." And no wonder Camus's austere hope did not suggest a literature of release. His work represented the literary future for a France that expected to be rebuilding for many years ahead, "a classic literature, without illusions, but full of confidence in the grandeur of humanity; hard, but without useless violence, passionate yet restrained, a literature which strives to paint the metaphysical condition of man while fully participating in the movements of society."

In this remarkable lecture, which focused on Camus as a writer and as a person, Sartre sounded a number of themes the two men shared: absurdity, a gritty humanism, the necessity of struggle, willingness to face extreme situations, refusal of any escapism, rejection of heroic gestures, rejection of any scheme of understanding that did not center on human experience and action. And, by extension, Sartre also recast his own prewar fiction, *The Wall* and *Nausea,* into politically committed works relevant to the postwar era. Appropriately enough, just before leaving for the United States, Sartre drafted an essay on commitment intended to introduce his new journal. In rooting the idea of *engagement* in the Occupation years, Sartre now seemed to assimilate Camus to himself. And for good reason. He saw in Camus what mattered most to him. This young man was already the person Sartre was trying to become: the engaged but not starry-eyed or ideological writer, at once "poet of freedom" and political activist.

Twenty-five years later, Sartre would comment on *The Plague* in an interview destined for his authorized biography: "When I think of Camus claiming *years later* that the German invasion was like the plague—coming for no reason, leaving for no reason—*quel con,* what a fool!" In this reevaluation of Camus's novel long after their break, Sartre forgot the main point about *The Plague,* which he had grasped in 1945. The book was not at all a reflection on the cause of the pestilence, whether human or natural, but, rather, the story of the collective spirit of combating it. That is why Camus began to be mentioned for the Nobel Prize from the moment the book appeared. Sartre's emphasis on Camus as a committed writer indicated that "commitment" was less Sartre's unique idea than a way of living and acting that he saw Camus as having achieved. He was just arriving there himself.

After changing his mind about the author, Sartre reworked his memory of Camus's book. In the 1970 interview he returned almost obsessively to Camus's deficiencies of commitment, while ignoring the way he had taken Camus as a model twenty-five years earlier. Although he admitted that he had changed during the postwar years, he neglected the fact that Camus was one of his influences. His earlier immense respect for Camus fit poorly with the retrospective sense of inevitable break-up. His earlier amalgamation of their outlooks became incompatible with his later conclusion that they had little in common.

: : :

Sartre's 1945 lecture in New York applied ideas he had worked out earlier. These were published in mid-October 1945 in his resounding introduction to *Les Temps modernes.* In contrast to Camus's avoidance of broad principles and preference to describe and to do, Sartre needed to formulate the major directions of his life as extended theoretical and programmatic concepts. His famous call for *engagement* was lengthy, theoretical, and explicitly tied to his philosophy. It was also Sartre at his most eloquent.

He rejected the notion of "art for art's sake" as a form of irresponsibility; he decisively placed individual persons, especially writers, into their historical world; and he then called for a committed literature:

> Since the writer has no means to escape, we want him to embrace his time tightly; it is his unique chance: it made itself for him and he is made for it. One regrets Balzac's indifference to the 1848 Revolution, Flaubert's frightened incomprehension of the Commune. One regrets it for *them.* There is something there that they missed forever. We do not want to miss anything in our time. There may be some more beautiful, but this one is our own. We have only *this* life to live, in the middle of *this* war, of *this* revolution perhaps.

He might have been admonishing the author of *Nausea* and of studies on the imagination and emotions, or the young man reading Husserl and Heidegger in Berlin in 1933–34. "Indifference" and "incomprehension" were presented with a lovely touch of sadness for missing out on one's own life. One *is* in one's historical situation, and one is therefore responsible for it.

> Every word has consequences. Every silence, too. I hold Flaubert and Goncourt responsible for the repression which followed the Commune because they did not write one line to prevent it. One might say that it was not their business. But was the Calas trial Voltaire's business? Dreyfus's condemnation Zola's? The administration of the Congo, Gide's? Each of these authors, in a special circumstance of his life, measured his responsibility as a writer. The Occupation taught us ours. Since we act on our time by our very existence, we decide that this action will be deliberate.

Like Camus's *Letters to a German Friend,* Sartre was expressing intimate feelings, though he wrote more programmatically. Just as Camus was obviously "France" in the earlier piece, so is Sartre obviously "the writer" here. And he was also writing as editor of a new journal, announcing the direction he would give it. Henceforth "we do not want to miss anything," and so our "action will be deliberate."

Sartre's call was immediately a cause célèbre. Beginning in early 1947 he developed at greater length a historical, philosophical, and political justification for engaged literature. He seemed to be working on a synthesis of Camus's practice and his own ideas—spelling out and generalizing what Camus was doing. After all, weren't Camus's editorials exactly what Sartre saw Zola and Voltaire (with whom he had already compared Camus) as having done? And wasn't his own call to action a poignant and powerful promise that he, Sartre, would no longer miss his own rendezvous with history? Might not Camus have read Sartre's New York lecture, or at least Sartre's ideas, with a deep sense of recognition and satisfaction?

In fact, he did not. Camus was unhappy with Sartre's demand. Even though praised and obviously appreciated by Sartre, he rejected any general claim that he was doing what the writer *should* do. And he rejected key aspects of Sartre's philosophy that underlay the demand, including its systematic character and its postwar insistence that we are situated in history. It is tempting to ascribe his decision not to participate in *Les Temps modernes* to these differences, but in fact, when the editorial team was assembled in late 1944, he was absorbed in *Combat.*

When Camus, before the war, had reviewed Paul Nizan's *The Conspiracy*, he expressed the opinion that political commitment—in this case becoming a member of the Communist Party—is like marriage, "a problem as pointless as that of immortality, a matter that a man settles himself and about which one mustn't judge him." In his postwar journals and interviews, Camus now defended the writer's freedom while never doubting the writer's need to "depict the passions of the day" and "the drama of our time." In a mid-1946 journal entry, Camus wrote: "I prefer committed men to literatures of commitment. Courage in one's life and talent in one's works—this is not so bad. And moreover the writer is committed when he wishes to be. His merit lies in his impulse. But if this is to become a law, a function, or a terror, where is the merit?"

It was Sartre who was looking for "a law, a function," which obviously Camus regarded as "a terror." "It seems," Camus continued—was he referring to those calling for commitment?—that writing a "poem about spring today would be to serve capitalism." But insisting that humanity needs "bread of the heart" as well as bread and justice, Camus remarked that he would delight unreservedly in such a work "if it was beautiful." Was he talking about Sartre when he said, "I should like to see them less committed in their works and a little more so in their daily life"? It seems so, because his next journal entry was about existentialism, and by 1946, when talking about existentialism, he was talking about Sartre, although not by name. He accused him of assuming Hegel's great error, "which consists in reducing man to history." He believed that Sartre had contradicted his own basic principle, because humans absorbed completely into history have lost all freedom.

In Camus's view, Sartre's demand for commitment placed history *above* the individual. Unlike nature, history prescribes responsibilities that the individual must meet, or it refers to vast forces that subordinate the individual. According to Camus, Sartre, although he began with contingency, was untrue to his own starting point because he ended up with history with a capital H. Existentialism was no less guilty than Christianity or Marxism of evading absurdity in ways diagnosed by *The Myth of Sisyphus*. Camus asserted this in a famous interview in fall 1945. After insisting that he was not a philosopher because he did "not believe sufficiently in reason to believe in a system," Camus pointed out that existentialism takes two forms, the religious and the atheistic. Atheistic existentialism, including that of Husserl, Heidegger, and Sartre, also ends up with "divinization, but it is simply that of history, considered as the only absolute. They no longer believe in God, but they believe in history." Camus recognized the value of religion and acknowledged history's importance, but he maintained he did not believe in either "in the absolute sense of the word."

What exactly was taking place in his disavowal of Sartre? Although Camus sought to separate himself from his friend's injunctions about commitment, he was also insisting on the fundamental opposition between "history" and "the world" or "life" that had been part of his own thought since the 1930s. In lamenting the beginning of war in September 1939, for example, he hoped that "after this war the trees will blossom again, because ultimately the world always conquers history." In one of his "Reading Room" reviews, he commented favorably on author André Chamson's view of history as "a ridiculous episode over which life always triumphs in the end." And in his *Letters to a German Friend* he had spoken of "entering history" in order to combat the Occupation. As Sartre later said, Camus believed himself *outside* history but saw himself as entering it from time to time. Committed as Camus always was, he saw history as alienating us from ourselves and from all that is most vital.

As we see, Camus was quite capable of articulating and analyzing the sometimes subtle and sometimes sharp differences between Sartre's thought and his own. He rejected the postwar direction Sartre took with his notion of "situation"—the historical and social reality in which we *always* find ourselves and for which we *always* bear responsibility. For Camus, if we admit that we are totally within a situation, history would overwhelm our own room for maneuver and absorb our own choices. For Sartre, our ontological freedom is absolute; yet it always means choosing how to live (or reject) our various determinations.

As Sartre was shifting from an ontological perspective to a historically grounded one, Camus perceived his Achilles' heel: Where is the basis for freedom and self-determination once we accept that these occur only in a concrete context? Sartre did not even attempt to reconcile the ontological or ahistorical nature of his original terms with a historical understanding of human reality, including ontology, until around the time of Camus's death, when winding up his labors on the never-to-be-finished (and only posthumously published) second volume of *Critique of Dialectical Reason*. For Camus, the stakes were high: to preserve an area outside any historical situation for individual freedom, autonomous values, and moral judgment. Had this issue been openly explored between friends of such rising fame and political commitment, the two would have created one of the most important of postwar political discussions. But instead, Camus made do with quips and shrugs, saving his sharpest remarks for his journal.

It is not surprising that Camus rejected the all-embracing character of Sartre's thought. He claimed not to be a philosopher because he laid claim to areas of life *not* governed by the principles of a synthesizing vision: art knows no logic but its own; morality judges politics; individuals are free *not* to commit themselves; the world is governed by specific people and processes, not just by a few broad forces.

Moreover, Camus was seeking to distinguish himself from Sartre for reasons of pride. Beauvoir noticed how he bristled when Sartre, who was widely regarded as the more powerful thinker, was always named first: "Sartre and Camus." In rejecting the label of junior partner, he withdrew from Sartre's field of force. He humorously but decisively separated himself in one of his interviews in fall 1945.

> No, I am not an existentialist. Sartre and I are astonished to see our names connected. We even are thinking of one day publishing a little announcement where the undersigned affirm that they have nothing in common and each refuses to repay debts that the other contracts. Because, finally, it is a joke. Sartre and I published all our books, without exception, before meeting each other. When we met, it was to verify our differences. Sartre is an existentialist, and the only book of ideas I have published, *The Myth of Sisyphus,* was directed against philosophers called existentialists.

The Myth of Sisyphus had criticized Chestov, Kierkegaard, and Jaspers for escapism because "they deify what crushes them and find reason to hope in what impoverishes them. That forced hope is religious in all of them." Sartre had much more in common with Camus than with any of these writers, but Camus was now insisting that since Sartre was opening himself to history and society, he and the new French "existentialists" were making the same sort of leap of faith he decried in *The Myth of Sisyphus.*

On his side, Sartre acquiesced in Camus's determination to distinguish himself from Sartre. He had begun his article in *Action* in December 1944 by describing Camus's philosophy of the absurd as "coherent and profound," crediting Camus with being "big enough to defend it all by himself" (*de taille à la défendre seul*)—a rather patronizing compliment. Then he launched into a defense of existentialism against his Communist critics.

In his 1973 conversations with Beauvoir, Sartre contradicted his earlier writing by insisting that Camus "had nothing in common with existentialism." We have seen Camus's disavowal of existentialism and suggested the reasons for it. The public linkage of Sartre and Camus was no mere misunderstanding, as was demonstrated by the stunning review that a former student of Sartre, Alexandre Astruc—then a reporter for *Combat* and later to become a filmmaker—wrote for the Communist weekly *Action* in October 1944. Astruc, infatuated with Sartre's thought, illuminated Camus's play *The Misunderstanding* by reference to ideas shared by Camus and Sartre. The play's hero returns home after many years, somewhat like Orestes in *The Flies,* but to a mother and sister who rob and kill their guests. He hopes that they will recognize him and thus confer a destiny upon him. Because "existence is absurdity and man is a stranger," the world answers no to his passive hope, and his mother and sister, taking him for a well-to-do stranger, kill him like all the others, and only then discover who he was. But this is a human mistake, not the unfolding of fate. Like *The Flies,* but unlike the works of Giraudoux, Anouilh, and Cocteau, this tragedy does not portray "the crushing of a man by destiny but the affirmation of human freedom in a struggle with itself." Astruc's review, like Sartre's American lecture a few months later, assimilated Sartre to Camus for a simple reason: they were similar.

: : :

Political writing was a major preoccupation of both Camus and Sartre during the postwar period. Camus wrote at least 120 newspaper editorials in the year after the Liberation. As a journalist, he rarely made or supported specific programmatic proposals but wrote mostly of broad themes such as justice, truth, order, morality, cynicism, purity, and dignity. Notwithstanding the revolutionary slogan on its masthead and its general commitment to a democratic and socialist transformation of France, *Combat* advocated rather limited change, that of "introducing the language of morality into the exercise of politics." Camus carried this out by short, thematic essays, which were often replies to other newspapers' editorials or to public statements by political figures.

On September 8, 1944, Camus posed in the most general terms the "problem that faces Europe today" : reconciling individual freedom with collective needs—that is, reconciling freedom with justice in such a way that life can "be free for the individual, but just for all." Camus always acknowledged the practical difficulties in realizing such goals, but his purpose was to set them before his readers as touchstones for political behavior. He sought to create, and make use of, a moral compass for political judgment.

When reflecting on the atomic bombing of Hiroshima in August 1945, Camus insisted that "technical civilization has just reached its highest level of savagery." He wrote a forceful editorial that stressed that civilization must choose between collective suicide and using its scientific conquests wisely. He insisted that it would be "indecent" to join the chorus celebrating such a discovery. Henceforth, a truly international society of equals would be the only solution, and the "only struggle worth engaging in" is for peace. Camus's editorial should be compared with the treatment given to Hiroshima by one member of the chorus, the Communist daily *l'Humanité,* which said little about the actual destruction wrought by the bomb and dwelled instead on "the most sensational scientific discovery of the century." In contrast to the Communist Party's celebration of technology, Camus vigorously asserted moral principles.

Only in one case—when discussing Algeria—did he pursue "the simple reporting of factual information." In spring 1945, he wrote a series of articles after a three-week visit to his native country. It took place around the time of the Sétif massacre of French settlers (May 8) and the subsequent reprisals. Camus described the economic and political situation behind the explosion. He discussed the widespread famine and the need for massive aid from France, the inequality in rations designated for French and Arabs, and the further inequality in rations actually received. He then explored the political situation, giving a sympathetic account of why Arab Algerians no longer desired assimilation (the official policy) and supported the "Friends of the Manifesto," who sought equal citizenship and power for Algerian Arabs alongside Algerian French in a republic within metropolitan France. It was "pure and simple stupidity" to respond to such demands with prison and repression. Camus ended with a vague demand for justice, for giving Algeria not the discourse of democracy but its reality.

Camus might be criticized for not mentioning the horrifying disproportion between European and Muslim victims of the uprising that followed the celebration at the end of the war in Europe: 102 French and at least ten times as many Arabs died in the rioting. He did not go into the systematic French oppression of Arabs in every area of Algerian life. Nor did he spell out what he meant by equality between Arabs and Europeans or by a democratic Algeria. But his perspective was totally new in mainstream French media of the time, as we can see by comparing Camus with *l'Humanité*'s articles on Algeria during the same period. These demanded that Hitlerite and Vichyite agents in the pay of the "one hundred fascist landowners" responsible for the troubles be arrested. *L'Humanité* agreed that Muslims must be given "bread and not bombs," but said nothing about the colonial system as such. The Communist inclination was to blame provocateurs, not colonial conditions, for Sétif and the aftermath. Given what was actually being said at the time, Camus's was a rare and courageous voice for facing reality, and, more implicitly, for doing so with the recognition of Algerian Arabs as equals.

Camus's editorials tended to moralize. One example: "The greatness of this age, so miserable otherwise, is that its choices have become pure." Another:

"There is only one thing left to try: the simple, modest path of honesty without illusion, of wise loyalty, of tenacity, which only strengthens human dignity." His editorials may seem naive, simplistic, or dogmatic a half-century later. But in reading them today we should appreciate both Camus's historical situation and his political purpose.

Combat, after all, called for a revolution that never happened. Not only did the Resistance represent a minority, but its non-Communist left wing was a minority among a minority. The moral capital of its adherents was enormous, but their social, political, and military power had to be shared with the Gaullists and the Communists, not to mention the military forces that did most of the work of liberating France, namely, the Allies. Sartre, with his outsider's sense of the Resistance as being little better than symbolic, perceived an essential element of the situation: however important it seemed on the ground in France, the Resistance was merely one aspect of an overall strategy for liberating France that had been largely developed in London. Accordingly, the resistants' postwar sense of being cheated of the fruits of victory—a real social transformation from "Resistance to Revolution"—resulted from an illusion, namely, that the French had liberated themselves and were fully masters of their own fate. France was in fact subject to far more powerful forces, which severely constricted its room for maneuver, both at the Liberation and during the years that followed. Camus was a skilled newspaperman and a fresh voice with a new approach to politics, but he was also a voice crying in the wilderness. The faults of his editorials, including what seems to be their inflated language, were inseparable from his role as a lone prophet.

At the same time, Camus's unstated purposes were to educate an intellectual readership, primarily a young one, in rejecting political realism, whether of the Left, Right, or Center; to insist on applying principles to politics; to counter cynicism. By demonstrating that political thinking need not abandon the terrain of values, his editorials were serious efforts at political journalism.

: : :

Sartre's first political reportage was written for Camus. As we have seen, Beauvoir claimed to have authored Sartre's first *Combat* articles. The second and third sets of newspaper articles bearing Sartre's name appeared in *Combat* and *Le Figaro* between January and June 1945. The twenty-one *Combat* articles, clearly left-wing in orientation, focused on American living conditions as experienced by a French observer—social and economic themes, Hollywood, and American factories and workers. The eleven articles for *Le Figaro* made more enjoyable reading, which annoyed Camus, but they skated across the surface of American life and mythology.

That fall, Sartre launched *Les Temps modernes* with his resounding call for political commitment. These first statements of his intellectual and political project, in a different register from Camus's writings, were no less moral and reflected the fundamentally ethical cast of his thinking. What else but ethical was his stress on action and the idea that in acting for ourselves we act for all of humanity, his insistence on the writer's political commitment, based on the individual's responsibility for all that happens in his or her historical world? Morality was at the very center of a philosophy that stressed freedom and choice, that insisted that in choosing we create our own values.

All choices are not equal, of course, as Sartre showed in one of his first truly committed writings, "Portrait de l'antisémite." Written in October 1944 and published in *Les Temps modernes* in late 1945, it was the early draft of a book published in 1946. This essay, one of the first discussions of anti-Semitism in the face of the revelations coming from the extermination camps, dissected the voyage into bad faith of someone who develops a vocation for anti-Semitism. It described the choice of evil as the decision to turn others into things, to have rights over them, springing from a fundamental denial of one's own contingency. Sartre had already suggested this vocation in some of his 1930s fiction: young Lucien Fleurier's choice in "The Childhood of a Leader" to become a fascist; Rémy Parrotin and Bouville's bourgeoisie in *Nausea,* who attempted to intimidate their subjects and claim a right to rule them; in the same novel, the Corsican librarian's homophobia and authoritarian violence. In a discussion based directly on the account of relations between the self and the other in *Being and Nothingness,* Sartre sought the ontological root of oppression, much as Camus would do with revolutions gone awry in *The Rebel.* Sartre's stress on choice, situation, historicity, and responsibility and his vision of a collectivity of equals added to his developing moral basis for political intervention. He was testing the power of his philosophy as an interpretative grid for contemporary social issues. Anti-Semitism, he said, "could not exist in a classless society." Where people "feel mutual bonds of solidarity, because they are all engaged in the same enterprise, there is no place for it."

In the discussion held a few days after Sartre's "Existentialism Is a Humanism," Pierre Naville, a Marxist philosopher who was not a Communist, used the term "pre-engagement" with reference to Sartre's philosophy. By 1945, as we have seen, Camus was already political, committed, and active in a way that Sartre could only talk about. As Sartre's call for commitment indicated, he was moving toward politics, but most of his statements—with the notable exception of his discussions of the United States—were still rather abstract. His first political interventions, still a few years off, involved crossing a major threshold, which he would continue to negotiate in his plays as late as 1954. Sartre's most impressive statement of the time was a ringing declaration of engagement, a kind of preface to politics. The politics would follow.

As Sartre became more political, Camus's own political development gathered momentum in a direction that was parallel but sometimes ran contrary to the one Sartre was taking. To appreciate this development we must turn to Camus's and Sartre's interaction with the major presence neglected by our story so far, namely Communism both in the Soviet Union and in the French Communist Party. The two men's attitudes toward Communism were already part of their political evolution: all of Sartre's and Camus's political-intellectual efforts in the period immediately after the war were aimed at strengthening the *non-Communist* Left. Their common rejection of "political realism" was in part a rejection of the Communist outlook. For both of them, the PCF would loom even larger. Communism would become Camus's enemy and Sartre's polestar.

4

camus's turning-point

One evening in mid-November 1946, at a party given by Boris and Michelle Vian, Camus showed up in a foul mood at about eleven. According to Beauvoir, telling the story long afterwards,

> He attacked Merleau-Ponty on the subject of his article, "The Yogi and the Proletarian," accused him of justifying the Moscow trials and was appalled that opposition could be made into treason. Merleau-Ponty defended himself, Sartre supported him; Camus, shattered, left, slamming the door behind him; Sartre and Boris rushed out and ran after him along the street, but he refused to come back. This quarrel was to last until March 1947.

Why the explosion? Beauvoir exploited her former closeness with Camus to cast his bad temper in strictly personal terms, asserting that he "was going through a crisis caused by the feeling that his golden age was drawing to a close." Her reminiscence dates from 1963, after Camus's death. In telling the 1946 story, she quoted from Sartre's 1952 letter "My Dear Camus," which broke off their friendship, and from Camus's narrator-protagonist Clamence's description of himself in *The Fall,* published in 1956. She presented Camus in the worst possible light:

> We were with him once at a concert which everyone who was anyone in Paris attended; he was accompanied by a young singer in whom he was interested. "When I think," he said to Sartre, "that we can foist her on this public tomorrow!" He swept the auditorium with a triumphant gesture. Sartre, at his request, wrote the first words of a song: "Hell is all my habit now." But that was as far as it went.

The young woman was Juliette Gréco. How slanted this entire reconstruction was can be seen from Beauvoir's silence about the main reason for Camus's anger toward Merleau-Ponty. While mentioning that Merleau-Ponty had criticized Arthur Koestler's anti-Communist *Darkness at Noon* and *The Yogi and the Commissar* in *Les Temps modernes,* she ignored two key details. Camus had just become personally and politically close to Koestler, and Camus was in the midst of completing a major rethinking of his political outlook in a series of articles with the overall title *Neither Victims nor Executioners.* The series was published in *Combat* from November 19 through 30.

However self-righteous Camus may have become, this dispute was first and foremost a political one. Merleau-Ponty, the political editor of *Les Temps modernes* and Sartre's political mentor, had explained the Moscow Trials as the understandable self-defense of a besieged revolution; Camus equated Communism with murder. Merleau-Ponty presented an independent but sympathetic Marxist understanding of Soviet violence; Camus rejected Marxism and revolution. Merleau-Ponty still regarded the Communist leaders as potential comrades; Camus had come to regard them as enemies. In forgetting that Camus was on the verge of articulating an important critique of Communism from within their common leftist intellectual world, Beauvoir trivialized the dispute. Looking back a decade and a half later, she ignored the arduous process he was going through and denied him both political intelligence and the courage of his convictions. Searching for seeds of the split in a way that cast blame on Camus, she was retelling the story from its ending backward.

The real story includes not only the friendship between Camus and Sartre, which was to continue for another six years, but also both men's interactions with Communism. Camus's and Sartre's political, intellectual, and personal development was inseparable from their individual and sometimes intertwined relations with the French Communist Party and the Soviet Union.

This part of our story reaches back to the early 1930s. It took Camus from 1935 until the fall of 1946 to arrive at a dramatic, public conclusion about Communism. That conclusion must have prompted his outburst against Merleau-Ponty, and it eventually pitted him against Sartre. An examination of the two men's interaction with Communism reveals why Camus, and not Sartre, was moved to regard Communism as humanity's foremost enemy on the eve of the Cold War, and why Sartre later came to side with Communism against the capitalist West.

: : :

During the high tide of the Resistance, the PCF had acted with such courage, discipline, and militant force that by the Liberation it had become France's largest party, with nearly 400,000 members. In 1946 the membership had almost doubled. The party won more than one-fourth of the votes in every postwar election; participated in the coalition government until mid-1947; dominated the country's largest trade union; published dozens of newspapers (including the two largest in France) and journals; created many organizations; had a payroll of more than 14,000 people; and placed its cadres throughout the government, including the educational system, the social security apparatus, and the police. A professedly revolutionary party, the PCF made it clear, after the heady and chaotic first few weeks of the Liberation, that it sought above all to be included in the government as the party of the working class.

The PCF, it was commonly said, was a party unlike any other. In theory its members formed a revolutionary priesthood, disciplined cadres rather than the more loosely committed supporters attached to other parties. They accepted an all-embracing ideology and submitted to an authoritarian decision-making process. Collectively they formed a cradle-to-grave countersociety, which sought to meet its members' needs in the present while pointing to the future classless society. Its claim to represent the industrial working class was widely accepted. Its rival party, the Socialists—the French Section of the Workers' International (SFIO)—had basically embraced parliamentary democracy in 1921, and since then had acted in the name neither of a single coherent ideology nor of the industrial working class. In contrast, the PCF that emerged from the underground in August 1944 was huge, largely proletarian, and militantly Marxist. While willing to consider a democratic path to socialism, it regarded electoral activity as only one terrain of struggle in a war without compromise.

PCF Marxism was at one and the same time politics, popular culture, science, philosophy, and aesthetic culture—answering all questions; fighting on all terrains; enlisting workers, farmers, shopkeepers, teachers, artists, writers, natural and social scientists, and philosophers. All intellectual questions were its province, and so the party had—*had* to have—an answer for everything. Much of the PCF's Marxism was routinized and dogmatic, the credo of half-educated pedants, but Communism also attracted brilliant minds in search of a compelling and hopeful worldview.

The PCF's primary allegiance was not only to the workers but also to the single successful revolutionary socialist society, the Soviet Union. The USSR dominated much of the PCF's ideological and organizational style and dictated its key policy decisions. At the decisive test in September 1939, most of the French Communist leadership chose the Soviet Union and neutrality over France and war with Germany. The PCF was outlawed; during the Phony War, some said that the French government fought the PCF more vigorously than it fought the Germans. Individual Communists who defied the Party line were left to resist the Occupation on their own or in small groups. Once the Soviet Union was attacked, the PCF's revolutionary fervor was liberated, and it became the heart, soul, and most militant arm of the Resistance. Supporting Soviet interests now meant fighting for France.

The PCF brought the cult of Stalin home; indeed, it doubled it in the cult of its own general secretary, Maurice Thorez. "The comrades tell us . . ." was the way PCF leaders brought the latest directives from Moscow to their Central Committee meetings. The USSR's survival and prosperity were arguably the single most important barometer of the Communist cause, and Stalin did everything to ensure that the national parties were controlled by disciplined, trusted, and—especially—obedient loyalists. The Party created its own ideal type, illustrated by Sartre in the character Brunet in the trilogy *Roads to Freedom.* It was the militant who surrendered his subjectivity to a universal, historically ordained cause and who was able to justify every twist and turn in the Party line, even a reversal of yesterday's line.

By the time of the Liberation, the Red Army had defeated Nazism in the east, and would soon liberate and occupy Eastern Europe. Many who had been outraged by Stalin's alliance with Hitler discovered the material and moral superiority of Soviet Communism. The antifascist cause of the 1930s had triumphed. The PCF, allied with a mighty, victorious nation whose army was now less than two hundred miles away, enjoyed its golden age between the Liberation and mid-1947.

Yet the Soviet Union had long ago become a dictatorship, first of the Communist Party, then of its leadership, then of one man. In some of its most prominent features it closely resembled Nazi Germany, and the word *totalitarian* was coined to describe such twentieth-century phenomena. Stalin had supplanted the other original leaders of the Bolshevik Revolution and had imposed the chaotic and bloody collectivization of agriculture, leading to famine and the deaths of millions of farmers. He then unleashed the Great Terror on the rest of Soviet society in wave after wave, climaxing in the Moscow Trials, in which surviving revolutionary leaders like Bukharin abjectly confessed to the most improbable crimes. Hundreds of thousands were executed during this paroxysm, including most of the senior military officers. The surviving Old Bolsheviks and millions of others were exiled to remote labor camps. To say that this society had achieved "socialism," as Stalin insisted after 1934, was either insanity or the most galling act of cynicism of the twentieth century.

All of this was widely known. To pick only one example, André Gide had begun actively to support Communism in 1932; in 1936 he published *Return from the Soviet Union,* in which he expressed disappointment with what he had seen in a ten-week tour. He acknowledged the effort to create a new civilization but stressed its conformity and uniformity, the cult of Stalin, and the suppression of opposition. "And I doubt whether in any other country in the world, even in Hitler's Germany, mind and spirit are less free, more bowed down, more fearful (terrorized), more vassalized." The small, restrained book soon sold 100,000 copies, more than any of Gide's others, and was translated into fifteen languages.

No less sensational ten years later was the French translation of Koestler's *Darkness at Noon.* Echoing the Bukharin trial transcript, Koestler has Rubashov, still in the grip of Marxism's totalitarian mindset, confess to crimes he has scarcely even contemplated. He does so to buy time for the Revolution until it can industrialize and modernize Russia—and then, hopefully, realize Communism's promises. Koestler's point is that Rubashov willingly sacrifices himself for the sake of a history gone wrong, in the deluded hope that it will right itself. He seeks to depict the disastrous effect of Rubashov's totalitarian mind both on himself and on the world around him. Caught up in the immensely seductive power of an evil claiming to be good, Rubashov rejects the truth and so perpetuates Communism's chain of destruction.

With such publicity being given to its negative features, how was it possible for so many, Communists and sympathizers, to sing the praises of Soviet Communism after the Liberation? By defeating absolute evil in a Manichaean war, allied with the capitalist democracies under the banner of antifascism, the Soviet Union had wrapped itself in the democratic mantle. And didn't its defeat of the world's most powerful military machine testify to its own colossal achievements in ten years of forced industrialization and modernization? Didn't the total war that destroyed the Nazi armies mobilize the entire society and reflect massive popular support for Communism and Stalin?

Moreover, the negative features—forced collectivization and the consequent starvation of millions of small farmers, the shooting of a million supposed conspirators, the forced confessions at the Moscow Trials, a vast system of labor camps, totalitarian tyranny—were so unprecedented, so unimaginable, that it was difficult for supporters even to admit their possibility. And Marxism encouraged the tough-minded understanding that you have to break eggs to make an omelet. In a violent and ugly world, human progress, especially in Europe's most backward country, could not be sweet and reasonable. After all, didn't the Second World War end only with the nuclear destruction of Hiroshima and Nagasaki?

Paradoxically, the very brutality of Russian Communism confirmed how serious it was about creating a new society. After all, Merleau-Ponty, in the articles that angered Camus and later became the book *Humanism and Terror*, spoke of Communist violence as a means, perhaps the only means, for removing capitalism's violence. He accepted the Moscow Trials as a legitimate mode of political struggle for a revolutionary government under threat, stressing the necessity of terror to protect that government. Moral judgments and questions of fact seemed to dissolve in the face of this sophisticated existentialist-Marxist dialectic, as Merleau-Ponty earnestly clarified the logic whereby even a loyal Bolshevik like Bukharin might "objectively" become an enemy of the Revolution.

Other key features of Marxism inclined its adherents toward accepting Stalinism. Marxism's stress on the authority of science, its claim to objectivity, and its eschatological mood predisposed many to embrace the victorious Soviet Union as its authentic, real-world embodiment. Taking the name of its founder, Marxism honored the authority of superior knowledge. If Lenin became its second eponymous prophet, then why not acknowledge the genius of Stalin in combining theory and practice? Marxism's stress on objective social structures and the need to transform them, and its neglect of subjectivity, lent support to the notion that *how* these structures were changed was of lesser importance. The thing was to abolish capitalism and industrialize by hook or by crook, and then democracy and other such human development would follow. This is why Koestler's Rubashov became an excellent recruiter for Communism. Furthermore, Marxism's utopian dimension disposed its supporters to anticipate, and embrace, a top-to-bottom transformation of the human condition, as was surely taking place in the Soviet Union. Caviling over short-term costs threw obstacles in the way of this total change, which could not help but be chaotic and even brutal.

But this emphasis on the Soviet Union neglects something closer to home. Russia mattered less than France. For Sartre and many others, the Soviet Union formed a distant horizon, not the heart of the matter. To get closer to the working class meant approaching the French Communist Party. For intellectuals and workers alike, France's largest party—whatever its affiliations elsewhere and however unappealing many of its traits—not only had been the leading force of the Resistance but was above all the party of the workers. Later, Sartre would remember wanting "to fight on the side of the working class" and thus being drawn to Marxism "as the moon draws the tides."

It certainly counted for something that Soviet Communism supported French workers in the conflict with French capitalism and French imperialism. After all, like Hitler, didn't those attacking Communism seek to protect a system that meant poverty and unemployment, colonialism and war? In the climate of struggle, Merleau-Ponty asked, wasn't anti-Communism a way of avoiding talk about the evils of capitalism? Accordingly, supporters of the working class and partisans of Communism were willing to tolerate or even deny many of its most terrible features, believing they were defamatory images concocted by the other side.

But not indefinitely. Gide's story shows that Communism raised the universal and highest hopes of millions of the best minds of the twentieth century. But it also shows that, especially among intellectuals, belief in the Soviet Union faded as the truth became known. No other movement betrayed its hopes so cruelly. The commitments that drew intellectuals to Communism after the war withstood some, but rarely all, of the revelations: Stalin's anti-Semitism, Khrushchev's "secret speech," the Soviet invasion of Hungary, and so forth. No other movement produced an international series of testimonies about "the God that failed." Millions went through Communism only to be disenchanted by it, to be expelled, to resign, to drift away. In France, each decade after the Bolshevik Revolution saw once-enthusiastic intellectuals turn away and write about their disenchantment. Pierre Pascal and Boris Souvarine did so in the 1920s, Gide and Malraux in the 1930s. Sartre's boyhood friend Paul Nizan, who became well known as the author of *Aden, Arabia* and as the foreign editor of *l'Humanité*, resigned from the PCF at news of the Hitler-Stalin pact in August 1939.

: : :

Camus's and Sartre's postwar relations with the PCF took place within this larger picture, connecting intimately with the experience, testimony, and analysis of such friends as Nizan, Arthur Koestler, and Maurice Merleau-Ponty. In Algiers in the 1930s it had been nearly impossible to be a young, leftist European, eager for radical change, without being drawn to the PCF. Camus became a member, as did many of his friends. As organizer of its theater troupe and, hence, one of the Party's most visible members in Algiers, he rejected the way it soft-pedaled the critique of colonialism just to maintain a coalition with rabidly anti-Arab European workers. His experience reflected French Communism's subjection to the shifting needs of the Soviet Union and its bizarre ways. Camus was tried by the Party and expelled as a "Trotskyite"—a code name for someone whose views were more militant than those of the Party leadership.

Camus's earliest response to his experience in the PCF is reflected in *The Myth of Sisyphus.* He developed his absurdist philosophy *after* having been exposed to Marxism and Communism. In the 1930s he had encountered Marxism's emphasis on meaning and coherence, but by the 1940s he had decided that the world had neither meaning nor coherence. Having lived and worked within Communism's vision of human progress, he decided that the true picture of the world was captured by Sisyphus's fruitless, endless labor. Having experienced the Party's sense of social connectedness, he decided that the individual was the locus of thought and action. Having lived in an ambiance of class struggle, he concluded that humanity's great question was whether or not to commit suicide.

To Marxism's claims, Camus's absurdism replied that none of our labors can solve the tragedy of death or give sense to the world. There is no direct mention of Marxism or Communism in *The Myth of Sisyphus,* but the critique is everywhere implied: "The leap in all its forms, rushing into the divine or the eternal—all these screens hide the absurd." In this deepest sense his Party experience entered into the text, which was therefore—unlike Sartre's *Being and Nothingness*—post-Marxist rather than pre-Marxist. Having rejected Marxism's hopes, Camus struck the dominant chord of his philosophy: Sisyphus continuing his labors in spite of everything. Ex-Communist Camus affirmed that "being deprived of hope is not despairing."

And Sartre? For many years his experience of the party was as an apolitical observer, an outsider. In the mid-1930s he watched as Nizan, his alter ego and best friend at the Ecole Normale Supérieure, became as prominent in the PCF's Paris circles as Camus was in Algiers. He read his friend's attack on their teachers and on bourgeois philosophy in general in a book called *The Watchdogs*. And he knew that Nizan had left the party in response to the Hitler-Stalin pact and was killed at the front shortly afterward. Through Nizan's commitment and disillusionment, and his later denunciation by PCF intellectuals, Sartre saw what drew people to Marxism, their sense of belonging to a cause larger than themselves, and the disciplines imposed by that cause. Nizan would become the model for the Communist militant Brunet in Sartre's trilogy *Roads to Freedom*.

When forming the Socialisme et Liberté group in 1941, Sartre tried to link up with the PCF, apparently not realizing that it would fail to oppose the Occupation until the Soviet Union became involved in the war. Not only did the PCF rebuff him, but Party members began to spread the story that Sartre had been allowed to leave the prison camp because he was a German agent. After Sartre's little Resistance group disbanded, its most serious members joined cause with the Communists, and Sartre returned to his writing. Then, during the high tide of the Resistance, the party created all manner of broad activities and organizations, such as the Comité National des Ecrivains, which published *Les Lettres françaises*. Nonparty writers like Sartre and Camus were invited to join the CNE and to contribute to *LLF*.

Around the same time, according to fellow resistant and writer Jean Lescure, a leaflet appeared denouncing "existentialist" writers who claimed to be in the Resistance. It specifically named Sartre, Camus, Lescure, and one other writer, ostensibly questioning their Resistance credentials. This strange tract, apparently the work of a Communist named Jean Marcenac, had the sinister intention of denouncing the named writers to the Germans.

Did PCF intellectuals see Camus and Sartre as potential future competitors even while Resistance comradeship was at its peak? In *Combat*, Camus challenged the *parti des fusillés* immediately after the Liberation. *Combat*'s slogan "From Resistance to Revolution" and its call for radical social change differed sharply from the Communists' patriotic call for greater productivity for the war effort. As an editorialist, Camus claimed that the Resistance had not sacrificed for all these years only to bring back the same politicians, the same corrupt republic, and the same mediocre ruling class. He called for "a collectivist economy to take away money's privilege." The PCF sought to revive the Popular Front of the 1930s but with itself as the leading force. Because the war wasn't over yet, it argued that all the nation's energies must be directed at destroying

Nazi Germany, which was battling on two fronts—against American, British, and French armies as well as Soviet armies. In contrast to the PCF, Camus declared that France must "make a revolution and at the same time fight a war." Although he was sympathetic to workers, Camus's stress on the individual was far from Marxism's sense of social class. He called for "a new liberal socialism" rooted in the Resistance and distinct from Marxism. But he also stressed the need for different political currents to clarify their differences in an open-ended way.

Right after the Liberation, editorials criticizing other individuals or organizations often avoided mentioning names. Resistance solidarity kept debate polite and lines of opposition open. Camus had come a long way from the twenty-three-year old writer and amateur director who had been hauled before a Party tribunal in Algiers. He now approached the Communists as an equal, a self-confident Resistance editor with a clear sense of his political principles. In October 1944, he intervened in a discussion that originated with an article in *Action,* which criticized his friend Jean Guéhenno for his stress on "purity." He was answered by *Action*'s editor Pierre Hervé in November. Without using names, Hervé spoke scornfully of "the young turks of the bourgeoisie" who emerged from the Resistance full of ambition. They called themselves socialists since socialism was the fashion, and saw themselves as "saints, pure ones" who claimed to speak in the spirit of the Resistance. Bored by Marxism, unwilling to speak to the proletariat, they spent their nights in the "stilted world of ideas" speaking of freedom but with no sense of what freedom means to an unemployed worker.

Even while he distinguished the Combat movement from the PCF in its commitment to socialism *and* individual rights, justice *and* freedom, Camus also criticized the Communists for thinking they had an exclusive claim on the truth and for being unwilling to discuss their ideas openly and undogmatically. Yet Camus rejected anti-Communism as "the beginning of tyranny." Although he was still speaking to the Communists, the Resistance sense of unity faded as the war dragged on. By December 1944, Camus was warning that the Resistance was in danger of being regarded as just another political sect rather than remaining the consensus of France.

At this same time, Communist and pro-Communist readers and their publications were encountering Camus and Sartre, usually mentioned together, as newly fashionable authors of fiction, plays, and philosophy. Communist editors sometimes ran strikingly non-Marxist articles—for example, those in *Action* by Alexandre Astruc, a former student of Sartre's. Astruc called *The Stranger* "the best novel published during the Occupation," and described Sartre's work as "the most passionate of his generation." And in an article on Saint-Exupéry,

Astruc described that author's movement from absurdity to hope as parallel to that of Camus and Sartre, whose work "is haunted by an essential incoherence, which reveals the world under the angle of a nightmare and absurdity." The three writers opened a window onto "morality, that is, values," which had become a crucial contemporary theme.

Les Lettres françaises, controlled by PCF members in a broad coalition with others, kept its pages open to Sartre. Both Sartre and Camus had contributed to it clandestinely during the Occupation. Within the three months of its first legal appearance, *LLF* not only published "The Republic of Silence" and gave *No Exit* a highly intelligent review but ran as a lead piece the first chapter of Sartre's forthcoming novel, *The Reprieve.* Then, in early December, *LLF* gave Sartre's response pride of place among a set of interviews about wartime prisoners' readings.

In the first months after the Liberation, Party criticisms and Sartre's and Camus's responses formed a genuine exchange, as with Camus's editorials. *Les Lettres françaises* ran an article by its publisher, George Adam, criticizing unnamed authors for flirting with despair and "individualist pessimism," which now, just after the Liberation, were "out of season." Camus, implicated but unnamed, defended himself as well as Sartre in a *Combat* article in November 1944 entitled "Pessimism and Courage." He distinguished himself from Nietzsche and Heidegger—and also, by implication, from Sartre, who was just then embracing the word "existentialism": "I do not have much liking for the all too famous existential philosophy, and, to tell the truth, I think its conclusions false. But at least it represents a great adventure of the mind."

Camus still regarded the Communists behind *LLF* as "comrades." "Their doctrines are not ours, but it has never occurred to us to talk of them in the tone they have just used toward us and with the assurance they show." Associating himself directly with Sartre, he agreed that "everything is not summed up in negation and absurdity. We know this. But we must first posit negation and absurdity because they are what our generation has encountered and what we must take into account." He pleaded for patience to be shown to these writers, who after all, were sincerely grappling with difficult issues. "Isn't it possible to address them more humbly?"

After being attacked in *Action*, Sartre wrote "A More Precise Clarification of Existentialism," which appeared in *Action* in late December. His article was markedly different from Camus's response two months earlier. Unlike Camus, who repeatedly but politely stressed his differences with Communism during this period, Sartre's article was confrontational and roughly drawn. He was clearly irritated at the PCF's "absurd criticisms."

> I'll give it to you straight: your attacks seem to me to stem from ignorance and bad faith. It's not even certain that you have read any of the books you're talking about. You need a scapegoat because you bless so many things you can't help chewing out someone from time to time. You've picked existentialism because it's an abstract doctrine few people know, and you think that no one will verify what you say. But I am going to reply to your accusations point by point.

He then proceeded in the same combative tone. In the name of Resistance solidarity, Camus had limited himself to objecting to the Communists' hostility. But Sartre's article was a masterpiece of provocation, allowing him to hawk his ideas in the guise of defending them, while never abandoning the offensive. Like Camus he did not try to integrate his philosophy with Marxism, but unlike him he did not strike a single conciliatory note. Also unlike Camus, even while accusing PCF intellectuals of lying about his philosophy, hypocrisy, bad faith, and stupidity, Sartre underscored his commitment to class struggle and his great respect for Marx's thought.

: : :

During this year after the Liberation, Communist intellectuals faced a dilemma in dealing with France's newly famous writers. They were clearly on the Left, speaking about "revolution" far more often than the PCF. Their works were new, alive, and fresh, reflecting a common mood, and their words and names were everywhere. Camus, the former Communist, rejected anti-Communism; and Sartre was critical but not politically unfriendly to the party—why not treat them as potential allies, agreeing to disagree? Sartre had heard that many Party members wanted to do just this.

The problem was that Camus's and Sartre's ideas of absurdity and freedom, their stress on morality and responsibility, and their very explicit commitment to the Left but not to the PCF, were very much in vogue among educated young people. And, as Beauvoir and Merleau-Ponty began to echo and extend these themes, starting in late 1944, it seemed as if Camus and Sartre were founding a school of thought. However friendly Sartre and individual Communist intellectuals might wish to be, he and the Party were competing for the same audience. In October 1945, this would become clear with the debut of *Les Temps modernes.*

The Communists were constitutionally incapable of agreeing to disagree. This, after all, is what Camus demanded in his call for humility, but doing so would relegate Marxism to being one point of view among others on the Left.

Claiming to possess the only valid world-historical outlook, and seeing all intellectual challenges as ideological reflections of class interests, PCF intellectuals would sooner or later have had to attack such alternative ideas and attribute them to antiproletarian ideologists even if Stalinism's witch-hunt mentality had not rubbed off on them.

For *Action,* running Sartre's article at the end of 1944 meant that the waning comradeship of the Liberation had not completely vanished. But in June 1945, *Action* finally ended its ambivalence, with a sharp attack on Sartre's ideas and, three weeks later, an assault on Camus.

Sartre's critic was Henri Lefebvre, author of a major exposition of Marxist philosophy, *Le Matérialisme dialectique*, and the most qualified person in the Party to take on Sartre. His article was steeped in Marxism's self-confidence. Lefebvre calmly laid out the historical and social perspective within which he situated the individualist philosopher, explaining why despair, solitude, anguish, and nothingness should be Sartre's main themes. Representing "an epoch condemned to disappear," Sartre might have renounced metaphysics and pure consciousness to critically move toward a perspective stressing collective action founded on objective knowledge. But he persisted in encountering existence with an isolated consciousness and in rejecting objective, historical content. Sartre viewed nothingness not as threatening "a social order on the way to being superseded"—capitalism faced with "historical death"—but, rather, as revealing "an eternal structure of human consciousness." Afflicted by an obscurantist skepticism toward science, Lefebvre contended, Sartre was unable, despite his stress on action, to see that humans make themselves socially and historically. Therefore Sartre's existentialist philosophy lent itself to being a "theoretical war machine against Marxism."

Coincidentally, Lefebvre's article appeared the day before Camus's *Combat* began publishing Sartre's last six articles from the trip he had just made to the United States, his descriptions and reflections on the American working class. These showed Sartre breaking new ground. The U.S. trip had already generated his first sustained social and political observations, and these lively and detailed articles were his first writings influenced by Marxist ideas. He stressed the centrality of social class, the alienating effect of industrial labor, and the exploitation of the workers; and he explored questions of workers' organization and ideology. On this trip he paid his first visits to factories and had his first conversations with workers and trade unionists. The United States seemed to provide a laboratory for Sartre to act on the idea of literary commitment that he was in the midst of developing. Back home, however, the Communists were declaring war on him and Camus.

At the end of June, Pierre Hervé began his column in *Action* by complaining that anti-Communism had entered into current political maneuvering among former Resistance groups. Then, obviously fed up with Camus's moralism, he turned his guns on Camus in a very personal way. He attacked Camus's and *Combat*'s habit of beginning or ending their editorials with self-righteous protestations of good faith: "We who are impartial. We who are objective. It is the custom of the popes of existentialism, who are our friends at *Combat,* to speak this way." Hervé himself would have described these *Combat* writers as "constipated." And then, zeroing in on Camus:

> I understand that the French editorialist who is the most widely read in the world doesn't find things to his taste and that he arrogates to himself the right to sovereignly distribute blame and encouragement one after the other. Like a bishop conducting a service, he objects to a dog's barking in his neighborhood. To him, the truth! To him, honesty! Unhappily, authorship of several remarkable literary works doesn't keep one from being, in political matters, a false spirit. When the cold-fish tone exasperates me, I say so. I don't hide my exasperation behind the hypocritical haughtiness of the moralist.

In discussing the maneuvering among members of the Resistance, *Combat* gave the "most inexact, the most false, and the most dishonest" accounts. Adding the voice of authority to his attack on such "bitter dilettantes," Hervé quoted from Lenin on the petite bourgeoisie: "the instability of their revolutionary impulses, their sterility, their facility in entering into submission, apathy, into fantasy, and even a rabid infatuation for this or that fashionable bourgeois tendency, all this is universally known."

Clearly a shift had taken place. The Resistance had fractured. In the fall of 1944, Camus had used the term *comrades*, but by June 1945 he was treated as an enemy, complete with a supporting quote from Lenin. Hervé's article was calculated to humiliate Camus. Indeed, after this public thrashing, Camus wrote only a few more editorials in *Combat* and then fell silent. As we have seen in his response to Hiroshima, and very much in disagreement with the PCF, he lamented the use of nuclear weapons. Later that same month, declaring that the purge had gone awry, Camus took issue with those who wanted to continue it—the Communists, above all. His admission that the political force of the Resistance was spent was one of Camus's last editorials for over a year.

In her search for the first sour notes between Sartre and herself and Camus, Beauvoir pointed to Camus's bizarre notion of asking scientists to suspend their research in order to eliminate nuclear weapons. The two years of Sartre's and Camus's most intense closeness was coming to an end at the same time as the Resistance fraternity, which had stretched from Gaullists to Communists, was falling apart. Certainly this was no coincidence. While Sartre and Camus would come to share many of the same criticisms of the Communists, their basic attitudes toward the PCF differed sharply. Ironically, as Camus was taking Communism as his main political enemy, Sartre was becoming the Party's main intellectual enemy.

Why Sartre and not Camus? Engaged with them in a totally different way than Camus was, Sartre relished arguing. Author of a complex and appealing philosophy and supported by several other proponents, Sartre openly challenged Marxism as an ideology, and PCF intellectuals had to grapple him as the "leader of a school."

They criticized *Les Temps modernes* ("nothing new" in Sartre's call for commitment) and the unhealthy characters and situations in the first two volumes of *Roads to Freedom* ("roads . . . or impasses?"). Then they devoted two whole articles to a "balance sheet of the existentialist offensive." About this time, Sartre was invited to a meeting with two of the most important Communist intellectuals, Roger Garaudy and Henri Mougin. He had been approached by a rising PCF intellectual and former student, Jean Kanapa, to meet with these men, with the idea of making peace and creating the basis for common work and dialogue. When the day came, Kanapa was not allowed to attend. Sartre recalled:

> I went to [the meeting] in a conciliatory spirit, and I found myself facing a tribunal where Garaudy and Mougin attacked me violently about my philosophy, declaring that it was rotten. Garaudy was the more violent, affirming that there was no possibility of agreement on any point between them and me. At which point I asked, surprised, why this meeting was taking place, since at no time was the possibility of a reconciliation raised.

On December 21, now fully embracing the PCF line, *LLF* published a lead article by editor Claude Morgan setting forth the newspaper's political and literary commitments and stating that "we fight against the literature of the absurd and despair"—which was how both *Caligula* and *Roads to Freedom* had just been reviewed. In the same issue, René Scherer insisted that Marxism needed no completing by existentialism, and that the two outlooks were totally opposed. On December 28 came Garaudy's front-page denunciation of Sartre as a "false prophet" and of existentialism as a "sickness." Garaudy attacked Sartre's entire range of writings, including "The Republic of Silence," which had been published in the same newspaper. He labeled Sartre a "gravedigger" and, in Sartre's own words, dragged him "more or less everywhere through the mud."

Sartre responded by dragging Garaudy himself in the mud in *Les Temps modernes*. In June and July 1946, he weighed in with a philosophical essay, "Materialism and Revolution," which criticized the mechanistic materialism of Stalinist Communism while proclaiming solidarity with the workers and with revolution, and which cruelly attacked Garaudy as being not very bright, only barely tolerated by the Party, and guilty of a "naive and stubborn" scientism. This essay demonstrated Sartre's supreme self-confidence, although he gave no indication that he had read Marx.

In arguing that materialist socialism was a contradiction in terms, Sartre stressed that any given state of affairs (for example, the workers' impoverishment) only produces another state of affairs: "A state of the world will never produce class consciousness." Even if enslaved, we are already free in some fundamental sense. Although the "myth of materialism" was useful in explaining oppression, it was utterly useless in explaining how and why humans act to emancipate themselves. Sartre developed his own key themes—action, situation, transcendence, freedom, being-in-the world, the centrality of subjectivity, opposition to any a priori ethics, hostility to the bourgeois idea of rights—in new social and political directions. In sharp dialogue with the PCF, Sartre offered existentialism *in place of* Marxism. Like Camus, Sartre had been attacked by the Party, but unlike Camus he kept talking back, fiercely and on his own ground.

: : :

Hervé's attack on Camus in June 1945, followed by Hiroshima, followed by Camus's conclusion that the purge had gone wrong, marked the end of Camus's postwar hopes. The Resistance's first wave of social reform having been exhausted, the movement was irremediably fractured. Notwithstanding the myth that France had been liberated by the Resistance, Hiroshima symbolized a deeper truth—namely, that France would now be subject to powers beyond its control. Camus's bitter reflections on the purge signaled the end of an era and a personal turning point. First he had hoped to move from "Resistance to Revolution," by which he meant socialism combined with freedom; then he lowered his sights, at least promoting political morality, mutual respect, and open, honest discussion. But by summer of 1945 these goals too seemed will o' the wisps. The old politics had returned, and Camus had nothing more to say.

Combat's masthead now sounded quaint. The Resistance was over, revolution unthinkable.

It was time for Camus to retreat and to contemplate what had gone wrong, and the direction he took was shaped by his experiences with the Communists. After a dozen years of interaction with the PCF, Camus's loss of postwar political optimism mingled with his feeling that *they* were responsible. Emerging as a prominent voice of the non-Communist Left, he had argued with the Party's outlook, but as an equal and as a comrade. This dialogue was now ended by Hervé's ugly denunciation. Such public mistreatment, especially from people he saw as fundamentally wrong philosophically and politically, meant that from now on he would speak *about* Communists, never again *to* them.

Camus signed off as editorialist on September 1, 1945, by summing up his experience over the past year as a journalist seeking to create dialogue. *Combat* had tried "loyally" to define where it agreed and disagreed with the Communists, but "we received no reply at all." Also addressed by the Catholic François Mauriac in a tone "which silenced us," Camus did not blame others for making dialogue impossible. Rather, it was a "temporary failure" due to the fact that "we have not yet found the language" to bring us together in discussion. These brave words would have entailed continuing the search for common ground, but instead Camus turned to his notebook. Little by little, he came to treat Communism as a civilizational disease, "the modern madness." Over the next sixteen months he worked at understanding its nature, its causes, its underlying premises, and its consequences.

Immediately after Hervé's article, Camus began to reflect on the tension between two terms central to his understanding of Communism, freedom and justice. In his editorials he had sought socialism *with* freedom, but the Communists, who, he argued, sought justice *without* freedom, seemed to demand that he choose between the two. And he did: "Finally, I choose freedom. For even if justice is not realized, freedom maintains the power of protest against injustice and keeps communication open." Open, that is, if it is not stifled by the Communists, who lack the intellectual freedom to admit "that the adversary is right." A few months later he contended that "Marxists do not believe in persuasion or in dialogue." And those among them "who have the responsibility of speaking for the masses"—the PCF's leaders—do not care about freedom. Still, many people side with them, choosing justice over freedom, because "justice alone can give them the material minimum they need."

These jottings moved back and forth between defiance and pessimism. Camus saw himself among a tiny minority doomed to martyrdom: "Program for tomorrow: solemn and significant execution of the witnesses of freedom."

He had worked to reconcile justice and freedom as the West's "last hope," but this was utopian in today's climate. "One or the other of these values must be sacrificed? What to think in that case?"

In a rare reference to religion, Camus said that he felt caught between two unacceptable faiths, Christianity and Communism: "Historical materialism, absolute determinism, the negation of all liberty, that frightful world of courage and silence—these are the most legitimate consequences of a philosophy without God." The only way to limit human claims and ambitions was to see God behind people and history, but this required a faith no longer possible. Was there a third way out? For Camus this meant an agonizing personal choice:

> How to choose between the two? Something in me tells me, convinces me that I cannot detach myself from my era without cowardice, without accepting slavery, without denying my mother and my truth. I could not do so, or accept a commitment that was both sincere and relative, unless I were a Christian. Not a Christian, I must go on to the end. But going on to the end means choosing history absolutely, and with it the murder of man if the murder of man is necessary to history. Otherwise I am but a witness. That is the question: can I be merely a witness? In other words: do I have the right to be a mere artist? I cannot believe so. If I do not choose both against God and against history, I am the witness of pure freedom whose fate in history is to be put to death.

When writing this—shortly after the beginning of November 1945—he could see no alternatives to "silence or death." To believe in history as the Communists did was the path of "falsehood and murder," but it was discouraging that religion seemed the only alternative. "I understand that a man can hurl himself into religion blindly to escape this madness and this painful (yes, really painful) laceration. But I cannot do it."

Slowly, with enormous strain, Camus was shaping his own alternative political path, trying to find a moral ground that would withstand the pressures he felt. And his key terms were absurdity, purity—and revolt. Around this time, Camus mentioned Sartre for the first time in his notebook. Having explained that he himself was an artist and not a philosopher because, he said, "I think according to words and not according to ideas," and having pronounced "against the literature of commitment," the pied-noir reflected that his spiritual home lay outside the cities—which were the home of thinkers such as Hegel, Sartre, and "all the modern philosophies of history"—and amid the "permanence and equilibrium" of nature. How did Sartre, who in 1945 was as far from Hegel as he was from Marx, figure in Camus's reflections? I believe Camus separated himself from Sartre in the process of clarifying his growing opposition to Marxism. According to Camus, Sartre, by demanding immersion in one's times, was siding with Marxism, while Camus continued to insist that "all mankind does not coincide with history." In his mind, Sartre failed to see this truth: "Man is not only social."

But Camus's descriptions of Sartre and of Marxism do not fit very well. The most striking feature of these ruminations is that they show no evidence of reading *Being and Nothingness* or anything Marx himself wrote. Camus may have been responding to Sartre's 1945 call for commitment, but he lumped it with Marxism without reflecting on the fundamental differences. A close reading would have shown him that Sartre's ontology of the in-itself and the for-itself rules out the possibility of being swallowed up by history. In fact, the tension between his unhistorical starting point and the historical world would remain unresolved as Sartre moved toward Marxism. Camus's subsequent pairing of Marxism and murder was another sweeping but unsupported assertion. Camus may have been thinking about party members' justifications of Stalin's crimes, but the bald equation of Marxism and murder made no sense, as the SFIO's Guy Mollet, a Marxist and moderate Socialist, could have told him. Camus may well have been touching upon certain of Marxism's flaws, but exactly how is unclear. The problem in his assertions about Sartre and about Marxism lay not in Camus's argument but, rather, in the absence of one. Working through these troubling questions, he often proceeded by making categorical claims without close analysis, reading, or actual textual references.

: : :

As Camus was pursuing these thoughts and finishing *The Plague,* the world around him was changing drastically. Nineteen forty-six was the year in which the wartime alliance broke apart into two camps, and when big-power tensions began to be cast as a war between civilizations—or, in the West, to preserve civilization itself. By February, the West's ideological foundation of the Manichaean struggle was spelled out in ambassador George Kennan's famous "long telegram" from Moscow. And in March, more publicly, British prime minister Winston Churchill gave his "Iron Curtain" speech in Fulton, Missouri. There was considerable East-West tension about Iran, Turkey, Greece, and Poland, but it was becoming clear that the Soviet Union was determined to keep control over the countries on its borders, no matter what the cost.

The world situation was shifting, and events in France were moving toward their Cold War definition. The Tripartite governing coalition of Socialists, Communists, and the Christian-Democratic Mouvement Républicain Populaire (MRP), which had initiated a series of breathtaking reforms in the months immediately after Liberation, putting in place France's modern system of social welfare and governmental economic intervention, was becoming immobilized. The first postwar elections for the Constituent Assembly, in fall 1945, had seen the two left-wing parties win an outright majority, with the PCF as the country's leading party. In May 1946, Socialist prime minister Léon Blum used the Communist threat to win debt forgiveness and new credits from Washington (funds that had originally been earmarked for the Soviet Union). One side of the government was being supported against the other by the United States, and the Communists, although in government, were not allowed access to power. Nevertheless, in the elections of November 10, the PCF tallied 28.6 percent of the vote.

Camus was absorbing the shift in the political climate, and the tensions that would lead to the Cold War. For him, as for the West as well as half of the French Left, ascendant Communism was becoming the main target. In early 1946, Camus first encountered Arthur Koestler's just-published *Darkness at Noon,* which immediately became grist for his mill. He read there descriptions of "historical reasoning"—which he was beginning to see as *the* problem. He also noticed Koestler's statement of Communism's contradiction: by making the individual a cog, it denied free will and yet demanded "that the cog should revolt against the clockwork and change its motion."

Camus visited the United States between March and May 1946. Resuming his journal upon his return, he focused his thoughts on two points—connecting Marxism with murder, under the influence of *Darkness at Noon,* and rejecting Sartre and existentialism's stress on history and commitment. Camus was working toward answering Hervé and the Communists, in his own way.

: : :

One last spark was needed to ignite this mixture. Right at this time, in Beauvoir's words, "a tumultuous newcomer burst into our group" —Arthur Koestler in person. Camus and Koestler felt an "instant comradeship" and from the beginning used the familiar *tu* with each other. *Darkness at Noon* was a best-seller, and Koestler's volume of essays *The Yogi and the Commissar* had been published recently. This book drew a sharp distinction between the historical and social orientation of the kind of person who seeks to change the world and the contemplative and artistic approach of the Yogi—a distinction that Camus had been laboring to validate. It also systematically demolished the Soviet myth with facts, figures, and analyses, concluding that the USSR was "a state-capitalist totalitarian autocracy." Koestler also sought to create an alternative vision for the Left. In person he was an agitator, pressing his anti-Communism on his new friends. Camus met him in the same month in which Merleau-Ponty broadcast his critical support for the Soviet Union while criticizing *Darkness at Noon* and Koestler's reading of Marxism. Koestler spent time drinking and socializing not only with Camus but also with Sartre and Beauvoir, in whose journal Merleau-Ponty attacked him. Camus fell in love with Koestler's partner, Mamaine, and Beauvoir had a sexual encounter with Koestler.

Beauvoir recounted their first meeting and their rollicking times together. They were "a bit embarrassed by his self-taught pedantry, by the doctrinaire self-assurance and the scientism he had retained from his rather mediocre Marxist training." He was filled with vanity and self-importance, but also with "warmth, life and curiosity; the passion with which he argued was unflagging; he was always ready, at any hour of the day or night, to talk about any subject under the sun." During Koestler's stays in Paris, Sartre and Beauvoir often met him, Mamaine, and Camus. On the night of October 31, 1946,

> we had dinner with him, Mamaine, Camus, Francine, and then went on to a little dance hall in the Rue des Gravilliers; then he issued an imperious invitation to the Schéhérazade; normally neither Camus nor myself would ever have set foot in that sort of place. Koestler ordered *zakouski,* vodka, champagne. The following afternoon, Sartre was to give a lecture at the Sorbonne, under the aegis of UNESCO, on "The Writer's Responsibility," and he hadn't yet prepared it. But the alcohol, the gypsy music and above all the heat of our discussion made him lose track of the time.

As they drank they opened up to each other. Sartre, Beauvoir, and Camus affirmed their closeness, while Koestler played the agitator.

> Camus returned to a theme very dear to him: "If only it were possible to tell the truth"; Koestler grew gloomy as he listened to "Dark Eyes"; "It's impossible to be friends if you differ about politics!" he said in an accusing tone. He rehashed his old grudges against Stalin's Russia, accusing Sartre and even Camus of trying to compromise with the Soviets. We didn't take his lugubriousness seriously; we were not aware of the passionate depths of his

> anti-Communism. While Koestler continued his monologue, Camus said to us: "What we have in common, you and I, is that for us individuals come first; we prefer the concrete to the abstract, people to doctrines, we place friendship above politics." We agreed, with an exaltation partly caused by alcohol and the lateness of the hour. Koestler repeated: "Impossible! Impossible!" And I replied, in a low voice, but clearly: "It *is* possible; and we are the proof of it at this very moment, since, despite all our dissensions, we are so happy to be together." Politics had opened abysses between some people and ourselves; but we still thought that nothing separated us from Camus except a few nuances of terminology.

Koestler led Camus by a few years in the project that was now stirring him. As a former Communist who remained on the Left, Koestler's achievements, ideas, and personality encouraged Camus's efforts both to figure out what was wrong with Communism and to find an alternative path. Camus's notebooks indicate that his own inflamed sense of Marxism was drawn from neither Marx nor Lenin but from the newcomer who proclaimed himself an expert and whose books were creating a storm in Paris. Under the heading "Conversations with Koestler," Camus reported:

> The end justifies the means only if the relative order of importance is reasonable—ex.: I can send Saint-Exupéry on a fatal mission to save a regiment. But I cannot deport millions of persons and suppress all liberty for an equivalent quantitative result and compute for three or four generations previously sacrificed.

To follow Koestler along this path of rejecting "Communist" reasoning had its perils, however. Koestler's model for Rubashov's genocidal ethics was allegedly Bukharin. But this "Marxism," which demanded sacrificing the present for the future, and so supported Stalin's most brutal acts, could have not have been further from that of the real-life Bukharin. A distinguished theoretician, he never believed in Koestler's logic that future happiness resulted from and justified present evils. He was, after all, the thinker behind the go-slow New Economic Policy, and spoke of pursuing "socialism at a snail's pace." Next to the Promethean tragedy of the real Bukharin on trial, Rubashov's drama was remarkably flat, lifeless, and ideological. This author of the Soviet constitution was no willing stooge of an evil process as in Koestler's morality play. On trial, Bukharin struggled with all his might against all specific accusations while trying to keep his bargain with his prosecutors. They promised to exchange his family's safety for a confession—but he also tried to save his honor and his revolutionary vision in the face of Stalinism. Others had read the trial transcript with greater understanding of the real life-and-death conflict taking place between the lines. It suggested an alternative way of being a Communist revolutionary, which Koestler—and, following him, Camus—refused to consider. Their vision of Communism had been shaped by the apparatchiks of the second generation with whom they had worked, products of a movement that had already been Stalinized.

As he was about to begin work on *Neither Victims nor Executioners*, Camus summarized an October 29 conversation about Communism that he had had with Koestler, Sartre, Malraux, and Manès Sperber. Koestler spoke about the moment when he stopped making excuses for the Soviet Union and saw Stalin as no better than Hitler: "something came undone at that point." Malraux doubted that the proletariat was the highest historical value. Sartre refused to turn his "moral values solely against the USSR" when the history of American racism was no less evil than the Soviet deportations. Koestler then stressed their obligation to denounce "what deserves to be denounced." Having reported this discussion, Camus added a skeptical note: it was impossible to determine "how much fear or truth enters into what each one says."

Around this time, Camus wrote a dramatic spoof, which he never published, "L'Impromptu des philosophes" (discussed more fully below, p. 235). One of its characters, M. Vigne, is a provincial pharmacist and mayor, and the other, M. Néant, is a traveling salesman of ideas—and a madman—who discourses on anguish and absurdity in a way that seems to poke fun at both Sartre and Camus. This farce (of thirty-five handwritten pages) plays with the existentialist vogue but does not allow any easy conclusions about Camus's personal feelings toward Sartre. It is more clearly ironic about the Communists and, perhaps, the election of November 10, as Vigne, in his quest for freedom, speaks of his intention to vote "for those who wish to suppress it." Shortly after October 29, Camus wrote in his notebook:

> Met Tar. as I came away from the public statement I made concerning dialogue. He seems reticent, yet has the same friendly look in his eyes that he had when I recruited him into the *Combat* network.
>
> "You're a Marxist now?"
>
> "Yes."
>
> "Then you'll be a murderer."
>
> "I have already been one."
>
> "I too. But I don't want to be anymore."

"You were my sponsor."

That was true.

"Listen Tar. This is the real problem: whatever happens, I shall always defend you against the firing squad. But you will be obliged to approve my being shot. Think about that."

"I'll think about it."

Marxism = murder. With this step, Camus's target was now defined. A few days earlier he had agonized about his "anguish at the idea of doing those articles for *Combat.*" Like Koestler, however, he would now say exactly what he felt needed saying.

: : :

Neither Victims nor Executioners appeared at the foot of the opening page of *Combat* between November 19 and 30, 1946. The individual article titles are worth noting: "The Century of Fear," "Saving Lives,' "The Contradictions of Socialism," "The Betrayed Revolution," "International Democracy and Dictatorship," "The World Is Changing Fast," "A New Social Contract," and "Toward Dialogue." Together they represented a new political credo. The very first article drew on *The Yogi and the Commissar* and Camus's conversations with Koestler.

> Terror is legitimized only if we assent to the principle: "the end justifies the means." And this principle in turn may be accepted only if the effectiveness of an action is posed as an absolute end, as in nihilistic ideologies (anything goes, success is the only thing worth talking about), or in those philosophies which make history an absolute end (Hegel, followed by Marx: the end being a classless society, everything is good that leads to it).

Rejecting political violence, Camus insisted that to accept "Marxism as an absolute philosophy" was no more and no less than to legitimize murder. "In the Marxian perspective," he wrote, "a hundred thousand corpses are nothing if they are the price of the happiness of hundreds of millions of men." To this he added his own binaries: either there is logic in History, and Marxist realism and violence are valid—or there are moral values independent of history, and Marxism is false.

But even as he spelled out his anti-Communism, Camus rejected in advance the Cold War. These same articles attacked the growing East-West confrontation, and condemned the atmosphere of terror caused by the new war "now being prepared by all nations." Camus sought a self-consciously utopian goal, "a world in which murder is not legitimate." The nonviolent orientation pitting him against Communism now led him to explore alternatives to war.

He tried to sketch a path for reform that would reduce the risk of a general conflagration. Key to this was abandoning any hope of revolution. But he still sought a "relative utopia": pursuing world unity and international democracy. National boundaries had become meaningless because "there no longer exists any policy, conservative or socialist, which can operate exclusively within a national framework." The point was to minimize domestic politics, which today were limited to "administrative problems," and to use the peace movement to create an international social contract. This was the conclusion, Camus asserted, of "all contemporary political thinking that refuses to justify lies and murder."

These articles voiced an anti–Cold War, anti-Communist, reformist leftism. Their strength lay in Camus's willingness to separate himself from all existing mainstream tendencies—the Right's move toward violent anti-Communism, the moderate Left's acceptance of the Cold War and abandonment of any hope of meaningful change, the Communists' easy rationalizing of violence and brutality en route to building a supposedly better society. After his experience of intense political activity, Camus had developed the capacity to create alternatives, the willingness to stand all by himself, if necessary, and to articulate what *ought* to be done. This strength sprang, in part, from Camus's deepest commitment: to avoid making a virtue of violence. Not that he was, or ever claimed to be, a pacifist. We have seen in his *Letters to a German Friend* his insistence on going into battle with clean hands—on the use of violence only when absolutely necessary, within limits, in response to a vital threat. And he took this step after first arguing against participation in World War II. Violence was a last resort.

Camus's antiviolent anti-Communism rejected the Cold War and did so with a clarity and consistency that other anti-Communists would be unwilling to emulate. Although he had justified taking up arms against the German occupiers, he would not justify taking up arms against the Soviet Union. While helping to provide the ideology for one side in the Cold War, Camus would never join up. His articles were a widely read early statement of a "third way" between the two sides that were just then forming.

With this lonely stand, Camus posed a new direction for the Left in France. For Sartre, Camus had been a model during 1944 and 1945. Was that still the case at the end of 1946? Much later, after the Sartre-Camus break, Beauvoir blamed Camus's personal failings and then his anti-Communism for the cooling of the friendship. But as Camus voiced his mature political position, Sartre was just beginning to develop his own political perspective. Unlike Camus, he became most concerned about French state violence and the built-in violence of its economic system. The democratic capitalist state had already perpetrated staggering brutality in Algeria in 1945 in the wake of the Sétif uprising; it was about to begin a ruinous war of colonial reconquest in Vietnam; and within a year it would impose martial law on the coalfields of northern France. In the face of these realities, Sartre would criticize the French Communist Party, its rhetoric about revolution notwithstanding, for *not* being revolutionary, for following a legal and conventional path to political power and influence. And soon he would chide his friend Camus, who had been one of the few in France to denounce the nuclear bomb and reprisals against Algerian Arabs in 1945, for his lack of concern about the violence in Vietnam.

Making a major issue of nuclear weapons and Marxist violence, Camus now rarely noticed the violence practiced by the French government overseas or at home. While he henceforth spent enormous energy dissecting what he regarded as Communism's intrinsic violence, especially *over there* in the Soviet Union, where it had triumphed, he made few critical comments with respect to governmental and systemic violence, and then only about excesses, when they originated *here* in France. Yet during the remaining years of Camus's life, France was immersed in colonial wars. How then could Camus say that Marxism equaled murder but capitalism or colonialism did not? Camus rejected every form of cooperation with the Communists. Yet in his effort to find a solution in Algeria, he sought to influence the French establishment. He supported electing the moderate Pierre Mendès-France, and he met with Jacques Soustelle, Algeria's governor-general, as well as with de Gaulle himself.

There was, then, a built-in contradiction in Camus's mature politics. Keeping the Communists out of power was the major domestic issue in French politics, which meant that in order to govern, the Socialists had to rely on the Right and give up any sort of meaningful change. Like the Socialists, who broke with the Communists in the spring of 1947, Camus hoped for a politics of leftist reform, while insisting that one-quarter of the French population, the industrial workers who supported the PCF, be excluded on principle.

This dilemma may help to explain the strained note in *Neither Victims nor Executioners*. As earlier, Camus began with morality and ended up by moralizing. The self-righteousness Hervé had denounced eighteen months earlier was now in full bloom, and was much discussed by Beauvoir retrospectively. Dismissing the Left's goals as "far-off and shadowy ends," Camus contended that his proposal for an international utopia was the sole possible choice of "honest realists" who refused to "compromise with murder." A social system that minimizes both poverty and fear, without giving way to revolutionary dreams and the inevitable murders they spawn, will call for "action and for sacrifices, that is, for men."

One reason for Camus's hostility to Communism had been its unwillingness to argue, but here he was treating all who disagreed with him with contempt. Without a clear reading of Marx, he equated Marxism with murder. In his own Cold War partisanship, Camus labeled those not on his side as not only wrong but also dishonest, less than men, and, like his friend Tar., murderers.

: : :

Camus was probably immersed in the task of writing these articles at the time of his outburst at the Vians' party. Jazz was playing, and the crowd was in a good mood when he arrived. And then he encountered the man whose pronouncements Camus now abhorred. Merleau-Ponty had just attacked Koestler, the person who was helping Camus find his direction, and had also justified the infamous Moscow Trials. Having privately written about martyrdom, Camus now faced the philosopher who, in his own mind, might call for his, Camus's, execution. His anger was understandable; Koestler certainly would have understood. But our accounts come from the other camp, long afterwards. Like Beauvoir, Sartre trivialized Camus's behavior: "He had recently spent a few days with a charming woman who had since died, and because of this love affair and separation he was rather closed up and morose." And so, after greeting everyone, he attacked Merleau-Ponty. "It was most painful," recalled Sartre. "I see them still. Camus, revolted. Merleau-Ponty courteous and firm, somewhat pale, the one indulging himself, the other refusing the delights of violence." As Camus left, he murmured something about "Left-Bank revolutionaries." Sartre followed his friend, hoping to patch things up, to no avail.

Camus's hostility reached beyond Merleau-Ponty, and resulted both from Camus's political choice and from the strains of that choice, including his personal sense of isolation. Koestler supported Camus, but he came to Paris infrequently. Not only was Camus unsupported by Sartre as he took this decisive stand against Communism, but in part he took it *against* Sartre. In the second article of *Neither Victims nor Executioners*, Camus had stated their differences sharply, without mentioning his friend. He criticized the Sartrean notion of commitment, still much discussed in 1946, now giving it a unique turn. "We cannot 'escape History,'" Camus said, "since we are in it up to our necks. But one may propose to fight within History to preserve from History that part of man which is not its proper province." Still misreading Sartre, Camus was arguing that outside of history lay morality—and it was from morality that Camus judged contemporary events. In so doing, he voiced his disagreement with his friend's theory of commitment.

Sartre was beginning to view Merleau-Ponty as his political mentor just as Camus was publicly abandoning his own hopes for radical change. Camus wrote to an American friend: "I have come to understand how lonely you can be as soon as you use a certain language. . . . You can't abandon [your position] and yet I don't enjoy the position of victim." From now on he approached political disagreements with a chip on his shoulder.

5

sartre's turning-point

By the end of 1946 Sartre had not yet begun to act politically. By most assessments, however, he had accomplished a staggering amount since the war: his name was everywhere; he edited France's leading intellectual journal, *Les Temps modernes*; he had developed a coterie around the journal; and everyone was talking about existentialism. His themes, such as *commitment,* were being hotly debated. Since the Liberation he had published two novels; staged two new plays and one revival; written dozens of newspaper articles on the United States and numerous longer articles for the journal; and had published a book on anti-Semitism, a biography of Baudelaire, and his lecture on existentialism. As an "engaged" writer, he seemed to be enjoying great success, critiquing Baudelaire's evasions, demanding other writers' political involvement on the side of the Left, taking a courageous stand on the still-suppressed issue of anti-Semitism, and giving Communist intellectuals a run for their money.

Far as he had come, Sartre knew that he was still talking rather than acting. But he was talking more clearly about what it meant to be involved in the world and have an effect on it. If existentialism was the militant humanism he had described to Communists at the end of 1944, he would sooner or later have to be judged by his own call for "action, effort, combat, and solidarity." To complete the journey that had begun over apricot cocktails with Beauvoir and Raymond Aron in 1933, when he blanched upon learning of Husserl's phenomenology, would require *political* action. What did this mean for Sartre? Camus continued to offer an example. Back in Algiers he had already been a Communist militant, created and run a theater company, run afoul of Party leaders, been expelled, and then become a crusading reporter and an editor. Then he had run real risks during the Resistance, and after the Liberation he put out a daily newspaper and wrote countless editorials read by hundreds of thousands of people. And now, at the end of 1946, Camus as a political intellectual had taken a major stand on the issues of the day. He had a real-world weight that still eluded Sartre, the literary and philosophical genius. At forty-one, Sartre still lagged behind the thirty-three-year-old who had been acting in a way that mattered politically since his early twenties.

Though edging closer to action in 1947, did Sartre actually make such comparisons? Did he see how far beyond his own writings were Camus's recent *Combat* articles? While he never admitted as much, Sartre would confess, in his 1952 letter breaking off with Camus, that in 1944 Camus had lived his "first contact with history . . . more deeply and fully than many of us (myself included)." Camus, he then said, was for several years "the symbol and the proof of class solidarity." Camus was "not far from being exemplary." Five and a half years before saying this, Sartre read a mature *prise de position* by his friend. Although Sartre might have disagreed with Camus's argument in a number of ways, it was unlike anything Sartre had ever attempted.

Even a comparison of Sartre's own literary concerns since *Nausea* with Camus's images of solidarity and action in *The Plague* tells us much. Sartre's great theme had become how to involve oneself authentically in the real historical world. From Orestes in *The Flies,* who leaves Argos after avenging his father, to Garcin in *No Exit,* the pacifist editor who heads for the border when the going gets tough, to Mathieu in the first two volumes of *Roads to Freedom,* who is painfully adrift in an uncommitted freedom, Sartre's characters feel unreal to themselves, or unable to act, or uncommitted, or swallowed up by necessity. Or they act in bad faith and through dramatic gesture.

At roughly the time Camus was publishing *Neither Victims nor Executioners*, Sartre was writing the screenplay *In the Mesh.* Conceived in the wake of *Darkness at Noon,* never filmed (although performed as a play), and not published until 1948, the screenplay tried to grasp the phenomenon of Stalinism. One of its characters, a revolutionary who is a nonviolent moral purist with no insight into the demands of history, is murdered by the central character, Jean Aguerra. Aguerra, the Stalin figure, has sought to buy time for his revolutionary government by bowing to the demands of a powerful neighboring country, in the process becoming a violent and tyrannical ruler. Eventually absorbed and broken by his own violence, he nonetheless remains lucid and committed to his original revolutionary goals. But then Aguerra, far more interesting and complex than his moralist friend Lucien, is overthrown by comrades who detest his methods and are trying to keep the revolution's promises. These comrades, however, are immediately forced by the threatening neighbor to compromise and to adopt Aguerra's methods.

The screenplay's theme, later brought to life with richer characterizations and more complex ideas, would become a reference point for Sartre's eventual alignment with Communism and for his side of the controversy with Camus: there is no way to transform a violent and oppressive world without becoming violent and oppressive oneself. *In the Mesh* groped toward, but did not yet arrive at, what Sartre came to regard as a genuinely historical politics as opposed to a simplemindedly moralistic one. Sartre's screenplay seemed an attempt to respond to Camus's *Neither Victims nor Executioners*, including an exploration of Camus's "purity" in Lucien. Sartre clearly heard and understood Camus's argument and, as we shall see, disagreed with it. Having taken Camus as a living example of the committed writer, Sartre was now beginning to shape his thinking *against* Camus.

Shortly after *Neither Victims nor Executioners* appeared, Sartre began to elaborate on his idea of engagement. And toward the end of *What Is Literature?*—first published as a series of articles in *Les Temps modernes* from February through July 1947—appeared Sartre's only published criticism of Camus's politics before their break. After acknowledging that the resort to violence was always "a setback," he went on to present, without attribution, Merleau-Ponty's argument that while it may be true that using violence against violence only perpetuates it, violence is nonetheless "the only means" for ending violence. Then Sartre commented directly on Camus's argument of a half-year earlier, all but mentioning him by name.

He began by noting that the day after *Combat* had published "a rather brilliant article saying that it was necessary to refuse any complicity with violence wherever it came from," the newspaper announced the opening shots of the French war in Vietnam. "I should like to ask the writer today how we can refuse to participate indirectly in all violence." Not to speak out against the war meant conceding that it would inevitably continue. "But if you got it to stop at once and at any price, you would be at the origin of some massacres [of French in Vietnam] and you would be doing violence to all Frenchmen who have interests down there." Sartre's point to Camus was that since violence would take place no matter what, "one must make a choice, according to other principles." For Sartre, the issue was whether one choice or the other brought France closer to realizing a socialist democracy. "Thus, we must meditate upon the modern problem of ends and means not only in theory but in each concrete case."

: : :

The argument is a bit confused, and we cannot ignore its slightly stilted tone—"I should like to ask the writer today," "If you say," and so forth. Perhaps Sartre was uncomfortable criticizing a friend in public, even though Camus had criticized him in the *Combat* articles. Or was Sartre himself the unequal, venturing onto the other man's terrain? Or perhaps the author felt he was not addressing an equal but teaching a pupil a lesson. We have already seen Sartre approach Camus in this way, and we will see it again. In any case, he clearly considered it important to answer Camus, and in the process he was developing his own position on political violence. Camus's *Neither Victims nor Executioners* and Sartre's brief reply were the beginnings of an important disagreement on the Left over the role of violence. Camus had declared himself, and Sartre, within a complex text pointing in a wholly different direction, disagreed. Later in the essay, Sartre acknowledged Camus, along with Malraux and Koestler—and by implication himself—as contemporary writers who were creating a "literature of extreme situations," and then praised Camus's just-published *The Plague.*

Also in the last sections of *What Is Literature?* Sartre turned toward the working class for the first time since his 1945 visit to the United States. He connected his own discovery of political commitment with what he saw as the contemporary worker's effort "to free himself and, by the same token, to free all men from oppression forever." As a writer, Sartre mused that the worker might conceivably be *his* public: "We share with him the duty of contesting and destroying; he demands the right to make history at the moment that we are discovering our historicity." In part, Sartre moved toward the working class because, like Marx almost a hundred years earlier, he divined that the writer's ideas would not become reality all by themselves: "the fate of literature is bound up with that of the working class."

What Is Literature? had a major theoretical function for Sartre, aligning his key philosophical themes with his growing commitment to the historical world and to the creation of a socialist society. Continuing the line of thought begun a year earlier in "Materialism and Revolution," Sartre gave a solid Kantian grounding to his reasons for commitment. Socialism, like the reader-writer relationship, was based on the mutual recognition of liberties and aimed at achieving the Kingdom of Ends. At the same time he spelled out a universalist vision of the writer's tasks and powers and a philosophical argument for socialism. Camus may have had this in mind when, sometime between June and October 1947, he confided ironically to his notebooks: "Sartre or nostalgia for the universal idyll."

Unlike Sartre, with his revolutionary zeal in these articles, Camus had decided that modest reforms were the most that could be achieved. No doubt he was more at home with Sartre's critical reflections on Communism. Writers wanting to speak to the workers, Sartre said, were blocked by the Party. "These men, to whom we *must* speak, are separated from us by an iron curtain in our own country; they will not hear a word that we shall say to them. The majority of the proletariat, strait-jacketed by a single party, encircled by a propaganda which isolates it, forms a closed society without doors or windows." Soviet Communism had become "a defensive and conservative nationalism," which, in turn, made the PCF conservative and incapable of revolutionary politics or open discussion. "The politics of Stalinist Communism is incompatible in France with the honest practice of the literary craft." And Camus may have recognized Hervé in Sartre's biting sketch of the way PCF intellectuals argued with the party's critics on the left:

> persuasion by repetition, by intimidation, by veiled threats, by forceful and scornful assertion, by cryptic allusions to demonstrations that are not forthcoming, by exhibiting so complete and superb a conviction that, from the very start, it places itself above all debate, casts its spell, and ends by becoming contagious; the opponent is never answered; he is discredited; he belongs to the police, to the Intelligence Service; he's a fascist.

Sartre's ever-stronger willingness to tangle with the PCF demonstrates that by 1947 he not only had shaped a radical non-Communist direction for himself and his journal but was also at the peak of his powers. When would he directly engage himself?

We have seen Camus raise the alarm about two huge, antagonistic blocs taking shape, bringing with them a new threat of war. He was right. In March 1947, the Truman Doctrine had enunciated a new role for the United States in Greece and Turkey, stressing the struggle for freedom versus oppression. In June, the Marshall Plan was unfurled, not only to revive Germany but also to offer other European countries assistance for their own postwar reconstruction. Not so coincidentally, between March and May the Communist parties were expelled from postwar coalition governments in Italy, Belgium, Luxembourg—and France. Cold war was in the air. Under Soviet pressure the Czechs and the Finns turned down Marshall Plan aid. Opposition parties in Poland and Hungary were eliminated over the summer, and the Bulgarian Peasant Party leader Petkov was hanged for treason. In a September meeting in Poland, the Soviet Union revived the Comintern with a new name, Cominform, and there Alexei Zhdanov proclaimed the angry Soviet response to the "imperialist" Marshall Plan and the inter-American bloc just created by the United States at Rio de Janeiro. East and West would henceforth be two hostile camps.

Events in France mirrored the worsening climate. Two years after the Liberation, the standard of living continued to decline. The bread ration, which had been 275 grams at the worst point during the Occupation, was reduced to 200 grams in June 1947. The government, ignoring the objections of a powerless Communist defense minister, had already initiated hostilities in Indochina as part of its disastrous postwar colonial policy of restoring domination, by war if necessary, throughout the French Union. In May, on the heels of a Trotskyist-initiated strike at Renault, which the Communists felt they could not disavow, the PCF ministers were dismissed from the Ramadier government. The Marshall Plan brought together the two major issues in French domestic politics—postwar economic reconstruction and isolating the Communists. The Socialists and their allies further to the right embraced American aid and created the domestic anti-Communist modus operandi that was to last a generation. The SFIO, the PCF's closest competitor and the largest party in the government coalition throughout 1947, articulated France's domestic and international anti-Communist alignment with the United States. Feared, hated, and all but proscribed, the Communists still drew nearly one-third of the vote in municipal elections that fall, marked by the spectacular rise of the Gaullist party, the Rassemblement du Peuple Français (RPF), which campaigned on a combination of Bonapartism and anti-Communism.

The international and domestic situations were merging. At the Cominform's founding conference, leaders of the PCF were roundly criticized for their three years of parliamentary illusions. In a well-worn Communist ritual, they affirmed Stalin's new line by admitting the mistakes they had made in following the previous line. Back home, they now went into fierce opposition, simultaneously opposing the integration of France into the American camp and supporting workers whose already disastrous living standards were continuing to decline. A wave of militant strikes began, initiated by the largest French trade union federation, the Communist-led Confédération Générale du Travail (CGT) and met by anti-Communist hysteria and a widespread fear of insurrection. A "great fear" stalked France from Marseille, which saw a general strike, to the northern mine regions, under occupation by undisciplined military forces, and reached its grim climax in an apparently intentional train derailment that cost twenty-one lives. Writing for a Gaullist newspaper a few months later, Arthur Koestler even suggested that the Communists were secretly preparing for civil war.

What Is Literature? had taken Sartre to within a step of acting. And now, in September 1947, he accepted an offer to present a weekly *Temps modernes* radio program in which he, Beauvoir, Merleau-Ponty and others from the magazine would discuss current events. Also in September, according to Beauvoir,

> a few socialists—Marceau-Pivert, Gazier—seeking to constitute an opposition within the SFIO solicited the support of those men of the Left who did not belong to any party; they would draw up together an appeal in favor of peace and the creation of a neutral and socialist Europe. We met every week at [Georges] Izard's home: [David] Rousset, Merleau-Ponty, Camus, [André] Breton and a few others. We argued over every word, every comma. In [November], the text was finally signed by *Esprit, Les Temps modernes,* Camus, Bourdet, Rousset, and published in the press.

The looming Cold War was provoking some non-Communist leftists to seek a way out of its "either/or" choice. The text, which appeared in several newspapers and then in the journal *Esprit* in November, was also read by Sartre to be broadcast on the radio show in December. The program had begun on October 20 with an attack on Gaullism just as the RPF was becoming the big winner in municipal elections. The following week's program, on Communism, began by conceding that the PCF represented the French working class and that the Soviet Union had to be understood in an international context and in relation to difficult internal conditions; but it went on to castigate both. Gaullists and

Communists alike were outraged by the broadcasts, and the third program dealt with the storm provoked by the first two. Most of the broadcasts spoke against the Cold War and the inevitability of war and critiqued contemporary socialism as well as Communism and capitalist democracy. One program focused on the current strike wave by interviewing a dissident leader of the CGT who opposed PCF strategy.

Very much a collective activity, the broadcasts stirred up much controversy. Sartre received dozens of hostile and even threatening letters. One contained a picture of Sartre covered with human excrement. Within the individual programs, political leadership and responsibility for the most concrete discussions usually belonged to Merleau-Ponty. Sartre was an active participant but reflected on issues in abstract and general ways. Three further programs were taped, the second with Sartre reading the text put together at Izard's. After the postelection replacement of the Socialist Ramadier by the more conservative Robert Schumann, however, the new government abruptly canceled the series.

The full story of the text for these broadcasts, on which both Camus and Sartre worked, contains an astounding fact: the first political intervention credited to Sartre was a collective redraft of a statement written by Camus. In response to Truman's speech at Rio de Janeiro in early September, Camus had written a statement intended to be signed by others. It began by calling Truman's speech "murderous," and rejected its logic of military confrontation. Camus brought the statement to meetings at which Sartre was present. Camus's draft was the one in which "every word, every comma" was disputed until it became reworked into the final text, which was published in November 1947. Sartre's bibliographers attribute it to him under the title "A First Call to International Opinion," without mention of Camus's original draft.

A comparison of the Camus draft and the Sartre final text shows that the group dropped Camus's initial reference to Truman, kept much of Camus's basic structure, and sharpened his rather fuzzy ending. They softened Camus's fear of a Soviet invasion but retained most of his ideas, as well as his exact wording in at least seven places. The main points of both Camus's draft and Sartre's text were that the creation of blocs opened the road to war; that "for Europe, war means occupation or battlefield ruins or both"; and that preparation for war disturbs economic life and "retards social liberation." The idea of a balance of terror made no sense at all. But war could "be avoided" if Europe were to become an active force. And then came the divergence—Europe had to lead the way in constructing an international organization which, beyond national sovereignty, would build societies neither depending on the police nor subjugated to money (Camus)—or would have to unite to regain its sovereignty against the blocs and pursue "a radical transformation of the existing social order" (Sartre). Although the second text was slightly more militant than the first, the proposals in both of them lacked focus and plausibility, which is one reason why the effort fell on deaf ears.

Sartre the tyro fashioned his first political intervention alongside Camus the veteran, and took off from his friend's text. For all their developing divergence, Sartre and Camus had been engaged in a joint project. That fall, Sartre and Beauvoir had seen quite a lot of Camus. Beauvoir described him to Algren as "an interesting but difficult guy. When he was not pleased with the book he was writing [*The Plague*], he was very arrogant; now that he has achieved considerable success, he has become very modest and sincere." Koestler had returned to Paris in October, and Beauvoir's letters at the time revealed that his anti-Communism was rather more virulent than Camus's and also that she and Sartre were far more hostile to the Communists, and closer to Camus in this respect, than they would later become. They all spent time together, including an evening at Camus's apartment that was almost spoiled by the anti-Communism of Koestler and an American friend, although Camus was very friendly and in good humor. Koestler then left Paris but returned after the New Year. According to Beauvoir,

> he wanted to repeat our night [of October, 1946] at the Schéhérazade. We went with him. Mamaine, Camus, Sartre and myself—Francine wasn't there—to another Russian nightclub. He insisted on letting the *maître d'hôtel* know that he was being accorded the honor of waiting on Camus, Sartre and Koestler. In a tone more hostile than the year before, he returned to the theme of "No friendship without political agreement." As a joke, Sartre was making love to Mamaine, though so outrageously one could scarcely have said he was being indiscreet, and we were all far too drunk for it to be offensive. Suddenly, Koestler threw a glass at Sartre's head and it smashed against the wall.

We will probably never know how much competition with Camus or with Koestler was contained in Sartre's self-mocking pitch for the lovely Mamaine. The tensions must have been complex indeed. Beauvoir had hoped to have an affair with Camus two years earlier but hadn't succeeded. She had had a one-night stand with Koestler the previous year, when Camus had fallen in love with Mamaine. Camus and Francine traveled to England later that year with Mamaine and Koestler.

> We brought the evening to a close; Koestler didn't want to go home, and then he found he'd lost his wallet and had to stay behind in the club; Sartre was staggering about on the sidewalk and laughing helplessly when Koestler finally decided to climb back up the stairway on all fours. He wanted to continue his quarrel with Sartre. "Come on, let's go home!" said Camus, laying a friendly hand on his shoulder; Koestler shrugged the hand off and hit Camus, who then tried to hurl himself on his aggressor; we kept them apart. Leaving Koestler in his wife's hands, we all got into Camus's car; he too was suitably soused in vodka and champagne, and his eyes began to fill with tears: "He was my friend! And he hit me!" He kept collapsing onto the steering wheel and sending the car into the most terrifying swerves and we would try to haul him up completely sobered by our fear.

For the following few days, Camus wore sunglasses to hide his black eye. At the time, Sartre, Beauvoir, and Camus "often went back to that night together; Camus would ask us perplexedly: 'Do you think it's possible to go on drinking like that and still work?' "

: : :

The Camus-Sartre statement led to the political activity into which Sartre would now throw himself—a new neutralist, socialist movement, the Rassemblement Démocratique Révolutionnaire (RDR). Its function was to oppose both blocs and the pressure for war while carving out space for an independent and genuinely socialist France. Made up primarily of ex-Communists, former members of the left wing of the SFIO, Trotskyists, Christian leftists, and other independent socialists, the RDR grew rapidly, flourished briefly, and then split apart, overwhelmed by the pressures of the Cold War.

In its first month, March 1948, the RDR held a rally attended by more than a thousand people, followed by another one with more than four thousand. The organization's first statement, drafted by Sartre, called for "a free people's assembly for revolutionary democracy [to give] new life to the principle of freedom and human dignity by linking them to the struggle for social revolution." For Sartre, the RDR's main purpose was to bring together precisely the two terms Camus despaired of reconciling: freedom and socialism. This would be France's, and Europe's, answer to the contest between Americans and Russians. Combining a revolutionary spirit with democracy, the RDR rejected the Cold War and criticized both the Soviet Union and the capitalist West. It insisted on being a "gathering" rather than a party—although it was widely known as

"Sartre's and Rousset's party"—thus allowing members of different political parties to join. It received considerable exposure in the press, held a few large rallies, and published a semimonthly newspaper.

But Sartre's colleagues Georges Altman and Rousset began to accept American money, which, we now know, came from the CIA, and by April 1949 the largest rally of all, attended by ten thousand people, heard praises of American nuclear weapons. Under the pressure of the Cold War and American funding, these non-Communist leftists moved rightwards. Feeling betrayed, Sartre resigned from the leadership that fall, and the organization soon fell apart.

Camus shared the podium with Sartre at one of the RDR's major rallies but was never as involved as Sartre. Yet both men planned to travel together to the United States on behalf of the RDR and then, when this plan fell through, to South America. Camus had several reasons for hanging back. He was writing *The Rebel,* which was enormously demanding. And he, after all, was no zealot but someone who had given up on grand schemes of social change because he now believed them to be impossible to carry out without massive violence and foreign intervention. His postwar hopes deflated, Camus was now probing the enemy on the left. Having become both anti-Communist and anti-Marxist, he now described himself as "intransigently reformist."

At one point Camus and Sartre collided publicly. An article by Sartre on political freedom appeared in the popular magazine *Caliban* (a kind of left-wing *Reader's Digest*) in October 1948, followed a month later by a sharply contrasting article by Camus. The appearance of the two pieces was arranged by Jean Daniel, a pied-noir friend of Camus, who supported the magazine. Sartre's piece, which Daniel published under the headline "To Be Hungry Already Means That You Want to Be Free," was a revised version of a talk Sartre had given at an RDR meeting in the spring of 1948. Sartre called freedom under capitalism a "hoax" because workers possessed no real economic power. Their hunger, on the contrary, was a demand to be free from need, to become full human beings. In his response, Camus spoke of democracy as "an exercise in modesty." He would not simplify human problems, as reactionaries and revolutionaries did, and embraced democracy as the "least evil" system of government. Like Sartre, he refused "to accept the condition of the proletariat," but he equally refused "to aggravate that misery in the name of a theory or a blind messianism." Sartre attacked "bourgeois" democracy, whereas Camus extolled democracy—eschewing the adjective "bourgeois"—as "the least objectionable system of government." Sartre was clearly not the "modest" democrat Camus was talking about. The two articles did not constitute a real debate, for the clever Daniel made Camus appear to be answering Sartre though his article had been published in July. They might well have been debating, however, because their paths were obviously diverging. Yet we should not make too much of the disagreement—after all, Camus's article had first appeared in the RDR's newspaper, *La Gauche*.

: : :

Sartre's play *Dirty Hands* was first performed shortly after the launching of the RDR, in April 1948. His most popular engaged play, it was written and first presented just as he was beginning to act politically. Its main character, Hoederer, the undoctrinaire Marxist leader willing to dirty his hands to achieve socialism, is Sartre's most positive hero. In some ways the story is suggestive of the murder of Leon Trotsky in Mexico in 1940. Hoederer's commitment is enriched by his warmth and his regard for people, his directness, honesty, flexibility, and sense of historical perspective. He treats people as individuals and tries to understand all situations concretely. In short, he is an ideal communist with a small *c* and not a typical Party representative—except that he tells Hugo that were he in his shoes—as an assassin planted by the opposing Party faction—he would not have backed down as Hugo did at first.

But Hoederer is not the center of the play. He is assassinated—out of jealousy—by Hugo, the alienated bourgeois intellectual who has been sent to kill him over tactical differences. Hugo is working for a minority Party faction at a moment when contact with Moscow has been lost. He surprises his wife Jessica and Hoederer embracing and hence, having given up the political project of assassinating him, finds a new motive for murder. But finally, after Hugo has served a prison sentence for the murder, the revenge killing is transformed by Hugo's retrospective declaration of a political motive. Which, in the end, is his way of affirming Hoederer.

The party had been formed by the fusion of Hoederer's Social Democrats with the Communists. Those who would murder Hoederer were the "real" Communists—sharpening Sartre's criticism of the Party. In response, the PCF went into paroxysms of fury, and picketed its performances. After all, it portrays the Stalinist hacks Olga and Louis treating Hoederer as an enemy to be eliminated because of differences over tactics. Unlike Hoederer, these Stalinists are doctrinaire and inflexible, incapable of independent thought. They parrot the latest twists and turns of the Party line, to the point of cleverly making Hoederer into a hero after his death because the line has changed. At the end a sense of despair is unavoidable: both Hoederer and Hugo are dead, the Party-liners are in charge, and history has been rewritten. We learn what Camus thought of the play from a reminiscence of Sartre's:

> Camus had gone with me to one of the final rehearsals (he hadn't read the script yet), and as he was walking back with me after it was over he said, "It's excellent, but there's one detail I don't approve of. Why does Hugo say, 'I don't love men for what they are but for what they ought to be' [a rough quotation from act 5], and why does Hoederer answer, 'And I love them for what they are?' The way I see it, it should have been just the opposite." In other words, he really thought that Hugo loved men for what they are since he didn't want to lie to them, whereas Hoederer, on the contrary, became in his eyes a dogmatic Communist who weighed men in terms of what they ought to be and who deceived them in the name of an ideal. This is just the opposite of what I meant to say."

Camus sided with Hugo, Sartre with Hoederer. But both opposed what they regarded as the dominant Party attitude: anything is permissible in the present to build tomorrow's good society. And Camus may have thought Hoederer's loves a bit abstract and formulaic, the only concrete love in the play being Hugo's for Hoederer. Moreover, Sartre gave both Hoederer and Hugo sufficient complexity, life, and moral-political validity that it was possible to identify with either man.

But the most interesting aspect of Sartre's anecdote is that he and Camus interpreted the characters' actual behavior in opposite terms. It was less a matter of the "correct" reading of *Dirty Hands* than of the attitudes each brought with him to the play. For Camus, sticking to principle and refusing to lie for the sake of politics was inseparable from respecting people and loving them. For Sartre, acting on principle dictated being true to long-term ends.

: : :

Between 1946 and 1948, both Sartre and Camus had called for a democratic and radically transformed Europe that would avoid war and pursue a path between the capitalist and Communist blocs. The RDR tried to do just this, and its collapse had a profound effect on Sartre, as his notes show. "Splitting up of the RDR hard blow. Fresh and definitive apprenticeship to realism. One cannot create a movement." Actual possibilities of political change would now become decisive. "Circumstances merely appeared to be favorable to the association. It did answer to an abstract need defined by the objective situation, but not to any real need among the people. Consequently they did not support it."

Sartre would now insist that social conditions and historical possibility were central to any discussion of political goals. But as the Cold War shrank the historical space available for meaningful action, Sartre the budding realist was "forced to choose" in a way that Camus could not accept. Willing to align himself with even the most compromised possibility of social progress, Sartre inclined toward Communism after trying an ideal third way and deciding that historical realities made it impossible. Having tortuously found his way to politics after a long apprenticeship, Sartre would understandably make realism the hallmark of his politics. To flow with the current of history, anathema to Camus, became essential to Sartre.

While the Cold War had been imposing itself with increasing urgency, Sartre and Camus had remained part of the dwindling world of independent leftist intellectuals who insisted on being critical of both East and West and sought to find a way between them. Within this tiny world they might disagree on the likelihood of change, how radical that change could be, and whether their deep criticism of the Communists sprang from the PCF's being revolutionary or not being revolutionary enough. But the collapse of the RDR finished off that world. Sartre now integrated his existentialism into Marxism, espoused violence and revolution, and took his stand decisively against the West. And on each step of the way, he confronted, and rejected, Camus's example and arguments without mentioning his friend by name.

In the meantime, Camus in 1948 became involved in a public exchange with fellow traveler Emmanuel d'Astier de la Vigerie, an important Resistance figure and editor of the pro-Communist newspaper *Libération.* Camus's response to Astier's criticisms of *Neither Victims nor Executioners* contains his famous remark that he did not learn about freedom from Marx: "I learned it from poverty." Camus, having been accused of complicity with bourgeois society, lashed out at Astier and all Communist and fellow-traveling intellectuals who sought to "dominate the world in the name of a future justice." Theirs was a complicity with murder, and theirs would be the victory of the slaughterhouse: "Those who pretend to know everything and settle everything finish by killing everything."

In September 1948, Camus became a supporter of Gary Davis, an American who renounced his citizenship and declared himself a world citizen during a sit-in in front of the United Nations headquarters in Paris. Although Sartre and Beauvoir wounded Camus by first refusing to involve themselves in an affair they regarded as "nothing but hot air," Camus held a press conference to support Davis's effort to speak at a United Nations meeting in November. Camus addressed two large demonstrations on behalf of Davis, the second speech being hailed by *Le Monde* as "brilliant and incisive." In June 1949, Sartre finally declared his critical support for the movement.

Camus's friends saw him as naively encouraging a crackpot scheme that had no chance of success. But unlike Sartre, he was not trying to be realistic in the sense of gearing himself to observable tendencies with a demonstrable prospect of success. In *Neither Victims nor Executioners*, Camus had advanced a self-consciously "utopian" program for world unity and international democracy. This stance entailed rejecting both sides in the Cold War as well as the conflict itself, and championing moral values against the terrifying direction in which the world was moving. Camus's decisions led directly to "unrealistic" alternatives—such as advocating world citizenship—while "realism" led to embracing one of the existing two blocs. Camus was certainly an idealist. Never becoming a Cold Warrior, his revulsion from violence would only grow stronger over time. If Sartre's growing commitment to effective action led him to abandon what he regarded as his early idealism, Camus's unapologetic idealism suggested less a weakness than a willingness to "leave" reality in order to change it. The "utopian" dimension would express itself again and again, right down to his proposal for a civilian truce during the Algerian War. To disparage him for such a proposal, as Beauvoir did in 1963, was to ignore the strength of Camus's approach. He insisted on *creating* alternatives, no matter how few people supported them at first.

: : :

From 1949 to 1951, Sartre and Camus were moving in opposite directions. Sartre's first major political activity since the Liberation, which might have led him in a number of directions, perhaps away from politics altogether, had fallen victim to the Cold War. In the face of the RDR's defeat, Sartre struggled to understand what had gone wrong with the movement and to find another way to have an effect on events.

Differences that might once have attracted each man to the other now became divisive. Already in 1948 an incident took place so serious that Sartre recalled it twenty-five years later in response to Beauvoir's inquiry about how things between him and Camus grew "worse and worse, to the point of reaching a break." There was "a personal episode that didn't make me in the least angry with him but that he found disagreeable." Was this, Beauvoir asked, "the business of the woman you'd had an affair with yourself?" Sartre's reply, so many years later, still danced around the issue:

> It was rather awkward. And as this woman had broken with him for personal reasons, he held it against me to some extent. In fact it's a complicated story. He'd had an affair with Casarès and fallen out with her. He broke it off and told us confidentially about this break. I remember an evening with him in a bar at the time when we often used to go to bars; I was alone with him. He had just made up again with Casarès and he had letters of hers in his hand, old letters that he showed me, saying, "Well, there you are! When I found them again, when I was able to read them again . . ." But politics separated us.

Camus and Maria Casarès reunited in June 1948. Although she had broken with him three years earlier over his refusal to leave his wife, they would now remain attached for the rest of Camus's life. Was Sartre saying that he had an affair with Casarès earlier, and that Camus now realized it and was furious? There is no other evidence that she was the woman. But given the other sexual tensions—Sartre protesting in early 1944 to Wanda Kosakiewicz that she shouldn't have fallen for Camus, Beauvoir expressing in late 1945 a wish to have an affair with Camus, Camus's love affair with Mamaine Koestler—and given Sartre's and Camus's nonstop pursuit of women, such a confrontation was perhaps inevitable. The two kept all other such rivalries tightly under wraps, so it is no wonder that this one should have been difficult to discuss, or to piece together, twenty-five years later.

During 1949 they saw each other less than before, letting slide their weekly lunch. Still, in November, Camus told an interviewer that the friendly relations between him and Sartre remained established: "Our meetings are less frequent but warm." Much later, Sartre agreed with Beauvoir that there was always "a certain intimacy on the private level," as long as they were on good terms together. "Even our political differences didn't worry us much in conversation." But their paths continued to diverge.

: : :

In 1949, Sartre published *Troubled Sleep,* the third volume of *Roads to Freedom.* In this novel, Mathieu finally swings into action, however absurdly, and the Communist Brunet connects with a deeply personal source of political energy. The novel's ending points to the combination of personal and political authenticity Sartre was striving to create. Camus published his first volume of collected political essays in 1949, but he was working mainly on *The Rebel* and its companion play, *The Just Assassins,* which premiered near the end of the year. In this exploration of the murder of a Russian grand duke at the turn of the century, as in *The Rebel,* Camus was concerned with intellectuals and their penchant for revolutionary violence. He focused on the complex attitude of the young intellectuals-turned-revolutionaries. His characters have many of the weaknesses Camus ascribed to his antagonists: they are concerned with justice in the abstract but take little notice of concrete individuals; they worship violence and believe in the future over the present; they hate life, including their own lives. Apocalyptic, they are willing to kill endlessly to end killing. Nevertheless, according to Camus—and he would spell this out at length in *The Rebel* —they are more honorable and attractive than those of the mid-twentieth century. They refuse to kill the Grand Duke's niece and nephew; they love deeply; and they are willing to take personal responsibility for their killing—that is, they are not yet nihilists. They are willing to die for taking a life. "Others, perhaps, will come who'll quote our authority for killing, and will *not* pay with their lives." "Others" meant Astier and other pro-Communist and Communist intellectuals.

Sartre was not yet numbered among these, and when Camus saw him and Beauvoir at the play's opening night in December 1949, "the warmth of his greeting brought back the best days of our friendship." A woman standing by told Camus that she liked the play better than *Dirty Hands.* Camus, no longer so irritable about such pairing, turned to Sartre "with a smile of complicity and said, 'Two birds with one stone!' "

: : :

Sartre had just signed his name to Merleau-Ponty's editorial in *Les Temps modernes* on the Soviet forced-labor camps, about which the French press was making new revelations. The article contained fundamental criticisms of the Soviet Union, asking by what right a country where one in ten citizens was in a labor camp might be called socialist. Merleau-Ponty rejected Sartre's former comrade David Rousset's effort to label the USSR as "enemy number one" and to subordinate all the world's struggles to opposing Communism. The article insisted on criticizing oppression both in the East and the West. The "decadence of Russian communism does not make the class struggle a myth, 'free enterprise' possible or desirable, or the Marxist criticism in general null and void." What was most important for Sartre was his support of two particular claims. First, the article reasserted Marxism's "humane inspiration," meaning that he and Merleau-Ponty had "the same values as a Communist." Second, "whatever the nature of the present Soviet society may be, the USSR is on the whole situated, in the balance of powers, on the side of those who are struggling against the forms of exploitation known to us." The labor camps marred, but did not cancel, the Soviet Union's progressive place in the world. This article reflected Merleau-Ponty's complex attitude toward Communism. Adding his name to it meant that Sartre, feeling forced to choose, was inclining toward Communism despite its flaws.

: : :

In June 1950, North Korea invaded the South, launching one of the most dangerous confrontations of the Cold War. Merleau-Ponty abandoned his last hope that the Soviet Union might play a positive historical role. He decided to remain silent, and *Les Temps modernes* lost direction as a result. Some warmth clearly remained between Sartre and Camus. When American troops moved north, there was talk in France about the possibility of a Soviet invasion of France, as Beauvoir recalls.

> "Have you thought about what will happen to you when the Russians get here?" [Camus] asked Sartre, and then added with a great deal of emotion: "You mustn't stay!" "And do you expect to leave?" asked Sartre. "Oh, I'll do what I did during the German occupation." It was Loustanau-Lacau, always one for secret societies, who started the idea of "armed and clandestine resistance"; but we no longer argued freely with Camus. He was too quickly carried away by anger, or at least by vehemence. Sartre's only objection was that he would never accept having to fight the proletariat. "You mustn't let the proletariat become a mystique," Camus answered sharply; and he complained of the French workers' indifference to the Soviet labour camps. "They've got enough trouble without worrying about what's going on in Siberia," was Sartre's reply. "All right," said Camus, "but all the same, they haven't exactly earned the Legion of Honor!" Strange words: Camus, like Sartre, had refused the Legion of Honor, which their friends in power had wanted to given them in 1945. We felt a great distance between us. Yet it was with real warmth that he urged Sartre: "You must leave. If you stay it won't be only your life they'll take, but your honor as well. They'll cart you off to a camp and you'll die. Then they'll say you're still alive, and they'll use your name to preach resignation and submission and treason; and people will believe them."

With distance and yet with warmth, Camus still saw himself on the same side as Sartre. Beauvoir described similar conversations with others, and concluded that although Sartre didn't really believe the Soviets would invade, merely thinking about it "played a great role in his subsequent development." At the end of July 1950, he published a foreword to a book on Yugoslav Communism, in which he celebrated the role of subjectivity in Tito's Marxism, and enunciated what would now become his own project: "We must rethink Marxism, we must rethink man." In the process, he took up where Merleau-Ponty, his mentor, left off.

At the beginning of 1951 he started to "rethink man" in earnest, in *The Devil and the Good Lord,* a play about the Peasants' War of the sixteenth century. In this major step in his moral-political development, Sartre has his protagonist, Goetz, move from being abstractly evil and then abstractly good to finally pursuing his own liberation in a concrete struggle alongside other people. In portraying a conversion, the play is, in a sense, Sartre's equivalent of *The Plague,* except that solidarity is not the fabric of the drama but the solution ultimately arrived at. Caught in unresolvable moral dilemmas, Goetz eventually becomes an engaged individual. Giving up the hope of being and doing good in a pure form—which leads to widespread disaster—Goetz accepts the demands of a prolonged struggle. As long as he and his fellow human beings are unfree, he comes to realize, the only way to love them is to agree to struggle alongside them, as their leader. Solidarity is the only possible love at a time of social struggle. At the end, Goetz declares: "I shall make them hate me, because I know no other way of loving them. I shall give them orders, since I have no other way of obeying. I shall remain alone with this empty sky over my head, since I have no other way of being among men. There is this war to fight, and I will fight it."

Henceforth for Sartre, ethics became indistinguishable from history and politics. Being moral involved acknowledging that we and our world are inescapably violent. Abandoning his cynical realism as well as his naive idealism, Goetz comes to appreciate both the goal of a nonviolent future and the necessity of using whatever means are at hand, including violent revolutionary action, to get there. The Kingdom of Ends, envisaged in "Materialism and Revolution" and *What Is Literature?* is now posed as the goal of a revolutionary struggle. *The Devil and the Good Lord* was the fruit of a long and complex process in which Sartre finally articulated the framework for an ethics that would satisfy him, namely, that radical political change is the only path for creating a world in which moral human relations are possible. Intellectually and then politically, that ethics would lead to the decisive rift with Camus.

Camus watched rehearsals—observing Goetz embrace violence as a way of realizing the good society—just as he was putting the finishing touches on his systematic critique of political violence. He ended the penultimate section of *The Rebel* with a provocative discussion of existentialism *as expressed in Sartre's play*. In this play Sartre was becoming a new kind of political realist, willing to join on their own terms what he saw as the only historical forces for human progress—just as Camus was reiterating his rejection of the "cult of history" and insisting on keeping one foot squarely on the terrain of moral judgment.

Beauvoir, using Sartre's notes, portrayed the play as "the mirror of Sartre's entire ideological evolution." She contrasted Orestes' departure from Argos at the end of *The Flies* with Goetz's determination to stay and participate in the peasants' battles. "In 1944, Sartre thought that any situation could be transcended by subjective effort; in 1951, he knew that circumstances can sometimes steal our transcendence from us; in that case, no individual salvation is possible, only a collective struggle." Sartre's previous plays, like his trilogy *Roads to Freedom,* had contrasted the subjectively free individual to the disciplined militant, but now, after a long evolution, Goetz projects a synthesis: "He accepts the discipline without denying his own subjectivity. . . . He is the perfect embodiment of the man of action as Sartre conceived him." Goetz lives both his solidarity and his freedom.

For the first time, Sartre's individual freedom was intimately connected with everyone's freedom, and working for others' freedom demanded joining up with their struggle. In *Dirty Hands,* for example, Hugo is alternately too neurotic or too principled to simply do what has to be done to advance the cause; and those interpreting and controlling "the cause" lack individual subjectivity and principle, which suggests that the cause itself is not the betterment of humanity. This explains why the Communists picketed *Dirty Hands*. But three years later, when Goetz associates his individual freedom with the larger struggle, he becomes what Sartre had long sought to become: a man among men. Goetz freely joins his fellows' struggle and submits to its discipline. Until now Sartre had been *talking about* history and commitment, or had been creating *his own* journal, or had been creating a *new organization.* But "one cannot create a movement." The time had come to take the next step: to *join* a struggle already taking place, one wholly beyond his control.

In the final moment of *The Devil and the Good Lord*, an officer rejects Goetz's leadership of the rebel army. Goetz warns the officer to submit and, when he refuses, stabs him to death. This appears as a shocking, gratuitous murder. Yes, Goetz needs to keep order if the peasant army is to have a chance, but this stabbing is no critical or cautious acceptance of the necessity of violence within limits. It is a theatrical gesture, containing, I think, something deeper. Sartre may have intended to shock the complacency of an audience which, like his friend Camus, wanted to measure and control violence. Beyond this, in Goetz's gesture, like that of Orestes in *The Flies,* violence seems itself to be a value. Camus had thrown down the gauntlet: to be a revolutionary is to be violent. And Sartre had picked it up, proclaiming his affirmative answer.

As Beauvoir said of the turning point, "The work he had begun in 1945 with his article on the writer's commitment was finished; he had utterly demolished all his illusions about the possibility of personal salvation. He had reached the same point as Goetz: he was ready to accept a collective discipline without denying his own liberty." And then she returned to Sartre's notes: "After ten years of rumination, I had reached a breaking point: one light tap was all that was required."

: : :

While *The Devil and the Good Lord* was in rehearsal, the Sartre-Camus friendship revived when Camus regularly stopped by the theater to pick up Maria Casarès, who was starring in the play. Sartre and Camus agreed that *Les Temps modernes* would publish the chapter on Nietzsche from *The Rebel,* which Camus was now completing. But although they didn't talk about it, the play's ideas and thrust were diametrically opposed to what Camus had already said and written. So despite their making a show of closeness, we should not be surprised that, as Beauvoir recalled, the celebration on opening night, June 7, 1951, with Camus, Maria Casarès, and their friends, was "a pretty dismal meal; the old warmth between Camus and ourselves seemed beyond recall."

6

violence and communism

For fifty years *The Rebel* has demanded of those who read it to *take sides*. And for good reason. Between the middle of October 1951 and the summer of 1952, Sartre and Camus dramatically took positions concerning the Cold War. First *The Rebel* appeared, a description of what Camus regarded as the civilizational malady that led people to embrace Communism. In April 1952, after many reviews and much controversy, the book was panned by Francis Jeanson in *Les Temps modernes*. Sartre proclaimed his identification with Communism, including his appreciation of Communist violence, in July. Camus's reply to Jeanson appeared in August, followed by ripostes from Sartre and Jeanson. Very suddenly, the final strands of a personal, political, and philosophical connection were broken.

Sartre and Camus had seen each other socially after rehearsals of *The Devil and the Good Lord* as late as spring 1951; *Les Temps modernes* had published *The Rebel*'s chapter on Nietzsche that summer; and Sartre and Camus had even had a drink together after a political meeting in February 1952. But it was time to choose sides. "The postwar period was over," Beauvoir wrote. "No more postponements, no more conciliations were possible. We had been forced into making clear-cut choices." And Camus, when warned by his old teacher Jean Grenier that the manuscript of *The Rebel* reminded him of Charles Maurras, the royalist who became a supporter of Vichy, replied, "Too bad, but one has to say what one thinks."

The title by which this work has been known in the English-speaking world has always given the wrong idea about what Camus was saying. A rebel is defined *in relation to* an existing and legitimate authority, against which he or she rises up. Had Camus wished to convey this meaning, with its further implication of frequent defeat, other French terms, such as *le rebelle,* were at hand. The expression he did select, *l'homme révolté,* can be rendered more closely as "man in revolt." If a rebel cannot be thought of apart from the authority against which he or she rebels, and which often suppresses the rebel, the "man in revolt" stands independent of authority, but without aiming at the victory desired by the "revolutionary." Camus's more ambiguous use of *l'homme revolté* conveyed his intention to distinguish the original impulse of revolt from the internally connected pair: the rebel, who sets up *and continually contests* a power against which he or she rebels, leading to the most horrible consequences; and the revolutionary, who in nihilistic frustration seeks to transform the world and successfully gains power to do so. Camus's title also preserved the sense of a person who is revolted by the society established by revolution. Considering Camus's intention, I will use *Man in Revolt*, despite the fact that no such English title exists.

The book's very title—*L'Homme révolté*—was a demand to take sides. The defiant individual at the heart of Camus's book was constructed *in opposition to* the revolutionary. Even in his first more exploratory and less polarized formulation, published in 1945, revolt is "an obscure protest involving neither system nor reasons"; it is "limited in scope" and is "only a testimony." Revolution "begins from a clear idea . . . , whereas revolt is the movement that leads from individual experience to the idea." By 1951, Camus had sharpened these contrasts into ideological antagonisms and contributed them to the Cold War. The healthy posture, revolt, was about respect and solidarity. The unhealthy one, revolution, was about attempting too much and killing to achieve it. The Communists did the latter.

We have seen Sartre evolving into a revolutionary, Camus into a man in revolt. Sartre's central intellectual-dramatic-political construct was Goetz, the leader who accepts violence as the price of social change. Camus labored no less profoundly or long to shape his own creation, the man in revolt, for whom violence could never be justified.

Despite growing differences, Sartre and Camus still regarded each other as friends. Camus hoped for a positive review, and Sartre, in order to protect the friendship, dithered about reviewing the book. Although Camus had criticized Sartre in *Man in Revolt*'s penultimate chapter, it was in a measured tone and with carefully chosen language that anticipated a response, not a rupture. It was as if Camus still thought he could convince Sartre to change his thinking. But each one had worked his way to an intellectual and political position that was diametrically opposed to the other, and, like it or not, they were becoming leaders of opposing camps. Their own choices, responding to the evolution of the larger political situation, now became forces in that situation and mortally damaged what remained of the friendship.

: : :

November 1951: Camus drops his bomb on Communism; July 1952: Sartre swears a lifelong hatred for his social class and sides with Communism. The political purpose of Camus's book was to develop his earlier equation of Communism with violence; Sartre's essay embraced this very equation to the point of showing such violence to be both legitimate and inevitable. Reading both today, even after the Cold War, it is hard to avoid being tugged in one direction or the other. Who was right, Camus or Sartre?

Of course, the Cold War largely determined who would choose each side. Leftist pro-Communist intellectuals in France mostly sided against *Man in Revolt,* while a much smaller and less vocal group of leftists welcomed it. Those further to the right hailed it, with the exception of a few like Raymond Aron, who rejected Camus's style of thinking outright. Not surprisingly, American and British reviews congratulated Camus on his courage and his insight.

As long as Soviet Communism survived, the pressure to take sides was revived frequently, with *Man in Revolt* resurrected in a new anti-Communist wave in the late 1970s. The "New Philosophers" appeared on the scene, former student leftists searching for the roots of their mistakes and the century's revolutionary debacles, and they self-consciously followed in Camus's footsteps. With the overthrow of Eastern European and then Soviet Communism by their own citizens, and with many cheering them on in English, Camus's conclusions have now become dominant across the political spectrum. Accordingly, anyone who wants to read *Man in Revolt* as part of the Camus-Sartre biography is pressured to side *with it* by today's prevailing view: Camus was always right and has only now, belatedly and sadly, received his due. Defying the new "of course" with "on the contrary," some Sartre partisans insist on siding against *Man in Revolt* and continuing the battle from the other, defeated, side. If Camus was right, Sartre was wrong, and vice versa; that was the logic of the Cold War, and we have not yet gone beyond it.

But to allow such Manichaeanism to frame our reading of *Man in Revolt* would defeat my purpose. I discuss this compulsion to take sides to show how it came to dominate Camus and Sartre—how they sided against each other, destroyed their friendship, and contributed to the Cold War divisions that shaped the second half of the twentieth century. We have to see their rupture in its true colors—as the product of a distorted choice. The Cold War confused political thinking, destroyed friendships and individuals, and deformed the Left and the entire political universe. As with the rest of the Camus-Sartre story, seeing and engaging both points of view critically as well as sympathetically may allow us to free ourselves from the dualistic thinking of the Cold War.

: : :

Revolt assumed for Camus the status in human experience that Descartes gave to the cogito, or that Sartre gave to the for-itself's activity in negating the in-itself: a primary, irreducible starting point. The first draft of the ideas in *Man in Revolt*, "Remarque sur la révolte," seems to have been written in 1943 or 1944 directly under the inspiration of Camus's encounter with *Being and Nothingness.* This little essay is startlingly suggestive of the way in which Sartre had sketched the negation of the in-itself by the for-itself, and in a most Sartrean fashion Camus stressed that revolt *creates* values. The act is positive no less than negative, generating at one and the same time human values, dignity, and solidarity. "I revolt, therefore we are." At its metaphysical core this is revolt against absurdity—against our own mortality and this absurd universe's meaningless and incoherence. In the half-dozen pages in his notebooks before an entry dated September 24, 1944, Camus mentioned *Being and Nothingness* twice, and in between talked mostly about *The Plague.*

In *Man in Revolt*, this effort to overcome absurdity is described as lying behind historical revolt. During the French Revolution the pursuit of absolute justice was announced in one decisive step, the killing of the king—which obliterated the original life-affirming, self-affirming, and solidaristic purpose of revolt. Camus's "history of European pride" reaches back to the Greeks and early Christianity, then moves on to the marquis de Sade, romanticism, dandyism, *The Brothers Karamazov,* Hegel, Marx, Nietzsche, surrealism, the Nazis, and the Bolsheviks. Camus talks of revolt as increasing its force over time and turning into an ever more desperate nihilism, overthrowing God and substituting man, wielding power more and more brutally. Historical revolt, rooted in metaphysical revolt, leads to revolutions seeking to eliminate absurdity by taking total control over the world. They make murder their central tool. For Camus, Communism was the contemporary expression of this Western sickness.

By an "inevitable logic of nihilism" Communism climaxes the modern trend to deify man and to transform and unify the world. Today's revolt yields to the blind impulse "to demand order in the midst of chaos, and unity in the very heart of the ephemeral," leading the man in revolt who becomes a revolutionary to kill and then to justify murder as legitimate. The man in revolt must learn to live and act within limits, to embrace more moderate, even more reformist hopes—"to live and let live in order to create what we are." Writing above all *against revolution,* Camus sought to clarify the fundamental spirit of revolt, to distinguish it from its fatal deformations, especially "Caesarean socialism," and to recall it to more modest origins.

This brilliant construction is of a different genre than, say, Victor Kravchenko's *I Chose Freedom* or Koestler's *Darkness at Noon* (the two top bestsellers in France between 1945 and 1955). It makes no explicitly political arguments or revelations, contains little in the way of actual social analysis or concrete historical study. It is, rather, a philosophical and literary history of underlying ideas and attitudes. In Sartrean terms, *Man in Revolt* is a history of bad faith, of increasingly organized and catastrophic refusals to face, accept, and live with absurdity. As the tone, style, and content of Camus's book make strikingly clear from the distance of a half-century, Camus was applying his absurdist ideas and insights to politics in the same way that psychoanalytically oriented social theorists such as Erich Fromm and Norman O. Brown were beginning to apply Freudian insights to social behavior and movements.

Because *Man in Revolt* claimed to describe what *lay behind* the evil features of contemporary revolutionary politics, it became a major political event. Even those who did not follow Camus page by page could hardly miss his description of how the impulse for emancipation turned into organized, rational murder. From its first appearance until now, many readers of *Man in Revolt* have seen themselves mirrored in the rebel's futile attempt to order an absurd universe.

The book's enduring strength lies in this, its exploration of the starting points, projects, weaknesses, illusions, and temptations of recent generations. As traditional religion has lost its force, young people have been growing up with an increasing sense that anything is possible. Modern secularism moves toward a nihilistic state of mind because it lacks what Camus regarded as the sole saving insight: that life is absurd, and even though we must rebel, nothing can create order or remove death's sting.

In presenting this message, Camus sought not so much to critique Stalinism as its apologists. His specific targets were intellectuals attracted to Communism—as he had been in the past and Sartre still was. His intended readers were those hundreds of thousands of educated leftists who bought and read serious literary, political, and philosophical texts, who thought about politics as much as they acted politically, and for whom ideas were decisive components of political allegiance. These were the students, teachers, and others usually described as "intellectuals" who read newspapers like *Combat* or journals like *Les Temps modernes.* Camus was speaking in tones that were individualist, deeply affected by modern literary movements, romantic and existentialist to their core. If in 1944 his audience had been the postwar youth who made Sartre's and Camus's ideas their own, by 1951 their hopes at the Liberation ("From Resistance to Revolution") had died, as had subsequent efforts to steer an independent leftist course between the United States and the Soviet Union. As Beauvoir recalled, people wondered what they would do if the Russians invaded. For readers such as these, a well-known political journalist and novelist's dissection of the mindset behind Communism could not help but be a significant political act.

: : :

Man in Revolt operates successfully as a worldview—a coherent amalgam of premise, mood, description, philosophy, history, and even prejudice that appealed to Camus's audience on many levels. Camus was intransigent in his insistence that both Communism's appeal and its sinister character sprang from the same source, a vital human impulse. Here is one of the ringing conclusions to his discussion of Marx:

> Once more we find, at the end of this long journey, metaphysical rebellion, which, this time, advances to the clash of arms and the whispering of passwords, but forgetful of its real principles, burying its solitude in the bosom of armed masses, covering the emptiness of its negations with obstinate scholasticism, still directed toward the future, which it has made its only

> god, but separated from it by a multitude of nations that must be overthrown and continents that must be dominated. With action as its unique principle, and with the kingdom of man as its alibi, it has already begun, in the east of Europe, to construct its own armed camp, face to face with other armed camps.

Validating revolt as a vital starting point, Camus rejects utopian solutions, the belief that history is the entire context of human existence. He criticizes totalizing politics, affirming that life should be lived in the present and the sensuous world; he explores the history of postreligious and nihilistic intellectual and literary movements; he attacks political violence with an outlook of limits and solidarity; and he ends by articulating the metaphysical role of art as well as a self-limiting radical politics. He concludes with a vision of Mediterranean moderation that he obviously hopes will be stirring and lyrical, binding the reader to his insights.

Camus's anti-Communist agenda skewed as well as shaped *Man in Revolt.* The book's weaknesses and limits can scarcely be separated from its strengths, and together they flow from Camus's choosing to write the book in this particular way. Starting with his initial equation of Communism and murder, Camus then deduces revolutions from ideas and states of spirit. He makes no close analysis of movements or events, giving no role to material needs or oppression, but presents his ideas sweepingly. The quest for social justice appears only as a metaphysically inspired attempt to replace "the reign of grace by the reign of justice," and assertions of human dignity are little more than efforts to overthrow God.

We can glimpse both Camus's power and his limits by looking at the book's first two chapters, companion introductions to the two main themes, murder and revolt. Camus begins stunningly:

> There are crimes of passion and crimes of logic. The boundary between them is not clearly defined. But the Penal Code makes the convenient distinction of premeditation. We are living in the era of premeditation and the perfect crime. Our criminals are no longer helpless children who could plead love as their excuse. On the contrary, they are adults and they have a perfect alibi: philosophy, which can be used for any purpose—even for transforming murderers into judges.

In the twentieth century, murder has become "reasonable," "theoretically defensible," justified by doctrine. In putting this at the center Camus tackles one of the century's master issues. He speaks of seventy million deaths since 1900 (by the end of the twentieth century the total was at least half again as large). As he points out, the twentieth century grew accustomed to "logical crimes"—mass death either planned or foreseen, and rationally justified. Therefore no intellectual task could be more pressing than to understand why such disasters happen—how the murders occurred and how they have been justified. Camus, quite rightly, calls "logical crime" the central issue of the time, seeks to "examine meticulously the arguments by which it is justified," and sets out to explore how the twentieth century became a century of slaughter.

But then *Man in Revolt* changes focus. Human reason is confused by "slave camps under the flag of freedom, massacres justified by philanthropy or by a taste for the superhuman"—the first two travesties are a reference to Communism, the third to Nazism. In the body of the text, Nazism virtually drops out (it was after all a system of "irrational terror"—not at all what interested Camus), sharply narrowing the inquiry. His shift is revealed by his question: How can murder be committed with premeditation and justified by philosophy? The "rational murder" Camus was concerned with is not committed by capitalists or democrats, colonialists or imperialists, or by Nazis—but by Communists. If at midcentury any single writer was able to take on the full range of these disasters, it was Albert Camus. Yet although he had written against Nazi violence, he did not now address the Holocaust. Although his had been a lone voice of protest against Hiroshima, he did not now ask how it happened. Although, after Sétif, he had been one of the few to indict French colonialism, he did not now mention it, except in a footnote. How, we may wonder, was it possible for Camus to focus solely on the violence of Communism in the very midst of the French colonial war in Vietnam and when he knew (he above all people) that a bitter struggle over Algeria lay ahead? Oddly, the writer most willing and able to tackle the question of murder in the twentieth century became blinded by ideology. He separated Communism from the other evils of the century and directed his animus at just this one. Camus's ideas, of course, had developed and matured over the years since he first began writing about revolt. But something else had happened: his agenda had changed. Revolt, his original and provocative theme, had been harnessed as an *alternative* to Communism, which had become the archenemy.

As a result, Camus was no longer interested in specific objectives of political movements, and he ignored concrete issues involved in struggling for change, including the business of achieving power. He did not look at societies and their structures, and he ignored the socioeconomic concerns of Marxism. To Camus, Marxism was not about social change; it was nothing less—and nothing more—than a revolt that "attempts to annex all creation." In a wonderfully ambivalent chapter on Nietzsche, which appeared in *Les Temps modernes* in July 1951, Camus distinguishes Nietzsche from the use made of him by the Nazis, and even urges: "We must be the advocates of Nietzsche." But he caricatures Hegel ("The conqueror is always right") and distorts Marx (he "found any form of beauty under the sun completely alien"). Neither of these is read for himself; they are mentioned only to advance Camus's argument. Reading *Man in Revolt*, one has no hint that moderate and reformist Marxist traditions, or even democratic revolutionary ones, exist at all. Instead, the political alternative to Marxism, in one of the book's most fascinating and idiosyncratic chapters, is cast as the activities of those Russian terrorists that Camus depicted in *The Just Assassins.* They refuse to attack the innocent and are willing to sacrifice their own lives. They kill, but only specific individuals and with the understanding that, having upset the moral order, they must pay with their own lives. In focusing on revolutionary leaders and their theories, Camus admires most of all the Russian terrorists, never discussing those who toil and rebel at the bottom of various ladders—colonial populations or the working class.

Perhaps this single-minded focus on demonstrating a theory is what turns Camus's customary spare, charged, absolutely precise style into ponderous and peremptory prose, which only occasionally comes alive. The text is punctuated with words of conclusion (*alors, donc, ainsi, c'est pourquoi*), which are rarely followed by consequences of what comes before but merely introduce assertions, based on no evidence or analysis. And it is studded with carefully composed topic sentences for major ideas—which demand to be followed by paragraphs, pages, and chapters of development but, instead, merely follow one another and sit undeveloped until the next equally well-wrought topic sentence. This is especially so in the book's final three chapters, which appear to be drawing conclusions from earlier discussions but time and again launch new themes. Rather than exploring issues with Camus's customary restraint, from its first page *Man in Revolt* frequently has an arbitrary, eccentric quality.

: : :

Its flaws are at the heart of *Man in Revolt* and, as we shall see, were duly described and denounced in *Les Temps modernes*. Camus's errors and obsessions made it easy for those who disagreed with his anti-Communism to ignore the book's importance, but fifty years later it still remains one of the most original and probing efforts to understand how the great modern impulse to freedom produced totalitarian societies. It would be unfair to criticize Camus for not fully answering this question; in asking it seriously and seeking the explanation within the West's basic attitudes he was already making an important contribution. Camus insists that the abstract, authoritarian, apocalyptic revolutionary, the person who would transform the world according to a science, in obedience to the laws of history, pretending to be governed by objective necessity, is thoroughly modern, thoroughly enlightened, and fully Western. Thus he looks closely at what has been one major strand of Marxism through the lenses of an antirevolutionary, intransigent, yet skeptical radicalism. *Man in Revolt* continues to attract readers today by looking askance at Western civilization, at progress, at the modern world itself—all ways in which Camus foreshadowed some of the main intellectual trends to come.

Man in Revolt still contains instructive ways of thinking about political action from the left. Its sober, concrete, and even humble sense of politics opposes itself to illusions as well as abstract ideas imposed from the outside. Camus resisted any notion that the peaceable kingdom is "coming true," insisting that perfection is only a dream. He stressed that morality must remain at the center of politics, and was unremitting in his advocacy of free speech, democratic institutions, and civil rights in any movement for social justice.

Foremost among the book's insights, Camus's sense of reciprocity and restraint and his understanding of violence remain relevant today. "Every human freedom, at its very roots . . . is relative." Each person's freedom limits that of others and, a fortiori, limits the freedom of rulers. Against the tendency of revolutionary philosophy to act as if we can know and settle everything, a philosophy of revolt "would be a philosophy of limits, of calculated ignorance, and of risk." This thinking does not mandate absolute nonviolence, but it certainly implies "the renunciation of violence committed on principle" —violence approached abstractly and justified by philosophy. Camus insists that violence is always unjustifiable. To avoid becoming corrupted by it, Camus rejects all efforts to theoretically justify using force to impose one's will on others. This is why Camus regards freedom of speech as so important. Imposing silence isolates people from each other and destroys their solidarity. It can create an artificial community, but never brings people in communication with each other. Only when communicating freely can people form reciprocal relationships based on self-limits.

While rejecting what revolutions have become in the twentieth century, these ideas certainly remain leftist at their core. Camus did accept that insurrections would take place against violent and oppressive governments. He tolerated the use of violence, but only in order to create "institutions that limit violence, not . . . those which codify it." He even gave some guidelines for political violence: it has to be provisional in character, tied to individual personal responsibility, used only when there is immediate risk and to "combat another form of violence."

: : :

Despite its weaknesses, *Man in Revolt* took hold, and Camus himself remained proud of it to the end of his life. Writing it was an act of great political and personal courage. Camus knew what it cost him, knew he would be hailed on the Right and derided on the Left, and knew he was attacking a broad consensus on progress, the Enlightenment, and the French Revolution. In Russian history, he sided neither with the Bolsheviks nor with the Mensheviks—neither with revolutionary nor with reformist Marxists—but, as he had already shown in *The Just Assassins,* with the hopelessly romantic and impractical Social Revolutionary terrorists. Camus also knew that East-West polarization had gone so far in generating its opposing realisms that little space was left for his more idealistic approach. Still, he persisted in using and enlarging that space. He was willing to fly alone into the storm, indeed, to provoke a storm, in order to say what he regarded as true, in order to produce and legitimize the alternative that no one else was advocating. It was a strength that Sartre, for all his genius, lacked: the ability to stand alone politically.

Was it because of rivalry with Sartre that Camus attempted so much—too much—in *Man in Revolt*? True, he was expounding at length on political ideas sketched in *Neither Victims nor Executioners* and was writing a sequel to *The Myth of Sisyphus.* But he turned all this into a book that sometimes seems to challenge *Being and Nothingness* as an effort to think through fundamental structures of human existence. In one sense, then, *Man in Revolt* may be called a work of philosophy. In the 1940s, Camus distinguished himself from the philosopher Sartre by describing himself as an artist and demurring from Sartre's systematic effort to understand the world. And yet I suspect that if it were not for his friendship with this philosophical genius, Camus would have continued to call himself a philosopher. At its beginning, after all, *Man in Revolt* casts rebellion as the equivalent of Descartes's *cogito ergo sum,* and by its end it seems to rival *What Is Literature?* by exploring at length the fundamental meaning of artistic creation, especially writing. Usually far more diffident than Sartre, Camus was now writing philosophy, history of ideas and literary movements, aesthetics, and political theory—as if replying to Sartre on several fronts at once.

Sartre, on the contrary, while never accused of restraint, usually focused each of his texts on a single dimension and developed that one carefully. *Being and Nothingness* restricts itself to describing the most fundamental ontological structures, and does so with immense power and depth. When he sought to develop this book's political, epistemological, and ethical consequences, Sartre did so in three separate texts. When he related literature to politics, however, he did so in a single set of essays. In fact, Sartre never wrote a book as ambitious in reach as *Man in Revolt.*

We will never know how far the two writers' relationship is a hidden component of *Man in Revolt.* But there is no doubt that a key section of the book was written explicitly *against* Sartre. Although it appears near the end as an aside on "the existentialists," it focuses on "the cult of history" against which the entire book is directed. The importance of this reference to existentialists is belied by the studied casualness of the "for example" introducing it, and by Camus's refusal to mention Sartre by name—although he did mention contemporaries André Malraux, André Breton, and René Char. In fact, it is a coded discussion of *The Devil and the Good Lord,* which Camus knew well, and specifically a criticism of the notion, central to the play, that Goetz is *growing* as he moves from revolt to revolution.

In the contemporary world, says Camus, rebellion denies itself by becoming revolution. To survive and remain true to itself, it must

> find a new object of faith and a new impetus. Before going any farther, this contradiction must at least be stated in plain language. It is not a clear definition to say like the existentialists, for example (who are also subjected for the moment to the cult of history and its contradictions), that there is progress in the transition from revolt to revolution and that the man in revolt is nothing if he is not revolutionary. The contradiction is, in reality, considerably more restricted. The revolutionary is simultaneously a man in revolt or he is not a revolutionary but a policeman and a bureaucrat who turns against revolt. But if he is a man in revolt, he ends up by taking sides against the revolution. So much so that there is absolutely no progress from one attitude to the other, but coexistence and endlessly increasing contradiction. Every revolutionary ends by becoming either an oppressor or a heretic. In the purely historical universe that they have chosen, revolt and revolution end in the same dilemma: either police rule or insanity.

However offhandedly he begins this passage, Camus is drawing a line in the sand. He does so without rancor, and in order to provoke a discussion. On the one side is his portrayal of revolt; on the other, Sartre's of revolution. Camus's readers knew that Goetz's evolution was *away from* metaphysics and *toward* becoming just another man in the world, and that accepting violence meant embracing reality in order to change it. In this passage Camus throws down the gauntlet, challenging Sartre to choose. Revolt either seizes power and falls victim to the entire pathology Camus describes, or remains true to itself and fights even the revolution in power.

: : :

At the very time that Camus was completing *Man in Revolt,* Sartre was completing his transformation into a revolutionary. Taking the pro-Communist Merleau-Ponty as his mentor, as Camus had done with the anti-Communist Koestler, Sartre went a step further and embraced violence as the necessary path for overcoming human oppression. Sartre's conversion took place in two half-steps: *The Devil and the Good Lord* in the spring of 1951, and *The Communists and Peace* in June 1952. Until this period, Sartre and Camus had been moving in directions that were simultaneously complementary and contrary. At least semiconsciously they seemed to be shaping themselves *against* each other. As Sartre later described in his biography of Gustave Flaubert, in a family where one sibling occupies, and so preempts, the space available for a certain identity choice, the younger sibling rarely chooses the same direction and tends to develop differently, sometimes in a quite unexpected way. Any French political intellectual trying to find direction between 1944 and 1951 would have been faced with Sartre and Camus commanding the field of intellectual-political choices on the non-Communist Left. No one in this universe could think through contemporary issues without regard to Sartre and Camus. Similarly, each of the two friends had to contend with the other, and each one's self-clarification demanded differentiating himself from the other.

Sartre's articulation of the ideas of situation and commitment led Camus to move toward his own alternative and spell it out more sharply. And Camus's forceful articulation of a nonviolent anti-Communism led Sartre to clarify his contrasting view of violence. If Camus's distinctive "utopianism" and "intransigent reformism" were viscerally opposed by the newly politicized and more radical Sartre, so Sartre was now finding his own path to change, embracing violence and revolution with a profoundly considered sense of realism.

: : :

In early 1952, members of the Communist Party asked Sartre's support for a campaign against the court-martial of Henri Martin, a naval officer who refused to participate in the war in Vietnam. By now completely isolated, the PCF leadership was reaching out to non-Communists. Sartre accepted their appeal and wrote a commentary for a book on the Martin case. He then left with Beauvoir for their annual vacation in Italy. Meanwhile, an American general, Matthew Ridgway, came to Paris en route to assuming command of NATO, and the PCF organized a militant demonstration, which led to rioting. The police suppressed the riots and arrested PCF leader Jacques Duclos. They confiscated from his car some pigeons he was taking home for dinner, charging that they were carrier pigeons used to coordinate the riots.

> I learned from the Italian newspapers of Duclos's arrest, the theft of his diaries, the farce of the carrier pigeons [wrote Sartre]. These sordid, childish tricks turned my stomach. There may have been more ignoble ones, but none more revelatory. An anti-Communist is a dog. I couldn't see any way out of that one, and I never will. . . . After ten years of ruminating, I had come to the breaking point, and only needed that one last straw. In the language of the Church, this was my conversion. . . . In the name of those principles which it had inculcated into me, in the name of its humanism and of its "humanities," in the name of liberty, equality, fraternity, I swore to the bourgeoisie a hatred which would only die with me. Rushing back to Paris, I had to write or suffocate. Day and night, I wrote the first part of *The Communists and Peace.*

In this July 1952 article, Sartre declares himself a fellow traveler. It is a strange, turgid text, a point-by-point argument with anti-Communists about the meaning of the May 28 demonstration. Sartre uses much of the article to settle accounts with various exponents of positions he has once held or is now rejecting, implicitly including Camus.

Then Sartre begins to defend the resort of workers and the Party to illegality and violence. This penetrating discussion, totally at odds with Camus's understanding of violence, begins with an account of how the new electoral law has reduced workers to second-class citizens. In the 1951 elections, five million Communist voters returned 103 deputies, while half as many Socialist voters returned 104 deputies! "Between ourselves, it is something which, broadly, might lead people to go out into the streets and break a few windows or bash a few faces." Long before these elections, the workers and the PCF had been placed in quarantine. Now, "of two dockers walking together on the quays of Le Havre, one hasn't the right to vote and the other has voted in vain." Their freedom to vote, the hallmark of bourgeois society, has thus been conjured away by the bourgeoisie.

At the root of this legalized trickery, Sartre claims, lies class war. As organized, France is "a society of oppression," and those reproaching the PCF for its illegality and violence ignore the fact that "today all violence, directly or indirectly, comes from the proletariat, which gives back to us what we have given it." In this sense, violence is ingrained in and legitimized by the social order.

> However far back he delves into the past, the worker finds himself already caught up in a society which has its code and its system of law, its government, and its idea of what is just and what unjust; more serious still, a society whose ideology he shares spontaneously. A destiny, limits are imposed on him; he is condemned to fragmented and semi-automatic tasks whose meaning and purpose escape him, and to industrial diseases. Forced to repeat the same gesture a thousand times a day he is discouraged by weariness and poverty from exercising his human qualities, he is shut up in a dull world of repetition; little by little, he becomes a *thing*. But when he tries to find those who are responsible for his condition, there is no one; everything is in order: he has been paid what is due to him.

Workers' violence, then, is a response to this "natural," normal violence.

> People pretend to believe that violence is born suddenly, at the moment a riot or a strike occurs. Not at all: in moments of crisis it comes out into the open, that is all. The contradiction is reversed: docile, the worker rejects what is human in himself; insurgent, he rejects what is inhuman. This rejection is itself a humanism, it contains the exigent demand for a new justice. But since oppression is not a visible offence, since the ideology of the ruling class defines what is just and what unjust, since nothing can be got unless an order that is sacred is smashed by force, the worker sees the affirmation of his own reality as a man in a manifestation of violence.

No sooner does the worker engage in violence than society escalates it, springing the trap. "His discontent *must* be transformed into a strike, his strike into a brawl, the brawl into murder." And then society imposes a repressive calm, "which is not pacification but a return to the original violence."

From this point of view, workers' violence is "positive humanism." "In fact, humanism and violence are the two indissoluble aspects of his effort to get out of his oppressed condition." Therefore, workers' violence "is the Communist Party's very substance and strength." Sartre accordingly ends the article by mocking all those who would like to see a well-mannered Left, "amiable, polite, ready to make distinctions, subtle reservations, which would fight capitalism but would be just to persons, which, without rejecting violence, would not make use of it except as a last resort, and which, while knowing how to stir up the generous enthusiasm of proletarians, would if necessary protect them from their own excesses."

This explosive, dramatic quality reappeared a decade later in Sartre's preface to Frantz Fanon's *The Wretched of the Earth*, as well as in his support for the violence and illegality of the revolutionary Left in the wake of May 1968. As a political moralist, Sartre condemned the violence of the rulers and approved in advance the violence of the oppressed. He would not even concede that the violence of the oppressed is regrettable but inevitable, acceptable within certain limits but not when it exceeds them. A supporter of revolution, refusing to waste time on any talk of violence as demoralizing or corrupting, ignoring its damage, Sartre had become a fierce and intransigent tribune of the oppressed. On exactly this point, Sartre's direction is most sharply opposed to Camus's. While Camus had been devoting all of his energies to writing against violence, especially revolutionary violence, Sartre had gradually been embracing violence, especially revolutionary violence.

7

the explosion

Near the end of *Man in Revolt*, Camus was clearly seeking to provoke a response from Sartre. But why the unwillingness to mention his friend by name? Disagreeing strongly with Sartre's position, demanding to know how a historically oriented philosophy can be moral, Camus seemed impelled toward a confrontation with Sartre, while at the same time avoiding it. Even before the book was published Camus became embroiled in controversy with the indefatigable surrealist poet, theorist, and polemicist André Breton. In retrospect, much of Camus's debate with Breton seems like a rehearsal. This controversy strikingly anticipated, in its differences as well as its similarities, the contest between friends to follow a few months later. Camus attacked a core idea of each man's philosophy, the idea that he considered to be politically most dangerous. In early 1951, *Cahiers du Sud* had published an excerpt from *Man in Revolt* containing Camus's criticism of the poet Lautréamont, beloved of the surrealists, in which Camus linked the poet's drive for absolute freedom with its opposite:

> Conformity is one of the nihilistic temptations of rebellion which dominate a large part of our intellectual history. It demonstrates how the rebel who takes to action is tempted to succumb, if he forgets his origins, to the most absolute conformity. And so it explains the twentieth century. Lautréamont, who is usually hailed as the bard of pure rebellion, on the contrary proclaims the advent of the taste for intellectual servitude which flourishes in the contemporary world.

This passage in *Man in Revolt* is followed immediately by a section titled "Surrealism and Revolution," which attacked not only Rimbaud but Breton himself as "parlor nihilists" with an addiction to violence. This remarkable discussion was bound to provoke a storm. The surrealists were native to France and, led by Breton, had had a glorious moment of influence immediately after World War I. They were still widely respected, if for no other reason than that they had counted among their number, at one time or another, most important contemporary French poets. Although now considered old-fashioned by Camus and Sartre and many others of the new generation, surrealism still had its passionately loyal followers. Camus, however, objected not only to their past flirtation with Communism and their continued alignment with the idea of revolution but above all to their theoretical devotion to the unconscious and the irrational as the path to liberation. If Camus believed in *measure,* the surrealists sought explosive release—and argued that all the forces restraining the psyche were in league with bourgeois society. They sought to express the unconscious, making themes and images of violence crucial to the process of freeing dammed-up psychic drives. Breton's most famous remark, circa 1933—"The simplest surrealist act consists of dashing down into the street, pistol in hand, and firing blindly, as fast as you can pull the trigger, into the crowd" —horrified Camus. For him, such intellectual playacting at violent expression fed the twentieth century's organized unleashing of violence.

Breton had not seen Camus's book before attacking the section on Lautréamont. Sensing where Camus was headed, he wrote an indignant riposte, published in the cultural weekly *Arts* on October 12 and timed with the book's appearance the following week. Breton professed himself offended that a well-known writer like Camus should attack someone a thousand times greater. In ignoring surrealism's liberating power and in attacking Lautréamont's nihilism, Camus was "siding with the worst elements of conservatism and conformism."

The tone of Camus's reply was self-righteous, sharp-tongued, and assertive: Breton "has obviously not really read me and . . . his purely sentimental argumentation has not modified one of my *actual* points of view on Lautréamont." We are all supporters of surrealism, Camus said, but in addition to its encouragement of revolt it also generates attitudes of servitude and conformity. He claimed that anyone who had really read his text on Lautréamont would have been able to see this between the lines. Conservatism? Camus yielded not one iota of his political radicalism to Breton: "If there were something to conserve in our society, I would not see any dishonor in being conservative. Unhappily, that is not the case."

This remark foreshadowed Camus's declaration to Sartre, ten months later, that "if the truth appeared to be on the Right, I would be there." In response, Breton affirmed that he had indeed read the book. He gave an interview to *Arts* in which he rejected Camus's central claim because it was so obviously at variance with surrealism.

> What is this phantom of revolt that Camus is trying to credit, and behind which he takes shelter, a form of revolt into which "moderation" has been introduced? Once revolt has been emptied of its passionate substance, what could possibly remain? . . . I have no doubt that many people will be duped by this artifice: it is a case of keeping the word and eliminating the thing itself.

In his reply and in the longer article that followed, Camus showed that the voice of the current generation was fully equal to that of the great spokesman of the older, post–World War I generation. In December 1948, Camus and Breton, along with Sartre, had been on the platform together during the most successful of the meetings organized by Sartre's RDR. Now the generations were arguing in a highly visible weekly journal over the political meaning of key themes of the national culture. During the next few months a number of other people were drawn into the fray.

The conflict might well have been described as "Camus versus Breton." Camus's faculty for such controversy was demonstrated by the fact that he dared to write one of the first negative analyses ever of Lautréamont, a poet greatly admired by French intellectuals, and then crossed swords with the pope of surrealism. Even though, as he said in his personal letters, he was now confronting a new fear that sapped his energy, he did not hold back.

The Camus-Breton controversy culminated in two events, both of which reflect Camus's social power. The first was a book-length symposium, *La Révolte en question,* published by younger followers of Breton, to which Camus refused to contribute. (Accordingly, its editor accused him of being "scornful" and "immodest.") The second was a remarkable personal reconciliation. In spite of their quarrel, Camus recommended that Breton be invited to speak at a rally against Franco's Spain toward the end of February 1952; and when the older man heard of this, he burst into tears. At the event, the two chatted amiably on the platform—because, Camus later said, he had refrained from answering the older man in the same intemperate tones Breton had used toward him. Camus may have interacted more easily with Breton than with Sartre because they were not personal friends or because their differences were about surrealism and not about Communism. More would be at stake between Camus and Sartre. After the meeting, Sartre, who had also been on the platform, went out for a drink with Camus and told him that there would be a critical review of *Man in Revolt* in the May issue of *Les Temps modernes.*

: : :

Between its publication date and May 1952, numerous reviews of *Man in Revolt* appeared: in political, literary, religious, and general-interest publications; in dailies, weeklies, and monthlies; in publications across the political spectrum; and by literary reviewers as well as by well-known figures, including Camus's comrades from the Resistance. The book was widely talked about, and generally well received. Of course there were critics, especially as the longer and more reflective articles began to appear. But the political reaction followed no clear pattern. Camus's response to *L'Observateur* shows how touchy he was. Claude Bourdet, who had given Camus his editorial position in the Resistance in early 1944, gave the book a positive and serious review in two issues of the weekly. Subsequently, another writer in *L'Observateur*, named Lebar, mentioned that the review in the Communist journal *La Nouvelle Critique* by Pierre Hervé, Camus's old antagonist, was "a remarkable study." Camus then mistakenly attacked *L'Observateur* for saying that the Communist article was "a fine study," apparently unaware that Lebar had gone on to explain *why* it was remarkable, namely, that "it was more of a pamphlet than an article." Getting it totally wrong, Camus sent a pompous letter insisting that the weekly must choose "between watchdogs and free men, the police-state Left and the free Left."

One interviewer fondly recalled the great peace rally at the Salle de Pleyel in December 1948, at which Sartre, Camus, and Breton had spoken, and lamented that the united non-Communist Left of that period had fragmented. Asked about this, the author of *Man in Revolt* was intransigent: what was over was "the time of disarray"; "this century's mystifications are being rejected by more and more people." All of us, Camus hoped, might be reunited again on condition that we no longer hide our differences and that everyone acknowledge the real problem of today, meaning Communism, and denounce it. In other words, anti-Communism, not socialism and neutrality, had to be the chief building block of a united Left before Camus would participate.

Camus was asserting the key political conclusion to be drawn from his new book. In this period he combined haughtiness, aggressiveness, and prickliness with his characteristic political independence and strength of conviction. Taken together, these dispositions led to a willingness to tangle with all comers, though not always by name. In his letter to *L'Observateur*, Camus expressed anger with Pierre Hervé and *La Nouvelle Critique* for taking seven months to review his book. How must he have felt toward *Les Temps modernes* and its editor Sartre for taking yet another month? Camus had been assertively distinguishing himself from the "existentialists" for years, and now one of them, Jeanson, finally responded in detail. If he was touchy about negative or (as he saw them) hostile comments, how would he react to a thoroughly critical review?

: : :

The question of how to deal with *Man in Revolt* had been causing a problem at *Les Temps modernes* from the moment the book was published. "In November," Beauvoir tells us, "Sartre asked for a volunteer to review Camus's *The Rebel.* He wouldn't let anyone say anything bad about it because of their friendship; unfortunately none of us could think of anything good. We wondered how we were going to get out of the dilemma." Every two weeks the question was posed at editorial meetings. Some of the editors had already been saying that the book was based on secondary sources, not on original ones. Francis Jeanson, the journal's nominal managing editor, indicates that Sartre thought Camus was discussing matters he had not understood and had read neither Marx nor Engels directly but merely used other writers' summaries. Why didn't Sartre himself review the book, since he knew what needed to be said and would have achieved just the right balance? Given his mastery of language and his friendship with Camus, his reticence was bound to raise eyebrows. Yet France's greatest thinker and editor of its most important journal avoided criticizing Camus by delegating the review to one of his followers. The most obvious explanation was that he was avoiding a confrontation that might hurt his friend and ruin the friendship. Both he and Beauvoir knew that Camus bristled easily, and they had learned to watch their words around him, especially as their differences increased. Firmly, sometimes dogmatically committed to his opinions, Camus tended to be critical, self-righteous, and defensive. As Beauvoir noted, this behavior worsened over time. It seems that Sartre took the easy way out—he knew how important his opinion would be to Camus, knew that expressing it would anger him and cause serious problems between the two old friends, and sought a way out by having someone else answer Camus, a reviewer who had no personal relationship with him. As Sartre said, "it is going to be even more disagreeable for him if we say nothing at all about his book." And so he gave the job to Jeanson, who, he thought, would at least be "polite." Avoiding the issue in this way was shortsighted and foolish, but understandable.

A second possible reason for Sartre's failure to review Camus's book himself, given the violence of Sartre's words when he did finally address its author, assumes less tenderness on Sartre's part. He did not deign to respond directly to someone who would not mention him by name. Recall how Sartre, after Camus had referred to him as a "writer of today," chided Camus for his superficial knowledge of philosophy. By now Sartre was world famous and in the same class as the thinkers named by Camus in *The Myth of Sisyphus* and *Man in Revolt*. Not mentioning Sartre by name was an insult that drew the attention of at least one reviewer. Discussed openly and directly, Sartre might well have replied openly and directly. But when he was argued with but simultaneously ignored, his best response would be to ignore Camus in turn by having a junior collaborator—whose negative stance toward Camus he had to have known about—perform the critique. Open affection for his friend? Avoiding conflict and protecting his friend? Suppressed anger? Returning a slight? Sartre's unwillingness to reply suggests all these motives. His anger eventually came into the open after Camus treated Jeanson as he had twice treated Sartre: by attacking him but refusing to mention his name.

Another reason for Sartre's unwillingness to review *Man in Revolt,* equally plausible given the chronology of Sartre's political development, may have been *inability* to answer Camus. Although *The Devil and the Good Lord* staked out the path of revolutionary change, Sartre's own stance on revolution was still posed on a highly abstract level. His friendship with Camus had revived briefly during the rehearsals of the play; they had been together at its opening night; and Sartre offered to publish Camus's Nietzsche chapter in *Les Temps modernes.*

I have already quoted Sartre's comment that "a certain intimacy was always there as long as we were on good terms. Even our differences didn't worry us much in conversation." Their friendship may have been no more than a shell, but the relationship persisted. They had grown apart, staking out the political positions of enemies. Each was about to embrace and become the main spokesperson for the political-philosophical position the other most detested, while still retaining a formal friendship and even some fondness for each other. Beauvoir and Sartre, as Beauvoir recalled, saw Camus "in a little café on the Place Saint-Sulpice in April. He made fun of a lot of the criticisms of his book; he just took it for granted that we liked it, and Sartre had great difficulty in knowing what to say to him." This was the last time Beauvoir would see him.

Sartre had written *The Devil and the Good Lord* in winter of 1951. In late spring 1952, he rushed home from Rome to write the first part of *The Communists and Peace.* His earlier words bear repeating: "An anti-Communist is a dog. I couldn't see a way out of that one, and I never will. . . . after ten years of ruminating, I had come to the breaking point, and only needed that one last straw. In the language of the Church, this was my conversion." The temporizing on the part of Sartre and *Les Temps modernes* over reviewing *Man in Revolt,* and Sartre's passing it off to Jeanson, had happened in the months *before* his conversion.

Before the summer of 1952, Sartre had theoretically decided on the path of revolutionary realism but had not yet walked it. He would take this step only after his decision to side with Communism. The chronology points to the conclusion that he could not review *Man in Revolt* himself for two reasons: Camus was still his friend, and the event he referred to as "that one last straw" had not yet happened. If Camus posed a challenge to him between fall 1951 and spring 1952, it was as a friend. Sartre resolved his political direction only after beginning to write *The Communists and Peace.* With this manifesto, he became the leading independent pro-Communist in France.

But was Sartre's avoidance any greater than Camus's? Both did what they could to put off the confrontation, and both took steps toward it. The evasions and provocations would only fuel the explosion. Camus was no doubt growing impatient, and in the meantime he was fighting on other fronts. Sartre, contacted by the Party to help in the Henri Martin affair, was moving toward open support of Communism. Reading *Man in Revolt* may have helped him complete this process by forcing him to sharpen his own position in opposition to Camus's. Camus mailed off his reply to *Les Temps modernes* on June 30, after Sartre had just finished the first part of *The Communists and Peace.* His attack on

Camus would be his first act as a fellow traveler. Upon reading Camus's reply to Jeanson's review, he did what he had avoided doing for nearly a year: he addressed Camus directly.

: : :

The provocative indirectness through which both men had avoided dealing with each other now had its explosive effect. Sartre presented his version of events in a dialogue with Beauvoir dated "August-September 1974," which was published after his death:

> The final break came about when [Camus] published his book *The Rebel*. I tried to find someone who would be willing to review it in *Les Temps modernes* without being too harsh, and that was difficult. Jeanson wasn't there at that time and no one among the other members of *Les Temps modernes* wanted to deal with it, because I wanted there to be moderation and everybody loathed the book. So that for two months, three months, *Les Temps modernes* did not mention *The Rebel*. Then Jeanson came back from his travels and he said to me "I'm quite willing."

Jeanson had met Sartre in 1947 at the *Les Temps modernes* office. Aged twenty-five at the time and, like Camus, suffering from tuberculosis, he had just written one of the first and best books on Sartre. Sartre contributed a preface to it. Jeanson published his first article in *Les Temps modernes* in 1948, and was named its managing editor after Merleau-Ponty stepped aside in early 1951. He was certainly (in his own words) a "disciple"—though never a "parrot"—of Sartre. He was not a member of the *famille* and never became a personal friend of Sartre's, although Sartre was a witness when Jeanson and his first wife were married. Jeanson was a penetrating and original thinker. He was probably the first writer to highlight the differences between early Sartre and Camus on absurdity: in his first book on Sartre he said that Sartre thought humans could in some way overcome absurdity, whereas Camus insisted on its centrality to all human experience. In articles published in early 1947, shortly before his book was finished, Jeanson made a telling criticism of Camus, far beyond anything Sartre was to say for many years. For Jeanson, Camus's insistence on "maintaining the absurd" did not imply consenting to the facts of experience but meant abandoning philosophical thought itself, renouncing "the mind's vocation." To him, Camus subscribed to a form of defeatism that led to "absurdism" by converting the fact of absurdity into a value. "To pose the absurd, even to consent to it, is still to will it."

By 1951, Jeanson had moved from within existentialism toward Marxism, incorporating both the individual, subjective dimension of experience and the historical and social demand for structural change in a single outlook. He felt "more Marxist than the Marxists." But he was never a Party member and never saw himself as a fellow traveler. In 1951 he had written an article on the working class, "its state of health, its tendencies, and its future," reluctantly supporting the PCF only because it was *the* party of French workers. In moving toward Marxism and in his willingness to give critical support to the Communists, as well as in his theoretical ability to integrate existentialism and Marxism, the younger man was ahead of his mentor in the late 1940s and early 1950s. Intellectually and politically he was probably more comfortable reviewing *Man in Revolt* than the master himself might have been.

But to preserve Sartre's friendship with Camus, while criticizing a book whose politics he himself detested by someone whose philosophy he rejected, was an impossible assignment for Jeanson. Since he had no personal relationship of his own with Camus, the first goal, Sartre's, could scarcely guide his writing. Sartre complained that Jeanson "wrote the article in the way I had not wanted, that is to say, it was violent and slashing, and it pointed out the book's faults, which was not difficult to do." Sartre then recalled an interesting detail. Merleau-Ponty, in Paris and in charge of the journal while Sartre was away, thought Sartre would not want such a violent review to appear. In his final words on the controversy, Sartre explained what then happened.

> [Merleau-Ponty] tried to get Jeanson to change his mind—they had quite a violent quarrel—and then all he could do was let the article appear. It did appear, but under special conditions—Jeanson had consented, and it was the only reservation that he did consent to, to show Camus his article before it was published and ask him whether he agreed.

Jeanson's twenty-one-page review reads as a critical study of *Man in Revolt* that engages its main themes by way of attacking both author and book. Before even touching on the book's substance, Jeanson criticizes the man, his previous writing, the book's reception, and its style. Only then does he relax his ironic tone—which he later ascribed to his desire to deflate Camus's reputation as a moral saint—to criticize Camus's ideas. Unlike Camus's transparent effort to provoke debate with Sartre, Jeanson treats Camus as an antagonist, dissecting his arguments, displaying his errors. Giving no ground to this political and intellectual opponent who is fundamentally wrong, Jeanson handles him roughly. This was the violence.

Jeanson's readers would first have noticed the title of the review. Camus was personally lampooned: "Albert Camus or the Soul in Revolt." In crossing "l'homme révolté" with "l'âme révolté," Jeanson's pun added a secondary meaning to "the revolted soul"—namely, "the revolted one." It was an implicit reference to Hegel's "beautiful soul" in *The Phenomenology of Spirit,* which explores how the effort to remain pure turns against itself. Camus himself had spoken of Hegel's launching the modern attack on purity with his "denunciation of the beautiful soul and of ineffectual attitudes." While he was thereby defending the devotion of the *belles âmes* to purity, Jeanson, and then Sartre, would scorn Camus for this. With the title of his review, Jeanson served notice that Camus himself was to be the target.

Irony is the article's dominant tone. Beginning with a review of the reviews, Jeanson at first seems to take Camus to task because the Right has lauded *Man in Revolt.* He then shifts ground to acknowledge that the book has also been well received by many on the Left, and suggests that this wide appeal is due to the book's weakness of thought, its "vague humanism," "a certain inconsistency of his thought, which renders it infinitely plastic and malleable, able to receive many diverse forms." Jeanson proceeds to criticize the book for being too well written. For Jeanson, Camus has violated his own guideline that "great style is invisible stylization" by creating a style that is "too beautiful, too sovereign, too sure of itself." Reversing his 1947 praise, Jeanson now attacks *The Plague* for its "Red Cross morality."

Summarizing Camus's main themes, Jeanson points out that Camus, by seeing revolutions as aiming at "the divinization of man," in fact rejects "any role for history and economics." The ironic summary becomes critique.

> One can see that this odd conception of history results in its being suppressed as such, because it eliminates all concrete situations in order to obtain a pure dialogue of ideas: on the one hand, the metaphysical protest against suffering and death; and, on the other hand, the equally metaphysical temptation toward omnipotence. The first constitutes true rebellion, the second its revolutionary perversion. At this elevated level of thought, theological quarrels can undoubtedly appear decisive, but this is certainly not the case for the simple existence of men who, for example, may be hungry and who, following their very inferior logic, might undertake to struggle

against those responsible for their hunger. From all evidence, Camus does not believe in infrastructures.

In place of studying "the concrete structures of revolutionary action," which involve the manner in which revolution emerges and develops as well as "the behaviors that constitute it," Camus gives "absolute primacy" to ideologies and blames everything that has gone wrong on thinkers and their thoughts. Accordingly, says Jeanson, Camus devotes more than one-fourth of the book to the analysis of modern revolutions by studying Rousseau's Social Contract, Saint-Just's speeches, Hegel's *Phenomenology of Spirit,* "nihilo-anarcho-terrorist professions of faith," theorists of fascism, Lenin, and Stalinist theory. "Is not this false history of failed revolutions nothing but a failed history of revolutionary ideologies?"

Underlying Jeanson's criticism was his sense that Camus was condemning revolutions *in advance* because of the intellectual defects he claimed were built into them; in other words, Camus was preaching a kind of quietism. After rejecting Camus's misinterpretation of Hegel, Jeanson goes on to criticize the futility of Camus's praising revolutionary syndicalism as the only genuinely efficacious political stance. Camus is championing "humiliated rebellion" against the "triumphant rebellion" embodied in the Soviet Union. Jeanson attacks what he sees as a cult of political defeatism—Camus's promoting as the only legitimate political attitude the one doomed in advance to Sisyphean suffering. The Communist Party, Jeanson contends, speaks for the working class, and to reject it out of hand is to prescribe failure.

The impulse behind doing so, according to Jeanson, is Camus's desire "to be done with history." At the heart of Camus's thought is the missing God: "He only wants to challenge him and, with respect to this Master, forever remain the rebellious Slave." But this God and his drama of absurdity make it "difficult to take seriously relative injustices, and rather pointless to claim to remedy them: 'children will always die unjustly, even in the perfect society.' " As Jeanson says, it cannot be denied that Camus's rebellion is "in a rather radical way *the refusal of history*—when rebellion is characterized by 'limits,' while [history] is made the very locus of 'excess,' of cynicism, of destruction and of limitless servitude, an indefinite series of 'convulsions' and 'a prodigious collective agony.' "

Jeanson was disturbed that Camus was against revolution, because revolution is often a people's only hope. Ruling it out in advance dooms them to futile protests. Revolutions, whether or not they are proposed by self-deifying intellectuals, come about in concrete situations where people's vital needs are being deprived, so that the people gather together collectively to overthrow those in power and radically change their situation. The consequences of such action may be ugly, but this is the cost of social change, especially given the massive forces usually available to those in power.

Jeanson's political and philosophical disagreement with Camus was fierce, but he stopped short of reading Camus out of the Left, or of using the language of betrayal that others might have chosen, schooled by the controversies engendered by the Bolshevik Revolution. Indeed, if this long and negative review had appeared in another journal—such as *Esprit,* the voice of the fellow-traveling Catholic Left—it would not have constituted a turning point in French intellectual life. But in Sartre's journal it meant much more. The main drama of this article lay in how Camus would have read it—*had to have* read it. Given his clumsy but sincere attempt to engage Sartre in discussion, and given their personal history, Camus must have been infuriated to see it in the monthly which, years earlier, he had talked about founding with Sartre and Beauvoir, a journal that had invited him onto its original editorial board and had published a chapter from *Man in Revolt* only eight months before Jeanson's review. Aside from any of these considerations, Camus would have been riveted by the byline. There was no getting past the fact that Sartre had not only *not* chosen to review *Man in Revolt* personally but had selected for the job a junior member of *Les Temps modernes*, not even a member of the editorial board, an acolyte—which Camus himself would never have become.

Given his own pride and secret self-doubts, Camus must have taken this as a deliberate effort to humiliate him, a demonstration for all to see that his ideas did not merit the attention of Sartre himself. Perhaps a wholly appreciative article by a junior collaborator might not have stuck in his throat—although *Man in Revolt* had already been discussed by a number of important reviewers. Camus's own hard-earned status might in other circumstance have made him sympathetic to a little-known younger man engaging him in dialogue. But in the context of *Les Temps modernes*, Jeanson's very obscurity was probably the greatest of insults. The fact of the younger man criticizing him *for Sartre* bespoke nothing less than Sartre's dismissal of Camus. The personal digs—"revolted soul," "beautiful soul," "Camus never undertakes anything," "Red Cross morality"—are likely to have angered Camus all the more because they came from Sartre's junior collaborator. For all these reasons, the article could not have been read by Camus as other than Sartre breaking with him.

: : :

Camus's seventeen-page reply was dated June 30, 1952. It was written to "M. Le Directeur" (To the Editor) and never once mentioned Jeanson. Although in his first draft he did refer to Jeanson, Camus then crossed out the name. Instead, he began his letter by referring to "the article your journal has devoted to me." Alternating between "your collaborator" and "your article," Camus treated Jeanson's article as if it were Sartre's, because he was sure that Sartre was "in solidarity" with the author's position. As a newspaperman, he fell back on the protocol of holding the editor responsible for the article and its opinions—a device that didn't fit a journal editor like Sartre, for whom contributors were entitled to speak freely and without editorial interference. With the decision to address Sartre directly, Camus ended his efforts to avoid a confrontation.

Camus expressed outrage at what he regarded as a blatant and unflattering distortion of him, his life, and what he intended to say in *Man in Revolt.* The reviewer had accused him of being in the clouds, of disengagement, of writing, "against all evidence, an antihistorical manual," of being "separated from reality," of being "an unrepentant idealist." After seven years of warm relations with the journal, Camus now turns on it:

> After all, no one, except your journal, would think of challenging the claim that, if there is an evolution from *The Stranger* to *The Plague,* it has gone in the direction of solidarity and participation. To claim otherwise is to lie or to dream. But how can one act differently if one is to prove, against all evidence, that I am detached from reality and history?

The break with Sartre was already contained in this remark, as Camus voiced frustration at being misinterpreted, his determination to *control* the way in which he was interpreted, and his disposition to see an unflattering reading as stemming from incompetence or malevolence. His letter typified his habit of peremptory responses to whoever disagreed with him. At least a dozen times he repeated, even lamented, that *Les Temps modernes* had ignored and then rewritten his clearly stated and obvious arguments.

Jeanson had raised a legitimate issue: Was Camus focusing on ideas to the exclusion of other historical processes, and what was the standing of a book that did so? Camus tried to make *Les Temps modernes* the issue.

> Your collaborator's method consists in saying . . . that I deny the crucial role played by economic factors and that "evidently" (it's a matter of internal evidence, no doubt) I don't believe in infrastructures. But why criticize a book if one has decided to pay no attention to what can be read in it? This

> procedure is a constant feature of your article and preempts all possibility of discussion. When I state that the sky is blue and you make me say that I think it's black, I have no other option than to acknowledge my madness or declare my interlocutor deaf. Fortunately, the real condition of the sky remains, as in this case does the thesis under discussion; and that is why I must examine your collaborator's reasons in order to decide between my madness and his deafness.

The "collaborator," Camus suggests, has revealed his motivation for entering into this battle:

> In truth, rather than being deaf, he appears to be someone who doesn't want to hear. His thesis is simple: what I have called blue is black. Indeed, his article essentially turns on a discussion of a position that I have not only not defended, but that I have even discussed and criticized in my book. This is how he sums it up, even though all of *Man in Revolt* gives the lie to it: all evil is found in history and all good outside of it. Here, I really must protest and tell you calmly that such tactics are undignified. That a supposedly qualified critic, speaking for one of this country's most important journals, takes it upon himself, without reason or evidence, to present as the thesis of a book a proposition against which a part of the book is directed only gives a disgusting idea of the contempt in which simple intellectual honesty is held today. Because one must think of those who, reading the article, will not have the inclination or the time to pick up the book, but will consider themselves sufficiently informed. Far from that being the case, they will have been deceived and your article will have lied to them.

This is a public statement to the friend he considered to have broken with him by publishing the review. In an even more direct aside to Sartre, he accuses the editors of being unwilling to voice their worries about him "to my face." More than once in his letter, Camus indicates what he had hoped to find in *Les Temps modernes.* A "loyal and wise critic" would not have distorted his book but, rather, focused on "my true thesis: namely, that whoever seeks to serve history for its own sake ends in nihilism." "For its own sake" obviously means history *apart from* norms and values. Such a critic would have "tried to demonstrate that history can on its own provide values that are not exclusively those of force, or else tried to prove that one can act in history without appealing to any value." These would be difficult demonstrations, but "that effort would have contributed to the joint progress of all of us, and, to be honest, I expected them from you. I was wrong."

Camus keeps on complaining about how badly he has been treated and keeps trying to set the record straight. The penultimate paragraph of his letter contains another direct and personal comment on Sartre: "I am beginning to get a little tired of seeing myself—and even more, of seeing former militants who have never refused the struggles of their time—endlessly receive lessons in efficacy from critics who have never done anything more than turn their theater seat in the direction of history." Recall Camus's words, when he woke his sleeping friend who was "occupying" the Comédie-Française during the insurrection in August 1944: "You have turned your theater seat in the direction of history!" And now Camus reminds Sartre of their original relationship, and of his own record compared to Sartre's. He recalls Sartre's difficulty becoming committed. He reminds Sartre of where things stood when Camus was the editor commissioning Sartre to write articles for his newspaper. Who was "outside of history" then? Camus is restraining himself, however. The only people who would have understood this reference were Sartre himself and the handful of people who knew about the incident.

: : :

Camus was right: Jeanson had avoided his main argument. But the reader can perceive a studied indirectness on both sides, begun by *Man in Revolt* and shared by Jeanson. After all, who was the main target of Camus's book? He was writing against those who *justified* murder, the intellectual accomplices of Communism, those who rationalized it to the rest of the world. And if Sartre had only now declared himself, he and his journal certainly had been heading in that direction all along. Camus had begun right after the Liberation to criticize Sartre's tendency to historicize his thought, and for years he had been distinguishing himself from Sartre, and then sounding a warning, which was unheeded. Their argument in 1946–47 was about two themes: violence and commitment. These themes were at the center of each man's development in the years leading up to their break.

Having taken a self-consciously heretical position in the political wars of the day, Camus might have understood that those disagreeing with him would fight back rather than treat him as a friend. But understanding this meant seeing his argument from their perspective rather than his own, which he refused to do. So we have the sad spectacle of Camus's crying "foul" and devoting the first half of his reply to the accusation that *Les Temps modernes* distorted his ideas.

Now, halfway through his letter, Camus turns the tables on Sartre and *Les Temps modernes* and begins to speak directly about what is at stake—Sartre's support for Communism. His critique of the review becomes a critique of Sartre. Returning to his brief comment at the end of *Man in Revolt* as well as to his remarks about existentialism since 1945, Camus now fully and directly tells Sartre what is wrong with his thinking and his politics.

Sartre and his journal have adopted a Communist perspective while refusing to state it honestly: "everything proceeds in your article as if you were defending Marxism as an implicit dogma." "Contrary to your previous positions" the review ignored all non-Marxist revolutionary traditions and so suggested "that there is no third solution, and that we have no alternative to the status quo or Caesarian socialism." The possibility of criticizing Marxism—of its becoming outmoded as any other superstructure—was not even considered, nor was the entire effort of *Man in Revolt* to explore the connections between twentieth-century revolutions and terror. "In any case, if one is of the opinion that authoritarian socialism is the principal revolutionary experience of our time, it seems to me difficult to not come to terms with the terror that it presupposes, particularly today—and, for example, . . . with the fact of concentration camps." Camus says he would "find it normal, and almost courageous, if, facing the problem frankly, you were to justify the existence of these camps. What is abnormal and betrays your discomfort is that you don't comment on it at all while discussing my book, simply accusing me of not getting to the heart of the matter." For Camus, the camps were the heart of the matter. In advocating revolution, he insists, the review "seems to say yes to a doctrine while remaining silent about the policies that it entails."

Camus did not see a commitment to freedom in Sartre's turn toward Marxism, but an aspiration to submission. Existentialism, especially its starting point of human freedom, was contradictory to Marxism's notion of historical necessity. To free humans from every sort of impediment is incompatible with imprisoning them in historical necessity. "The truth is that your collaborator would like people to rebel against everything except the Party and the Communist state." This brings Camus back to the review's unwillingness to tackle his argument.

> It is not for nothing that your article cannot deal directly with the reality of a text and is obliged, in order to criticize it, to substitute another one for it. It is not for nothing that, confronted by a book that is totally preoccupied with the political situation in Europe in 1950, your article makes no reference to the questions of the moment. That's because in order to refer to them, it

> would have to speak out and, although it is not difficult for your writer to take a stand against racism and colonialism, his contradictory attitude prevents him from speaking out clearly about Stalinism.

The point of Camus's argument is obvious: existentialism, a philosophy of freedom, has embraced necessity and entered into complicity with Stalinism. At the moment Sartre explicitly came out in support of Communism, Camus explicitly turned the entire argument of *Man in Revolt* against Sartre and *Les Temps modernes.* In his reply to the review, a peevish author's complaint about his ideas being ignored is combined with an aggressive argument. Restating his main points, Camus courageously escalated the debate.

: : :

"My Dear Camus: Our friendship was not easy, but I will miss it. If you end it today . . ." From the beginning, Sartre made clear that Camus's reply, not Jeanson's review, was to blame for ending their friendship. But the direct, conversational tone of Sartre's letter, in contrast to Camus's awkward distance, indicates that he, at least, was going to use the personal to justify their break. So from the moment he took up his pen, readers of *Les Temps modernes* were treated to the gripping spectacle of a public settling of private accounts between one former friend and another. Jeanson also contributed a response, which he wrote without seeing Sartre's. But another thirty-page attack, on top of Sartre's twenty pages was simply too much; together they gave the impression of a total assault by *Les Temps modernes* both on Camus's person and on his ideas. Jeanson's article was scarcely noticed, not only because it was redundant but because the break between friends made everything else look like a sideshow.

Cruelly, Sartre castigates and explains his former friend's weaknesses in full public view. In vivid contrast to Camus's restraint, Sartre holds nothing back:

> Unfortunately, you have so deliberately put me on trial, and in such an ugly tone of voice, that I can no longer remain silent without losing face. Thus, I shall answer you, without anger, but unsparingly (for the first time since I have known you). Your combination of dreary conceit and vulnerability always discouraged people from telling you unvarnished truths. The result is that you have become the victim of a dismal self-importance, which hides your inner problems, and which you, I think, would call Mediterranean moderation. Sooner or later, someone would have told you this. It might

> just as well be me. But have no fear. I am not trying to paint your portrait, as I do not want to incur the reproach which you so gratuitously made to Jeanson. I shall speak of your letter, and of that only, with a few references to your works, when necessary.

Sartre then publicly flays Camus in the most personal terms. Ingeniously and viciously he explains Camus's anti-Communism as an evasion of personal growth and a refusal to fully live in the changing and demanding real world. Calculatingly unrestrained, Sartre put on a dazzling and disturbing performance. Violent beyond measure, Sartre's reply was justified by nothing that went before.

In October 1951, Sartre had wanted to protect the friendship and avoid an ugly encounter. What had happened by the summer of 1952? Did he attack Camus because he now saw anti-Communists as "dogs"? Sartre's conversion would surely not have led him to so wholly redefine his friend if Camus had not broken off the friendship, allowing Sartre to judge him in a purely political way. Until this moment Sartre may well have held back because of Camus's tendency to lose his temper and to moralize—to play the "Saint-Just" of the postwar years. Released from the obligations of friendship by Camus, and indirectly by his own choice of Jeanson as reviewer, he was now able to treat Camus "objectively"—as someone who had broken with him and who was no more and no less than an anti-Communist. For the first time, Sartre was free to say to Camus *what was on his mind.*

And so he gleefully used the friendship as a weapon in the conflict. Its restraining effects removed, Sartre could now bring up all those things that had troubled him about Camus during the past ten years, his behavior as well as his writings, and to do so *in order to discredit him.* All the more so because Camus's response to Jeanson's review had shown the same prickly, self-righteous, and judgmental traits that had bothered Sartre while they were friends, as well as what Sartre regarded as Camus's intellectual shallowness and laziness.

Most objectionable to Sartre was Camus's handling of Jeanson. Knowing Sartre, we should not be surprised. If any hostility remained constant in Sartre, all the way back to his two books that Camus had reviewed in 1938 and 1939, it was his revulsion at humans' treating others as things and arrogating to themselves rights over them. Such exploitative arrogance appears in Sartre's young fascist-in-the-making in "Childhood of a Leader" and in the Corsican librarian in *Nausea*; it was his explanation of anti-Semitism in 1946 and of colonialism later; and it was his reason for hating torture and regarding torturers as irredeemable. The determination to combat such behavior reached into the core of his philosophy. Ignoring Jeanson but attacking him meant treating him as "an *object,* a dead man." Camus, Sartre charged, spoke "*of him* as though he were a soup tureen or a mandolin, never *to him.*" What did this mean, if not Camus's placing Jeanson outside of humanity? Assuming the right not to treat Jeanson as a fellow human, Camus regarded him with a moral superiority that Sartre described as "racial": "Are we dealing here with a racism of moral beauty? You have a beautiful soul, his is ugly: communication is not possible between you."

This attack on the "beautiful soul's" sense of moral superiority departed completely from the restraint and allusiveness that marked both Jeanson's review and Camus's letter. Near the beginning of his reply, Sartre indicated his strategy: "I would have so much preferred that our present quarrel went straight to the heart of the matter, without getting confused with the nasty smell of wounded vanity." With these jarring words Sartre pulled out all the stops and addressed Camus directly, indicating that, unlike Camus, he would call a spade a spade, which meant bringing Camus's personal motivations into the picture. And such personalizing had a political meaning, namely, that Camus had become a counterrevolutionary: "Your letter amply demonstrates—if one must speak of you the way an anti-Communist speaks about the Soviet Union, the way, alas, that *you* speak of it—that you have made your Thermidor."

The first half of the letter is a malicious attack on Camus. "You do us the honor of contributing to this issue of *Les Temps modernes*, but you bring a portable pedestal with you." Camus had trotted out references to his former poverty to make "the jury weep." After accusing Camus of placing himself outside the debate and writing didactically, of setting himself above criticism by scandalously invoking the dead of the Resistance, and of using tactics of intimidation, moral blackmail, and verbal violence, Sartre zeros in on Camus's style.

> What is disconcerting about your letter is that it is too *well written.* I do not reproach you for its pomposity, which comes naturally to you, but rather for the ease with which you handle your indignation. I realize that our times have some very unpleasant aspects and that on occasion it must be a relief for sanguine natures to pound on the table, shouting. But I am sorry to see you base your rhetoric on this character disorder, even when there are excuses for it. The indulgence that may be granted to involuntary violence must be rejected when that violence is managed. How cleverly you play at being calm, so that your thunderbolts will take us more by surprise. And with what art you reveal your wrath, only to hide it immediately behind a falsely reassuring smile. Is it my fault if these procedures remind me of criminal court? Only the Attorney General, in fact, is so skilled in becoming expediently enraged, in retaining mastery of his wrath until its final

> transports, and then changing it, if need be, into an air for cello. Perhaps the Republic of Beautiful Souls should have named you its Chief Prosecutor.

To Camus's statement that he would "find it normal, almost courageous," if *Les Temps modernes* were to discuss and perhaps even justify the Soviet labor camps, Sartre replies:

> We are now at the police station, at the Quai des Orfèvres; the cop walks by and his shoes creak, just like in the movies. "I tell you, we know everything. It's your silence that makes you suspect. Go on, say it, you are an accomplice. You know about these camps. Well, admit it, and the jury will take your confession into account." My God, Camus! How *serious* you are, and to use your own words, how frivolous!

Responding to Camus's "calumny" about the journal's approach to the Soviet labor camps, Sartre defends *Les Temps modernes* by pointing out that he devoted an editorial and several articles to them as soon as information was published in France, and then returned to the issue several months later with a second editorial. But now he is concerned with the political issue: "Yes, Camus, like you, I find these camps inadmissible, but equally inadmissible is the use that the 'so-called bourgeois press' [Camus's formulation] makes of them every day." After all, didn't anti-Communists greet Rousset's "revelations" about the Soviet camps with joy rather than with horror?

> If we opened our mouths to protest against some extortion, they would close it for us immediately with: "And what about the camps?" They *summoned* people to denounce the camps under pain of being accomplices to them. Excellent method: either the poor wretch turned his back upon the Communists or he became an accomplice to "the greatest crime on earth." It was then that I began to find these blackmailers despicable. For, to my way of thinking, the scandal of the camps puts us all on trial—you as well as me, and all the others. The Iron Curtain is only a mirror, in which each half of the world reflects the other. Each turn of the screw *here* corresponds with a twist *there*, and finally, both here and there, we are both the screwers and the screwed.

Sartre excoriates Camus for using the camps in his letter "to demolish a critic who did not happen to praise you." And he also criticizes him for refusing to distinguish between masters and slaves: "If we are to apply your principles, the Vietnamese are the colonized, and thus slaves, but they are also Communists, and thus tyrants." No wonder, Sartre implies, that the war in Indochina was so difficult for Camus.

Sartre then replies most directly to Camus on the question of his willingness to cooperate with Communism. There is, he claims, no way of escaping the cage all of us are in today,

> and if you really hope to prevent any movement of the people from degenerating into tyranny, don't begin by condemning it without appeal, and by threatening to retreat to a desert. To merit the right to influence men who are struggling, one must first participate in their struggle, and this first means accepting many things, if you hope to change a few of them.

Sartre did not, however, address the moral question, implicit throughout the controversy, of means and ends in history: Can accepting a system that engenders labor camps ever lead to a positive end? Don't its obvious horrors bespeak some fatal flaw in the revolutionary project itself and call for a clear rejection of Communism? At what point does revolutionary violence become a weapon of destruction and dehumanization rather than emancipation? Sartre was willing to side with the Communist movement, in spite of the evils of the Soviet Union, because he saw it as the only real hope and political expression of the majority of France's workers. He criticized Camus for rejecting it without searching for an alternative. But Camus's critique of revolution *was* his critique of Communism: both were built on a fundamentally wrong and destructive approach to humans, history, and reality itself. Sartre never provided a full response to Camus's main challenge, any more than Jeanson did. As he moved to conclude, he *changed the subject.* He turned back to Camus and unleashed his final tour de force.

The last pages are still astonishing fifty years later. Recalling Camus when they first met, Sartre explores Camus's project, his encounter with history through the Resistance, his standing at the Liberation, and his place in French letters, including quotations from Camus's writings. It is a miniature version of Sartre's studies of great French writers; he had already dissected Baudelaire and Genet, was planning a study of Mallarmé, and would then fill nearly three thousand pages analyzing Flaubert. In this thumbnail sketch, Sartre aims to capture Camus's fundamental impulses, his impressive strengths, and the way he combined the political and the personal as the editor of an underground newspaper. He then recalls Meursault's startling honesty.

> You had been for us—you could again be tomorrow—the admirable conjunction of a person, an action, and a work. That was in 194[4]. We discovered Camus, the Resistant, as we discovered Camus, the author of *The Stranger.* And when the editor of the clandestine *Combat* was joined with Meursault, who carried honesty to the point of refusing to say that he loved his mother and his mistress, and whom our society condemned; when we knew, above all, that you had ceased to be neither one nor the other, when this apparent contradiction made us progress in the knowledge of ourselves and of the world, then you were not far from being exemplary. For in you were resumed the contradictions of our times, and you transcended them through your ardor to live them.

This appreciation continues for four more pages, describing the man who for several years was "the symbol and the proof of class solidarity" as well as indicating his place in "our great classical tradition." This is the Camus of whom Sartre says: "How we loved you then."

What is driving Sartre at this point? Why didn't he let matters rest a few pages earlier, ending with what might well have been his final quip: "you have condemned yourself to condemn, Sisyphus"? Hadn't he already scored enough points, discredited Camus, relieved the anger he denied but expressed so intensely, made as much of the political argument he was going to make, and successfully defended Jeanson and *Les Temps modernes?* What explains these final pages recalling Camus at such length and so admiringly in order to then show why he failed to change with history? Why, after all, did Sartre now *go too far?*

One of the sources of Sartre's explosion may have been Camus's most personal dig at Sartre in his otherwise impersonal letter. Sartre mentions it near the beginning of his response but skips over its allusion to himself. It is the aside where Camus complains about "critics who have never done anything more than turn their theater seat in the direction of history." Sartre now recalls that original relationship more explicitly: "If I say 'your first contact with History,' it is not to infer that I had another kind and that it was better. All of us intellectuals had the same one then, and if I call it *yours,* it is because you *lived* it more deeply and fully than many of us (myself included)." Beneath Camus's discretion lay, among other things, his characteristic sense of restraint. But if his reference to history shows Camus's unwillingness to go for Sartre's jugular, it can also be seen as a veiled threat: Camus knew, even though he was not dwelling on it, just where matters stood in August 1944 when Sartre fell asleep in the theater seat.

The last half of Sartre's letter is a typically Sartrean reversal: the winner loses and the loser wins. He is posing the question, why did the exemplary

Camus not adapt to history after the Liberation? Strangely enough, Sartre made the Liberation the year zero of history, as if the Resistance had been the first moment calling for such adaptation. Sartre's question calls for translation. His missing premise, contained within parentheses "(myself included)," was the comparison between himself and Camus: I, Sartre—who was so much less involved in 1944—subsequently changed, and learned to live in history, and now I am fully committed and taking risks. You, Camus, so courageous and fully integrated then, didn't grow, have since been fleeing from history, and have decided to avoid taking any further risks. The central reality is what Sartre has discovered and what Camus, though born into the working class, has ignored since the war, "the struggle of man."

> You rebelled against death, but in the industrial belts which surround cities, other men rebelled against social conditions that raise the mortality rates. When a child died, you blamed the absurdity of the world and the deaf and blind God that you created in order to be able to spit in his face. But the child's father, if he was unemployed or an unskilled laborer, blamed men. He knew very well that the absurdity of our condition is not the same in Passy as in Billancourt.

Camus's postwar image, his interests, his pursuits, all carried the message that "personal salvation was accessible to all." But this was patently false. What else might Camus have done? "You should have changed if you had wanted to remain yourself, but you were afraid to change." Changed, that is, by both keeping some of his beliefs and "answering the needs of these oppressed masses." Sartre recalls a major reason for Camus's turning his energy against Communism: perhaps it was because "their representatives"—the PCF—insulted him, "as is their habit," that he "decided against history." As a result, Camus sought to retain his acquisitions while losing touch with the connection that made them possible. "Your personality, which was real and vital so long as it was nourished by events, became a mirage."

As an analysis of Camus, Sartre's remarks have the ring of one-sided truth. We know that Camus had never stopped being involved in "history," but he was involved in his own way. Yes, his hostility to Communism and commitment to peace ignored other issues, but they were based on an appreciation of real evils. But that was not the key question here. Expressed privately between two friends, such remarks, wounding as they may be, would have had the force of honesty, of getting (in Sartre's words) to the "heart of the matter," of seeking to reconnect the friend with his own vital currents. Their one-sidedness wouldn't have mattered so much. Written publicly "to," but really about, the leading voice of a rival political current—precisely because they contained so much that was true—they had a wholly different meaning. The personal became a devastating weapon in a political conflict. Sartre, standing apart from history in 1944—even in Camus's original remark at the Comédie-Française—was now fully engaged; Camus, fully engaged in 1944, was now depicted as standing aloof. Their contrasting personal development was put forth as the source of their opposing attitudes toward Communism. Exposing a former friend in this way was an act of war, the more effectively violent the more honestly done. Sartre, embracing violence, was now giving a demonstration of just how violent he could be. His sketch was nothing less than an attempt to annihilate Camus or, if not to destroy him, to silence him. And now Sartre ends with a final cruel note—his own vow of silence.

> In any case, it was good that I could tell you what I thought. The journal is open to you if you want to reply to me, but I will not reply to you further. I have said what you meant to me, and what you are to me now. But whatever you may say or do in return, I refuse to fight you. I hope that our silence will cause this polemic to be forgotten.

8

arranging many things, performing real acts

On September 5, 1952, Camus, having just returned to Paris from summer in Le Panelier, wrote to Francine on what awaited him:

> *Les Temps modernes* has appeared with twenty pages of response by Sartre and thirty by Jeanson. Even before the journal appeared in bookstores, extracts appeared in *L'Observateur.* Things are off to a running start, even if not elegantly. As far as the responses are concerned, one is nasty, the other stupid.

For the next few weeks, Paris would be abuzz with what was

described in the headlines as the "polemic," the "disagreement," and the "literary quarrel."

L'Observateur appeared to avoid taking sides. Its editor, Roger Stéphane, observed that "two attitudes toward the world" were at stake in the confrontation, which "therefore concerns all of us." Yet Camus noticed that *L'Observateur*'s editors betrayed their partiality in a decisive way—Stéphane gave three times as much space to Sartre as to Camus. And as if to suggest how Jeanson's fifty pages would come to be treated, Jeanson received a fraction of the space given to Camus. When the August issue of *Les Temps modernes* appeared in bookstores, it immediately sold out, was reprinted, and sold out again. Within a few days the headline on page two of the weekly tabloid *Samedi-Soir* proclaimed that "the Sartre-Camus break is consummated," hypocritically lamenting the pleasure that would be afforded to their common enemies. *Le Monde* noted that Sartre's and Camus's attitudes toward Communism were at the heart of the dispute, but that their personalities made it more than a debate over political ideology. Then *Combat* filled two whole inside pages, seven columns each, with substantial extracts. The editors noted that Sartre had admirably captured "how after the Occupation, with its spiritual disarray, with its confusion of values, Camus appeared to the country as the very embodiment of its essential hope." Today, they stressed, "two human temperaments clash with each other—and two ways of dealing with life." During the rest of September, one weekly after another sensationalized the rupture, slanting it according to its particular agenda. The quarrel became so famous that by the end of September *Le Monde* and *L'Observateur* each devoted a retrospective article to it, the one taking Camus's side, the other poking fun at all those commentators who kept score while failing to see that their own fate was at stake, as well as "their bad faith, their comedies, their petty nastiness."

: : :

For Camus, all this attention only made matters worse. Sartre was comfortable with such publicity, but Camus, plagued by self-doubt, was in agony for months. His first reaction was to seek support—from Francine, from Maria Casarès, from close friends, from colleagues at Gallimard. On one occasion he stormed into Maria's apartment nearly in tears. To an old Algerian friend, Jeanne Terracini, he contemplated posturing as a street tough from his working-class Algiers neighborhood: "What do you want me to do about it, punch him in the kisser? He's too little!" To his close friend Urbain Polge, who as a pharmacist could not be farther from Parisian literary quarrels, he expressed doubts about whether he had been right in the first place.

The day after the issue of *Les Temps modernes* appeared, Camus tried to drum up support at Gallimard, but had little luck. No one questioned the legitimacy of Sartre's violent attack, as if it was entirely natural to tear someone apart in public using evidence drawn from a friendship with that person. Turning to his colleagues, Camus soon discovered that most seemed to believe that Sartre had won, and that the fight had been fair. People cynically gave out points to both, with Sartre overwhelmingly in the lead. Camus walked in on several people working in one office, the issue of *Les Temps modernes* in his hand, and asked: "Did you see this?" Nobody answered. There were no words of consolation for Camus, but finally Dionys Mascolo broke the embarrassed silence: "We'll talk about it later at l'Espérance" (a neighborhood bar). Camus turned around and marched out.

As the hurt and shock were settling in during these agonizing days, which stretched into weeks, Camus struggled mightily to come to terms with what was happening. In his very first letter to Francine, on September 5, he criticized Sartre's and Jeanson's letters:

> Neither answers my questions, except for Sartre on one point, but the fifty pages are deliberately insulting. Thus I have the pleasure of being called a cop and a ham actor, among other things. All told, it's a long disquisition on my pride, which nevertheless takes a real hit, as you can see. That will delight a lot of people. Decidedly, this book is costing me dearly. Today I'm wondering whether it's worth anything, and whether I'm worth anything since I resemble it too closely.

But it was not enough for Camus to consider Sartre and Jeanson wrong. He continued working away at what the attacks meant to him. On September 17, he wrote to Francine again:

> I've lived almost alone all this time, with somber thoughts, not sleeping well. I'm trying to accommodate myself to this as best I can, the way one tries to find a good position on an uncomfortable bed. It isn't always easy. I understand that they are discussing my work, and I was the first one to find it questionable, even on the deepest levels. But I have nothing to say if they are accusing me personally, because then every defense becomes a self-apology. This explosion of long-suppressed hatred is striking, and it proves

> that these people were *never* my friends and that I have always offended them by what I feel, hence this show of nastiness and this incapacity to be generous. There is no other explanation for the extreme vulgarity of these attacks, but I won't reply to them, because it's impossible to do so.
>
> I just have to try to tell true from false in the midst of all this shit, and not be vexed or humiliated by other people's logic. I must resist the temptation of despising *too much,* as well as of not despising enough. In short, I must know how to break with others (yes, indeed), but without resentment. Such acrobatics are not easy, but they are my fate, while unfortunately I have many things to arrange and less vital energy than before. The only benefit of this operation ("operation pedestal") is that it has thrown light on the disagreement. These gentlemen want, call for, demand servitude. They will probably be both served and subjugated. Good luck to them!

Camus was searching for a way to react, and laboring to come to terms with his lost friendship with Sartre. The "never" and the "always" were the beginnings of an effort to erase that relationship. Sartre's letter certainly spoke of long-simmering hostility but also of initial love. Camus focused on the former and ignored the latter. He set out an entire program for "arranging things"—managing his own reactions. While he acknowledged the possibility of being wrong, he completely rejected "operation pedestal"—Sartre's slashing personal analysis of him.

Why, then, did Camus simplify Sartre's motivation? Wouldn't it have eased his pain to realize that the attack on him and his work was primarily political, rooted in the historical world, and so, since he used the term for himself, a matter of "destiny"? But what is most striking in Camus's response is the specific way in which he personalized the rupture. First he narrowed the political dimension of the quarrel, and second, while still smarting from it, he tried to ignore the personal criticism. The political side became captured in a single idea, namely, that in supporting Communism Sartre sought servitude. The personal became dominated by what now appeared to him so suddenly and so brutally: Sartre had *never* been his friend, had *always* despised him. And beneath this he discovered an equally ugly fact, which he began to voice in his notebooks: "Sartre, as a man and as a mind, is disloyal."

Why was Camus so shocked by the treatment he received from Sartre? After all, Sartre had complained of Camus's behavior before the break: "Every time we met he bawled me out. It wasn't yet a breaking up but it had become less and less pleasant." Further, Camus had intended *Man in Revolt* to challenge the Left; and in December 1951 he had a premonition of disaster that must have been connected with the book: "I patiently await a catastrophe that is slow in coming." Sartre noted that a cooling had certainly taken place between them; the celebration they had hoped to have at the opening night of *The Devil and the Good Lord* had fallen flat; and Camus, doubtful about Sartre's existentialism for many years, had criticized its prorevolutionary direction in *Man in Revolt.*

But it is also true that such strains were experienced in a different way by the working-class pied-noir than by the Parisian graduate of the Ecole Normale Supérieure. For Sartre in his new phase, anti-Communists were the enemy, and that was that. He had broken with old friend Raymond Aron for similar reasons, and he would soon break with Merleau-Ponty and others. But just as history was not everything for Camus, neither was politics. To him, something deeper was at stake—personal loyalty. He responded to Sartre as if their attitudes toward Communism could never shake *that.* And Sartre's and Beauvoir's memories agree that up to a point his disagreements did not affect Camus's caring—for example, when they discussed a possible Soviet invasion—or his assumption of personal closeness.

Camus prized personal loyalty above all. He was shattered by Sartre's brutal treatment of him and bore this for the rest of his life. Together with his lost friendship with Pascal Pia, the break with Sartre would cast a cloud over Camus that even the Nobel Prize could not dissipate. In his mind, he would have remained unreservedly loyal whatever their disagreement. One of the few transparently personal moments in his long complaint to *Les Temps modernes* came when he used the word *loyal.* He complained about the journal's treating him as an enemy rather than considering his ideas fairly and directly. Unlike Sartre, Camus retained a core of unconditionally loyal friends, mostly from his Algiers days, as well as the pharmacist Urbain Polge and the poet René Char. Sartre, on the other hand, had only one male friend who was his peer after the war, and that was Camus. The icy tone of Camus's "To the Editor" notwithstanding, Camus's anger had been restrained; he had only hinted at Sartre's nap during the occupation of the Comédie-Française. "Operation pedestal" was beyond him.

Robert Gallimard, one of the few people who remained friends with both men, has called the rupture between Camus and Sartre the end of a love story. It certainly had an effect of this kind on Camus. At first he was overcome by shock, disbelief, a feeling of betrayal, and a sense of having been wrong in some indefinable way. He struggled to work through his immediate pain and then grappled with his feelings on several levels. Initially he sought to retain his self-esteem. As he looked around, Paris had suddenly become a minefield. If Sartre was the gatekeeper who, ten years earlier, had welcomed him to its literary world, wasn't the attack an expulsion? Camus grew bitter about the city itself. He avoided public places in Saint-Germain-des-Prés, and stayed away from restaurants where he used to meet Sartre. He felt under siege. When invited to participate in a symposium by the same Pierre de Boisdeffre who had just sided with him in *Le Monde,* Camus declined because he felt that "this whole business is still in its journalistic phase," and anything he might say would be used against him. Although being treated, mistakenly, as someone who might be publicly insulted with impunity, he would now find it impossible to be polite. "I consider, for example, that my opponents in *Les Temps modernes* are henceforth disqualified and would say so if I had to speak about it."

Proceeding as he had done seven years earlier when trying to understand why the Communists had heaped ridicule on him, he ruminated on the sources of the attacks. His notebooks anathematized Sartre, "the existentialists," and *Les Temps modernes.* His first entry after the magazine appeared in September read: "*Temps modernes.* They admit sin and refuse grace. Thirst for martyrdom." Then, after being criticized in *Arts, Carrefour,* and *Rivarol,* he extended his disgust to all of Paris. "Paris is a jungle, and the beasts there look seedy." And, before remarking on Sartre's disloyalty, Camus labeled his antagonists "upstarts of the revolutionary spirit, nouveaux-riches, and pharisees of justice." He continued to judge Sartre:

> T.M. polemic.—Knavery. Their only excuse lies in the terrible epoch. Something in them, finally, aspires to servitude. They dreamed of getting there by some noble road, full of thoughts. But there is no royal road to servitude. There is cheating, insult, denunciation of brothers. After which, the appearance of thirty pieces of silver.

Now with a Manichaean mind-set equal to Sartre's, Camus linked Sartre's sympathy for Communism—his "servitude" and hypocrisy as a "pharisee of justice"—to his betrayal and denunciation of his "brother." Apparently those who embraced the first evil were likely to do the second. Even in his notebooks, Camus was too much of an artist to use a world like *brother* carelessly. It suggests how deeply Sartre's attack had wounded him but perhaps also how close he felt they had once been.

At the end of October, Camus told one of his friends, the scholar Roger Quilliot, that he felt confirmed in his original arguments, which had not been addressed: "I therefore consider myself authorized to continue the same road, which I know, besides, is the road of many." This view was supported by letters he received from friends, colleagues, and readers, which he prized. Char, his closest friend, told him he thought *L'Homme révolté* was his best book; the Polish painter and writer Josef Czapski told him he had more friends than he realized. In November he replied to Czapski: "If the words 'left wing' no longer have much meaning, it's because leftist intellectuals in particular have chosen to be the gravediggers of freedom, which may be seen from the example of *Les Temps modernes.* That's what must be fought head-on and neutralized." Camus tried to do this when asked by a third party to contribute to, of all things, the book on behalf of Henri Martin, which Sartre was helping to prepare. Camus sent his own individual protest to the daily *Franc-Tireur,* explaining why he had refused to participate in the collection of essays: "My reason is simple: henceforth, the values of freedom, among other values, are compromised if they are defended along with *Les Temps modernes* and those who approve of that magazine."

: : :

Despite such bold pronouncements, Camus was not out of the woods. He continued to "arrange things." Jeanson's and Sartre's words rang in his ears, and he could not stop answering them. He worked on a point-by-point reply, which he sent to his former teacher, Jean Grenier, for comments. Responding at the end of December, Grenier suggested that Camus's tone was a bit too harsh and recommended a number of changes to soften it. But Camus neither revised nor published this reply, and his "Defense of *Man in Revolt*" was published posthumously by Quilliot, five years after Camus's death. In it, Camus presents the personal and historical reasons behind *Man in Revolt,* and shows that far from being a counterrevolutionary, as Sartre claimed, he was very much of the Left. Without self-righteousness, he also corrects many of the specific accusations made by Sartre and Jeanson, defending himself forcefully and escalating the attack on his accusers.

Echoing Sartre's personal style, Camus begins in an unusually direct and autobiographical manner, describing how his experience of the Occupation led him to develop justifications for resistance. Trying to root *Man in Revolt* in the experience of an entire generation, Camus explains how, when faced with the need to struggle against the Germans, he was "almost completely devoid of reasons drawn from a living morality." Finding religion impotent to guide him, bourgeois values totally compromised, and the Communists in effect arguing (in justifying the Hitler-Stalin pact) that "you had to collaborate with the enemy before fighting him," those who were determined to resist the Nazis found themselves searching "for an elemental value." Rebellion and revolution became their two key themes, and in this "Defense" Camus refuses to choose between them, insisting that each needs the other.

By situating *Man in Revolt* squarely within the Left's commitment to socialism and workers' liberation, Camus rebalances and, in a sense, reinterprets key themes of the book, which did, after all, privilege revolt over revolution and sought to grasp the civilizational sickness underlying contemporary revolutionary societies. Now he asserts that "in spite of all distortions" *Man in Revolt* does not pronounce "a blanket condemnation of the revolutionary attitude." He argues that he has critically evaluated "the only instrument that claimed to liberate the workers, in order that this liberation might be something other than a long and disheartening mystification." He now trumps Sartre's accusation that he is a counterrevolutionary and a bourgeois by not only rejecting the bourgeoisie as "unworthy of its leading role," but also by avowing kinship with the working class, which Sartre was incapable of doing: "I want the definitive liberation of [the workers], first for those who share my blood, but also for the love of all that I respect in this world." He stresses that he is not seeking "the victory of a few scholars" but, rather, concrete forms of workers' liberation. And he connects what he wants for workers with his reasons for opposing Communism: "their daily happiness, their leisure, the humanization of their work, and their participation in a great and courageous enterprise—I don't believe that this liberation will have taken a single step forward if we replace bank directors with policemen."

Sartre attacked him for moralizing, and Camus now turns this around: "I didn't put anyone on trial without at the same time putting what I believed on trial." In other words, *Man in Revolt* was a dissection of his own attitudes as well as those of others. Sartre and Jeanson had attacked him as seeking "comfort," especially in his theme of limits, or *mesure,* but his critics were guilty of "childishly playing with words and especially by withdrawing authority from lived experience." At our best we live within limits, recognizing the dignity of other people. Pursuing moderation means living in a relationship of constantly renewed tension, rejecting excess, which leads to servitude. But perhaps his critics disliked his language, given the current fashion for more aggressive phrases, based on the "hunger for military exploits in our literary society." They had falsely claimed that he condemned history in the name of the individual and placed the individual above history, but "the individual, in order to be, must at the same time collaborate with history and resist it." Demanding both rebellion and revolution, Camus now abandons the oppositions that abound in *Man in Revolt* and focuses on interaction and productive tension. He also adjusts his former emphasis on the individual as *opposed to history,* now making each necessary to the other, and observing that their best relationship is one of tension.

Man in Revolt affirmed "that a morality is possible and that it costs dearly." This is what Camus had concluded in struggling against nihilism and murder. Now he turns to face Sartre directly. He attacks those who try to have it both ways—those who preserve their innocence *and* proclaim that all men and this terrible universe are responsible for the evil of our times. "They wish to save mankind and, finally, from one day to the next, are only capable of trying to insult and degrade it." Drawing this remarkable reply to a close, Camus plays the trump card, his role in the Resistance, compared to that of Sartre. Sartre and Jeanson have offered nothing that would have been useful to those seeking their moral-political bearings during the Occupation.

> I do not find anything in what has been proposed to us that would have been able to help me at the moment of that struggle without hope. On the contrary, at the conclusion of the experiences and reflections I recounted in *Man in Revolt,* I can forcefully affirm that, were it necessary to relive today what we went through during the 1940s, I would know both why and against whom I am fighting. I have not presented anything more than a testimony, and I am not tempted to make of it more than it is. But when the vain uproar that has taken place around this testimony has been exhausted, it will be possible to return to it and fairly evaluate its significance. Then, if it could only help some people survive, that would be enough for me.

Although now writing self-consciously from within the Left and its goals, Camus sharpened his disagreement with Sartre. Why did he not publish this reply? Considering the publicity given to their split, many periodicals would have been eager to print anything that followed it up, especially a reply by one famous man who had been savaged by the other. *Arts* or *L'Observateur* would have snapped it up, even if they disagreed with Camus, because it was so obviously newsworthy.

Yet Camus kept this spirited essay in the drawer. From the start he had agreed that Sartre was the more intelligent, but Camus the greater artist. *Man in Revolt* clumsily challenged this allocation of spheres, and the result was disastrous: the master himself gave him a philosophy lesson and scolded him for not reading his work. To reply now, Camus confided to his notebooks, was to risk looking ridiculous. And so he gave in to what he regarded as the code of the times, namely, that the writer must endure abuse in silence: "You have to allow yourself to be insulted by a lackey of literature or the Party without flinching!"

We may conclude that at that moment, and in the face of his doubts and the blows he had received, Camus wrote the "Defense" not to win the argument but out of an urgent need for self-affirmation. Writing the "Defense" helped him negotiate the immediate crisis, and he would live to fight another day, on his own terrain. He had "arranged," clarified, and reaffirmed his own thoughts and feelings, and that was enough for now. The artist would bide his time.

: : :

Sartre seemed to have put Camus out of his mind. In the next few months and years he made almost no mention of his former friend—leaving no traces in journal entries, letters, or conversations recalled by Beauvoir or friends. Not until Camus's death in January 1960 did Sartre discuss his lost friend. Yet although Sartre's letter to Camus and his subsequent behavior seemed to dismiss him as beneath consideration, Sartre would confess in his moving eulogy that this was not true at all. Camus retained the intellectual and moral force that Sartre had always credited him with. Sartre said that in his "dubious battle against events of these times," Camus continued to reaffirm "the existence of moral fact within the heart of our era and against the Machiavellians, against the golden calf of realism." This comment criticizes Camus, to be sure, but ends with a suggestion of self-criticism—that Sartre in his years of closeness with the Communists, 1952–56, had fallen victim to this idol. And he insisted that "Camus could never cease to be one of the principal forces in our cultural domain," representing in his unique way the history of both France and the century. Sartre's eulogy thus cast a retrospective light on how he himself had lived the seven years between the break and Camus's death:

> We had quarreled, he and I. A quarrel is nothing—even if you never see each other again—only another way of living together and not losing sight of each other in the narrow little world which is given us. That did not prevent me from thinking of him, from feeling his gaze upon the page of the book, upon the newspaper he was reading, and from asking myself: "What is he saying about it? What is he saying about it *at this moment*?"

Asked about this eulogy many years later, Sartre spoke of giving in to the temptation to write "some fine prose," which he hadn't meant, although he gave no specifics. In another interview he did admit that there was "a little falsehood in the obituary I wrote about Camus, when I say that even when he disagreed with us, we wanted to know what he thought." Was the eulogy insincere? It was the fourth time Sartre had spoken publicly about Camus the man: the earlier occasions were his 1942 review discovering Camus, his 1945 lecture on France's committed writers, and his published letter to "My Dear Camus." Each mention contained a tribute, and even though each of them was driven by purposes beyond the tribute, there is no reason to suspect Sartre of insincerity in any of the others. Had he been insincere in saying that he "lived with" his estranged friend after the rupture?

Interviewed at seventy about the inconstancy of his friendships, especially his breaking with Camus, Sartre replied that "my friendships have not counted as much as my love relationships." In response to the observation that "there are really a lot of people who have dropped out of your life—mostly men," Sartre protested that he did have long-standing male friendships; the only ones he could cite were with much younger men, members of the Sartre-Beauvoir *famille.* After saying that the break with Camus did "not really" affect him, he reminisced about the good times they had together and, surprisingly, called Camus his last good friend.

There is good reason to accept the notion that anticipating Camus's reaction could have affected the way Sartre thought about his own actions. Even if they had not been friends, given Camus's place in the political-intellectual landscape Sartre may well have been tempted to reflect on each new step of his itinerary as if seeing them through Camus's eyes. Others did. Of course, Sartre would never admit to having being influenced by his erstwhile friend; nor would Camus. Still, time after time each man wrote against, responded to, and argued with the other after going their separate ways.

: : :

The break with Camus focused a dramatic change in Sartre. He continued to work out the logic of his "conversion" in the second installment of *The Communists and Peace,* which appeared in the October–November issue of *Les Temps modernes.* The turgid, repetitive style makes this essay one of Sartre's worst pieces of writing, and suggests that his alignment with the Communists cost him considerable internal strain. Without mentioning it, Sartre was presenting an alternative to Camus's explanation of Communism in terms of the spiritual needs of the era's intellectuals. Communism was shaped by a more telling fact: it sought to transform the exploited, isolated, and passive French workers into an active, fighting social class. Arguing against all those who criticized

Communism from the right or the left as being either too revolutionary or too slavish to the Soviet Union, Sartre now sided with the PCF *just as it was.* He was presenting the logic of his choice, not by arguing for a better and less authoritarian Communist Party, but by telling his readers why it *had to be* as it was. Sartre rejected all criticism of the PCF, whether from ex-Trotskyists like Claude Lefort, who dreamed of a more radical and democratic party, or from anti-Marxists, Camus among them, who wanted the workers to choose less doctrinaire leaders and more moderate goals. The discussion had a strangely necessitarian cast—the PCF's faults, including its rigid, authoritarian organization, were not correctable mistakes but the appropriate means for the mass of separated workers to overcome their alienation and dispersion. Only thus could they become united as a class.

Sartre's move toward the Party had begun earlier in 1952 during the campaign on behalf of imprisoned sailor Henri Martin. After *The Communists and Peace* and the break with Camus, *Les Lettres françaises,* which had attacked him unstintingly since 1945—right through to Elsa Triolet's 1951 review rejecting *The Devil and the Good Lord* as raising false problems and restating commonplaces —now signaled the Party's thaw toward Sartre. On September 18, editor Claude Morgan commented on the first part of *The Communists and Peace,* which he saw as championing peaceful coexistence: "I don't like Sartre's literary work or his philosophy. But when Sartre denounces those who under cover of anti-Communism are preparing for war, I note—and I am happy to note—that we can, and thus we should, work together to protect peace."

Then, on October 8, one of Sartre's works received a positive review in *LLF.* It was symptomatic of changes both in Sartre and the times, said the reviewer, that the ending of the new film version of *The Respectful Prostitute* had been rewritten by Sartre, working with Bost and Astruc, so that the white prostitute Lizzie and the black man join hands and stand up defiantly to the racist white mob. According to the reviewer, this film's "very noble nonconformity," unlike the "ignoble conformity of *Dirty Hands*, teaches us as much about Sartre's evolution as the resounding dispute that pitted him against Camus last summer." In short, the break earned Sartre points with the Party.

Sartre's "conversion" and the Communists' new friendliness toward non-Party intellectuals drew him into a new world and a new role. The World Peace Congress in Vienna in December was part of Stalin's strategy to create an international movement against nuclear war and for peaceful coexistence. Anti-Communists pointed out the asymmetry of the event and its participants: Party-selected individuals from the East who were incapable of independent action or free criticism of their governments, much as they might criticize Western governments, would dialogue with independent individuals from the West (including members of French political parties of the Right and Center) as well as Communists and fellow travelers. Arriving in Vienna, Sartre became the star of the Congress. He was asked to speak at its opening session. He reconciled with Communists who had attacked him in the past, including Alexander Fadeyev, who in 1948 had called him a "hyena with a fountain pen"; actively participated in deliberations; gave many interviews; and spent time with Communist intellectuals from all over the world, including Ilya Ehrenburg, Pablo Neruda, and Jorge Amado.

An entry ticket to the Vienna Konzerthaus, where many of the meetings were held, was required of Sartre. *Dirty Hands* was scheduled to be performed elsewhere in Vienna during the Congress. Communists had long regarded this play, sometimes quite personally, as an attack on them. Although no one asked Sartre directly, he decided to prohibit the performance, and even paid damages to do so. He insisted that all future productions of the play, wherever it was performed, be approved by the local Communist Party! Sartre regarded this condition not as an infringement on his freedom or integrity as a writer but as a concession to historical realities. At a press conference concerning a performance given without his permission in Vienna two years later, Sartre explained: "My play has become a political battlefield, an instrument of political propaganda. In the present atmosphere of tension, I do not think that performing it in sensitive key points like Berlin or Vienna can serve the cause of peace."

When Sartre rose to speak in Vienna, he focused on anti-Communist attacks on the meeting. Did he sense Camus looking over his shoulder as he delivered his speech? His first theme echoed Camus, but with a Sartrean twist: "Today's thought and politics are leading us to slaughter because they are abstract. . . . Each man is the Other, the possible enemy; we *mistrust* him. It is rare to meet men in France, my country: you meet labels above all, and names." He then argued against Cold War dualism and explained how the World Peace Congress was helping to reduce it. Those who think that World War III "will be the struggle of Good against Evil" are wrong: "the people have seen each other, they have spoken to each other, they have touched each other, and they are united in saying that the peace they want to make and shall make is a Good. No one's going to pull that crusade stuff on us again." After rejecting any pacifism that would allow peace to be imposed through terror, Sartre might have been arguing directly with Camus. Of all things, he returned to their four-year-old disagreement about Gary Davis, the former American airman who had declared world citizenship, whom Camus had championed but Sartre had only grudgingly supported. "Unlike Gary Davis, we know that we have to get involved in politics, and that peace is not a stable state we obtain one day like a medal for good behavior but a long and exacting labor of construction, which has to be carried out on a worldwide scale and requires the collaboration of all the world's peoples."

Sartre ended his speech to the World Peace Congress in the Vienna Konzerthaus with his mind on Paris, anti-Communism, and, remarkably enough, reconciliation back home.

> Personally, I know many good people who ought to be here with us and aren't. Why? Well, out of pessimism, resignation, and then they've been made to fear that the Congress is a cooptation. . . . They have to say to themselves: we wanted peace, sincere men gathered to try to make it, and we weren't there. The day that their regrets make their mistrust and fear melt a little, that no-man's-land, anti-Communism, will have retreated, and we shall be able to say that before helping bring about international pacification, we have helped bring about reconciliation at home.

Once home, in interviews and speeches Sartre gushed about Vienna as one of the great events of his life, stressing above all the sense of direct contact with people from all over the world, and the experience of discussing major issues with them freely and openly. But how openly? In reality this was no abstract question of whether or not the Communist delegates might speak freely, but one far more immediate and sinister. Two weeks before the Congress, Rudolf Slansky and other Czech Communist leaders, most of them Jews, were found guilty of treason in a show trial trumpeting an international Jewish conspiracy. Slansky confessed to charges of being a Zionist agent spying for the West. He and ten others were hanged in Prague on December 3. Before leaving for the Congress, Sartre responded to a question asked of French notables by the conservative *Le Figaro*: "Would you send a telegram to President Gottwald to save those condemned in Prague?" His reply: "Refuse systematically to make any statement to *Le Figaro*." This was his second entry ticket. Sartre did not protest against those vile murders, nor did the Congress. Nor would Sartre protest against the "doctors' plot" and the wave of anti-Semitism it initiated in the Soviet Union just before Stalin's death in March. In "My Dear Camus," Sartre had explained his alignment with the Communists: "To merit the right to influence men who are struggling, one must first participate in their struggle, and this means accepting many things if you hope to change a few of them." This silence, and canceling *Dirty Hands*, were among the "many things" he accepted.

Camus reflected laconically in his notebooks: *"A Vienne, les colombes se perchent sur des potences"*—"In Vienna, the doves perch on gallows." Elsewhere, and still privately, he spoke in greater detail and perhaps more directly about his former friend's pursuit of "the golden calf of realism": "Ordinarily, going to Vienna means participating in a Cold War act, but going there with a backdrop of eleven hanged men whose names were followed by the word 'Jew' in Czech newspapers is beyond description. . . . Just as our right-wingers were fascinated with Hitler's power, so our leftists are entranced by Communist power, tarted up with the name 'efficiency.' "

In June 1953, Sartre published an article furiously protesting the execution of Julius and Ethel Rosenberg. The United States government had ignored a worldwide campaign for clemency, and Sartre denounced the "criminal insanity" that was "capable tomorrow of throwing us helter-skelter into a war of extermination."

> In killing the Rosenbergs, you simply tried to stop scientific progress by a human sacrifice. Magic, witch hunts, autos-da-fé, sacrifices: we've reached that point. Your country is sick with fear. You're afraid of everything: the Russians, the Chinese, the Europeans. You're afraid of each other. You're afraid of the shadow of your own bomb.

On the day Sartre's article appeared, the East German government fired on demonstrating workers. Camus spoke at a protest meeting at the end of the month. His talk was directed against the pro-Communist press, for he took up more strongly than ever the role of the Left's conscience, for which Sartre had mocked him the previous summer. With Sartre's article (published in *Libération,* edited by Camus's old enemy Astier) and similar ones in mind, Camus excoriated those "in the left-wing press and its collaborators who neutralized—and the word is correct—the Berlin tragedy" by focusing on the Rosenbergs. Camus might have been hectoring Sartre himself, doggedly but eloquently insisting on the need to address *both* issues.

> But if I believe it impossible for the riots of Berlin to make us forget the Rosenbergs, it seems even more frightful that people who call themselves "leftists" can try hiding the Germans who have been shot behind the shadow of the Rosenbergs. It is, however, what we have seen and what we are seeing every day, and it is exactly why we are here. We are here because, if we were not here, no one apparently, among those among whom it is

> the avowed vocation to defend the worker, would be here. We are here because the workers of Berlin risk being betrayed after having been killed, and of being betrayed by the very people from whom they had hoped for solidarity.
>
> When one claims to be devoted to the emancipation of the workers, the uprising of workers who, in Germany and in Czechoslovakia, refuse to have their working hours increased and who logically wind up demanding free elections, thus demonstrating to all dynamic intellectuals who preach the contrary to them that justice cannot be separated from freedom, this uprising, and the great lesson we learn from it, and the repression which follows it, yes, doesn't this uprising deserve some reflection? Doesn't it deserve, after the many positions proclaimed all over, a firm and clear affirmation of solidarity? When a worker, anywhere in the world, holds up his bare fists before a tank and cries that he is not a slave, what kind of people are we if we remain indifferent? And what does it then mean when we intervene for the Rosenbergs if we remain silent before [Willy] Goettling [who had been shot by a Soviet firing squad as a pro-Western agitator]?

Although Camus's needling was aimed at pro-Communist intellectuals, perhaps at him directly, Sartre lost no sleep over it. When he was interviewed by *Combat* the following November on the occasion of the publication of *L'Affaire Henri Martin*, and was questioned about the intellectual's role, he recycled his original idea of commitment, saying that the "intellectual's duty is to denounce injustice wherever it occurs." Embarrassingly, these words became the article's headline even though Sartre was mainly concerned to explain why he did *not* denounce injustices in Communist countries. Having moved 180 degrees from Camus, he claimed that protests by Western intellectuals had no influence on Communist governments and, given the Cold War, turned into "acts of war." He wanted French intellectuals to comment on events in the half of the world they could influence and not find themselves siding with the bourgeois powers against the Soviet Union. This facile homage to "the golden calf of realism" replaced morality by political calculation, and contrasts sharply with Camus's determination to influence the Soviet Union with all available means. At this point in his embrace of Communism, Sartre was making a mockery of his own call to denounce injustice everywhere. Apparently in good conscience, he treated West and East according to two different standards.

As he had dramatized in *The Devil and the Good Lord*, Sartre accepted complicity in many evils in his pursuit of changing the world. If anything, his choices and pronouncements grew even more grotesque. Yet however contorted his reasoning was about the intellectual's responsibilities, it stemmed from a considered decision: accepting Communism's evils in order to participate in its project of transforming the world while changing Communism for the better. As he would explain in 1961 in his essay on Merleau-Ponty, an individual outside of Communism "faced with the unholy alliance of the bourgeoisie and the socialist leaders" had absolutely no way of making a positive difference. Alongside the Communists, at least he had some slight hope. His naïveté lay not in claiming that Communism had no flaws but in his ambition to influence it for the better. Beyond his brave words, he never explained how he aimed to do so.

However unrealistic Sartre was, in his mind adherence to Communism was not "servitude" as Camus saw it but, rather, political action from an independent perspective. This helps explain a much-remarked fact about Sartre's activities in relation to the PCF: Sartre moved toward Communism as many others were moving away from it. Merleau-Ponty gave up on the Soviet Union at this time. A bit earlier, Edgar Morin had been expelled from the Party. Charles Tillon and André Marty, two historic leaders of the PCF, were among those being purged from the Party just as Sartre was becoming the most famous fellow traveler. By the time of Sartre's connection with it, Communism's charm was gone, finished off by the revelations about Soviet work camps, the Eastern European show trials, the Cominform's hysteria about Tito, the "doctors' plot," and the shooting down of German workers in June 1953. Even Camus's old enemy Pierre Hervé would soon be expelled for daring to call for more democracy in the Party, and Khrushchev would give his "secret speech" about Stalin's crimes. As the 1950s wore on, few non-Communist intellectuals still saw the Soviet Union as moving toward a future free society.

The timing of Sartre's embrace of Communism is puzzling because of his strong record of criticizing it all the way back to 1944. His criticism in essays, works of philosophy, novels, plays, and interviews had helped make him French Communism's main ideological enemy during the postwar period. The image of *Dirty Hands* being picketed by Party members conveys Sartre's long-standing relationship to the Party. The timing of his alignment becomes clear, however, if we realize that his reasons were quite different from those of other intellectuals. For Sartre, Communism was neither a foretaste of the future nor a repository of hope—he did not embrace it as an attractive idea being realized in reality. Merleau-Ponty's article about the Soviet camps, endorsed by Sartre, mentioned the absurdity of talking about socialism in a country where one in ten people was in a forced-labor camp. If many intellectuals in the 1930s and even the 1940s regarded Communism as an *idea* or a *moral force,* Sartre knew about its ugly reality.

Communism appealed to Sartre because the workers were in the Party, and the Soviet Union was their main support outside of France. Jeanson had observed this in his 1951 article. For Sartre, as he had urged in *What Is Literature?* and now repeated in *The Communists and Peace*, commitment meant connecting with the writer's natural audience, those most capable of changing society: the working class.

> In the France of today, the only class with a doctrine is the working class, the only one whose "particularism" is in full harmony with the interests of the nation; a great party represents it, the only one which has included in its program the safeguarding of democratic institutions, the re-establishment of national sovereignty, and the defense of peace, the only one which pays attention to economic rebirth and an increase in purchasing power, the only one, in fact, which *is alive,* which crawls with life when the others are crawling with worms; and you ask by what miracle the workers follow most of its orders?

Political commitment did not entail a case-by-case deliberation about the correct moral choice. Rather, Sartre declared, it demanded an understanding of the main source of the world's ills—the capitalist system—and the forces and trends capable of overcoming it. To act morally and effectively on behalf of the oppressed meant siding with this party, accepting its ugly side, appreciating its violence, and even enduring the costs of political action. These were inevitable concomitants of becoming real and acting seriously. The violence with which Sartre attacked Camus as well as his silence about Communism's major problems and oppressions resulted from his taking this path.

As he would write in 1961, his direction posed questions about Communism at every moment: "And it is the same thing to ask 'Just how far can they go?' as 'How far can I follow them?'" Did this or that Soviet action or policy finally render it so destructive of humans and their freedom that the USSR no longer deserved the slightest privilege, indeed, had to be regarded as an evil system? This was of course the issue between Sartre and Camus, which Sartre himself summed up with relative honesty in his eulogy of Merleau-Ponty the year after Camus's death: "There is a morality in politics—a difficult subject, and never clearly treated—and when politics must betray its morality, to choose morality is to betray politics. Now, find your way out of that one! Particularly when the politics has taken as its goal the reign of the human." Camus had betrayed real-world effectiveness, or politics. But total honesty requires inverting the formulation: what if choosing politics in such circumstances, as Sartre had done, destroys morality? Camus had chosen one path, Sartre the other.

It was by taking chances, living with complexities and contradictions—even to the point of complicity with Stalinism—that Sartre finally entered the real world. Only by feeling some organized connection with the workers did Sartre see himself as just one person among others. Having firmly placed his feet on real political ground, having decided to take effective political action, he had to accept reality in order to change it. By the end of *The Devil and the Good Lord* he had solved this problem abstractly, but Goetz's brave declaration was only the beginning. In the next two years, Sartre for the first time lived this commitment rather than pondering it.

He captured this mood on the stage in adapting Dumas's *Kean.* This play, performed in November 1953, presents actor Edmund Kean's decision to leave the theater and get married. *Kean* concerns itself with the tension between the real and the imaginary so central to Sartre's theater and fiction, but unlike most of his other works it does not wrestle with the obstacles to acting effectively. Kean the actor has made himself into a thoroughly unreal person. Longing "to weigh with my real weight in the world" and "perform real acts," he decides to abandon his life of playacting and its artificial grandiosity and to become a modest, sober, private citizen. One of Sartre's least reflective plays, *Kean* was a great success. In adapting Dumas, Sartre embraced his optimistic energy. And each of his subsequent three plays was meant as an action, as were virtually all of his future political and theoretical writings.

: : :

Meanwhile, Camus busied himself with the kind of projects in which a well-known author could easily lose himself—gathering and republishing old writings, composing prefaces, giving speeches, writing letters for publication. He also returned to directing theater at the Angers summer festival. His life resembled the endless round of activities, none of them especially creative, which he would later describe in his short story "The Artist at Work." In that story, a painter is so devoured by his own success that he loses the ability to paint. Politically, Camus drew closer to a group of anarcho-syndicalists around *Révolution prolétarienne,* marginal but intelligent and idealistic radicals. He would continue to publish there and in a sister publication, the Swiss monthly *Témoins,* letting his name appear on that journal's editorial board.

The break with Sartre was never far from Camus's thoughts and activities. In his notebooks he continued to castigate Paris, existentialists, revolutionary intellectuals, left-wing intellectuals, nihilists, and intellectuals in general. On nihilism: "little dunces, levelers, arguers. Who think of everything to deny everything, not feeling anything while leaving it to others—party or leader—to feel for them." Reading a passage from Tocqueville's *Democracy in America* reminded him of "those spirits 'who seem to make the taste for servitude into a kind of ingredient of virtue.' Applies to Sartre and to progressives." He imagined a *commedia dell'arte* performance of the farce he had written in 1946, "L'Impromptu des Philosophes," which was about himself, Sartre, and the intellectual climate of the time. And, on a far grimmer note, he composed a list of the various historical facts that the "left-wing collaborators"—a scathing reference to French collaborators with the Nazis during the Occupation—approved of, ignored, or accepted as more or less inevitable:

> 1) The deportation of tens of thousands of Greek children.
> 2) The physical liquidation of the Russian peasant class.
> 3) Millions in concentration camps.
> 4) Political kidnapping.
> 5) Almost daily political executions behind the Iron Curtain.
> 6) Anti-semitism.
> 7) Stupidity.
> 8) Cruelty.
> More could be added. But that's enough for me.

He then sarcastically extolled his "noble profession," which entailed accepting the insults of lackeys without responding. "In other times, considered backward, one at least had the right to challenge [to a duel] and to kill without being ridiculed. Idiotic to be sure, but this made it less easy to be insulting."

In October 1953, *Actuelles II* appeared, dealing with the controversy surrounding *Man in Revolt.* This book of Camus's previously published articles and interviews was intended as a settling of accounts with those who had criticized him. Both the introduction and one of the interviews look beyond the conflicts concerning Communism, focusing on the artist and his or her primary goal, to create. Given that "the time of artists who remain seated is over"—no doubt a coded reference to Sartre's dozing at the *Comédie-Française*—Camus appeals to artists to look to the future without bitterness. The artist, being one among many who work and struggle, seeks to "open the prisons and to give voice to everyone's unhappiness and happiness." Art seeks to nourish a rebirth of justice and freedom. "Without culture, and the relative freedom it presupposes, even a perfect society is only a jungle. This is why all authentic creation is a gift to the future."

In the fall of 1953, Camus hoped, just as he had hoped at the end of the "Defense" a year earlier, to quit politics and to return to artistic creation. After the heading "October 53" in his notebooks, he wrote: "Publication of *Actuelles II*. The inventory is complete—the commentary and the polemic. From now on, creation."

9

recovering their voices

By mid-1954, Camus had lost his voice. Despite his brave pronouncements about returning to writing, he felt tongue-tied and on the edge of sterility. Twice during the winter, Francine had tried to commit suicide, and between attempts she lay on a hospital bed weeping, sleeping, and talking about Maria Casarès. Although moved by obligation, Camus could not find in himself the deep and consistent love that alone, he believed, might make a difference. Since the publication of *Man in Revolt*, he had been working on two stories, "The Adulterous Woman"—commissioned by a publisher in Algiers—which conveyed a powerful sense of isolation and betrayal, and "Jonas, or the Artist at Work," which was about a painter adrift in the Parisian whirlwind of fame who could no longer paint. As Camus struggled with silence throughout 1954, he began to tally the days in his notebook, trying in vain to find his way back to creativity. In July he told Roger Quilliot that he had been unable to work all year, and then, after completing a brief foreword, he told his friend René Char, "I no longer know how to write." In one letter he described himself as "vegetating," in another as not knowing when he might return to writing. Francine was faring no better, and her mother, who moved in to take care of her, asked Camus to move out. Emotionally and creatively, he said, "I feel all dried up . . . like ink by a blotting paper."

For Sartre, too, the years after the rupture were his emptiest as a writer. His silence seemed self-inflicted. How else can one explain Sartre's banning performances of his own play in Vienna? Wasn't it like cutting out his own tongue? And what of his silence about Soviet horrors such as the Slansky trial, the "doctors' plot," and the East Berlin uprising? Perhaps it was just a coincidence, but while visiting the Soviet Union, Sartre became exhausted and wound up spending ten days in the hospital. Then he returned and gave euphoric accounts of Soviet life.

During the four years after his reply to Camus, Sartre's only writing of any weight was the work of his "conversion," *The Communists and Peace*. In this series of loosely connected articles in *Les Temps modernes* between 1952 and 1954, the lumbering, agitated writing shows the strain of Sartre's embrace of Communism and violence. The eighty-eight-page final piece is an original study of French working-class history. It was Sartre's first Marxist writing, relying on historians and economists as never before, explaining in considerable depth how the history and structure of French capitalism led the proletariat to develop in such a way that the Communist Party became its necessary and appropriate expression. Sartre was mastering a new language, and although the style is more concrete and less labored than the earlier parts of *The Communists and Peace,* his thinking and expression are still far less elegant and clear than in any of his philosophical works.

This article represents the only instance between the rupture and Camus's death when Sartre mentions Camus more or less directly. He describes the waning of the skilled-labor hierarchy that had dominated the French working class in the early part of the century, and shows how unskilled workers dominated by the process of production needed an agency such as the Communist Party to unify and mobilize them. Earlier, the workers themselves had both created and staffed the unions, which then defended them. "That seems to have been the good time: a quarter of a century after its end, our beautiful souls [*belles âmes*] discovered revolutionary trade unionism, and they are still pushing it."

The chief *belle âme* was of course Camus, as Sartre (following Jeanson) had characterized him in "My Dear Camus." At the end of *Man in Revolt*, Camus had argued for revolutionary trade unionism as an alternative to Communist revolution. Weighing in on the side of the industrial working class, Sartre felt momentarily impelled to break his vow of silence toward Camus. He could not resist once more accusing him of being stuck in the past, en route to making the point that, like it or not, capitalism's evolution, creating today's unskilled industrial workers, necessitated creating the Party as a quasi-independent body of professional revolutionaries.

: : :

The Camus-Sartre friendship was over, but not their relationship. The two never saw each other again, but as Sartre would say in his eulogy for Camus, their break opened "another way of living together and not losing sight of each other in the narrow little world that is given us." For Camus's part, his political passion remained unchanged, as shown by a note following the fall of Dien Bien Phu on May 8, 1954. Here he seemed to take a middle position between Right and Left, while grossly distorting the Left's culpability in the death of French soldiers in the battle: "Right-wing politicians placed those unfortunates in an indefensible situation, while left-wingers were shooting them in the back." Having devoted in the previous September a double issue to critical studies of the war and, in its current issue, an attack on French policy, *Les Temps modernes* was certainly among those "left-wingers." A few pages farther on in his *Notebook,* Camus more pointedly attacks Sartre's thinking on social issues as contradicting his notions of freedom and responsibility:

> According to our existentialists, every man is responsible for what he is. Which explains the total disappearance of compassion from their universe of aggressive old men. Yet they claim to struggle against social injustice. There are therefore people who are not responsible for what they are; the poor person is not responsible for his poverty. Well then? The amputee, the ugly woman, the timid. And in the end, compassion, all over again?

In late fall 1954, Camus traveled to Italy for two weeks as a guest of the Italian Cultural Association. When in Rome on December 12, he learned that Beauvoir's newly published novel *The Mandarins* had won France's highest literary prize. He saw both the book and its success as directed against him.

> By chance I came across a newspaper. The Parisian comedy I had forgotten about. The Goncourt farce. About *The Mandarins* this time. It seems I am its hero. Indeed, the protagonist is described in his context (the director of a newspaper that began in the Resistance), but all the rest is false, whether dealing with thoughts, feelings, or acts. Even better, the dubious acts of Sartre's life are generously dumped on my shoulders. Otherwise, it's garbage, but not intentionally so, just naturally, the way one breathes.

Two days later he was still fuming: "Existentialism. When they accuse themselves, we can be sure that it is always to condemn others. Judge-penitents." In attacking Beauvoir's (and earlier, Sartre's) seeming self-revelation as a device for attacking others, Camus was not just fulminating. In hitting upon this concept of the "judge-penitent" in response to *The Mandarins,* he discovered the germ of what would, in the months ahead, become *The Fall.*

Even in confiding to his notebook, Camus protected himself by affecting indifference, beginning the day's entry by stressing his distance from Paris and its follies but ending with the deepest condemnation he could muster. The "hero is really me" because the novel's principal male character, Henri Perron, is a novelist who emerged from the Resistance as editor of the leading non-Communist newspaper on the left, *L'Espoir.* He has a reputation for morality, no longer loves the woman he lives with (she is becoming mentally ill), and longs to get away from politics and back to creative writing. Perron breaks with his close friend Robert Dubreuilh, husband of Anne and an older and more famous writer, after insisting that *L'Espoir* print revelations about the Soviet labor camps.

Focusing on French leftist intellectuals between the Liberation and 1948, the novel is filled with parallels to Camus, Sartre, Beauvoir, and Arthur Koestler, and includes the painful story of a relationship resembling Beauvoir's love affair with Nelson Algren. To this day it is read as a roman à clef, a coded presentation of postwar individuals, relationships, and situations—especially the Sartre-Camus rupture and the Beauvoir-Algren love affair. In interviews at the time and then in several detailed pages in her memoirs, Beauvoir took pains to stress the fictional nature of *The Mandarins.* Near the novel's end she put into Henri's mouth the attitude she would later present to reporters. Nadine, daughter of Anne and Robert, has complained that Henri went around "telling everyone all about us."

> "Look," Henri said, "I didn't write about us. You know very well that all the characters were made up."

> "Nonsense. There are dozens of things in your novel that apply to Father and you. And I very clearly recognized three lines of mine," she said.
>
> "They're spoken by people who have no connection with you," Henri said. He shrugged his shoulders. "Of course, I tried to depict present-day people, men and women who are in somewhat the same situation as ours. But there are thousands of people like that; neither your father nor I is specifically portrayed. On the contrary, in most respects my characters don't resemble us at all."

Thus does the Camus character reply in advance to Camus's objections. Beauvoir wanted the novel to be read as a work of fiction, and to make this happen she did some things that any contemporary reader would have spotted immediately. Real events are transposed chronologically by overlapping the story's disillusionment after the Liberation with the efforts of Robert and Henri to create a non-Communist Left organization—when in reality the RDR did not begin until the Cold War. The novel condenses into four years a series of events that actually took place over twice as long a period, and it distills postwar political conflicts on the Left into what in fact had been a non-issue—whether or not to tell the world about the Soviet camps. This fictional question is, however, set in the lived historical reality of post-Liberation disillusionment and France's shrinking room for maneuver between the United States and the Soviet Union. Each of the four main characters is based on an actual person, but their beliefs and actions are developed for fictional and not biographical reasons. The story becomes such a rich and complex work of imagination that its conclusion is unrelated to the real individuals who served as its starting point. At the end, Henri and Robert reconcile and begin work on a new leftist newspaper; Henri marries Robert and Anne's daughter, and the two become parents.

Robert certainly shares Sartre's "curiosity, concern with the world, and fanaticism in work," but the character is twenty years older than Sartre, and his total political absorption dates from the 1920s. As for Henri, Beauvoir tells us:

> The joy of existence, the gaiety of activity, the pleasure of writing, all those I bestowed on Henri. He resembles me at least as much as Anne does, perhaps more.
>
> For Henri, whatever people have said, is not Camus; not at all. He is young, he has dark hair, he runs a newspaper; the resemblance stops there. Certainly Camus, like Henri, was a writer, enjoyed being alive and concerned himself with politics; but they both shared these traits with a great many other people, with Sartre, with myself. Henri's language, his

> attitudes, his character, his relations with others, his vision of the world, the details of his private life, his ideas—all these things differ completely from those of his pseudo model; Camus's profound hostility to Communism would alone be sufficient—both in itself and in its implications—to set a deep gulf between them; my hero, in his relations with the Communist Party and in his attitude to Socialism, resembles Sartre and Merleau-Ponty, and not Camus in the slightest; and in fact most of the time they are my own emotions, my own thoughts that inhabit him. . . . The intimacy which exists between Henri and Dubreuilh is much more like that which in fact existed between Bost and ourselves than like the distant friendship that linked us to Camus. I have described [in *Force of Circumstance*] the way in which the final quarrel between Camus and Sartre was simply the final moment of a long disagreement; the rupture between Henri and Dubreuilh is so entirely unlike theirs that I had written a first version of it in 1950, and it is followed by a reconciliation, which did not happen between Sartre and Camus. As soon as we had been liberated, their political attitudes were already beginning to diverge.

Beauvoir wanted this work of fiction to convey real experiences and conflicts, but not in any one-to-one correspondence with the vicissitudes of actual people such as Camus. Did Beauvoir drag Camus in the mud, as his partisans insist? Even if Camus, as victim of Sartre's attack, could not avoid seeing Henri as standing for him, Henri emerges as a solid individual whose personal and political growth is perhaps the strongest thread of the novel. By the end he successfully integrates the tensions that have been driving him: he combines the will to live happily with an understanding that he cannot avoid acting to make the world a better place. On the level of feelings and outlook, he is far more attractive than Robert, who has a philosophical answer for every question but no subjectivity and little flesh and blood. Henri's transgressions—two-timing his mistress Paula, his dalliance with a ravishing actress who has had an affair with a German officer, and his lying in court to save this actress—are in the context of the novel not faults at all but stages of an individual's authentic moral and political evolution. Even if Camus insisted on seeing Henri as himself, he might have noticed that Beauvoir rewarded him with a happy ending, imagined a reconciliation with him, brought him into "her" family, and set him and his former antagonist to work together on a non-Communist leftist weekly.

Like Algren, however, Camus had good reason to complain. Why did she name Henri's newspaper after the series Camus was editing at Gallimard, *L'Espoir,* if not to tug the reader into an association *with* Camus? Why have

Anne open the paper so evocative of *Combat* and see—as virtually every one of the novel's readers had seen in September 1952—"the two letters in which [Robert] and Henri exchanged insulting repudiations"? In several places Beauvoir went so far as to borrow actual words used during the Sartre-Camus break. So much for her claim to have created an imaginary universe! Either something deeper was at work toward Camus, as toward Algren—perhaps an attempt to exorcise or fictionally transform certain painful relationships that had once meant a great deal to her—or Beauvoir was exploiting details of personal intimacies, in Camus's case right down to the late-night conversation they once had. At the very least, Beauvoir was guilty of insensitivity, pillaging her relationships for fictional materials.

Perhaps it was inevitable that Camus would see the novel as a settling of accounts. He told one old friend, "They've thrown all their goddamn slime on my back." When the Polish poet Czeslaw Milosz suggested he publish a response, Camus refused "because you don't discuss things with a sewer." Two years earlier, he had held back publishing his political reply to Sartre's attack so as not to appear ridiculous. Now, after nearly a year of being unable to write, he was equally unready.

: : :

In December 1954, Sartre was elected vice-president of the France–Soviet Union Friendship Association. The following year continued for Sartre in much the same way as the previous one: speeches and interviews extolling the Soviet Union, a trip to China followed by glowing reports. And in 1955 he wrote his least memorable play, *Nekrassov,* a satire of the anti-Communist press that was a far cry from the searching dramas he had written before his break with Camus.

The conflict marked a decisive moment in each man's life. Each one was stifled as a writer for years. Sartre was transforming his identity at this time to put politics in the center, where it would remain until his death. Assimilating this profound change took away his voice for several years, alternately suspending his critical faculties and putting into his mouth words from somewhere else. In a 1973 discussion, Sartre spoke of overcoming his earlier "moralism" at this time.

> I began to give way to the political realism of . . . Communists: all right, you do it because it works, and you check it out, you evaluate it according to its efficacity rather than some vague notions having to do with morality, which would only slow things down. But as you can well imagine, that whole idea didn't sit too well with me, it upset me no end, despite the fact

> that—ignoring my own better judgment—I carried it through and finally arrived at a pure realism: what's real is true, and what's true is real. And when I had reached that point, what it meant was that I had blocked out all ideas of morality.

Sartre was now saying that his pro-Communism of the 1950s—and by extension his break with Camus—meant replacing "vague notions having to do with morality" with "pure realism." In his mind, this substitution demanded taking several steps at once. First, he became cured of his lifelong neurosis, namely, that "nothing was more beautiful than writing, that to write was to create lasting works, and that the writer's life ought to be understood through his work." Second, he freed himself "almost immediately" from being idealistic, moralistic, and uncomfortable with the real world and its ways. Without mentioning a third measure, his treatment of Camus, he now acknowledged that he had gone too far during this period in suppressing an authentic side of himself that would eventually reemerge. He failed to see that silencing his friend was linked with silencing this side of himself.

And how far were Camus's own profound silences, his seeming loss of identity as a writer, connected with their breakup? The pied-noir was expelled by the gatekeeper of Paris; the reticent writer was publicly exposed and flayed by someone capable of saying *anything* in print; the anti-Communist leftist insecure about his audience was scorned by left-wing intellectuals; the provincial parvenu was mocked by the mandarins for his shoddy education and intellectual laziness. The stories he did manage to draft during 1954 and 1955 speak of betrayal, isolation, intense suffering, living in a fish bowl, and artistic sterility. His most disturbing story, "The Renegade," describes a "progressive" intellectual—perhaps resembling Sartre, but perhaps also himself—a missionary in North Africa who has his tongue cut out by the natives he had come to save. In "Jonas," the artist's final canvas contains a single word so small that one cannot discern whether it is *solitaire* or *solidaire*. How will the artist end up—totally alone or in solidarity with others? Camus might well have asked himself such a question even without the rupture with Sartre, especially because of Francine's illness and his guilt toward her, and because of the overwhelming demands of his fame and his habitual self-doubt. But I believe that the end of his friendship with Sartre came to him as a kind of political and personal expulsion, intensifying his sense of isolation, making him feel betrayed, and deepening his self-doubt. In mid-February 1955, Camus told his Algerian publisher, "I can't write anymore!" But that spring he received his most significant opportunity to speak out politically since the publication of *Man in Revolt*. He was invited to write regular back-page articles in the new moderately leftist American-style news weekly, *L'Express*. Its publisher, Jean-Jacques Servain-Schreiber, hoped to bring Camus's personal favorite, Pierre Mendès-France, back to office as prime minister. A nationalist rebellion had broken out in Algeria the previous November, and Mendès-France, who had overseen peace in Indochina, was one of the few people on the political scene Camus trusted to settle the conflict. Most of Camus's articles would be about Algeria.

But before settling down to this topic, Camus felt impelled to write about the *other* question as being the "real" issue. Sartre's attack and the "treason" of pro-Communist intellectuals like Sartre were still very much on his mind. In early 1955 he was still defending himself in his notebooks against Sartre's charge that he had become bourgeois, which was a "congenital impossibility." He reflected bitterly on his "great superiority over the *cheaters*"—the fact that he was unafraid of death, and that their effort to "preserve the revolutionary principle in the USSR, all the while progressively correcting its perversions," excused in advance Communism's totalitarian methods. By May he was again speaking out publicly against such leftist intellectuals, embroiling himself in a controversy with *L'Observateur*. In a May 26 article devoted to "Camus and journalism," the editors of that weekly claimed that Camus's anger toward them dated back to his break with Sartre, and criticized his "egocentrism." He in turn recalled their "lack of objectivity in the argument that pitted me against Sartre." In his second *L'Express* article, "The Real Debate," he replied that although he had finished with that conflict without ever discussing his "personal feeling about how the polemic was carried out," something beyond his personal quarrel with Sartre was still very much at issue, namely, "revolutionary decadence." On this question, he insisted, *L'Observateur* remained on the same side as Sartre, and Camus would continue to oppose them.

> I believe, for my part, that the idea of revolution will only recover its grandeur and its effectiveness the moment it renounces the cynicism and the opportunism which has been its law during the twentieth century, when it reforms its ideological material used and bastardized by a half-century of compromise, and when, in conclusion, it places at the center of its appeal the irreducible passion for freedom.

But to fulfill these conditions presupposed, among other things, "the rejection of collaboration with contemporary Communism." Since Communism was the "major problem of our time," the issue should not be hidden behind personal attacks. And so, setting out to rediscover his public political voice, Camus returned to his conflict with Sartre. Restating their underlying difference in *L'Express,* he extended his criticism "to the journalists of *L'Observateur* and to those who resemble them."

One of these, in Camus's view, was Jean-Marie Domenach, editor of the Catholic monthly *Esprit.* His controversy with Domenach dated back to the previous summer, when Camus had written a brief foreword to a book about the Resistance, in which he called for overcoming hatred and, at the same time, bitterly attacked pro-Communist intellectuals. *Témoins,* the anarchist journal that listed him on its editorial board, republished the foreword in its spring 1955 issue under the headline "The Rejection of Hatred." In it, Camus accused Communist intellectuals of being potential collaborators with the Soviet Union in the event of an invasion. Politically and morally, he said, they resembled the pro-Nazi collaborators of 1940. Domenach, author of one of the most intelligent and balanced discussions of the Camus-Sartre dispute three years earlier, was scandalized. He sent a stinging reply to *Témoins* accusing Camus of using a memorial to the Resistance to pursue his literary battle with Sartre. "One should not settle one's quarrels at the gates of cemeteries."

Camus replied, as was now his wont, with a letter not to Domenach but to *Témoins*'s editor, J.-P. Sampson. Because he believed the stakes to be the same as in his quarrel with Sartre, he reasserted his original position explicitly: "This struggle between the free Left and the progressive Left is the essential problem of our movement." As far as his former friend was concerned, he said,

> Sartre is not an enemy, I did not have a literary quarrel with him; he has been my adversary only on a single point, which I consider central for all of us. I consider also, it is true, that he was not a loyal adversary, but this only concerns myself. The quarrel that divided us, on the other hand, transcends both of us, and I will continue to wage it against Sartre, if necessary, and against our progressives in general. Because it was progressive intellectuals I was speaking about in my foreword; if Sartre is among these, so is Domenach.

Camus's remarks show how the personal and the political continued to intermingle in his attitude toward Sartre three years after their break. On the one hand, Sartre had not been loyal, which was a personal issue between the two of them; on the other hand, their quarrel was about their respective stands in relation to major political issues. His last sentence underscored that by 1955—and this would remain true for the rest of his life—Camus saw himself standing against a single and intellectually powerful bloc of leftist intellectuals who were more or less sympathetic to Communism or, at least, opposed anti-Communism; the bloc included *Les Temps modernes, L'Observateur,* and *Esprit,* and its dominant force was Sartre.

Yet by 1955 Camus was no longer fighting alone against an overwhelming tide. Writing for the mainstream weekly of the moderate Left meant that he too had supporters, colleagues, and an audience. Indeed, he felt confident enough to make the heaviest possible accusation from one former resistant to another—that Sartre and his colleagues, including *L'Observateur* and *Esprit,* resembled the pro-Nazi collaborators of 1940, who were fascinated by a foreign country that claimed to embody their ideals. For Camus, here was the litmus test: if the Soviet Union were to invade France, would Domenach and the others resist or welcome the invaders? But because he was fighting for its soul, he would not break with the Left, to which he proclaimed his loyalty. "I was born into a family, the Left, in which I will die."

: : :

Having reasserted his political presence, Camus settled down to the pressing business at hand. Over the next eight months he wrote thirty-two articles for the weekly and then daily *L'Express*; half of these were about Algeria and appeared mainly during July, October, and November. The Algerian conflict—the term "war" was not being used, even on the Left—was Camus's main reason for returning to journalism. These articles were his third major intervention concerning Algeria. In the first and second, in 1939 and 1945, Camus had been far ahead of even the most sophisticated political opinion. He had said things that virtually no other writer would dare discuss in public, even in the most radical newspapers. But every effort at reform had been subverted in Algiers, and now radical nationalists took the initiative. On November 1, 1954, the National Liberation Front (Front de la Libération Nationale, or FLN), calling for the "restoration of the Algerian state, sovereign, democratic, and social, within the framework of the principles of Islam," launched an insurrection, attacking government installations throughout Algeria.

The French authorities immediately rounded up thousands of Algerians and forcefully responded to FLN attacks; the FLN extended its attacks to Arabs who participated in the administration; it also committed acts of terrorism against French settlers, especially in outlying areas. Although charts in Algiers would show a rising number of incidents, Algeria was not yet making frequent headlines in Paris. Thus Camus's two articles published during July, presenting an overview of the Algerian situation, cast him once again in the role of seer.

But with a difference. Although still in advance of mainstream opinion, by mid-1955 Camus had fallen far behind the actual situation. As in his earlier articles, he tried to tackle "the profound causes of today's tragedy," and he went out of his way to say that he felt personally closer "to an Arab peasant, a Kabyle shepherd, than to a businessman of our northern cities." He spoke about missed opportunities and the need to put colonialism in the past. But he was vaguer than in the earlier articles and unwilling to confront how the situation had evolved. His explanation of the Arab motivation for terror—"despair"—now sounded psychological and patronizing, as if Camus was still interpreting Arab Algerians to French readers even after the FLN had enabled Algerians to take matters into their own hands. However genuine his sympathy for these people living "without a future, in humiliation," Camus had not absorbed, as the FLN certainly had, the fateful lessons of Dien Bien Phu. Above all, he had not understood the meaning of the insurrection that began on November 1, 1954.

This was strikingly demonstrated in the articles' main proposal. Rejecting the "bloody error" of terrorism as well as the government's "blind and idiotic repression," Camus called for a conference that would have a single goal: to stop the flow of blood. Who would participate? Camus named the old-line religious, nationalist, and assimilationist organizations, but not the FLN—at the very time it was absorbing all existing opposition groups! Camus also seemed blind to the intentions of the Algerian insurrection by proposing that the conference, after achieving a cease-fire and launching economic reforms, would call new elections, run by the French government in "the role of arbiter." He knew that the 1948 elections had been subverted by the colonial administration itself, and he blamed the government for most of what was wrong in Algeria, but he still imagined that the French state could guarantee, and could be seen by the insurgents as guaranteeing, fairness in a new election. So the FLN, whose name he refused to utter, was supposed to lay down its arms on this promise.

Camus was in denial. In the midst of this discussion he went so far as to cite, in italics, the conclusion to his 1939 articles on Kabylia: *"If colonization could ever find an excuse, it would be to the extent that it encouraged the personality of the colonized people."* This after showing conclusively that French colonialism had done nothing of the kind. In the drastically new situation, Camus gave the impression that his thinking about colonialism had remained stuck in the 1930s.

He did nod in the direction of the new reality, but in a way that betrayed him. His 1939 statement had included wording that he now suppressed: in the original he had spoken plainly of "colonial conquest," and of its only justification as being to help "the *conquered* people to *keep* their personality." Now in 1955 he shifted from "colonial conquest" and "conquered" to "colonization" and "colonized." The rewrite cushioned the destruction of freedom and conjured away its violence. More, a "conquered" people inherently has the right to throw off its conquerors and, violence having been done to it, might legitimately respond with violence, as the author of *Man in Revolt* well knew. His new wording suppressed these realities. The shift from "keep" to "encourage" is no less revealing. More than once in his 1955 articles, Camus would indicate that French colonialism had done what it could to *suppress* the Algerians' personality, but that the Algerians, having preserved it themselves, were now asserting it. Rejecting their "terrorism," Camus refused to mention two other key aspects of the way they were asserting their personality: their demand for independence and their organization, the FLN.

On August 20, any illusion that the conflict might be contained was dispelled by the brutal massacre of dozens of Europeans at Philippeville, followed by vicious reprisals against thousands of Arabs by the military and the settlers. Algeria, which had all but disappeared from the front pages, now returned shockingly, and immediately became *the* issue of the coming election. For the next seven years it would dominate French life. The government continued to rely on mass reprisals and torture to crush the rebellion, increasing its military presence by fits and starts to more than a half-million troops, while the FLN kept the struggle alive through terror against settlers as well as Algerians who supported the French, including those living in France.

After Philippeville, Camus wrote with a growing sense of urgency for *L'Express*, now a daily. In the new situation, he said on October 15, only "a free confrontation of the forces" at play might lead to a solution. Since French and Arabs were "condemned to live together," he wrote on October 18, all sides, "from colonizers to nationalists," must be brought together. He insisted that the popular image of the colonizer, brandishing a whip and driving a Cadillac, bore no resemblance to the overwhelming majority of the one million deeply rooted pieds-noirs, mostly workers and civil servants, who earned far less than their counterparts in France. On the first anniversary of the outbreak of hostilities, with 60,000 soldiers ready to be added to the 125,000 already in Algeria, and daily newspaper reports of attacks and executions, Camus still tried to head off the growing "xenophobic delirium." He once more pressed home the importance of bringing together the two sides and turned his concern to minimizing civilian casualties. Camus addressed the violence head-on, floating a proposal for a civilian truce. An undertaking by each side to respect civilian lives would reduce suffering and might lead to dialogue.

On January 2, 1956, the moderately leftist Front Républicain won enough votes to form a government; but within the Front, Mendès-France's Radicals disappointed the hope of the Front's supporters that they would outpoll the Socialists, and the post of prime minister was offered to the Socialist Guy Mollet. While Mollet was still forming his new government, Camus flew to Algiers to put himself on the line for his proposal. Friends in Algiers, including prominent Arabs who, unbeknownst to Camus, were members of the FLN, had joined together in a Committee for a Civilian Truce. Hoping to generate widespread support for the idea and to bring Algerians and French together, they planned a mass meeting for Sunday night, January 22, at the Cercle du Progrès on the edge of the Casbah.

The hall was filled with as many as twelve hundred people, equally divided between Europeans and Algerians. Outside, a virulent pied-noir crowd protested the meeting, led by Jo Ortiz, an Algiers bistro owner and rabid racist who would play a major role in the antigovernment insurrections to come. This furious crowd was surrounded by a silent and highly disciplined mass of Algerians, apparently FLN militants protecting the meeting, as well as French police deployed to keep the peace. Inside the tense hall, Camus, who had become French Algeria's most famous son, was the featured speaker. The ultras outside shouted "Camus to the gallows" and directed menacing slogans at Mendès-France and the liberal mayor of Algiers. Camus's old acquaintance, Algerian moderate Fehrat Abbas, entered the hall after the meeting started, joining Camus, his friends, and religious leaders on the dais. The two men embraced. As the shouts outside grew louder, the audience could hear stones clattering against the windows.

Camus's close friend Charles Poncet chaired the meeting. Ashen-faced, Camus rose to speak. His delivery was stilted as he read from a prepared speech, but the thoughts were strong and clear. Talking of the Algerian situation as his "personal tragedy," he observed that everyone inside the hall was united by our "love of our common soil." Speaking of the "ancient and deep origins of the Algerian tragedy," and referring darkly to "foreign ambitions" endangering France, Camus launched a "final appeal to reason" before the "fratricidal war" degenerated into "xenophobic madness." Stressing that Arabs and French were "equally worthy of respect," he declared that "French and Arab solidarity is inevitable," especially if his proposal for a civilian truce could succeed in changing the "very character of the struggle." As the tumult outside forced him to hurry, Camus called upon his listeners not to "bow before reality" and to reject any kind of fatalism that would swallow up their freedom—above all to "refuse to practice or suffer terror."

Courageously opposing terror, insisting on mutual recognition, and speaking with a generosity virtually unknown to his fellow pieds-noirs, the great

Camus once more insisted on going against the current and on creating possibilities where there seemed to be none. Yet he also skirted the core problem, thinking no deeper than "irrationality" and "hatred" and remaining mute about what lay beneath, namely, the colonial system itself. In urging the protection of civilians, he refused to recognize that the issue behind both sides' terrorism was precisely the *presence* of each side's civilians—one million privileged, nine million disenfranchised. The grim logic of both Algerian and French terrorism stemmed from the fact that each saw the other side's population as a threat. Camus would simply not look behind settler myths and speak honestly about the structured oppression in which Algerian Arabs lived, including the dozens of daily pied-noir privileges—nor would he face the ultimate frailty of the pied-noir position in Algeria.

When Camus had finished speaking, the din outside forced Poncet to wind up the meeting quickly. The listeners agreed to ask all parties to "assure the protection of innocent civilians" and then filed out of the hall, finding their way safely past the menacing pieds-noirs, who then marched across town continuing to shout their slogans. The next day Camus pitched the truce to the outgoing governor-general Jacques Soustelle, who dismissed the idea, contending that the rebels would never agree to it. So ended the last major effort at French-Arab reconciliation in Algerian history. Camus knew it had failed miserably. He resigned from *L'Express* and ended his last period of journalism with a column in early February praising the consolations of Mozart's music.

: : :

Five days after that last-chance mass meeting in Algeria, an equally historic event took place at the Salle Wagram in Paris. Several times during the past few months, military reservists had protested being posted to Algeria, but this was the capital's first mass meeting against the war. Camus's Algiers meeting had been held on a Sunday, the pied-noir day of rest, and so drew a large audience; this Paris meeting supporting Algerian nationalism was held on the Muslim day of rest, a Friday, and accordingly drew a crowd which was three-fourths Arab. A broad range of people spoke, including Algerians, Communists, independent leftist intellectuals, Sartre, and a radical University of Algiers professor, André Mandouze, who brought greetings from the FLN.

Sartre took the podium and delivered a carefully reasoned speech on "colonialism as a system." While Camus was about to take a vow of silence in the face of a conflict whose intensity he had failed to dampen, Sartre was reaching beyond the orbit of the Communist Party for the first time in nearly four years.

The Party was not ready to support Algerian nationalism—within six weeks it would approve granting emergency powers to the Mollet government to pacify Algeria. In contrast, Sartre was laying out the theoretical basis for what would become his political passion of the next ten years, Third-World liberation.

In the speech we can also discern a point-by-point reply to Camus's *L'Express* articles. Having read Camus's demand for mutual recognition under continuing French rule and then his call for a civilian truce, Sartre rejected such demands out of hand by denouncing the "pitiless" system, which had just been described in detail by Francis Jeanson and Colette Jeanson in their pro-FLN book about the rebellion. Sartre conceded in a footnote that petty functionaries and European workers were not only the regime's "profiteers" but also its "innocent victims." Still, they incarnated colonialism's "infernal cycle": a million settlers, "sons and grandsons of settlers, who have been shaped by colonialism and who think, speak and act according to the very principles of the colonial system." Their life was racist to its core, making "a subhuman of the Algerian" and then using this "subhumanity" to justify denying Algerians their basic human rights. The colonists being a small minority, "their only resort is to maintain themselves by force." In short, "There are no good colonists and bad colonists. A colonist is a colonist." Living under this oppression, the Algerians had learned their lesson well: "Thus the settlers have themselves formed their adversaries; they have shown the hesitant ones that no solution is possible other than a solution by force."

Sartre was answering an unnamed "realist with a tender heart." Camus had spoken of "reforms"; Sartre mocked the naive neocolonialist who "still believes that we can better manage the colonial system." Camus had sought rapprochement between the two populations; Sartre declared such "intermediate" solutions to be "reformist mystification." Camus had spoken of colonialism encouraging the colonized people's personality; Sartre insisted that the Algerians were forming their own personality in "reaction to segregation and in daily struggle." Camus had hoped for immediate economic reforms to improve the life of the Algerian masses; Sartre insisted that colonialism and French rule must first be suppressed. The task of all sympathetic French people was obviously not to soften colonialism but "to help it die." It was up to the Algerian people to make their own reforms, and Sartre and his fellow citizens should struggle alongside them "to deliver both the Algerians and the French from colonial tyranny." This talk, published in the March–April 1956 issue of *Les Temps modernes*, shows a much more comfortable relationship between Sartre and Marxism than at the beginning of Sartre's fellow traveling. The powerful moral force of his philosophy is starting to combine with a social and historical outlook, and his call to arms flows from his concrete analyses. On the tortuous path of political evolution, including apprenticeships to idealism (the RDR) and to realism (the PCF), Sartre is nearing his destination.

: : :

Camus in the meantime was finally getting over his writing block. Within the past year he had publicly commented twice on his break with Sartre, while engaging in two lower-intensity public disputes, the one with *L'Observateur* and the other with Domenach. He regularly entered the public arena as an editorialist, becoming deeply involved in the issue closest to his heart, Algeria, and writing with the courage of his convictions. Now he returned to work as a novelist. A story he had begun in mid-1955 outgrew its original plan and turned into a novella, which then became a short novel. This time, abandoning his usual method, Camus wrote quickly, breathlessly, with a minimum of planning and rewriting. He signed the contract with Gallimard a few days after his last article appeared in *L'Express,* and in a matter of weeks he produced a masterpiece. *The Fall* appeared in June 1956 and was immediately a sensation. Within six months it sold over 125,000 copies. A year later its author was awarded the Nobel Prize for literature.

Anyone who had followed Camus's career closely might be astonished upon opening the book. From the epigraph by Lermontov to the narrator's description of himself as a "judge-penitent," the conflict with Sartre was on every page. It was there subtly, cleverly, and even brilliantly, but there was no ignoring it. In writing *A Hero of Our Time,* Lermontov had intended to depict "the vices of our whole generation in their fullest expression." *The Mandarins* had won the Goncourt Prize eighteen months earlier for describing Beauvoir's and Camus's generation; and now, like Lermontov, Camus would describe it and, at the same time, show its vices. But Camus quotes Lermontov as recalling that many in his audience misunderstood him. Did he take *The Mandarins* as a dare to *really* present his generation? If so, *The Fall* was his answer.

The first sentence announces the book's style and point of view: the narrator, Clamence, immediately intrudes on the reader, who thenceforth become an imaginary patron in an Amsterdam bar and the narrator's confidant. In the second sentence, Clamence calls the bar's owner a "worthy ape." Recall, four years earlier, one of the most dubious assertions in Sartre's attack on Camus: "The superiority which you accord yourself and which gives you the right not to treat Jeanson as a human being must be a *racial* superiority." Just in case the reader might miss the allusion, Clamence then describes the owner as grunting; speaks of his "silence of the primeval forest," of his ignorance of "civilized languages"; and calls him a "creature" comparable to a Cro-Magnon man "lodged in the Tower of Babel." Camus portrays Clamence as embodying the racist attitudes that Sartre accused him of holding.

Sartre's and Jeanson's most biting accusations became the stuff of this ostensible Camus-character. Clamence immediately reminds the reader of Jeanson's criticism of *Man in Revolt* for its weakness of thought and for being too beautifully written, and of Sartre's words: "What is disconcerting about your letter is that it is too *written*." Catching himself using the subjunctive, Clamence muses: "I confess my weakness for that mood and for fine speech in general. A weakness that I criticize in myself, believe me. . . . Style, like sheer silk, too often hides eczema." It was a strange spectacle, Camus's protagonist donning the public criticisms that had silenced Camus himself for over three years. In a monologue of electric intensity, the creative artist Camus found his way back with a character's confessing the sins for which the author had been attacked.

However bitter and even violent *The Fall* seems, it also has its playful side. Sartre had called Camus "the chief prosecutor of the Republic of Hearts and Flowers." Now Clamence, the trial attorney, speaks of wearing his heart on his sleeve: "I am sure you would have admired the rightness of my tone, the appropriateness of my emotion, the persuasion and warmth, the restrained indignation of my speeches before the court." Sartre: "My God, Camus! How *serious* you are and, to use one of your own words, how frivolous!" Clamence: "To be sure, I occasionally pretended to take life seriously. But very soon the frivolity of seriousness struck me and I merely went on playing my role as well as I could." Sartre: "For you *are* bourgeois, Camus, like me. What else could you be?" Clamence, playing the detective to his interlocutor: "You are well dressed in a way, that is as people are in our country; and your hands are smooth. Hence a bourgeois, in a way!" Sartre: "You were not far from being exemplary." Clamence, after admitting he has stolen a painting called *The Just Judges* from the Amsterdam bar, fantasizing about being guillotined: "Above the gathered crowd, you would hold up my still warm head, so that they could recognize themselves in it and I could again dominate—an exemplar." Sartre: "Suppose your book simply attested to your philosophic ignorance? Suppose it were to consist of hastily assembled and second-hand knowledge?" Clamence: "Can it be that your culture has gaps?"

In liberally seeding this confession by a hypocritical defender of the poor and weak with echoes of Jeanson and Sartre, Camus places a deeper irony within it. Not only do Clamence's negative traits correspond to Sartre's and Jeanson's criticisms, but his positive ones recall Camus's public image after the war. Clamence describes his successful self and in a way strikingly reminiscent of Sartre's description of his "exemplary" friend in his letter to Camus:

> Familiar when it was appropriate, silent when necessary, capable of a free and easy manner as readily as of dignity, I was always in harmony. Hence my popularity was great and my successes in society innumerable. I was acceptable in appearance; I revealed myself to be both a tireless dancer and an unobtrusively learned man; I managed to love simultaneously—and this is not easy—women and justice; I indulged in sports and the fine arts—in short, I'll not go on for fear you might suspect me of self-flattery. But just imagine, I beg you, a man at the height of his powers, in perfect health, generously gifted, skilled in bodily exercises as in those of the mind, neither rich nor poor, sleeping well, and fundamentally pleased with himself without showing this otherwise than by a felicitous sociability. You will readily see how I can speak, without immodesty, of a successful life.
>
> Yes, few creatures were more natural than I. I was altogether in harmony with life, fitting into it from top to bottom without rejecting any of its ironies, its grandeur, or its servitude. In particular the flesh, matter, the physical in short, which disconcerts or discourages so many men in love or in solitude, without enslaving me, brought me steady joys. I was made to have a body. Whence that harmony in me, that relaxed mastery that people felt, even to telling me sometimes that it helped them in life. Hence my company was in demand. Often, for instance, people thought they had met me before. Life, its creatures and its gifts, offered themselves to me, and I accepted such marks of homage with a kindly pride. To tell the truth, just from being so fully and simply a man, I looked upon myself as something of a superman.

After thus evoking Sartre's 1952 paean to "the editor of clandestine *Combat* . . . joined with Meursault," Camus recalls Sartre's accompanying accusation that after such success Camus was unwilling to change with history. Clamence: "I literally soared for a period of years, for which, to tell the truth, I still long in my heart of hearts." And Camus points to further irony in Sartre's praise. Sartre had spoken of Camus as carrying a portable pedestal, and Camus had called the attack "operation pedestal"; yet in 1945, Sartre had been one of Camus's major publicists. Just who, Clamence now reflects bitterly, has elevated him so? "May heaven protect us, *cher monsieur,* from being set on a pedestal by our friends!"

Camus also makes clear—as in Clamence's references to dancing, to his own sensuousness, to his love of women and of rugby and the theater—that the fictional character contains more than Sartre's and Jeanson's opinions of his creator. Clamence also contains elements of Camus's own subjectivity. One aspect of the way Camus experienced the 1952 controversy is caught in Clamence's story of being trapped behind a stalled motorcycle at a red light. When the light turned green, the motorcyclist refused to pull over while trying to start his engine. With horns honking behind them and in ever-firmer tones, the usually courteous Clamence insisted that the motorcyclist pull over, only to be sworn at by this man. At wit's end, Clamence got out of his car to thrash the motorcyclist, who was much shorter than he, but was struck on the ear by a pedestrian who leapt to the other's defense as "an exasperated concert of horns rose from the now considerable line of vehicles." In a state of shock, Clamence got back in his car and drove off. Instead of teaching anyone a lesson, "I had let myself be beaten without replying, but I could not be accused of cowardice. Taken by surprise, addressed from both sides, I had mixed everything up and the horns had put the finishing touch on my embarrassment." We have heard this before: in 1952, Camus was humiliated in public but was unable to reply.

The entire novel both leads to and flows from a central experience not drawn from the Sartre-Camus conflict but lodged deeper in Camus's intimate life. Clamence describes how he once passed a young woman while walking over one of Paris's many bridges. He kept going, heard the sound of her jumping in the water, stopped, but didn't turn around. "Almost at once I heard a cry, repeated several times, which was going downstream; then it suddenly ceased." After standing motionless, Clamence walked away. He told no one. After this, his life fell apart, he left his law practice, and eventually moved to Amsterdam to inhabit this seedy bar and spend the rest of his days accusing himself and pleading his case. The novel is driven by Clamence's intense sense of guilt, his verbose effort to confess and yet evade it, the ways it overtakes him, and the game of mirrors in which he seeks to have others reveal their own guilt. Clamence is at once defendant, defense attorney, and judge. When Francine, now more functional after her suicide attempts of 1953 and 1954, read the novel, her response was: "You owe me this one."

Centering the novel on Clamence's complicity in the young woman's suicide, Camus goes beyond jousting with Sartre's and Jeanson's accusations. He takes them seriously. He now reveals that during his crisis of the past four years he has struggled long and hard with their criticisms, some of which hit home. One of them has become the stuff of Clamence's character and action. In 1952, Sartre had spoken of Camus's accusing the universe to avoid being judged.

> You pity me for having a guilty conscience (which isn't true), but even were I thoroughly poisoned by shame, I would feel less alienated and more open minded than you, because, in order to keep a clear conscience, you need to condemn. A guilty party is required; if it isn't you, then it must be the universe. You pronounce your sentences, and the world doesn't say a word. But your condemnations cancel each other out when they touch it. You always have to start again, for if you stopped, you'd be able to see yourself. You've condemned yourself to condemn, Sisyphus.

Now judgment becomes the defense attorney's very essence. Immediately after his public humiliation, Clamence realized that his dream of being a complete man—"Half Cerdan [the pied-noir world middleweight champion], half de Gaulle, if you will" —"had not stood up to facts." He had thought of himself as somewhat macho, "But, after having been struck in public without reaction, it was no longer possible for me to cherish that fine picture of myself." As a result, "I was eager to get my revenge, to strike and conquer." The champion of the accused became an accuser "who wanted, regardless of all laws, to strike down the offender and get him on his knees." After the young woman's suicide, he turned his judgment on himself, feeling that his friends had "lined up in a row as on the judges' bench. In short, the moment I grasped that there was something to judge in me, I realized that there was in them an irresistible vocation for judgment." In court he talked of his own guilt, but no one took him seriously. Clamence was left to live out his preoccupation with "moralizing and judging" by searching for ways of "extending judgment to everybody in order to make it weigh less heavily on my shoulders."

Camus himself wrote the "*prière d'insérer*" (publisher's blurb), which makes clear the strategy:

> The narrator in *The Fall* makes a calculated confession. . . . A refugee in Amsterdam, a city of canals and cold light, where he pretends to be a hermit and a prophet, this former lawyer is waiting for sympathetic listeners in a sleazy bar. He has a modern heart, which is to say that he cannot bear being judged, and therefore he hastens to prosecute himself, but only in order to better judge other people. He looks at himself in a mirror, but finally pushes it toward others. Where does he stop confessing and start accusing others? Is the narrator putting himself on trial, or his era? Does he represent a specific case, or is he the man of the hour? There is only one truth in this game of mirrors: pain and all that it promises.

What did Camus intend his readers to make of Clamence's game of mirrors? Clamence himself says that "it's very hard to disentangle the true from the false in what I'm saying." Only one reviewer, Gaétan Picon, pointed out that Camus had been wrestling with the accusation that he was a "beautiful soul" who was revolted by violence and sought to keep his hands clean at all costs. In *Man in Revolt*, said Picon, Camus had rejected the revolutionaries who dirtied their hands and had extolled those who, like Rieux and his comrades in *The Plague,* managed to remain morally whole while fighting evil.

After Camus's death, Simone de Beauvoir recalled that in 1956 she had opened *The Fall* "with a great deal of curiosity." At first, she said, "I recognized the same Camus I had known in 1943: his gestures, his voice, his charm, an exact portrait, without any overemphasis, of a person whose severity was in some secret way softened by his very excessiveness." She was "deeply touched by the simplicity with which he talked about himself now." But something about the book made her angry. "Then suddenly, this vein of sincerity ran out; he began to gloss over his failures with a series of conventional anecdotes; he switched from the role of penitent to that of judge; he took all the bite out of his confession by putting it too explicitly at the service of his grudges."

Pleased by the confessional tone and by the vulnerable side of Camus's subjectivity, Beauvoir dimly sensed something else at work. We have seen Camus himself make an explicit connection in his notebooks: the original *juges-pénitents* were Sartre and the "existentialists," including Beauvoir herself. Camus had hit on the term in response to *The Mandarins.* Just before Clamence introduces himself, he says: "If you want to know, I was a lawyer before coming here. Now, I am a judge-penitent." What Beauvoir barely glimpsed with her misplaced concern for sincerity was that Clamence begins as the Camus of Sartre and Jeanson, then takes on features of Camus's own subjectivity, and is finally transmuted into Sartre himself! In 1957, Camus explained in the *New York Times Book Review* that

> my character is a build-up. There are touches from difference sources. From the existentialists comes the mania for self-accusation, so that they can accuse others more easily. That has always seemed to me to be an extra dirty little trick; it's what shocks me the most in these gentlemen's activities. This passion for accusation always ends by a defense of the servitude which is the direct issue of existentialism.

Those who knew Sartre's wartime record and had read his postwar article "Paris under the Occupation," which described the Resistance as a symbolic "individual solution," as well as those who recalled that Sartre had been dubbed the "pope" of existentialism after the Liberation, would have discerned Sartre in Clamence. Clamence tells us that he was mobilized during the war, "but I never saw action." After the fall of France he found his way back to Paris and then he traveled to the unoccupied zone, possibly to hook up with the Resistance. "The undertaking struck me as a little mad and, in a word, romantic." Admiring but unable to imitate its participants' heroism, he crossed to North Africa "with the vague intention of getting to London." Sartre fit the first part of this description, although it was Jeanson who tried to get to the Free French and was interned in Spain. When Clamence's friend, who was involved with the Resistance, was arrested by the Germans, Clamence was picked up as well. Sent to an internment camp, he was crowned as pope by a demented Frenchman, and the others went along "in fun, but with a trace of seriousness all the same." Clamence himself then took the role of pope seriously.

Clamence as Sartre: from the beginning Clamence's verbal ease is far more reminiscent of Sartre's endless flow than of Camus's more restrained way with words. But only after he was publicly shamed did Clamence become preoccupied with judging and eluding judgment. In describing "the profession of judge-penitent," Clamence's Camus-confession moves into the Sartre-confession that Camus had seen operating in "My Dear Camus."

> Don't get the idea that I have talked to you at such length for five days just for the fun of it. No, I used to talk through my hat quite enough in the past. Now my words have a purpose. They have the purpose, obviously, of silencing the laughter, of avoiding judgment personally, though there is apparently no escape. Is not the great thing that stands in the way of our escaping it the fact that we are the first to condemn ourselves? Therefore it is essential to begin by extending the condemnation to all, without distinction, in order to thin it out at the start.

Then Clamence gives the gist of Camus's meditations on existentialism over the past several years, in a parody of Sartre's notion of responsibility evocative of *Being and Nothingness* and *No Exit*.

> No excuses ever, for anyone; that's my principle at the outset. I deny the good intention, the respectable mistake, the indiscretion, the extenuating circumstance. With me there is no giving of absolution or blessing. Everything is simply totted up, and then: "It comes to so much. You are an evildoer, a satyr, a congenital liar, a homosexual, an artist, etc." Just like that.

> Just as flatly. In philosophy as in politics, I am for any theory that refuses to grant man innocence and for any practice that treats him as guilty. You see in me, *très cher,* an enlightened advocate of slavery.

Having included Camus ("satyr" and "artist") among categories otherwise drawn directly from *Being and Nothingness,* Clamence now recalls the time when he "was always talking of freedom. At breakfast I used to spread it on my toast, I used to chew it all day long, and in company my breath was delightfully redolent of freedom. With that key word I would bludgeon whoever contradicted me; I made it serve my desires and my power." The fact that Sartre had run few real risks, especially compared with Camus, was never far from Camus's mind. Clamence says he has defended freedom "two or three times without of course going so far as to die for it, but nevertheless taking a few risks." The philosopher of freedom goes on to describe his attraction to slavery, and ends up recalling Camus's first comment to his notebook after the public explosion. Those who proclaim their freedom, says Clamence, "have to shift for themselves, and since they don't want freedom or its judgments, they ask to be rapped on the knuckles, they invent dreadful rules, they rush out to build piles of faggots to replace churches. Savonarolas, I tell you. But they believe solely in sin, never in grace." Sartrean existentialism led to Communist servitude according to Camus, and now Clamence the believer in freedom "decided on the sly that it had to be handed over without delay to anyone who comes along."

Having finished his confession, including the story of his theft of the painting, Clamence now turns to his listener and springs his trap. "Then please tell me what happened to you one night on the quays of the Seine and how you managed never to risk your life." As the first reviewers recognized, Camus is placing his reader in hell. Early on in Clamence's monologue he makes the connection explicit:

> Have you noticed that Amsterdam's concentric canals resemble the circles of hell? The bourgeois hell, of course, peopled with bad dreams. When one comes from the outside, as one gradually goes through those circles, life—and hence its crimes—becomes denser, darker. Here we are in the last circle. The circle of the . . . Ah, you know that?

Remembering his Dante, Clamence's interlocutor is trying to reply that the *Inferno*'s last circle was reserved for betrayers. Camus had betrayed his wife; Sartre had betrayed Camus; each had betrayed his many friends and causes through vanity, cowardice, and hypocrisy. Unceasing, excruciating, self-tormenting and tormenting, Clamence's monologue draws his reader into this hell.

As Camus promised, it is a dark vision. In creating it, he worked through his break with Sartre by universalizing what he saw as Sartre's and his own betrayals and by showing the relevance of their conflict for all humanity. With this bitter novel, Camus also challenged the greatest contemporary representation of hell, the one he had gotten to know in rehearsal in Beauvoir's hotel room during the last winter of the Occupation. Rivaling the timelessness of *No Exit*, Camus created a thoroughly contemporary hell of betrayers and hypocrites, sophisticated wordsmiths and political humanitarians, who at every moment are lost in and seeking to escape their own self-judgment. Despite *and because of* his confession Clamence lacks the slightest hope of redemption, becoming evil with desperate good cheer. He succeeds as a complex, many-layered character because he comes alive, worms his way into the consciousness with his intensity, his self-consciousness, his pretensions, his honesty, his guilt, and his bad faith. After Camus's years of pained silence it was a creative triumph, a victory of the spirit—simultaneously revenge, self-understanding, and a modern vision of damnation.

: : :

It was not coincidental, I believe, that 1956 was also the year of Sartre's return to himself. His year had begun with a fellow traveler's New Year's greetings in *Pravda* to "our Soviet friends." Then historical events began to have their effect. First Algeria: we have seen, at the Salle Wagram on January 27, his growing self-assurance as a Marxist thinker independent of the Communist Party. Sartre and others had begun to mobilize against the war, and Mollet betrayed his promise to move toward peace after being pelted with tomatoes by angry pieds-noirs during his February visit to Algiers. Mollet's proposal for emergency powers sailed through the Assembly in March, and from then he escalated the war relentlessly. The Battle of Algiers began in September.

Events in the Soviet world were no less dramatic. In February, Khrushchev's "secret speech" exposed Stalin's crimes. Stalin, object of twenty-five years of veneration, had been disavowed by the Soviets themselves, along with the "cult of personality." How much longer could Communists pretend to be indifferent to the moral fervor with which the independent Left, which included many Catholics, was criticizing the Algerian War? When would Communists, who were at long last feeling empowered to speak out against Stalinism, find their own outrage? A space was created to the left of the Party. France and the Communist world were stirring. What would the great Sartre do and say, he who had chosen the Party as the only effective voice of the oppressed, and whose own voice had been muffled for so long? In the summer of 1956, Camus's new novel added another ingredient to this combustible mixture.

Sartre knew, and said immediately on its appearance, that *The Fall* was a masterpiece—one in which Camus had both completely revealed and completely hidden himself. Later, in his eulogy for Camus, he called it "perhaps the most beautiful and the least understood" of Camus's books. If he genuinely understood it, he no doubt saw himself being skewered by Camus. He would have seen in Clamence a response to his own promise in "My Dear Camus" to one day "speak of myself and in the same tone" he had used to describe Camus. He would have recognized Camus talking about his letter when Clamence accuses himself "up and down" but, as Clamence says, not "crudely, beating my breast. No, I navigate skillfully, multiplying distinctions and digressions, too—in short I adapt my words to my listener and lead him to go me one better."

Picon, in his review in July 1956, was virtually alone in perceiving that Camus had raised the stakes in the Sartre-Camus argument. Without mentioning them by name, Picon noted that Sartre and Jeanson frankly advocated using the means of this terrible world to build a better one. Seeking to deepen the discussion, Clamence outdoes them, as someone of humane intentions who has become complicitous with evil. Clamence then seeks to remove the stench of evil by accusing others, thereby making himself totally evil. He gives up his freedom and devotes himself to laying traps for others. But his final pessimism is not Camus's: by presenting the problem, Picon explains, Camus was clearly seeking a way out beyond both Sartre's "dirty hands" and his own deliberately "clean hands."

Did Camus now influence Sartre? We have seen Sartre confess that he had been ignoring his "own better judgment" and had "blocked out all ideas of morality" for a few years. As 1956 wore on, not only was he faced with searching criticisms from former friends and newfound opponents, but the world itself was changing under his feet. Non-Communist radicals were becoming a new political force as the Party dragged its feet on Algeria. What was "realistic" now? In the fall of that year, with the Soviet invasion of Hungary, Sartre suddenly began to see things differently.

Interviewed by *L'Express* while the fighting was still going on in Budapest, Sartre announced his new stance toward the Soviet Union. "Regretfully, but completely, I am breaking my ties with my friends among Russian writers who are not denouncing (or cannot denounce) the Hungarian massacre. It is no longer possible to be friendly toward the ruling faction of the Soviet bureaucracy." Curiously enough, his vitriol was saved for the French Party liners who justified the invasion: "It is not and never will it be possible to reestablish relations with the men who are presently leading the French Communist Party. Each one of their phrases, each one of their gestures, is the end result of thirty years of lying and sclerosis."

As he learned more about events in Hungary, Sartre completed what was becoming not only a political but also a personal breakthrough. *Les Temps modernes* published a 487-page triple issue on the Hungarian uprising, including comments by dozens of Hungarians, and Sartre introduced it with his own 120-page study *The Ghost of Stalin.* After four years of apprenticeship to Marxism and Communism, this was his declaration of independence. Sartre continued to believe that "Communism appears to us, in spite of everything that has happened, to be the sole movement which still carries within it the likelihood that it may lead to socialism." But its goals could be served only by total honesty. Sartre's days of self-censorship and realism were now over.

Exulting in his independence, as if he had finally found the moral and political space in which he could be truly comfortable and fully himself, Sartre returned to the old debate about means and ends, formulating a sharp riposte to all sides, including Camus: "We are of those who say: the end justifies the means; adding, however, this indispensable corrective: these means define the end."

In returning to morality, Sartre was integrating it into his more recent intellectual and political commitments. He denounced the Soviet invasion of Hungary both because it was an attack on the oppressed and because it damaged the chances for a socialism worthy of the name. In the following story he shows the strength of the Hungarian workers, even in defeat:

> After the crushing of the rising, on November 16, a representative of the factory committees spoke on Radio Budapest asking his comrades to return to work, on conditions. He spoke like a conqueror, with wonderful pride: the strike was to be ended so as to go to the help of the inhabitants of Budapest; it would be resumed immediately if the strikers' demands were not satisfied. And in a building stuffed with police, in a ravaged town where Russian tanks were on patrol, he added these words, "The whole world knows our strength."

Sartre took pains to refute the thinking of his erstwhile comrades in the PCF who justified the invasion, highlighting the central role played by risk, contingency, and choice: "No one has the right to say that events in Hungary made intervention inevitable." Indeed, for a Sartre forcibly weaned from his flirtation with necessity, the key lesson learned from the Hungarian invasion was about the profound *mistakes* made by Soviet leaders.

Sartre's old genius, philosophical and moral, rhetorical and argumentative, had revived along with a new sense of historical concreteness joined with his passion on behalf of the oppressed. In 1952 this passion had led him to support the Party; in 1957 it led him to attack it as "an outfit with hardening arteries which can no longer make recruits among the young." Yet he still insisted that the Soviet Union had been, and might again become, a force for socialism. "Must socialism be called that bloody monster which tears itself to pieces? I answer candidly: yes. That was socialism even in its primitive phase; there has been no other, except perhaps in Plato's heaven, and it must be desired as it is or not at all."

: : :

The Ghost of Stalin launched the most remarkable period in Sartre's life. Now in his fifties and long regarded as one of the world's great thinkers, he burst forth with political and creative activity. Just as Camus's breakout from the effects of the rupture led him to the Nobel Prize for literature, so Sartre's break with Communism resulted in an astonishing series of works, which in 1964 won him the same award. During this period and to the end of his life, Sartre was unlike any contemporary. Passing out of the Communist orbit, he became even more scandalous than he had been in 1945 or 1952. Refusing to become "sensible" or "realistic," he became a pillar of revolutionary anger on behalf of the oppressed. Rejecting the perquisites of his reputation and never taking himself too seriously, Sartre remained intransigent toward the established order until his last breath. As he aged and in spite of his many infirmities, Sartre retained a vitality immensely attractive to younger people. He made mistakes, said stupid and one-sided things, but was fearless about risking his reputation and even his safety. Having eventually found his way to history, he never again lost touch with his times; having struggled his way to effective political commitment, he remained engaged even when blindness overtook him. Having lost and once again found his voice, he remained unpredictably independent until he died.

For the next ten years, in his own unique way, Sartre resembled the Sartrean version of the exemplary Camus after the Liberation. As Camus had been from 1944 to 1947, Sartre after 1957 was "the admirable conjunction of a person, an action, and a work." Sartre now became a major independent political force, speaking to the political parties without needing to belong to any of them.

Commenting freely on the day's issues, he became a moral presence whose views mattered. He combined philosophy, politics, and literature in a voice that was profound and unmistakable.

Sartre achieved unusual status as a Marxist during this period. Avoiding the fate of Hungary, Poland in October 1956 had negotiated its way to a nationalist government under Gomulka, which then encouraged a "Polish Spring" in 1957. In keeping with the new openness, a Polish journal invited Sartre to write an article on the current state of existentialism; he complied with an article that became *Search for a Method.* In it Sartre developed two seemingly contradictory themes, namely, that Marxism had stopped developing and that it was the "philosophy of our time." Until "lazy Marxists" began to use the powerful tools at their disposal and, above all, until Marxism did justice to the individual, existentialism must continue as a semiautonomous ideology within and alongside it.

Here was Sartre himself writing as a non-Party authority on Marxism. He was beginning to use Marxist tools—which he would exploit in his future biography of Flaubert—to demonstrate how a specific individual might be understood through his or her social determinations. He even went a step further and spelled out some of the key themes of a method to honor both one's social being and one's individual self-determination. His ideas became essential for future efforts to develop non-Communist Marxisms, especially in the 1960s and 1970s. Sartre worked nonstop on the *Critique of Dialectical Reason*, for which *Search for a Method* became the preface, first laying Marxism's philosophical foundations, and then trying to understand the political and historical reasons why Marxism stopped developing; that is, he was attempting to grasp Stalinism. In the second volume of the *Critique,* Sartre replied fully to Camus's *Man in Revolt*: Communism's evils were not due to a wrongheaded project but, rather, to the Bolshevik Revolution's search for ways of surviving in an impossible situation.

In these years of national liberation struggles and Communist passivity, many European left-wing intellectuals, like Sartre, shifted their focus from the hopes of the working class to those of colonial peoples. Sartre's angry and eloquent voice, freely mixing Marxism with morality, made him into the principal European spokesperson for the Third World. This cause became his major political interest, from "Colonialism is a System" to his activity with the International War Crimes Tribunal (convened by Bertrand Russell), whose findings he voiced in *On Genocide.*

: : :

One of the fruits of Sartre's new creative and political outburst was his play *The Condemned of Altona,* situated in postwar Germany so as to focus dramatically on a key issue of the French war in Algeria, the question of torture. The Gerlach family home presents a new hell, where the eldest son, Franz, a former Wehrmacht captain, has locked himself in his room in order to escape his guilt for torturing and murdering partisans on the Eastern Front. Four others are locked into this hell: old Gerlach, the head of the family-owned shipyards at Altona; Franz's sister Leni and brother Werner; and Werner's wife, Joanna. As in *No Exit* and *The Fall,* the themes of guilt, responsibility, judgment, and evasion are at the core of the play, right down to the device of using others as a mirror for one's own self-judgment and manipulating them as a means for evading it.

Camus had accused Sartre of blaming others in order to escape condemnation, but Sartre now turned the tables. Franz does indeed blame his century, becoming its prosecutor and defense attorney in speeches he tapes and replays. But unlike Clamence he ends his evasions and eventually makes a full confession to Joanna. She finds him unforgivable, and he pays the price for facing his past lucidly by going with his father to their death. Old Gerlach is no less guilty, having cooperated with the Nazis because he foresaw, being a cynical realist, that his shipbuilding business would survive the regime and continue to prosper. If Clamence suggests a Camus who simultaneously absorbs Sartre's criticism and accepts having "dirty hands," Franz suggests a Clamence no longer able to manipulate others' complicity with his game of mirrors and thus forced to face his guilt.

Sartre goes yet another step beyond *The Fall*: the century too is guilty. Or, rather, the capitalist economic system imposes its demands on the individuals who think they are running it; its political and military systems create "prefabricated crimes that are only waiting for their criminals." And, as the impotent firstborn son of a powerful family, Franz discovers that "war was my destiny." Sartre is excoriating the policies and systems that remove all sense of responsibility from individuals like Franz while assigning them hideous and inhuman tasks. The play ends with Franz and his father crashing to their death offstage, Joanna and Werner becoming free to live their lives, and Leni shutting herself up in her dead brother's room while the tape recorder replays Franz's appeal to the thirtieth century for his own century's acquittal.

The Condemned of Altona is many things at once: a portrayal of some of the worst features of the century; a new reflection on torture, a theme that had preoccupied Sartre for many years; a sharp attack on France's conduct of the Algerian War (Franz symbolizing France); an indictment of capitalism; and a dramatic presentation of the insights into the social and the individual sketched in *Search for a Method.* In constructing a contemporary hell, Sartre seems to be rethinking *No Exit* in terms of everything he has learned and done in the fifteen years since that work. And, although he quotes no actual words from *The Fall,* in *The Condemned of Altona*, one of his greatest works, Sartre seems to have in mind one of Camus's greatest works. Beyond their conflict and its dreadful consequences, Sartre and Camus remained connected in the next stage of their creative lives. It would be pleasing to think that *The Condemned of Altona*—the richest product of Sartre's liberation from the grim realism on behalf of which he had attacked Camus—was in its own way a response to *The Fall,* the novel in which Camus liberated himself from the effects of Sartre's attack.

10

no exit

Sartre and Camus had each worked his way past the effects of their rupture, and each had fully returned to himself. Both had criticized the Soviet invasion of Hungary, and the worst tensions of the Cold War had eased. Beauvoir had imagined a fictional reconciliation between the two former friends, right down to Henri's becoming a son-in-law to Anne and Robert. More realistically, Sartre and Merleau-Ponty, never as close as Sartre and Camus but estranged over Sartre's "ultra-Bolshevism," found themselves in March 1956 at the speakers' table at a conference in Venice chaired by Ignazio Silone. Realizing how much he still had in common with his old schoolmate, Sartre began tentatively to reconnect with him, a process still under way when Merleau-Ponty died in 1961. Wasn't it conceivable that Sartre and Camus, who retained their relationships with Gallimard and still lived in the Quartier Latin of Paris, might run into each other, each offering the other an embarrassed greeting, and one or the other following up with a note?

Robert's note to Henri in *The Mandarins* highlights some of the personal issues that would have to be dealt with. "I just read your farewell letter to *L'Espoir*. It's really absurd that our attitude accentuates only our differences when so many things draw us together. As for me, I'm still your friend." Beauvoir brazenly quotes from Sartre's letter of rupture in creating Robert's gesture of reconciliation, changing the past tense ("drew") to the present ("draw"). This must have outraged Camus. He had endured Jeanson's attacking his intellect and political wisdom and Sartre's tearing his personality apart; then, in late 1954, Beauvoir was treating his political commitment and personal life as grist for her mill. In the grip of his writer's block, he concluded that Sartre and company would use anything against him, even Sartre's former affection for him.

By 1956, Camus had battled his way back, but what Sartre had done to him personally he could never excuse. Already in 1955, as he was beginning to feel more self-confident, Camus had publicly spoken of Sartre's disloyalty. In *The Fall,* the Sartrean dimension of Clamence epitomizes bad faith. Worse, Clamence seeks to trap and torment others. He is the contemporary incarnation of the devil. Despite the mingling of elements of Sartre's and Camus's characters in Clamence, Sartre had become Camus's bête noire, the negative image of Camus's own sense of himself—his Other.

Although their differences had once complemented each other, since their break each had made the other into the example of what he had chosen *not* to be. Camus condemned a half-invented, half-real Sartre: pro-Soviet, violent, hypocritical, abstractly intellectual, terrified of death, facile with words and concepts, enamored of Hegel and Marx and history with a capital H, unwilling to take personal risks, blaming others to hide his own guilt, disloyal, blathering on about freedom while tolerating oppression, a bourgeois, privileged Parisian. Camus had built a personal, moral, and political self around his opposition to the individuals who shared those traits: "leftist intellectuals," or "existentialists." Cold War polarities had merged with personal polarities. And then, with the Cold War beginning to thaw, a new conflict imposed itself—the Algerian War.

: : :

During 1956, the number of FLN guerillas grew from about 6,000 to 20,000, and French troops in Algeria increased from 180,000 to 400,000. This created a demand that could no longer be met by sending reservists; conscripts were now required. At the end of September, when FLN women bombed the Milk-Bar and the Caféteria, graphically captured in Pontecorvo's *The Battle of Algiers,* a new phase in the war began. The rebels were beginning to turn on civilians, and the French answer was torture and terror—exactly what Camus had tried to avoid. Although the French authorities and military still tried to conjure up a middle ground between themselves and the FLN and to fill it with acceptable Algerians, brute force was their standard colonial means of dominating the situation, and so they inevitably turned the natives against them. In October the army intercepted a Moroccan aircraft that was flying to Tunisia, with Ahmed Ben Bella and other FLN leaders aboard, and imprisoned them in France for the duration of the conflict. This brilliant military coup was a political disaster because it froze any hope of a negotiated solution. Moreover, Algerians still trying to occupy the middle ground or operating independently were met by FLN terror, most brutally in the massacre of hundreds of members of a competing guerilla army at Melouza in 1957. Camus's vision of reconciliation between equals under the French flag turned out to be a fantasy. It gave way before the either/or perceived by Sartre: French colonial violence would only be ended by FLN violence.

By September 1957, French torture and terror, combined with technical and numerical superiority, won the Battle of Algiers; and the Morice Line along the border with Tunisia effectively sealed off Algeria from the growing guerrilla army waiting on the other side of the electrified fence. Winning militarily, the French were losing the war politically, for the FLN, through its disciplined and ruthless revolutionary leadership, had become hegemonic among Algerians and had achieved international recognition. In the meantime the war was losing support in France, as it became clear that military prowess was not defeating the FLN. In February 1957, PCF leader Maurice Thorez first pronounced the fateful word *independence.* In the summer of that year, France's leading establishment intellectual, Raymond Aron, published a small book of his articles from the conservative daily *Le Figaro* advocating Algerian independence as the only realistic course. The million pieds-noirs whose very identity was dependent on the national myth of *Algérie française* and a frustrated officer corps that had known constant defeat during the twentieth century, both groups afraid of being sold out by the Left, the intellectuals, and pusillanimous politicians in Paris, began to conspire. They hatched the project of overthrowing the Fourth Republic and bringing Charles de Gaulle back to power: he would save *Algérie française* by releasing the brakes that held back the military machine.

: : :

Here was a historical moment when Sartre and Camus both seemed destined to play major roles, and each remained in the other's sights. As we have seen, Sartre's first public comment on Algeria in January 1956 was a point-by-point reply to a "realist with a tender heart." In that same month, Camus denounced intellectuals who signed a petition to Soustelle protesting the war. He railed to his friend, Jean Daniel, about the "murderous frivolity in this vision of an occupied Algerian nation that is trying to free itself from the occupier and consequently has the right to use all means to gain its freedom, even taking revenge on non-Muslims." Sartre was one of several hundred signers.

Sartre now made the most of his fame, his leadership of a major journal, his radicalism, and his ringing voice. *Les Temps modernes*, after beginning the year with special issues on Hungary and Poland, published ten articles on colonialism and Algeria over the next ten months. In spring 1957, *Le Monde* asked Sartre to comment on a pamphlet in which reservists home from Algeria had described torture, summary execution, and murder of civilians. Sartre's article was rejected by the newspaper as too violent, so he published it in *Les Temps modernes* and then presented it at a meeting in June. He spoke of the "irresponsible responsibility" of anyone who failed to denounce the army's crimes: "There is the proof, there is the horror, ours: we cannot see it without tearing it out of ourselves and crushing it."

The success of *The Fall* did not alter Camus's decision to remain silent on Algeria. Even the revelations about torture did not change his mind. In the twenty-one months after the Algiers meeting, he spoke out only once, when he was criticized in *Encounter* for being silent on Algeria while denouncing the Soviet invasion of Hungary. In his reply he recalled his record and declared that colonialism should be ended by the creation of a Swiss-style confederation that would grant all communities a high degree of autonomy.

Camus's fellow North African, Albert Memmi, whose first novel, *The Pillar of Salt,* Camus had graced with a foreword, developed a term to explain his kind of silence, the "colonizer of good will." Memmi had agreed with Camus during his conflict with Sartre, but now, in April 1957, *Les Temps modernes* ran the first two chapters of his forthcoming book, *The Colonizer and the Colonized.* According to Memmi, the left-wing settler sympathized with the plight of the colonized but could not genuinely support their struggle without attacking his own existence as well as his community. "There are, I believe, impossible historical situations and this is one of them." Unable to imagine the end of his own people, incapable of fully identifying with the colonized, the colonizer of good will would come to feel politically impotent, slowly realizing that "the only thing for him to do is to remain silent." Memmi's book appeared later that year, with a foreword by Sartre. In December, Memmi published a brief article, "Camus or the Colonizer of Good Will." Here, with considerable sympathy, he made the link explicit: "Far from being able to speak of North Africa, because he comes from there, Camus has been rendered silent because everything that touches on North Africa paralyzes him." Camus was unable to transcend his tribe and remain on a universal plane. "Indeed, such is Camus's situation that he was assured of becoming the target of the suspicion of the colonized, of the indignation of the Left of metropolitan France, and the anger of his own people."

As this article was being read in France, the "colonizer of good will" was in Stockholm receiving the Nobel Prize. Asked to comment now on all manner of topics, Camus broke his silence about Algeria. On December 11, the day after receiving the prize, Camus met with students at Stockholm University. He brought up the subject of Algeria, and the room immediately grew tense. A young Algerian student peppered him with criticisms and interrupted him constantly. Angered, Camus demanded to be allowed to complete his thoughts, and insisted that he had always worked for "a just Algeria, where the two peoples should live in peace and equality." He suggested that the student hectoring him no doubt had comrades who were alive today thanks to his own intervention. And then he shocked his audience: "I have always condemned terror. I must also condemn a terrorism that is carried out blindly, in the streets of Algiers for example, and may one day strike my mother or my family. I believe in justice, but I will defend my mother before justice."

Camus's honesty immediately created a stir in France, and he reaffirmed his words in a letter to *Le Monde.* His mother before justice: his courage in posing what he felt to be the real choice was not accompanied by any understanding of why he was being harassed from all directions. Rather than thinking of how it might appear to those who didn't face his choice, he blamed them. Not the Algerians, who at least were fighting for their own cause, though in the most horrible of ways. In his letter to *Le Monde* Camus declared that he felt closer to the Algerian student who had badgered him "than to many French people who speak of Algeria without knowing about it."

Sartre had not stopped being one of Camus's targets. Four days after receiving the Nobel Prize, Camus argued with Sartre in his address at Upsala University. Complaining at first that "writers of today" found themselves attacked for not speaking up on political issues and then attacked again when they did speak up, Camus took aim at Sartre's notion of commitment. He strongly restated his old criticism, this time by stressing that the theory of engaged literature, by requiring the writer's political involvement, destroyed his freedom: " 'Pressed into service' seems to me a more accurate term in this connection than 'committed.' Instead of signing up for voluntary service, the artist does compulsory service. Every artist today is aboard the contemporary slave galley."

Even as a Nobel laureate, Camus seemed to see Sartre as blocking his path, as his nemesis. His allusions to Sartre appeared not only in the theme of commitment but also in coded phrases like "the period . . . of the armchair genius is over." The thrust of Camus's Upsala address was to reject an unnamed writer's insistence—I can only conclude that it was Sartre's—that artists *should* commit themselves politically *and* in specific ways. Camus asserted his artist's sense that the very nature of their freedom *would* lead them to involve themselves in their time and "create dangerously."

: : :

Within the next few months, Sartre wrote a sensational review, published in *L'Express*, of Henri Alleg's book *The Question*, an account of being tortured by paratroopers in Algiers. Beginning with the memory of the Germans torturing the French at Gestapo headquarters in 1943, Sartre recalled that the French had declared it to be impossible that "one day men should be made to scream by those acting in our name. There is no such word as impossible: in 1958, in Algiers, people are tortured regularly and systematically." Some readers would have recognized a reference to Camus's *Combat* articles of a dozen years earlier:

> Appalled, the French are discovering this terrible truth: that if nothing can protect a nation against itself, neither its traditions nor its loyalties nor its laws, and if fifteen years are enough to transform victims into executioners, then its behaviour is no more than a matter of opportunity and occasion. Anybody, at any time, may equally find himself victim or executioner.

Sartre had not forgotten the articles that had followed Camus's violent scene with Merleau-Ponty at the Vians' party. His powerful denunciation of torture caused *L'Express* to be confiscated by the authorities on March 6, 1958, and during the next several weeks the article became famous by being published as a pamphlet, confiscated, then appearing as a scroll that could only be read with a magnifying glass, and finally being published in Switzerland as a foreword to a reprinting of Alleg's text. In March, Sartre also published an article protesting the death penalty given to an Algerian couple for complicity in sabotage.

Meanwhile Camus, angered by Sartre and his colleagues, analyzed by Memmi, and attacked for his silence, was preparing his final answer. He selected from his writings on Algeria a number of pieces to appear as a book under the title *Algerian Reports.* In its preface and conclusion, Camus made a general response, defended himself against his critics, explained why he became silent after so much involvement with Algeria, and clearly stated his position on the current situation. He squared his accounts while demonstrating his lifelong commitment to Algerian Arabs, pointing out that if his "voice been more widely heard twenty years ago there would perhaps be less bloodshed at present." And then he signed off.

While making a show of condemning both Right and Left, Camus's comments directed to the Right have a formulaic quality, while his criticism of the Left is specific and shows a definite animus. He refuses to "protest against torture in the company of those who readily accepted Melouza or the massacre of European children." The Left, he charges, believes that Algerian Arabs "have earned the right to slaughter and mutilate," whereas he complained years ago "of Arab misery when there was still time to do something, at a time that France was strong and when there was silence among those who now find it easier to keep heaping abuse, even from abroad, upon their weakened country." Then Camus directly addresses those who, like Sartre, speak of the responsibility of *all* the French for what was unfolding in Algeria:

> If some Frenchmen consider that, as a result of its colonizing, France (and France alone among so many holy and pure nations) is in a state of sin historically, they don't have to point to the French in Algeria as scapegoats ("Go ahead and die; that's what we deserve!"); they must offer up themselves in expiation. As far as I am concerned, it seems to me revolting to cry "mea culpa," as our judge-penitents do, while beating on someone else's breast, useless to condemn several centuries of European expansion.

By situating himself within his tribe and reaffirming his choice of family over abstractions, Camus was responding to Memmi. He clearly believed that he could be true to principles of universal justice *and* a member of his community.

> When one's own family is in immediate danger of death, one may want to instill in one's family a feeling of greater generosity and fairness, as these articles clearly show; but (let there be no doubt about it!) one still feels a

> natural solidarity with the family in such mortal danger and hopes that it will survive at least and, by surviving, have a chance to show its fairness. If that is not honor and true justice, then I know nothing that is of any use in this world.

The introductory and concluding essays were efforts by a pied-noir to do justice to *both* communities in Algeria by holding tenaciously to the middle ground despite its disappearance from the political and intellectual landscape—by judging both sides' violence by the same standard, seeking equality between both peoples, and refusing a justice for the Arabs that would be unjust to the French. His intentions were honorable, yet Camus dismissed Algerian nationalism as "a conception springing wholly from emotion" and resulting from Nasser's "Arab imperialism" and Russia's "anti-Western strategy." He buttressed these outrageous claims with another: "There has never yet been an Algerian nation." But their national "unreality," said Raymond Aron, replying to Camus in his own book (his second on the Algerian conflict), "appears to me to be tragically real" among the FLN guerrillas. Aron, the great realist, not known for supporting leftist causes, continued to rebut Camus: "These Muslims have not been a nation in the past, but the youngest among them want to create one. Emotional demand? Of course, like all revolutionary demands. This demand is born in revolt against the colonial situation and poverty." Aron's analysis led to an inescapable conclusion: Algerian nationalism was no more unreal than the pied-noir demands asserted by Camus. Camus—and here Aron was borrowing from Memmi—revealed himself as the "colonizer of good will" by claiming to favor a compromise while simultaneously rejecting the legitimacy of Algerian nationalism and insisting on giving up "none of the rights of the Algerian French." All of which made a genuine compromise unthinkable.

The solution endorsed by Camus, the Lauriol Plan, was a masterpiece of bad faith. Camus wanted the French government to proclaim that "the era of colonialism is over" and that it was time "to grant full justice to the Arabs of Algeria." The neocolonial scheme would then give each community autonomy in areas pertaining to it alone, but the mainland French Assembly, enlarged by Arab representatives, would decide all matters pertaining to *both* communities. Decisive areas involving military and police power and economic and foreign policy would continue to be run from Paris. In this way Camus claimed to serve justice as well as his own people, while actually serving neither. It was, of course, impossible to end colonialism *and* leave existing French rights intact, a fact that Camus never faced. Instead, he warned of "dreadful consequences" if his solution did not prevail. "This is the last warning that a writer who for twenty years has been devoted to the service of Algeria can voice before resuming his silence."

But why was it necessary to be silent? Camus's real reason led back to his family and to "terrorism as it is practiced in Algeria." He feared that "by pointing out the long series of French mistakes, I may, without running any risk myself, provide an alibi for the insane criminal who may throw his bomb into an innocent crowd that includes my family." After saying this, Camus recalls his remark about "my mother before justice" and then, whether deliberately or not, separates himself from his critics by ending with a word that unconsciously refers back to the controversy over *Man in Revolt* and to the first pages of *The Fall.* "But those who, knowing it, still think heroically that one's brother must die rather than one's principles, I shall go no farther than to admire them from afar. I am not of their race."

The racial reference aside, Camus's remarks demand a closer look. They were followed by his statement about his "natural solidarity" with his family in danger and his primary commitment to the family's survival before worrying about fairness. But how could something Camus had written have provided an "alibi" for an FLN terrorist or endangered his own family? In his discussion with students in Stockholm, Camus had said that his interventions might have risked "aggravating the terror." If he were to comment publicly, he would criticize not only French government policy, as in fact he often did, but also, perhaps more importantly, his own community's intransigence, which he had never explicitly mentioned. Hearing of his criticisms, "insane" FLN members might feel justified in killing French civilians. Thus, to protect his endangered community, Camus would have to avoid speaking his mind.

Keeping quiet, however, did not mean remaining uninvolved. After Camus received the Nobel Prize, the war was clearly his major concern. He spoke to friends about it, made notes about it, brooded over it. In March 1958, he arranged a meeting with de Gaulle, trying to convince him in the event of his return to power that Camus's middle way was the best solution. And he did what he could, privately and behind the scenes, to intervene on behalf of dozens of Algerians accused or convicted by the French authorities. Camus placed Algeria at the center of his new novel, *The First Man,* which swept across the entire pied-noir experience from the first settlers to the war. It contained sweet childhood memories of a poor but gifted pied-noir as well as *Algérie française* myths about the working-class and indeed socialist settlers creating their country with their own hands.

: : :

As Camus was preparing his *Algerian Reports*, barricades went up in Algiers, trumpeting the great revolutionary and Resistance watchwords on behalf of a dying colonialism. De Gaulle not only insisted on ascending to office constitutionally but, after visiting Algiers, slowly realized that *Algérie française* was no longer possible. Hesitantly and in stages, in 1958 and 1959, he offered a "peace of the brave" to the FLN, then "self-determination," and then peace negotiations. He was faced on the Right by increasingly extreme supporters of *Algérie française*, especially among the officers and the pieds-noirs. They had brought him to power, and as soon as they sniffed betrayal, they began to hatch plots against his life. On the Left, de Gaulle's rise to power had been opposed by some in the small antiwar movement and also by the Communists, with Sartre among those leading the attack.

By mid-1959, Camus's anguish over Algeria seemed to ease. The previous October, after twenty years of feeling exiled from Algiers and homeless in Paris, he had used the money from his Nobel Prize toward the purchase of a house at Lourmarin in southern France. His writer's block, which had recurred after he became the Nobel laureate, had receded again, and he was deep at work on *The First Man*. He seemed resigned to the loss of his homeland. Although retrospectively celebrating French Algeria in the novel, Camus kept his promise to say no more about the conflict.

: : :

While returning from Lourmarin to Paris on January 4, 1960, Camus was killed in an automobile crash. He was forty-six. The manuscript he had been working on was in a black leather briefcase in the car. His death stunned Paris, Algiers, and much of the world. Beauvoir later described how, when hearing the news, her overwhelming sense of loss slowly overcame her determination not to let Camus's death matter, until she no longer thought of him as "that just man without justice" but once again as "the companion of our hopeful years, whose open face laughed and smiled so easily, the young, ambitious writer, wild to enjoy life, its pleasures, its triumphs, and comradeship, friendship, love and happiness."

Sartre's farewell to Camus was published in *France-Observateur* on January 7. From the outset, he made much of Camus's silence over Algeria, respecting his conflicts but not wanting to take his last remarks as final: "it was important that he emerge from silence, that he decide, that he conclude." He had died before he had the chance. Notably, Sartre now included himself among "all those who loved" Camus. This fit his reflection that their quarrel was "just another way of living together and not losing sight of each other in the narrow little world that is given to us." And he was correct to say that the break "did not prevent me from thinking of him," for we have seen how the two men had continued to "live together" during the seven years since the quarrel.

Sartre's strongest recollection of Camus was as a moral presence that he had either to avoid or to fight. Camus embodied "this unshakeable affirmation. For, as little as people may read or reflect, they collide against the human values which he held in his closed fist. He put the political act in question." This was a rather ambivalent tribute. Sartre said that he found Camus's silences "too prudent and sometimes painful," and noted that Camus had fought "against history." He had "refused to leave the sure ground of morality, and to engage upon the uncertain paths of the *practical.*" Yet the negative became positive. "His stubborn humanism, narrow and pure, austere and sensual, waged a dubious battle against events of these times. But inversely, through the obstinacy of his refusals, he reaffirmed the existence of moral fact within the heart of our era and against the Machiavellians, against the golden calf of realism."

Sartre did not admit that in pursuing the "practical" he himself had worshiped at the altar of realism for over four years, and then—after a chain of events that included reading *The Fall,* which he described as "above all, perhaps the most beautiful and the least understood" of Camus's books, and without the usual fanfare that accompanied his changes—had recovered his own way of connecting morality with politics. He hinted that in his way, no longer diametrically opposed to Camus, he too had begun doing battle with realism. And he acknowledged Camus's importance as one of the "principal forces of our cultural domain" and as a thinker who framed the questions for others: "One lived with or against his thought . . . but always through it."

Later that month, pied-noir Algeria rose up again in a revolt, which fizzled out after de Gaulle faced down the plotters. The government prosecuted Jeanson and his network. Defiant, Sartre and other celebrities signed the "Manifesto of the 121," urging conscripts to desert. The government also initiated prosecution against the signatories to the petition, and the whole business became such a cause célèbre that demonstrators shouted "Shoot Sartre," and de Gaulle had the charges dismissed with the words, "You do not imprison Voltaire." In spring 1961, the "generals' putsch" also failed in Algiers. The Organisation Armée Secrète (OAS) emerged among intransigent settlers and the military, its strategy being to kill as many Arabs as possible in order to sabotage any agreement.

As the government pressed on with peace negotiations, the OAS carried out a campaign of slaughter among Algerians and their supporters that rivaled in little more than a year the number killed in seven years of FLN terror. It hatched plots against de Gaulle and others in France, including Sartre. In Algeria this frenzy created the very conditions, once the FLN took power, that would force the pieds-noirs to abandon Algeria completely. It was a bloodbath. When Algerian independence was finally declared in July 1962, one million French Algerians were in the midst of fleeing to France and Spain, destroying everything they could not carry with them. Camus was dead, and so was his Algeria.

: : :

The first OAS bomb aimed at Sartre, in July 1961, had been mistakenly placed on the floor above the one he lived on; the second, in January 1962, damaged his apartment. Sartre and Beauvoir had holed up at an acquaintance's, but Sartre's mother was home. Luckily, she was in the bathroom when the bomb went off, and was unhurt. Camus had worried publicly about FLN violence against his mother, but it was Sartre's mother who came within a hair's breadth of being murdered by OAS violence. This irony points to the deepest reason why reconciliation had been impossible between Sartre and Camus. The difference had been apparent since they met in 1943—recall Orestes embracing violence in *The Flies* as a way of becoming real, Camus justifying the violence of the Resistance in *Letters to a German Friend.* Violence has been the basso ostinato sounding through this story, and it came to its climax over Algeria. Not that Camus was nonviolent and Sartre was violent, but the one was preoccupied with keeping his hands clean, and the other with the necessity of getting his hands dirty.

As Camus had said in 1939, and then tried to unsay in 1955, the story of French Algeria was one of "colonial conquest." By the time of the Algerian War, Sartre understood, and Camus tried to ignore, the fact that violence against the natives was not only a sin but a daily feature of the relations between French and Arab Algerians. The settlers had constantly reasserted domination over the natives, had constantly asserted their claim to the physical reality of the place that originally belonged to the natives. And at every moment even the poorest among the settlers enjoyed, in Memmi's words, the "small crumbs" differentiating them from the natives. In the great novel of French Algeria, Camus's Meursault revels in its sensuous reality, bonding with its sun and sea, its heat and landscape. On the other hand, Meursault's violent and inexplicable murder of the anonymous Arab, following on his complicity with Raymond's beating of the young man's sister, conveys without the slightest sentimentality Algeria's texture of colonial brute force. And in both *The Stranger* and *The Plague* Camus re-creates the settlers' personal and political worlds as strangely devoid of non-Europeans, portraying the original occupants as occasional, silent, brooding, and threatening presences.

Camus the journalist had tried to give the natives their due, but he was ultimately arguing with the Meursaults and the Raymonds, men without reason. And then, after the native rebellion broke out, although hoping for the end of colonialism and its inequalities, he avoided telling them the harshest but most urgent truths. Sensing both their intransigence and their ultimately untenable position, Camus did not dare talk to his fellow pieds-noirs about either their privilege or their violence. Thus the man who so decried violence and sought clean hands could not escape complicity with the brutality that was a normal part of his homeland's daily life.

At his Nobel Prize ceremony, Camus presented his writer's credo. His function of "serving truth and freedom" was based, he said, on "two commitments difficult to observe: refusal to lie about what we know and resistance to oppression." Truth and freedom. Yet in striving to achieve these goals, he remained silent about certain truths, just like those intellectuals he despised, including Sartre. Camus never realized that his keeping silent in order to help a people that felt itself as beleaguered was little different from Sartre's silences with respect to Communism. Of course Camus knew, as he heard Communist parties or new revolutions overseas being justified, that their intellectual partisans spoke with a forked tongue—Sartre had done this in relation to the Soviet Union and the French Communist Party between 1952 and 1956. By his own selective honesty and his own silences, Camus acted the same way in relation to French Algeria between 1955 and his death. Yet Camus had imposed a different standard on Soviet Communism and French capitalist democracy since 1946—just as Sartre had toward capitalist democracies and anticolonial movements starting in 1956.

It was Memmi who explained where Camus had gone wrong. Before going silent, Camus had tried to square the circle, declaring that colonialism was over while insisting that its essential political relations be retained. He spoke of the equality of French and Arabs while privileging the former and ignoring the latter's central demand, refusing even to mention their representatives. He spoke of recognizing the Algerians' dignity while imagining permanent French rule. This dishonesty, or delusion, was based on an underlying reality—the vulnerable position of French Algeria. Once the French government, under de Gaulle, had had enough, the pieds-noir*s* of Algeria faced a dead end. The OAS, that crazed movement of fascist killers, perfectly expressed its disastrous dialectic. Unwilling to recast their identity as a dominating force, nurtured on violence, the adherents of *Algérie française* chose a genocidal explosion, and then political and social suicide, rather than risk transforming themselves into a nonruling minority.

There was an inner link between the final silence of this great, generous spirit and the *Götterdämmerung* of the OAS after Camus's death. Probably no one and nothing could have induced a million settlers to abandon their privileges, especially that of their white skin, and to embark on a path of reform that would lead to their becoming a minority in an Arab-ruled society. Pieds-noirs participated in the massacres after Sétif in 1945, rigged the elections of 1948, and furiously resisted any concession to the majority after November 1954, until Algerian nationalists became as hard and intransigent as they. Never faced down by fair-minded but equally deluded politicians like Mendès-France, the pieds-noirs continued to drug themselves on the myth of French Algeria, ignoring until it was too late the nine million people who were making themselves into Algerians in response to the settlers' economic, political, and cultural domination. Camus, who both saw and publicly expressed the worst about Communism, who had exposed himself to great personal danger, was incapable of telling the simple truth to his own people.

By 1958 the case for Camus's people had been weakened considerably. Profound racist violence was stirring in his community. Camus must have heard the mob calling for his death, led by Jo Ortiz, in January 1956; and he must have learned that mob had mounted the barricades in spring 1958. The OAS, emerging as the dominant expression of *Algérie française*, declared its final program a year after Camus's death by assassinating another generous spirit of reconciliation, Pierre Popie, a pied-noir attorney. Its goals were to murder the remaining people of good will on both sides, to create a climate of retaliation and all-out violence that would throttle the peace talks, and, if victorious, to institute a system of apartheid. Camus's friend, the Algerian novelist and teacher Moloud Feraoun, had disdainfully described their precursor organization as "masturbating in a corner." Paradoxically, their final orgy of violence, capping their total refusal of every accommodation since 1945, only made inevitable what they were desperately trying to ward off. During one of the most murderous days, an OAS death squad stormed into a meeting Feraoun was attending with French and Algerian teachers. The names of Feraoun and five others were read out; the six were taken out of the room, stood up against a wall, and shot dead. This happened on March 15, 1962; within four months, Algeria was independent and French Algeria was finished.

Certainly Camus's hatred of Communism was legitimate and was understandably fueled by his opposition to violence. But like many another anti-Communist, he wrecked his own moral and political coherence by avoiding talking about his own society. Casting blame on Soviet ambitions, Camus seemed to analyze everything but the fundamental changes required to end colonialism. Unable to speak about what his people would have to give up to become merely equal citizens, indeed a minority in postcolonial Algeria, Camus fell silent.

: : :

What Camus lacked, as did the liberal Cold Warriors who embraced him, was the saving insight that Sartre had been struggling toward since *Dirty Hands*: in many of its key structures our world is constituted by violence. In *The Communists and Peace,* the first part of which he wrote just before breaking with Camus, Sartre confronted the violence of the democratic capitalist system. And when he turned his attention to colonialism in 1956, Sartre showed how, in the colonies, violence created the social order and its people. He proclaimed the reality of Algeria to which Camus had closed his eyes. His most intense statement came a year after Camus died, in his foreword to Fanon's *The Wretched of the Earth.* Where Camus was constitutionally unable to hear the Algerian point of view, Sartre invites his readers into their world: "Europeans, you must open this book and enter into it. After a few steps in the darkness you will see strangers gathered around a fire; come close, and listen, for they are talking of the destiny they will mete out to your trading-centers and to the hired soldiers who defend them." While Camus denied any guilt, Sartre spreads the net of responsibility. "It is true that you are not settlers, but you are no better. For the pioneers belong to you; you sent them overseas, and it was you they enriched." Then Sartre turns to what he regards as the central issue.

> Violence in the colonies does not only have for its aim the keeping of these enslaved men at arm's length; it seeks to dehumanize them. Everything will be done to wipe out their traditions, to substitute our language for theirs and to destroy their culture without giving them ours. Sheer physical fatigue will stupefy them. Starved and ill, if they have any spirit left, fear will finish the job; guns are levelled at the peasant; civilians come to take over his land and force him by dint of flogging to till the land for them. If he shows fight, the soldiers fire and he's a dead man; if he gives in, he degrades himself and he is no longer a man at all; shame and fear will split up his character and make his inmost self fall to pieces.

Inevitably the natives would make the settlers' violence their own, internalizing it, and then they would rise up against their masters. We, says Sartre, "are living at the moment when the match is put to the fuse." Even the Left would be upset by the explosion.

> They would do well to read Fanon; for he shows clearly that this irrepressible violence is neither sound and fury, nor the resurrection of savage instincts, nor even the effect of resentment: it is man re-creating himself. I think we understood this truth at one time, but we have forgotten it—that no gentleness can efface the marks of violence; only violence itself can destroy them. The native cures himself of colonial neurosis by thrusting out the settler through force of arms. When his rage boils over, he rediscovers his lost innocence and he comes to know himself in that he himself creates his self. Far removed from his war, we consider it as a triumph of barbarism; but of its own volition it achieves slowly but surely the emancipation of the rebel, for bit by bit it destroys in him and around him the colonial gloom. Once begun, it is a war that gives no quarter. You may fear or be feared; that is to say, abandon yourself to the disassociations of a sham existence or conquer your birthright of unity. When the peasant takes a gun in his hands, the old myths grow dim and the prohibitions are one by one forgotten. The rebel's weapon is the proof of his humanity. For in the first days of the revolt you must kill; to shoot down a European is to kill two birds with one stone, to destroy an oppressor and the man he oppresses at the same time: there remain a dead man, and a free man; the survivor, for the first time, feels a *national* soil under his foot.

Now the peasants will see their real situation, create "new structures which will become the first institutions of peace." According to Sartre, they are discovering their humanity "beyond torture and death," and are making themselves people at our expense: "a different man of higher quality," creating a socialist society. But here Sartre ends his gloss on Fanon's narrative, for he knows that the argument is continuing within his reader. Through the Algerian War, he claims, Europeans themselves are being decolonized: "the settler which is in every one of us is being savagely rooted out." And then Sartre recalls Camus's words of fifteen years earlier.

> A fine sight they are too, the believers in nonviolence, saying that they are neither executioners nor victims. Very well then; if you're not vic-

> tims when the government which you've voted for, when the army in which your younger brothers are serving without hesitation or remorse have undertaken race murder, you are, without a shadow of doubt, executioners.

Calling his readers "exploiters" and guilty of a "racist humanism," Sartre tells how French violence, blocked in Algeria, is seeping back into France. "Rage and fear are already blatant; they show themselves openly in Arab-hunting in Algiers. Now which side are the savages on? Where is barbarism? Nothing is missing, not even the tom-toms; the motor-horns beat out 'Al-gérie fran-çaise' while the Europeans burn Muslims alive."

We have, in this incredible journey, accompanied Sartre from his insights into colonialism, to his projection of its psychic damage, to an assertion of how that damage is being repaired through the natives' violence, to his bathing in that violence, to his exultant and self-flagellating attack on Europeans! In one of his most powerful pieces of writing, Sartre's argument and his worldview are as brutal as his language. If Camus denied settler violence, Sartre now composes the twentieth century's ode to violence as liberation and therapy. If Camus tried to lay down rules for conducting conflict, Sartre now approves of the natives' getting rid of colonialism "by every means within their power." If Camus adjusted his statements according to his sense of his community's intolerance, Sartre now guiltily attacks his own community in making himself the European spokesperson for the Third World. If Camus's anti-Communism masked his inability to listen to the natives' own voices, Sartre the revolutionary, away from the field of battle, now gives a blank check of support for even the ugliest anticolonial brutalities.

The theme of "dirty hands" had been Sartre's way of accepting violence into struggles for social change, but he now erected it into an ethic of struggle, even beyond the claim that the ends justified the means. Sartre now gave violence itself a value, a liberating function. Sartre later said that he exaggerated in order to please his friend, Frantz Fanon. But his main ideas were no momentary aberration. Since *Dirty Hands* Sartre had never been much concerned to place limits on violence as a tool of social struggle. Goetz's dramatic murder of the officer who balked at his command turned out to be annunciatory. Sartre sided with the Communist Party in part *because of* its alleged penchant for violence. His understanding of the PCF was part and parcel of a sustained exploration of the meanings, uses, sources, and structures of violence. At its deepest root, violence is about *scarcity*, the fact that the means of subsistence have always been inadequate to meet human needs. In a climate of scarcity, every human is potentially a threat to every other human.

> Nothing—not even wild beasts or microbes—could be more terrifying for man than a species which is intelligent, carnivorous and cruel, and which can understand and outwit human intelligence, and whose aim is precisely the destruction of man. This, however, is obviously our own species as perceived in others by each of its members in the context of scarcity.

Violence is inscribed in our world in the eyes of others, in things themselves. This world is itself Manichaean, and all class societies are rooted in this fact. Its people are "serialized"—isolated and alienated from each other by oppressive structures. Thus they do not come together naturally but only under the collective threat of death. Violence thus plays a unifying role in a worldview that stresses antagonism and passes over the thousand daily ways of unforced cooperation.

How, then, might it be possible to change such a world for the better? In an unpublished 1958 interview with Jean Daniel, Sartre wondered whether it was possible for anticolonial movements, like revolutionary movements and even the French Resistance, to do without secrecy and terror. Because intellectuals like himself who support their goals cannot influence their conduct, Sartre concluded that it was "not opportune" to publish certain ugly facts, such as the massacre at Melouza, because these truths aid the enemy. "They have to remain hidden because we are acting politically. We have to accept that politics imposes a constraint to remain silent about certain things. Otherwise one is a 'beautiful soul' and then one isn't acting politically."

Camus's and Sartre's inability to reconcile was not just a continuation of their disagreements. Each man was in bad faith about what turned out to be his key political theme, violence. At his best, Sartre broke the taboo against discussing the violence built into daily life, seeing and describing the systemic violence of capitalism and colonialism. Yet he also saw *all* social life as a bitter struggle for domination. He made a fetish of violence, deeming it necessary for human liberation and social change without calculating its costs. Camus at his best understood the corrupting and destructive effects of violence, especially in movements that claimed to liberate humans and whose long-term goals he supported. Yet he also denied and repressed violence insofar as it was central to the life of *his* Algeria, all the more vigorously to campaign against it elsewhere.

It shouldn't surprise us, then, that in the prefaces they wrote—Camus for *Algerian Reports* in 1958, and Sartre for Fanon's book in 1961, after Camus's death—each wrote about violence and each attacked the other. Camus singled out the "judge-penitents," Sartre singled out those who claimed to be "neither executioners nor victims." During these years, their antagonism hardened as each man took the other as the exemplar of the attitude he was fighting against. It was a situation of tragic ironies. In the name of serving the oppressed, Sartre accepted oppression. In loving his people, Camus muted his usual denunciations of oppression. Each one was half-right and half-wrong, locked into two separate but mutually supporting systems of bad faith. No longer could either learn from the other.

epilogue

Sartre survived Camus by twenty years and so had the last word—indeed, many last words—on their relationship. A few days after Camus's death, Sartre told a student that "Camus never did anything 'nasty' to me, as far as I know, and I never did anything like that to him." Perhaps his amnesia stemmed from the fact that Sartre, unlike Camus, did not hold tightly to friendships with men, having broken with many onetime colleagues during the 1940s and 1950s, always over politics. The list includes Aron, Altman, Rousset, Etiemble, Lefort, and Merleau-Ponty.

After Camus's death, Sartre the anticolonialist remained critical of his former friend, mocking Algerian settlers who tried to be neither victims nor executioners and rejecting the "false intellectuals" who thought they could avoid all violence in Vietnam and Algeria. Sartre's 1961 article on Merleau-Ponty, a former schoolmate whom he regarded as his political mentor but never spoke of as a close friend, contrasts strikingly with his eulogy for Camus. The hundred-page piece is a detailed and warm appreciation that avoids looking deeply into his former colleague's motivations but speaks at length about his influence on Sartre. Above all, it shows an unforced respect for Merleau-Ponty as a thinker—he was after all a fellow philosopher and graduate of the Ecole Normale—which was always lacking in Sartre's writings on Camus. The letters from his 1953 break with Merleau-Ponty reveal another side of Sartre's relationship with him, which was absent between him and Camus: strong professions of affection. These letters, intended to be private and published only in 1994, are marked by personal warmth and the use of *tu*. Sartre was still able to say, at the end of a pointed political argument over the proper attitude toward Communism, "I am and want to remain your friend." The two or three times they saw each other shortly before Merleau-Ponty's death were characterized by a pained and restrained friendliness. Although Merleau-Ponty published a book taking Sartre to task for his "ultrabolshevism," this separation and its aftermath had none of the drama we have seen in Sartre's break with Camus—the angry intensity, the public performances, the cries of betrayal, the continuing argument.

In 1963, Beauvoir presented her statement on the end of the Sartre-Camus relationship and on Camus's evolution. It is worth quoting in full.

> As a matter of fact, if this friendship exploded so violently, it was because for a long time not much of it had remained. The political and ideological differences which already existed between Sartre and Camus in 1945 had intensified from year to year. Camus was an idealist, a moralist and an anti-Communist; at one moment forced to yield to History, he attempted as soon as possible to secede from it; sensitive to men's suffering, he imputed it to Nature; Sartre had labored since 1940 to repudiate idealism, to wrench himself away from his original individualism, to live in History; his position was close to Marxism, and he desired an alliance with the Communists. Camus was fighting for great principles, and that was how he came to be taken in by the hot air of Gary Davis; usually, he refused to participate in the particular and detailed political actions to which Sartre committed himself. While Sartre believed in the truth of socialism, Camus became a more and more resolute champion of bourgeois values; *The Rebel* was a statement of his solidarity with them. A neutralist position between the two blocs

> had become finally impossible; Sartre therefore drew nearer to the USSR; Camus hated the Russians, and although he did not like the United States, he went over, practically speaking, to the American side. I told him about our experience [of recoiling at the sight of American soldiers in late 1951] at Chinon. "I really felt I was back in the Occupation," I told him. He looked at me with an astonishment that was both sincere and feigned. "Really?" He smiled. "Wait a little while. You'll see a real Occupation soon—a different sort altogether."

These "differences of opinion," were the political reasons why the friendship split apart. There were also personal ones.

> Compromise was not easy for a man of Camus's character. I suppose he felt how vulnerable his position was in some way; he would not brook challenge, and as soon as he saw one coming he would fly into one of his abstract rages, which seemed to be his way of taking refuge. There had been a sort of reconciliation between him and Sartre at the time of [*The Devil and the Good Lord*], and we had published his article on Nietzsche in *Les Temps modernes,* although we weren't at all satisfied with it. But this tentative attempt had not lasted. Camus was ready, at the slightest opportunity, to criticize Sartre for his permissiveness with regard to "authoritarian socialism." Sartre had long believed that Camus was wrong all along the line and that furthermore he had become, as he told him in his letter, "utterly insufferable." Personally, this break in their relations did not affect me. The Camus who had been dear to me had ceased to exist a long while before.

As time passed, Beauvoir and Sartre came to regard the break as the essence of the relationship. Like Beauvoir's sketch, Sartre's recollections invariably had the aroma of self-justification. He recalled Camus as the negative mirror image against whom he had defined himself, as in the 1971 discussion with his designated biographer, John Gerassi. Reflecting back on himself in 1943, Sartre said,

> I was then like Camus was in the fifties. . . . I did not understand that war is the consequence of certain inner conflicts in bourgeois societies. Workers don't go to war, peasants don't go to war, unless they are pushed into it by their leaders, those who control the means of production, the press, communications in general, the educational system, in one word, the bourgeois. When I think of Camus claiming, *years later,* that the German

> invasion was like the plague—coming for no reason, leaving for no reason—what a jerk!

This was an amazing turnabout, for we know that Sartre had taken Camus as a model in 1945 and had warmly praised his novel about the Resistance.

In a 1975 interview, Sartre was pressed on his disloyalty in friendship, especially in the relationship with Camus. He continued to feel fully justified in his attack because, as he said, he "called me 'Monsieur le directeur' and was full of crazy ideas about Francis Jeanson's article." In this same interview, however, Sartre uncharacteristically let a very different note slip out, which I have mentioned more than once in this story: "He was probably the last good friend I had." After acknowledging that he had replied "quite harshly" to Camus, Sartre implied that his personal affection survived alongside their differences. "I retained a liking for him although his politics were completely foreign to mine, particularly his attitude during the Algerian war." This "particularly" was an odd recollection, because it had been their differences about Communism five years earlier, and not about Algeria, that had driven them apart. Was he now suggesting that he had softened toward Camus after Hungary and with the thawing of the Cold War, but that their separation had been reconfirmed by their new political differences?

Certainly, he retained positive feelings toward Camus. When hearing that Camus had won the Nobel Prize in late 1957, he told his secretary, "Il ne l'a pas volé"—he didn't steal it. In his eulogy we have seen him pay tribute to Camus both as a writer and as a moralist. And after recovering his own sense of the importance of morality in politics, Sartre would continue to develop this perspective in new directions. Moreover, the unfinished second volume of *Critique of Dialectical Reason* poses precisely the same question as does *Man in Revolt*: How did a revolution aiming at human emancipation create hell on earth?

As for Camus's final view of Sartre, we have seen his last direct public comment in 1955, where he said that Sartre "was not a loyal adversary," as well as his various indirect reflections, especially in *The Fall*. Sartre remained his negative mirror image to the end, especially in relation to Algeria. In 1958, Camus wrote a foreword to a new edition of his mentor Jean Grenier's *Les Îles*, and it contains his final reference to Sartre. Intellectuals are fascinated, he says, by the half-truth that every consciousness seeks the other's death. The French reformulation of Hegel's Master-Slave conflict was Sartre's depiction of the Self-Other conflict in *Being and Nothingness*. Its conclusion was captured on stage in Garcin's final realization, in *No Exit*, that "hell is other people"—one of the lines Camus rehearsed during the war in Beauvoir's hotel room. Now Camus was paying tribute to his master Grenier by talking about their "relationship of respect and gratitude" as opposed to one of servitude or obedience. It was rather odd for Camus to pick an indirect philosophical quarrel with Sartre and then to seek to prevail by referring to his own relationship with Grenier. Unless, of course, he was suggesting a contrast between the relationship with Grenier, fifteen years his senior, and the one with Sartre, eight years older: the first one built, "happily," on admiration, while the second was among those relationships which "are equally often built on hatred."

There is, however, a sequel to the personal side of the story. By 1963 the Algerian War was over, Camus had been dead for three years, and French Algeria had ceased to exist. Had Camus been alive, he would no doubt have observed one final instance of Sartre's disloyalty to him. As he was winding up "My Dear Camus," Sartre had said: "If you find me cruel, have no fear. Presently, I shall speak of myself and in the same tone. You will try in vain to strike back at me, but have faith, I shall certainly pay for it all. For you are completely insufferable, but you are still my 'fellow human being' by the force of circumstances." Taunting, Sartre promised Camus an equally cruel *self*-analysis. He had in mind his autobiography-in-progress, *The Words*.

Did Sartre keep his promise to his fellow human being? To do so, in his autobiography, as at the beginning of *The Fall*, he would have had to lay himself bare, displaying his stratagems and hypocrisies as well as what lay behind them. Sartre would have had to adopt the same critical stance as he did in "My Dear Camus," and perhaps even demonstrate his own bad faith into the present. In *The Words*, Sartre does explore the way his childhood imposture took shape as he was raised by his grandparents and mother after his father died. He then describes how he became a writer as a boy who learned to put pen to paper and write stories, thus transforming himself into a socially acceptable imposter. Framed by a world of suffering and inequality he only learned about much later, the boy's beautifully told story slowly reveals a painful childhood. It tells how he became a fake child, having no real identity and no sense of belonging. So far, Sartre seems to be redeeming his promise to Camus.

Much like Clamence's confession, however, Sartre transforms the honesty and directness of his narrative into something else. His pain, authentic at first, is remade aesthetically, as the child's story comes to resemble not only a novel but a game of mirrors. Then Sartre draws it to a close, promising a sequel. By the end, the play of multiple levels wins out over self-revelation. Childhood pain takes on charm as the boy's story turns ambiguous and delightful. In the present I have stopped taking my pen for a sword, Sartre tells his readers, but he never makes clear exactly what he means. At some point in his adult years he has gained some profound self-understanding, but what and how? Sartre never finishes the story.

In creating this great literary success, then, Sartre both kept and failed to keep his promise to Camus. He revealed himself, but he let himself off the hook. Yet despite, or perhaps because of, this ambiguity, *The Words* was immediately recognized as a literary masterpiece. A year later Sartre was awarded the Nobel Prize for literature. Creating an even greater furor than Camus's "mother before justice" remark, Sartre refused the prize, arguing that it had become an instrument of the Cold War. So the one man, raised in Algerian poverty, reached the pinnacle of success with an award that also suggested that his life's work was finished, and used the money to buy his only permanent home; the other, a child of comfort, turned down the prize, money and all, as a political protest.

: : :

Camus, no doubt, will remain the more sympathetic of the two men. Because he died young, and so suddenly, he will never grow old in our eyes, whereas we can see the aging Sartre becoming a spent old man, seeming to outlive himself, leaving behind unseemly quarrels about whether his last words are really his own voice. Although Camus's success seemed to turn his head, and the rough and tumble of debate embittered him, he always was a visibly feeling, suffering, self-doubting, and vulnerable person, and even his literary powers seemed hard-won and more human than Sartre's incredible intellectual gifts.

But to conclude the story by speculating which of the two men "won" resembles the political either/or that has kept their full relationship from being seen for fifty years. Today's political climate, given the post–Cold War campaign to assign praise and blame, seems to impose this question. As surely as Sartre scored more points according to the office chatter at Gallimard in 1952, and as surely as the FLN won in Algeria ten years later, so Camus is the victor today according to those who are compiling *les erreurs de Sartre*. In the words of the best known of these, the political Sartre was a "fanatic," a "preacher of voluntary servitude," who suffered from "totalitarian delirium," while Camus was right at nearly every turn.

This reversal began while Sartre was still alive. One of its key moments occurred in June 1979, when a group of leading intellectuals gathered for a press conference followed by a visit to the Elysée Palace to urge President Giscard d'Estaing to intervene on behalf of the Vietnamese boat people. Sartre, in steep physical decline, encountered his old schoolmate Raymond Aron for the first time in over twenty years. Sartre demanded that people be helped from a "purely moral exigency; . . . people's lives must be saved." Camus's daughter Catherine, who was present, saw Sartre tossing ideological consideration to the winds and placing humanity before politics. Sartre was perceived as yielding to what Jeanson had earlier dismissed as Camus's "Red Cross morality."

Other key moments in the reversal took place in November 1989 and August 1991—the dates of Communism's collapse. Today's turnabout in Camus's and Sartre's fortunes cannot be separated from post–Cold War mopping-up operations. These include, most notably, the posthumous trial of Communism begun by François Furet's *The Passing of an Illusion* and continued by Stéphane Courtois and his collaborators in *The Black Book of Communism.* In these and related works we find strong praise for Camus and scorn for Sartre. Sartre the revolutionary has been declared anathema, while those who know little else about Camus's politics hear him praised for his insights into violence and revolution.

These currently fashionable half-truths resemble the two men's views of each other after their break: they justify and accuse rather than explain, and they block a fuller understanding. But the story I have just told points to a deeper criticism and appreciation of both men. In fact, *both* went very wrong. Camus stated the choice starkly: my mother or justice. But after declaring forthrightly that his concern for the other side's freedom must be framed by his own people's survival, Camus denied the Algerians' very sense of themselves. No justice without violence, said Sartre. But after painstakingly working his way through the impossibility of bringing peace and light to the world without overthrowing its oppressive and unequal social structures, Sartre proclaimed the necessary evil, violence, as a positive good.

Yet despite their mistakes, each had a characteristic power of insight, voice, and moral-political stance that placed him in the great French tradition of Voltaire, Hugo, and Zola. Upon becoming famous, both Sartre and Camus plunged into politics, each pursuing, with his own characteristic energy and conviction, a coherent project of political understanding and action. This was not just dabbling, but drew on all of each man's strength. No distinction could be made between Camus's or Sartre's literary, philosophical, or political work; their deepest ideas merged with, stemmed from, and fueled, their politics. No wonder they could never reconcile. As political intellectuals, each man was willing to take risks, to appear inconsistent, to make mistakes, and to become unpopular, disliked, even hated. And when it became necessary, each one risked his personal safety as well, showing more courage as a celebrated writer than he had as a young unknown.

Both stood up, spoke out, and were listened to—Camus for his intransigent denunciation of the totalitarian spirit, Sartre for his no less intransigent denunciation of colonialism; Camus on behalf of a politics of freedom and self-restraint, Sartre on behalf of attacking oppression fiercely; Camus against justifications of political violence, Sartre against systemic violence. And so, when Camus and then Sartre received the Nobel Prize for Literature in 1957 and 1964, the awards were widely taken as recognition of an entire man—not only of each one's fiction, theater, philosophy, political writings, journalism, and political activity, but of each man's presence in France and in the world.

Both took shape in argument with the other, only in this way becoming the fully developed political intellectuals that the world came to recognize as Camus and Sartre: the polar opposites who defined the choices for their generation. Each man's talent was so great, his immersion in his times so deep, his political commitment so strong, and his drive to clarify his own point of view so forceful, that in the end it came down to Camus *or* Sartre. The ending of their friendship was an inevitable casualty of this process, and was inscribed in the issues that pulled them apart.

Their break is distorted by the claim, made by many from then until now, that it stemmed from two fundamentally opposed approaches to life exemplifying the timeless antagonism of reform and revolution, the concrete and the abstract, nonviolence and violence, the artist's attitude and the philosopher's—the rebel and the revolutionary. To transmute the two men's specific personal, historical, and strategic differences into ontological principles would be to mistake the watchwords produced by their conflict for its causes. Their different choices stemmed from the Cold War, the possibilities bequeathed to them by French history and society, their own starting points and pathways through the world, and their opposition to each other. Their breakup is a historical fact but no more than this. In shaping themselves into who they became, in going along with the Cold War's "need to choose," these two particular individuals always had particular reasons for responding to, and trying to affect, their political family and the wider world.

Has history decided the issues that defined them and drove them apart? Yes. Is our situation so changed today that we can now declare the Camus-Sartre conflict over, resolved by events? No.

The deepest issues motivating and dividing Camus and Sartre are still with us. Much of humanity continues to struggle for self-determination, or to be ground down by inequalities of wealth and power, or to be caught up in the North's domination of the South. Terrorism seems to go hand in hand with the global economy. Violence and war are still the order of the day. Nuclear terror persists. Much remains radically askew in our world, and as we grapple with it, Sartre and Camus continue to be relevant—as does their relationship, their arguments, and each man's wisdom and blind spots. Yet Communism has been defeated by democratic capitalism, and almost all colonialisms have been abolished. The Cold War is over. The specific issues dividing the two men have vanished, and to this extent we live in a different world. We can now appreciate both Camus and Sartre and reject the either/or that broke them apart. Accordingly, I cannot keep from speculating that the time is ripe for a new type of political intellectual who might bring together each man's strengths and avoid each man's weaknesses. We can imagine someone speaking the truth *at all times,* and opposing oppression *everywhere,* uniting each man's characteristic power of insight under a single moral standard. Such an intellectual would illuminate today's systemic violence while accepting the challenge of mounting an effective struggle against it without creating new evils. A Camus/Sartre? As Sartre once said in another connection, this may be imagining an angel, an abstract embodiment of exactly what is needed in our situation. Angels do not exist, but they can be a yardstick for human beings.

postscript

As this book was entering into production I traveled to Aix-en-Provence, France, to study the manuscript of Albert Camus's major remaining unpublished work, "L'Impromptu des philosophes." I was surprised to find this one-act play, written in 1946, so charming and amusing—and so filled with allusions to Sartre. Olivier Todd and Herbert Lottman had both written summaries of this delightful farce in their biographies of Camus, but both concluded so ambiguously that I doubted that it warranted a trip to France. Because it might possibly add something to the story, however, I finally decided to consult this manuscript, which is not scheduled for publication until the new Pléiade edition of Camus's works appears.

Once I resolved to look at it, Catherine Camus graciously granted me permission to consult the forty-page typescript and thirty-five-page manuscript in the Bibliothèque Méjanes in Aix. Marcelle Mahasela, director of the Centre de Documentation Albert Camus, made it accessible, and she and I had several lively discussions about the manuscript, as well as about Camus's relationship with Sartre. She, the staff of the Salle Peiresc, and Catherine Camus helped me decipher Camus's handwriting, including the several pages of notes he added in 1947.

I came to "L'Impromptu des philosophes" late for another reason: the war in Iraq. My son-in-law was mobilized as the invasion was being prepared in early January 2003, a few days after my daughter gave birth to their son. She moved back home for several months to benefit from her parents' willingness to help care for her two children, which meant that I would not travel to France until after the book had been shaped. This historical accident places my discussion of the manuscript as a postscript to the complex and tragic story of a friendship and its end. It is by caprice and by chance, then, that the reader now has the opportunity to savor one of the relationship's interesting and delightful moments with the entire story in mind. We can enjoy the time when, as Catherine Camus said to me, they were still *copains*—pals. After seeing their relationship tossed and torn in the winds of the history that created it, this unpublished manuscript recalls us to a calmer and lighter moment when Camus was able to mock himself, Sartre, and the Parisian journalists and fashion-merchants who had put their seemingly outrageous pronouncements on everyone's lips.

: : :

Monsieur Vigne, a provincial pharmacist and mayor possessed of more vanity than good sense, is visited by a "traveling salesman of new doctrines," Monsieur Néant. Had this play been performed, attention would immediately have been drawn to the latter's name and his trade. Who else, in Paris and France, would people think of when hearing the name M. Néant, so deliberately taken from the title of Sartre's magnum opus? In a plot suggestive of *Tartuffe,* the intellectual confidence man preys on the foolish Vigne, eager to be taken in by the "new Gospel" from Paris contained in the enormous tome Néant lugs around—a not-so-subtle allusion to Sartre's voluminous *Being and Nothingness.*

Camus is ridiculing the vogue for both his and Sartre's views, and the colossal misunderstandings to which their ideas were subjected in the press. Even a supposedly sophisticated reporter such as Janet Flanner, writing as "Genêt" in the *New Yorker,* could do no better in one of her first letters from Paris than to say that Camus's "wisdom consisted of thinking that life was ridiculous." And, a few months later: "As nearly as can be made out by dullards who would have thought that an important new French philosophy must be founded on something more than a 'disgust for humanity,' Sartre's form of existentialism is, indeed, founded on a disgust for humanity." In addition to ridiculing such rubbish, the cavorting of the big-city hustler and the provincial fool reveals a certain pleasure in turning convention upside down, a delight in nonsense, and a penchant for paradoxical formulations—as well as poking fun at several of Sartre's ideas.

In Paris ideas are commodities, and so Vigne vows to pay Néant for his trouble. Enthused by his new religion, Vigne tells his daughter Sophie that her beau Mélusin, if he loves her, will ask her to share his bed. Indeed, he'll make her pregnant, and having an illegitimate child will give her a deeper grasp of what it means to exist. Camus is sending up Sartre's philosophical stress on extreme situations, and he is directly playing with Sartre's *Age of Reason,* the literary sensation of fall 1945. This novel revolves around Marcelle's pregnancy and Mathieu's search for a solution which would avoid committing him to marry her (he even steals the money for an abortion). Vigne tells his daughter that her young man can't love her without being *engagé*—committed—and he can't be committed without placing her in a terrible situation. One can't love without responsibility—Mathieu had failed this test—and one can't be responsible without pregnancy.

Mesmerized by such ideas, Vigne orders his wife to prepare a room for Néant, who will be moving in with them. Néant ravenously devours a ham Mme. Vigne has brought while he and the mayor discourse about anguish, "the best thing in the world." It gives one a sense of existing and, after all, the dead know no anguish: "Anguish, more anguish, always anguish, M. Vigne, and we will be saved." When Mme. Vigne and Néant rub each other the wrong way, the hustler urges Vigne to repudiate her. His heart throbbing like a twenty-year-old's, Vigne declares himself free from his obligations.

In talking with his daughter's beau the pharmacist-mayor insists that the young man is not who he is—this is a play on the Sartrean notion that we are always becoming and only become who we are in any fixed and stable way when we are dead. Young Mélusin responds with a breathlessly delivered speech in which he presents a summary of Néant's ideas taught to him by Sophie to convince her father, echoing the Sartrean buzz-words of "responsibility," "commitment," and "freedom." Vigne replies to the very proper Mélusin that to qualify for Sophie's hand it would be an advantage to have stolen something or to be a criminal. What is more, he should admit sexual desires toward his mother and sister and, even better, other men. Camus is jesting about the sense of scandal with which his and Sartre's works were often greeted, about both men's preoccupation with abnormal characters and extreme situations, and also about Sartre's fascination with homosexuals. In Sartrean language Vigne tells the young man that his consent depends on the birth of their illegitimate child. "If there is no child, you are without responsibility, and if you are without responsibility you are not at all committed. And if you are not committed, you don't love my daughter—that is obvious." It would have been no less obvious to anyone seeing the play in 1946 that Camus's newspaper, *Combat*, had been running a series of famous authors' reflections on this theme of commitment, which had become all the rage since Sartre's introduction to the new *Les Temps modernes* the previous October.

In the one exchange that diverges from the family farce, Camus recalls Sartre's famous line that the French were never so free as they were under the German occupation, as Néant declares that being free depends on being oppressed. As in *Tartuffe*, the charlatan makes the entire family miserable. Because the young man has not slept with Sophie, Vigne rejects him with the parting counsel: he should exercise his love of humanity behind closed doors [*à huis-clos*]. This obvious allusion to Sartre's most celebrated play also toys with its theme that hell is other people. Vigne announces that he is divorcing his wife and wishes to have Néant and Sophie produce an illegitimate child. They are ripe for Néant's declaration that such suffering means that they are all admirably experiencing the human condition—also an echo of "The Republic of Silence."

It turns out that Néant has escaped from an insane asylum. This reflects one strand of popular opinion, which saw Sartre and Camus, as well as some of their characters, as demented. We learn that Vigne was not the first to be taken in: Néant had many followers in Paris. But if he is a madman, what about his book? Vigne has not read it—nor has Néant. This would have drawn laughs from the audience as another reference to France's famously most-owned and least-read book, *Being and Nothingness.* Before being committed Néant had earned his living as a critic. Everyone knows that critics never study the books they talk about and that Parisians are too busy discussing ideas to read them.

: : :

Camus signed the pseudonym "Antoine Bailly" to "L'Impromptu des philosophes." He worked on the play a bit during 1947, adding one note as late as mid-summer. But he never sought to stage it, even when directing his own theater company. He did, however, think about it into the 1950s as one of his unfinished projects, and even mentioned staging it as a commedia dell'arte.

It is interesting to speculate about whether Camus ever showed the play to Sartre, and about why Camus never had the play performed. It is equally interesting to speculate about why it continued to have a life for him after his breakup with Sartre. But the most striking fact about "L'Impromptu des philosophes" is simply that it exists, an unusually lighthearted testimony to a certain moment—in Camus's life, in his relationship with Sartre, and in French history.

Its parody of Sartrean philosophy is good-natured and, even if it might be taken to suggest that Camus thought that Sartre was talking nonsense, could easily have been shared and laughed about between friends. It is noteworthy that even while distinguishing himself from existentialism during these months, Camus begins this farce by parodying the popular understanding of both his and Sartre's thinking under the rubrics of absurdity and heroism. Camus, so keenly determined not to be seen as Sartre's satellite, drafted a play which, if staged, would have been seen as simultaneously feeding and poking fun of the Sartre-phenomenon of 1945–6. Boris Vian's *L'Ecume des jours,* published in the spring of 1946, featured the philosopher Jean-Sol Partre, the author of *Vomit,* who publishes no less than five articles a week, was at work on a twenty-volume "encyclopedia of nausea," and was at the center of a riotous public lecture. And now Camus, too, had drawn an extravagant and even zany caricature of the man who was dazzling Paris and the world, ending up by packing him off to an insane asylum.

Had the play been staged, the asylum director's last words would also have drawn attention—keep your children from philosophizing. Here was the philosopher of *The Myth of Sisyphus,* abjuring philosophy! The serious thinker was, as a playwright, making fun of serious thinking. Or was he showing the impossibility of applying serious thinking to everyday matters, as Sartre insisted on doing? The play stays very close to the surface and indulges in much wordplay, making it difficult to conclude that Camus is seriously critiquing his friend's ideas. In fact silliness seems everywhere, and the satire has little intellectual depth. Why is it that the wise old asylum director concludes that one set of ideas is as good as any other, that philosophy is useless for daily life, and that we should avoid philosophers?

Was Camus just joking? Or does the play hint at what would become sharp divergences between the two, and even suggest seeds of the split? Nearly sixty years later, though it was never meant to see the light of day, the public life of "L'Impromptu des philosophes" has not yet begun. Answers to these questions may slowly emerge once the play is read and reread and, above all, once it is performed and discussed. We can look forward to this with pleasure.

notes

PROLOGUE

1 ***"Les Temps modernes. . . ."*** Albert Camus, "Révolte et servitude," *Essais* (Paris, 1965), 754.

1 **"still too many. . . ."** Jean-Paul Sartre, "Reply to Albert Camus," *Situations* (New York, 1965), 71.

2 **"consummated"** *Samedi-Soir,* 6 September 1952; see Herbert R. Lottman's excellent *Albert Camus: A Biography* (Corte Madera, CA, 1997), 532.

2 **"Sartre against Camus"** Jean Caillot, *France-Illustration,* 21 September 1952, 280.

2 **"the burning issues of our time"** Francis Jeanson, "Albert Camus ou l'Ame révoltée," *Les Temps modernes,* April 1952, 2070.

2 **"national dispute"** Raymond Aron, *Opium of the Intellectuals* (Boston, 1957), 51.

3 **issues between Camus and Sartre** One of the best of the brief accounts is Ian Birchall, "Camus contre Sartre: quarante ans plus tard," *Actes du colloque de Keele, 25–27 mars 1993,* ed. David H. Walker. Longer studies include Germaine Brée, *Camus and Sartre: Crisis and Commitment* (New York, 1972); Leo Pollmann, *Sartre and Camus* (New York, 1970); Peter Royle, *The Sartre-Camus Controversy* (Ottawa, 1982).

4 **"great principles"** Simone de Beauvoir, *Force of Circumstance* (New York, 1965), 106–12.

4 **"had 20/20 political vision"** Lottman, *Albert Camus*, xiv–xv; translation modified. This theme is developed by Bernard-Henri Lévy, *Le Siècle de Sartre: Enquête philosophique* (Paris, 2000), and Tony Judt, *The Burden of Responsibility: Blum, Camus, Aron, and the French Twentieth Century* (Chicago,1998). Both are discussed below.

4 **"He was my last good friend"** Jean-Paul Sartre, "Self-Portrait at Seventy," in *Life/Situations* (New York, 1976), 107.

5 **"the least understood"** Jean-Paul Sartre, "Albert Camus," in *Situations, IV* (Paris, 1964), 127; *Situations,* 109.

5 **larger forces than themselves** Jean-Paul Sartre, *Critique de la raison dialectique, II* (Paris, 1985); see Ronald Aronson, *Sartre's Second Critique* (Chicago, 1987), 51–75.

6 **of the relationship** Doris Lessing, *The Golden Notebook* (New York, 1962), 227–29.

6 **their true colors** For a negative view of Camus see John Gerassi, *Jean-Paul Sartre: Hated Conscience of His Century* (Chicago, 1989); for a negative view of Sartre see Olivier Todd, *Albert Camus: A Life* (New York, 1997).

7 **"another way of being together"** Sartre, "Albert Camus," 109.

CHAPTER ONE

9 **"was Albert Camus"** Simone de Beauvoir, *The Prime of Life* (Cleveland, 1966), 427.

10 **"likeable personality"** Ibid., 443.

10 ***pris des choses*** Camus's letter to Ponge about his book, dated 27 January 1943, appears in the Pléiade edition of Camus's *Essais* (Paris, 1965), 1662–68; Sartre's essay, dated December 1944, is entitled "L'Homme et les choses," *Situations, I* (Paris, 1947), 226–70.

10 **"in North Africa"** Beauvoir, *The Prime of Life,* 444.

10 **role of Garcin** *Quiet Moments in a War: The Letters of Jean-Paul Sartre to Simone de Beauvoir 1940–1963*, ed. Simone de Beauvoir (New York, 1993), 263.

10 **"group or clique"** Beauvoir, *The Prime of Life,* 444.

11 **"part of me"** Letter to Lucette Meurer, quoted in Todd, *Albert Camus*, 85.

11 **"expressed in images"** Albert Camus, "On Jean-Paul Sartre's *La Nausée*," in *Lyrical and Critical Essays* (New York, 1970) 199.

11 **"lavished and squandered"** Ibid., 199–200.

12 **"threshold of consent"** Ibid., 201.

12 **"impatient to see"** Ibid., 202.

12 **"Sartre's stories"** Albert Camus, "On Jean-Paul Sartre's *The Wall and Other Stories*," in *Lyrical and Critical Essays*, 204; translation modified.

12 **"own ends"** Ibid., 205.

13 **"truth of his work"** Ibid., 206; translation modified. The article appears in Camus, *Essais*, 1419–22.

13 **fall 1942** Beauvoir, *The Prime of Life*, 415.

13 ***Myth of Sisyphus*** The essay, published in the winter of 1943, was, in Annie Cohen-Solal's words, "Sartre's first occasion for boundless praise." Cohen-Solal, *Sartre: A Life* (London: Heinemann, 1988), 189. Sartre, we should bear in mind, was capable of withering criticism. At the exact moment Camus was praising him, he published his attack on François Mauriac, concluding famously: "God is not an artist. Neither is M. Mauriac." Jean-Paul Sartre, "François Mauriac and Freedom," in *Literary and Philosophical Essays* (New York, 1962), 25.

13 **"hopeless lucidity"** Jean-Paul Sartre, "Camus's *The Outsider*," in *Literary and Philosophical Essays*, 28–29.

13 **" 'a stranger' "** Ibid., 29, referring to Albert Camus, *The Myth of Sisyphus and Other Essays* (New York, 1955), 5; translation modified.

14 **"in the face"** Camus, Ibid., 9; translation modified.

14 **mentioned explicitly** Ibid., 10–11.

14 **"also the absurd"** Ibid., 11.

14 **"against the absurd"** Sartre, "Camus's *The Outsider*," 44.

14 **Nietzsche's forerunners** Ibid., 27.

14 **"classic temperament"** Ibid., 28.

15 **"classical dialectic"** Ibid., 4.

15 **"acid tone"** Albert Camus and Jean Grenier, *Correspondence, 1932–1960* (Lincoln, Neb., 2003), 66; 156; translation modified.

16 **literature and ideas** Todd notices Sartre's slap and not Camus's slight (*Albert Camus*, 155). He attributes the normal condescension of the genre to Sartre the person. For example, Todd calls the title of the review condescending, as if Sartre had some special animus toward Camus and "explication" were not a perfectly customary literary activity.

16 **Camus himself knew** See Camus's reference to the differences between the sky of Algiers and Le Havre in the indispensible French edition of Todd's *Albert Camus* (Paris, 1996), 495. The English version has cut about half of the text of the original; accordingly, I indicate the version to which I am referring by "F" or "E."

17 **education and culture** Anna Boschetti, *The Intellectual Enterprise: Sartre and Les Temps Modernes* (Evanston, 1988), chap.1.

17 **"Spaniards and Algerians"** "Conversations with Jean-Paul Sartre," in Simone de Beauvoir, *Adieux: A Farewell to Sartre* (New York, 1984), 266.

17 **"innumerable stories"** Ibid.

17 **down their relationship** Most of Sartre's and Camus's biographers follow their subjects' own retrospective tendency to play down their relationship. John Gerassi's interviews with Sartre and Beauvoir between 1970 and 1973, for example, present their memories filtered through their shared conclusions about Camus's moralism and withdrawal from politics and through Sartre's later political radicalism. "Sartre liked Camus" at first. They briefly enjoyed themselves together. Gerassi, *Jean-Paul Sartre*, 8. Gerassi presents Camus as a foil for Sartre's revolutionary commitment. Ronald Hayman mentions Camus frequently in the sections of his biography of Sartre dealing with the Occupation, the Resistance, the Liberation, and the postwar years, and then again at the time of the rupture. But he gives no sense of a strong attraction or an important relationship. Ronald Hayman, *Sartre: A Biography* (New York, 1987). And in his biography of Camus, Patrick McCarthy goes out of his way to scotch all such talk. "Camus was not specially drawn to Sartre. . . . Sartre felt a stronger attraction." Patrick McCarthy, *Camus* (New York, 1982), 183–84. His argument, developed at length, is that although "in 1943 Sartre could see in Camus a kindred spirit" (186), the two were not close, shared little, and that only briefly: "The Camus-Sartre relationship is misunderstood if one imagines either that there was a long period of friendship before the furious break or that the two men had much in common" (183). Cohen-Solal, however, helps focus the discussion of the years and months before they met by pointing to their appreciation of each other's writings. In his first article on Camus, Sartre, in Cohen-Solal's words, "sketches a sort of kinship that mesmerizes him." *Sartre*, 189.

17 **to each other** When they first met, Sartre and Camus "seemed to fall for one another," in Todd's words. *Albert Camus* (E), 173.; "Ils ont eu un coup de coeur l'un pour l'autre." *Albert Camus* (F), 336.

17 **so similar** Todd describes him as the "surly, meditative Camus, who could be heavy-handed though seductive, [and] came from the working class." *Albert Camus* (E), 173.

17 **a rationalist** As reported by Denis de Rougement to Cohen-Solal; see her *Sartre*, 233.

18 **"celebrating victory"** Beauvoir, *The Prime of Life,* 450.

18 **" 'is just right' "** Ibid., 444.

18 **Camus together** Cohen-Solal and Gerassi include the photograph, but Todd and Lottman, the only Camus biographers to include photographs, do not.

18 **"less expertly"** Beauvoir, *The Prime of Life,* 454.

19 **"and friendships"** Ibid., 444; translation modified.

19 **years later** See the discussion in my "Sartre's Last Words," in Jean-Paul Sartre and Benny Lévy, *Hope Now: The 1980 Interviews* (Chicago, 1996).

19 **rebuffed her** Camus told Arthur Koestler that she offered herself to him but he rejected her advance. Todd, *Albert Camus* (E), 231.

19 **"bluestocking, unbearable."** Ibid.; translation modified.

19 **his love life** Beauvoir gave the official version of this in *Force of Circumstance*, 52–53, but a much more revealing account in a letter to Sartre dated December 1945, in which she said she hoped the result would be a love affair: "If everything works out well, we'll go and spend a fortnight winter-sporting in February—he seemed really to like the idea too." Simone de Beauvoir, *Letters to Sartre* (New York, 1992), 392.

19 **protect Sartre** These conclusions emerge from my reading of Deirdre Bair's thorough and insightful *Simone de Beauvoir* (New York, 1990).

20 **was enormous** This is made clear by Beauvoir's interviews with Bair; ibid., 289.

20 **ugly genius** Beauvoir, *Letters to Sartre*, 377–78; for this discussion see Bair, *Simone de Beauvoir*, 290.

20 **"both wanted it"** Bair, *Simone de Beauvoir*, 292.

20 **"infatuation" with Camus** Ibid., 290.

20 **full life of his own** Ibid., 292.

20 **financial support** Since the mid-1930s Sartre and Beauvoir had together pursued tutelary and amorous relationships with attractive and intelligent students. Bair tells the story of the "family" in detail in *Simone de Beauvoir*, beginning in chapter 14.

20 **Sartre-Beauvoir family** Ibid., 291.

20 **"better known"** Beauvoir, *Adieux*, 267.

21 **central frustration** See Todd, *Albert Camus* (E), 174.

21 **between the two men** McCarthy reports (185), and Beauvoir confirmed to Bair (287 and 641), that at the beginning of their friendship they went out together to seduce young women.

21 **"distinction" like Sartre** Bair, *Simone de Beauvoir*, 291.

21 **"bit jealous"** Gerassi, *Jean-Paul Sartre*, 181.

21 **to go sour** Ibid.

21 **"watch out"** Sartre, *Quiet Moments in a War*, 263.

21 **Camus's women** Beauvoir, *Adieux*, 268.

21 **"More intelligent"** Todd, *Albert Camus* (E), 174.

22 **"Combat movement"** Beauvoir, *Prime of Life*, 444.

CHAPTER TWO

24 **"bad mess"** Simone de Beauvoir, *A Transatlantic Love Affair* (New York, 1998), 108; translation modified.

24 **"Liberation period"** Beauvoir, *Prime of Life,* 470.

24 **mass audience** Cohen-Solal, *Sartre,* 216.

24 **"collective life"** Jean-Paul Sartre, "Un Promeneur dans Paris insurgé," quoted in Michel Contat and Michel Rybalka's exhaustive *The Writings of Jean-Paul Sartre*, vol. 1, *A Bibliographical Life* (Evanston, 1974), 101.

24 **"a new order"** Ibid., 103.

24 **"bullets were fired"** Beauvoir, *A Transatlantic Love Affair,* 108.

24 **"Sartre's supervision"** Michel Rybalka, personal communication, March 26, 2002.

24 **"too busy"** Bair, *Simone de Beauvoir*, 293. Contat and Rybalka list the articles in Sartre's bibliography, mentioning Beauvoir's "collaboration"; *The Writings of Jean-Paul Sartre*, 1:100.

24 **these days** Lottman, *Albert Camus,* 328.

25 **"direction of history"** This is cited, without an explicit reference, by Todd, *Albert Camus* (E), 188; translation modified. The original reads: "Tu as mis ton fauteuil dans le sens de l'histoire!" (F) 355.

25 **effortlessly assumed** For the structural impediments in his original ideas, see Ronald Aronson, *Jean-Paul Sartre: Philosophy in the World* (London, 1981).

25 **the young Arab** See Conor Cruise O'Brien, *Albert Camus of Europe and Africa* (New York, 1970).

25 **Arab nationalism** Lottman, *Albert Camus,* chap. 12.

26 **"their destiny"** Albert Camus, "Misère de la Kabylie," in *Essais*, 938.

26 **"beasts has begun"** Albert Camus, *Notebooks 1935–1942* (New York, 1996), 141.

26 **"new carnage"** Albert Camus, "La Guerre," September 17, 1939, *Essais,* 1376.

26 **"are our positions"** Albert Camus, "Notre Position," November 6, 1939, in *Essais,* 1380. Editor Roger Quilliot, after placing *réclamant* (demanding) in the original, notes that it is obviously a typographical error and proposes replacing it with *respectant* (respecting), which I have done.

27 **peace in the barracks** McCarthy, *Camus,* 125.

27 **collaboration with the Germans** Jean-Pierre Azéma, *From Munich to the Liberation, 1938–1944* (Cambridge, UK, 1984), 95–96.

28 **by the Resistance** McCarthy, *Camus*, 177.

29 **"cut the pages"** Beauvoir, *The Prime of Life,* 112.

29 **Jew or a Freemason** For the controversy over whether Sartre took the post of a dismissed Jewish professor, see Ingrid Galster, *Sartre, Vichy et les Intellectuels* (Paris, 2001), and Jacques Lecarme, "Sartre et la question antisémite," *Les Temps modernes,* June–July 2000.

29 **"Lycée Pasteur anyway"** Gerassi, *Jean-Paul Sartre*, 175.

30 **voted to empower** See Azéma, *From Munich to the Liberation,* 50–58.

30 **Germans and Vichy** Claude Bourdet describes the social background of the first resisters in *L'Aventure incertaine* (Paris, 1975) 21–36.

30 **"full of pamphlets"** Gerassi, *Jean-Paul Sartre*, 176.

30 **dissolved the group** The story is told by Cohen-Solal, *Sartre*, 159–78 and Gerassi, *Jean-Paul Sartre*, 174–79.

30 **war: he wrote** See Cohen-Solal, *Sartre*, 159–215.

30 **"eyes underground"** Pierre Piganiol, quoted in Cohen-Solal, *Sartre*, 198.

31 **Occupation was over** Published in *Les Temps modernes,* June–July 2000, and *Sartre Studies International* 8, no. 2 (Fall, 2002).

31 **"8:00 or 9:00"** Gerassi, *Jean-Paul Sartre*, 176.

31 **"resistant who wrote"** Interview with Gerassi; see Cohen-Solal, *Sartre*, 190.

31 **"walk[s] on air"** Jean-Paul Sartre, *The Flies*, in *No Exit and Three Other Plays* (New York, 1949), 62, 61.

31 **"burden on [his] shoulders"** Ibid., 93. See Aronson, *Jean-Paul Sartre*, 181–85.

32 **during the Occupation** "Theâtre de circonstance," *Action,* November 24, 1944, 13.

32 **"battle more effective"** Albert Camus, preface to the Italian edition of *Letters to a German Friend*, in *Resistance, Rebellion, and Death* (New York, 1974), 3.

32 **"misery of this world"** "Letters to a German Friend," in *Resistance, Rebellion, and Death,* 8.

32 **"right was on our side"** Ibid.

32 **"human dignity"** Ibid.

32 **"defeat is inevitable"** Ibid., 9.

32 **"mother country"** Ibid., 14.

33 **"be courageous"** Ibid., 10; translation modified.

34 **solidity and weight** See Aronson, *Jean-Paul Sartre*, 181–84.

34 **violence against civilians** Albert Camus, "Reflections on the Guillotine," in *Resistance, Rebellion, and Death.*

34 **powerfully repelling it** For Sartre, see Pierre Verstraeten, *Violence et éthique* (Paris, 1972).

34 **honor and importance** Continuing the Camus-Sartre battle, Todd points out: "Almost all active members of the Resistance were given false papers. Sartre never had any." *Albert Camus* (E), 178.

34 **got to the printers** Lottman, *Albert Camus*, 318–19.

35 **at Ravensbrück** Todd, *Albert Camus* (E), 181.

35 **she swallowed it** McCarthy, *Camus*, 194.

35 **village of Ascq** "For Three Hours They Massacred Frenchmen," in *The Republic of Silence*, A. J. Liebling, ed. (New York: Harcourt Brace, 1947), 425–30.

35 **"stage of the war"** He says: "je suis entré dans son groupe de résistance, peu avant la Libération," which suggests much more than simply attending a single meeting. Beauvoir, *La Cérémonie des adieux* (Paris: Gallimard, 1981), 342; *Adieux,* 267; translation modified.

35 **"run over in the street"** This is the recollection of Jacqueline Bernard, cited by Todd, *Albert Camus* (E), 179. Also see Lottman, *Albert Camus,* 319.

35 **"bursting out in the streets"** Albert Camus, "Le Combat continue . . . ," in *Essais,* 1520; Albert Camus, *Between Hell and Reason* (Hanover, NH 1991), 39; 21 août 1944, *Camus à "Combat"* (Paris, 2002), 140.

35 **"called a Revolution"** Lottman, *Albert Camus,* 331.

36 **"individuals, if not societies"** Bourdet, *L'Aventure incertaine,* 310.

36 **"even being killed"** Herbert Lottman, *The Left Bank: French Writers, Artists, and Politics from the Popular Front to the Cold War* (Boston, 1982), 169.

36 **"would write *afterwards*"** Albert Camus, "Introduction aux *Poésies Posthumes* de René Leynaud," in *Essais,* 1474.

36 **"died alongside me"** Ibid., 1464.

36 **Camus the resister** McCarthy, *Camus*, 177.

37 **made long afterward** It was restated in my interview with Francis Jeanson in Claouey, France, July 23–25, 2001. See Ronald Aronson and Francis Jeanson, "The Third Man in the Story," *Sartre Studies International* 8, no. 2 (2002).

37 **political detachment** See Gerassi, *Jean-Paul Sartre*, 183. We will return to this in chapter 3.

37 **"degraded and vilified"** Jean-Paul Sartre, "Reply to Albert Camus," in *Situations*, 71; translation modified.

37 **"myself included"** Ibid.

37 **"thirty years old"** Jean-Paul Sartre, "New Writing in France," *Vogue,* June 1945, 84.

38 **"not a damn thing we can do!"** Jean Daniel, *Le Temps qui reste: Essai d'une autobiographie professionelle* (Paris, 1984), 34; this is quoted slightly differently by Lottman, 391, whose translation I have otherwise used.

38 **"we loved you then"** Ibid., 72.

38 **"salvage the country"** Jean-Paul Sartre, "Paris under the Occupation," *Sartre Studies International* 4, no. 2 (1998): 11.

38 **for *Les Lettres françaises*** September 9, 1944, 1; reprinted in *Situations, III* (Paris, 1949) and translated widely, above all in Liebling, *The Republic of Silence.*

38 **"under the Occupation"** *La France libre* (London), November 15, 1944; reprinted in *Situations, III*, and translated in *Sartre Studies International,* Fall 1998.

39 **"An Apocalyptic Week"** In Michel Contat and Michel Rybalka, eds., *The Writings of Jean-Paul Sartre*, vol. 2, *Selected Prose* (Evanston, 1974).

39 **"human condition"** "La République du silence," *Les Lettres françaises,* September 7, 1944, 1; "The Republic of Silence," in *Sartre by Himself,*" a film directed by Michel Contat and Alexandre Astruc (New York, 1978), 55.

40 **"police—against Nazism"** "The Republic of Silence," 56–57.

40 **actively resisted** See Azéma, *From Munich to the Liberation,* 145–65.

40 **with our own hands** Sartre adds a note at this point: "If one had to find an excuse for the phenomenon of 'Collaboration,' it could be said that it was also an attempt to provide France with a future."

40 **"torture was real"** Sartre, "Paris under the Occupation," 8.

41 **inevitable frustration** See Aronson, *Jean-Paul Sartre*, 51–103.

41 **occupation, and struggle** "New men" were specifically called for in an article in the underground *Libérer et fédérer,* no. 30, October 1, 1944. See *Les Idées politiques et sociales de la résistance* (Paris: Presses Universitaires de France, 1954), 120–21.

42 **"adapted to the circumstances"** And also to include Michel Leiris; Sartre, *Quiet Moments in a War,* 264.

42 **"era with its ideology"** Ibid., 445.

CHAPTER THREE

43 **Gabriel Péri** A leading Communist journalist and member of the Party's Central Committee, Péri was arrested in May 1941 and executed as a hostage that December. In his final letter he wrote, "I will soon be going out to shape all the singing tomorrows."

43 **winning the war** See Jean-Pierre Rioux, *The Fourth Republic, 1944–58* (Cambridge, UK, 1987).

44 **"broadest sense"** Albert Camus, "Combat Continues . . . ," August 21, 1944, in *Between Hell and Reason*, 39; *Camus à "Combat,"* 140.

44 **June 1940** A September 1 editorial, attributed to Camus by Alexandre de Gramont, the editor of *Between Hell and Reason*, but not included in *Camus à "Combat,"* said that that the Resistance had awakened "society's dormant forces, which are the forces of the individual." A "new order" based on an "essentially humane" tradition was being established. "Politics is no longer dissociated from individuals. It is addressed directly by man to other men" ("Resistance and Politics," in *Between Hell and Reason*, 48).

44 **end of 1945** During this time, according to Beauvoir's retrospectively bitter comment, "that fallacious entity, the Resistance, no longer existed." *Force of Circumstance,* 43. Beauvoir reported that "in December 1945, Malraux mentioned it in the Chamber of Deputies and caused nothing but embarrassment, whereas a year earlier the mere word would have produced an automatic burst of applause." Ibid., 43–44. Her main explanation was that the Resistance had split apart. For a discussion of the fate of the Resistance see Rioux, *The Fourth Republic,* 188–92.

45 **values of the Resistance** Sartre and Camus have become so strongly identified with the Resistance that, for example, in discussing France in *The Intellectual Resistance in Europe* (Cambridge, MA, 1981), James D. Wilkinson refers primarily to the ideas and activities of the two.

46 **arm's length** See Boschetti, *The Intellectual Enterprise*, 171.

46 **"synthetic anthropology"** For a detailed account of the journal's content, see Howard Davies, *Sartre and "Les Temps modernes"* (Cambridge, UK, 1987).

46 **serious journal** Ibid., 143–70.

46 **"opening our mail"** Beauvoir, *Force of Circumstance,* 16.

46 **"talk of Paris"** Lottman, *Albert Camus,* 360.

47 **"representing *Combat*"** Beauvoir, *Force of Circumstance,* 17.

47 **"Arabia an Existentialist"** Ibid.; and Maurice Nadeau, *Combat,* October 30, 1945, 1.

47 **"makes of himself"** Jean-Paul Sartre, *Existentialism and Human Emotions* (New York, 1948), 15.

48 **"at us and whispered"** Beauvoir, *Force of Circumstance,* 39; translation modified.

49 **the postwar era** Cohen-Solal, *Sartre*, 256.

49 **nightclubs of Saint-Germain** Lottman, *The Left Bank*, 233; translation modified.

49 **"in a dozen languages"** Beauvoir, *Force of Circumstance,* 40.

49 **"It's not much"** Camus, *Notebooks 1942–1951* (New York, 1995), 118.

49 **"a misunderstanding"** Ibid.

49 **ruined by it** See Lottman, *Albert Camus*, 457.

49 **"for me, was hatred"** Quoted in Beauvoir, *Force of Circumstance,* 45.

50 **"complete clarity"** *Sartre by Himself*, 62.

50 **Café des Deux Magots** Beauvoir, *Adieux,* 271.

50 **"shouldn't go too far"** Beauvoir, *Adieux,* 266.

50 **his closest friend** Bair, *Simone de Beauvoir*, 298.

50 **staggering home** Lottman, *Albert Camus,* 389.

51 **"life and pleasure"** Ibid., 61.

51 **death sentence** Ibid., 29.

51 **"further from the Communists"** Ibid., 115–16.

51 **whom they did** Todd, *Albert Camus* (F), 213.

51 **"having with people"** Beauvoir, *Adieux,* 266.

51 **such as Francis Jeanson** Interview with Francis Jeanson, Claouey, France, July 23–25, 2001.

52 **"ten others"** "A guerre totale, résistance totale," *Camus à "Combat,"* 123.

52 **"praiseworthy actions"** Albert Camus, *The Plague* (New York, 1948), 120.

52 **"themselves to do it"** Ibid., 121.

53 **"the wheel again"** Ibid., 232–33.

53 ***Vogue* in July, 1945** This brief talk on "new writing in France" was, as Cohen-Solal put it (*Sartre*, 233), "a veritable ode to Camus."

54 **"no longer pertinent"** Jean-Paul Sartre, "New Writing in France," *Vogue,* June 1945, 84.

54 **moment in France** The *Vogue* translation renders *engagement* as "involvement."

See Jean-Paul Sartre, "Nouvelle littérature en France," *Oeuvres romanesques* (Paris, 1981), 1919.

54 **"limits of man"** Sartre, "New Writing in France," 85; translation modified.

55 **"submission to things"** Sartre explicitly linked "realism"—bending to the weight of events—to collaboration in his "Qu'est-ce qu'un collaborateur?" published that August in a French periodical in New York and later in *Situations, III.*

55 **"movements of society"** Sartre, "New Writing in France," 85.

56 **"what a fool"** Gerassi, *Jean-Paul Sartre*, 183; translation modified.

57 **"will be deliberate"** Jean-Paul Sartre, "Presentation aux *Temps modernes,*" *Situations, II* (Paris, 1948), 12–13.

57 **engaged literature** It had the interesting philosophical function of operating a transition between *Being and Nothingness* and Sartre's new radical political commitment. See Aronson, *Jean-Paul Sartre*, 122–41.

57 **absorbed in *Combat*** The draft was circulated in late 1944 when the two were very close, and Camus decided not to participate during this time. In fact, when the journal first appeared, in late October 1945, Camus was no longer so busy with *Combat.* As we will see in chapter 4, he virtually stopped writing editorials after June. By this time he had begun clearly to differentiate himself from Sartre.

58 **"mustn't judge him"** Albert Camus, "*La Conspiration* de Paul Nizan," in *Essais,* 1396.

58 **"drama of our time"** "Encounter with Albert Camus," May 10, 1951, in *Lyrical and Critical Essays*, 353.

58 **"where is the merit?"** Camus, *Notebooks 1942–1951,* 140–41.

58 **"serve capitalism"** Ibid, 141. In *What Is Literature?* Sartre would make much of the fact that he considered poetry exempt from his call for an engaged literature.

58 **"believe in history"** Albert Camus, "Interview à *Servir,*" in *Essais,* 1427.

58 **"absolute sense of the word"** Ibid., 1428.

59 **"conquers history"** Albert Camus, *Le Soir républicain,* September 17, 1939, in *Essais,* 1377.

59 **"triumphs in the end"** *Alger républicain*, May 23, 1939, in *Essais,* 1400; see Rosemary Gina Loveland's excellent discussion in "Antecedents of the Quarrel between Sartre and Camus," doctoral dissertation, University of California at Los Angeles, 1976, 132–33.

59 **time to time** Jean-Paul Sartre, "Albert Camus," 109–10.

59 ***Dialectical Reason*** See Ronald Aronson, "Sartre's Return to Ontology: *Critique de la raison dialectique II* Reflects on *L'Etre et le Néant,*" *Journal of the History of Ideas,* Winter 1987, and Aronson, *Sartre's Second Critique.*

60 **"called existentialists"** Albert Camus, "Non, je ne suis pas existentialiste . . ." in *Essais,* 1424; interview of November 15, 1945, "Three Interviews," in *Lyrical and Critical Essays,* 345.

60 **"in all of them"** Camus, *The Myth of Sisyphus,* 24.

60 **"all by himself"** Jean-Paul Sartre, "A More Precise Characterization of Existentialism," in *Selected Prose*, 156.

60 **"common with existentialism"** Beauvoir, *Adieux,* 266.

60 **mere misunderstanding** Nor was Hazel Barnes—one of the philosophers who first brought existentialism to the United States—wrong to refer to Camus as an existentialist in her memoirs. Hazel E. Barnes, *The Story I Tell Myself* (Chicago, 1997).

61 **"in a struggle with itself"** Alexandre Astruc, "Le Malentendu dissipé," *Action,* October 20, 1944, 9.

61 **"exercise of politics"** Albert Camus, "*Combat* rejects anticommunism," October 7, 1944," *Between Hell and Reason,* 61; *Actuelles, I,* in *Essais,* 274; *Camus à "Combat,"* 240.

61 **"faces Europe today"** "[Justice and Freedom]," in *Between Hell and Reason*, 52; September 8, 1944, in *Essais,* 271; "Justice et liberté," in *Camus à "Combat,"* 176.

61 **"level of savagery"** "[On the bombing of Hiroshima]," in *Between Hell and Reason*, 110; *Camus à "Combat,"* 110; August 8, 1945, in *Essais.*, 291; *Camus à "Combat,"* 569.

62 **"discovery of the century"** "La bombe atomique a son histoire," *l'Humanité,* August 8, 1945, 1.

62 **"factual information"** Albert Camus, "Crise en Algérie," *Actuelles, III,* in *Essais,* 943; May 13–14 1945, *Camus à "Combat,"* 501.

62 **subsequent reprisals** In spring, 1945 Camus spent three weeks in Algeria, from April 18 to May 7 or 8, which suggests that he had returned to Paris before learning of the May 8 Sétif massacre of French settlers and the air and naval bombardment that followed in reprisal. In any case, he was moved by events to contribute an eight-part series in *Combat*, beginning on May 13 and the editorial of June 15. See *Camus à "Combat,"* 497–534, 549–52.

62 **prison and repression** *Essais,* 957; *Camus à "Combat,"* 527.

62 **as many Arabs** Other estimates of Arab dead have ranged from 6,000 to 45,000.

62 **"and not bombs"** "Pour mettre fin aux troubles d'Algérie," *l'Humanité,* May 15, 1945, 1.

62 **system as such** Months earlier *l'Humanité had* decried the second-class status of Algerian Muslims, and had spoken vaguely of getting rid of "the colonial regime and its corrupt agents." "Waldek Rochet nous expose: Pourquoi les musulmans d'Algérie ont créé 'Les Amis de la Démocratie,' " *l'Humanité,* October 10, 1944, 1–2. After Sétif, however, it spoke of "the union of the Muslim population with the people of France against their common enemies"—the mostly fascist one hundred landlords, and their actively fascist friends in the Algerian administration. "Un communiqué officiel qui n'apporte rien," *l'Humanité,* May 16, 1945, 2.

62 **Arabs as equals** The French and Algerian Communist parties, for example, were far behind Camus on this score. *L'Humanité* spoke of "Hitlerite" provocations. See Todd, *Albert Camus* (F), 378.

62 **"have become pure"** Camus ["France must reject concessions and complacency"], *Between Hell and Reason*, 75; *Camus à "Combat,"* October 29, 1944, 296.

63 **"strengthens human dignity"** "[On purity and realism]," in *Between Hell and Reason*, 77; November 4, 1944, *Camus à "Combat,"* 313.

63 **a half-century later** This is nicely captured by McCarthy, *Camus*, 204.

63 **years that followed** Rioux, *The Fourth Republic,* part one.

63 **factories and workers** For a discussion see Michael Scriven, *Sartre and the Media* (London, 1993).

64 **life and mythology** Ibid., 31–32.

64 **cast of his thinking** See, for example, his sketch of a theory of knowledge, written in 1947–48 and only published posthumously, Jean-Paul Sartre, *Truth and Existence* (Chicago, 1992).

64 **create our own values** I say this to counter the fashionable misreadings of Sartre. See, for example, Tony Judt, *Past Imperfect: French Intellectuals 1944–1956* (Berkeley, 1992), and, more recently, Judt, *The Burden of Responsibility: Blum, Camus, Aron and the French Twentieth Century* (Chicago, 1998).

64 **a book in 1946** Jean-Paul Sartre, *Anti-Semite and Jew* (New York, 1948).

64 **authoritarian violence** Jean-Paul Sartre, "Childhood of a Leader," in *The Wall and Other Stories* (New York, 1948); Sartre, *Nausea.*

64 **"classless society"** Sartre, *Anti-Semite and Jew,* 149.

64 **"no place for it"** Ibid., 150.

64 **Sartre's philosophy** This was during a lengthy comment following Sartre's *Existentialism is a Humanism,* 107.

65 **as late as 1954** His 1954 adaptation of *Kean* explores an actor's decision to abandon the imaginary and live in the real world.

CHAPTER FOUR

66 **"until March 1947"** Beauvoir, *Force of Circumstance,* 111.

67 **Juliette Gréco** Michel Rybalka, personal communication, October 2002.

67 **toward Merleau-Ponty** Beauvoir does, however, report that the two attended the same meetings in 1947, aimed at forming a non-Communist left-wing group, until the effort broke up under the pressure of Camus and André Breton to include opposition to the death penalty in the list of their causes. *Force of Circumstance,* 148.

69 **in small groups** And that resistance became substantial. See Irwin Wall, *French Communism in the Era of Stalin* (Westport, 1983), 20–23.

69 **Central Committee meetings** Ibid., 131.

69 **yesterday's line** See especially Jean-Paul Sartre, *The Age of Reason* (New York, 1947) and *Troubled Sleep* (New York, 1950).

70 **"more vassalized"** André Gide, *Retour de l'U.R.S.S.* (Paris, 1993), 436.

71 **democratic mantle** François Furet, *The Passing of an Illusion* (Chicago, 1999) 209–65. Furet implies that the primary concern of all who joined the Communist Party should have been the worst features of the Soviet Union. But he ignores the Left's struggle against capitalism and bourgeois society—those who subscribed to it with intelligence and good faith are immediately dismissed as being under the spell of the "illusion" Furet is dissecting.

71 **a new society** Edgar Morin, *Autocritique* (Paris, 1959).

71 **enemy of the Revolution** Maurice Merleau-Ponty, *Humanism and Terror* (Boston, 1969).

71 **real-world embodiment** See Ronald Aronson, *After Marxism* (New York, 1995), part one.

72 **"draws the tides"** Jean-Paul Sartre, *Search for a Method* (New York, 1963), 20, 21.

72 **French imperialism** Taking this fact into account (as do none of the current postmortems on the evils of Communism) situates both sides in their life-and-death conflict and necessarily extends any moral retrospective to include both sides. From 1917 to 1991, the great story of the twentieth century was the struggle between Communism and capitalism. Locked in battle, partisans of both sides stressed only their own side's good, the other side's evil. The Left made much of slavery, colonialism, racism and racial apartheid, the genocide of native peoples, poverty amid plenty, and the mechanized murder of modern warfare. The Right dwelled on the horrors of Communism. In the climate of total ideological war, before "peaceful coexistence" was even thinkable, neither side admitted its own evils—except as something in the past, or as attributable to the other side, or as shortcomings remediable within the "democratic" or "socialist" framework (each side rejected even the other's main self-descriptive term).

The point is not simply the psychological one that conflict creates a natural tendency to self-justification as well as selective moral bookkeeping. At war, our sides' faults are kept from the other side, which would certainly use them as a weapon if it could. Just as Communist violence cannot be fully understood without being placed in the context of what the Left saw as bourgeois violence, from Verdun to Hiroshima, so Communist moral blindness can only with great distortion be treated all by itself, lifted from the life-and-death struggle with bourgeois society and capitalism's own historical crimes. To demand symmetry between the two is artificial, but it is no less myopic to ignore capitalism's evils in discussing Communism's.

As much as anything it was the total war between the two systems that shaped either side's responses—the downright lying, the one-sidedness, the moral blindness, the selective amnesia. Certainly modern democratic capitalist societies, committed as they have been to equality and productivity, have constantly generated criticism for not being sufficiently egalitarian and for their economic irrationalities, especially the narrow concentration of wealth. And such disaffection quite naturally envisions a socialist alternative—a society more democratic, more equal, more collectivist but no less modern or productive. The Communist idea had enormously wide currency, in spite of the brutal realities of Stalinism, because of its achievements and because the struggle shaped the Left's commitment and thus its vision. See Ronald Aronson, "Communism's Posthumous Trial," *History and Theory,* Spring 2003.

72 **"God that failed"** Prepared by Richard Crossman, a British Labour Member of Parliament, its authors were André Gide, Richard Wright, Ignazio Silone, Louis Fischer, Stephen Spender, and Arthur Koestler. Crossman, ed., *The God that Failed* (New York, 1950).

73 **"hide the absurd"** Camus, *The Myth of Sisyphus*, 67.

74 **German agent** Jean-Paul Sartre, David Rousset, Gérard Rosenthal, *Entretiens sur la politique* (Paris, 1949), 72–78.

74 **contribute to *LLF*** In his history of the publication, presented in the first post-Liberation issues in September 1944, Claude Morgan recalled a detail that has never been mentioned since: both Sartre and Camus were at *LLF*'s organizing meeting at Edith Thomas's Paris apartment in January 1943, five months before they met face to face. Camus's single contribution, which reflected his critical, independent direction, occurred while *LLF* was still underground. He entered into a controversy in April and May 1944 with Morgan and poet Paul Eluard, both Communists, over how severely to judge a former Vichy official, Marcel Pucheu, who defected to the Free French in North Africa. In an article scheduled (along with an article by Sartre) for the April issue, Camus claimed that Pucheu "lacked imagination" for authorizing executions of Resistance members. Editor Morgan held back Camus's article for a month in order to first present the leadership's much harsher position on Pucheu; then in May he published Camus's article and Eluard's disagreement.

74 **writers to the Germans** Lescure is quoted in Todd, *Albert Camus* (E),182; another version of the story, told by Sartre, had Marcenac mention Sartre alone, attacking him for his studies of German philosophers. See Cohen-Solal, *Sartre*, 263; Rosenthal et al., *Entretiens sur la politique*, 7.

74 **"money's privilege"** Albert Camus, ["*Combat* wants to make justice compatible with freedom"], in *Between Hell and Reason*, 57; *Camus à "Combat,"* October 1, 1944, 223.

75 **"fight a war"** ["France must both make a revolution and fight a war], in *Between Hell and Reason*, 68; *Camus à "Combat,"* October 21, 1944, 274.

75 **distinct from Marxism** ["Everyone in France is Socialist"], in *Between Hell and Reason*, 83; *Camus à "Combat,"* November 23, 1944, 347.

75 **open-ended way** ["*Combat* rejects anticommunism"], in *Between Hell and Reason*, 59–61; *Camus à "Combat,"* October 7, 1944, 237–41.

75 **political principles** Already in a September editorial his endorsement of a deliberately vague use of "revolution" had a target: the "mental laziness" of those taking October 1917 as their model. ["The N.L.M.'s first public meeting"], in *Between Hell and Reason*, 56 (translation modified); *Camus à "Combat,"* September 19, 1944, 199. He was immediately answered in the "Read Elsewhere" column of the Communist weekly *Action*: Hadn't Hitler borrowed Marxism's words, likewise emptying them of their content? "Not anyone who wants to can make a revolution." "Lu Ailleurs," *Action,* September 23, 1944, 3.

75 **stress on "purity"** Camus's argument is summarized in "Revue de la presse libre," *Combat,* November 3, 1944, 2. Guéhenno answered in *Le Figaro,* attacking not the PCF but the kind of realism that would use any means for achieving good ends. Camus editorialized in support of Guéhenno, speaking broadly for purity and against the party's kind of political realism.

75 **unemployed worker** Pierre Hervé, "Ils vont au peuple," *Action*, November 24, 1944, 3.

75 **"passionate of his generation"** Alexandre Astruc, "le roman américain," *Action*, October 7, 1944, 8.

76 **contemporary theme** Alexandre Astruc, "De l'absurde à l'espoir," *Action*, October 13, 1944, 5.

76 **intelligent review** Claude-Edmonde Magny, " 'Huis clos' par Jean-Paul Sartre," *Les Lettres françaises*, September 23, 1944, 7.

76 **prisoners' readings** "Lectures de prisonniers," *Les Lettres françaises*, December 2 and 3, 1944. It is worth noting that, under attack for promulgating the thought of a Nazi philosopher in an outrageous article in the Christian-Democratic newspaper *L'Aube* (Gaston Rabeau, "Nazisme pas mort?" October 21, 1944, 1), Sartre did not mention the seminars he led at the Stalag on *Being and Time.*

76 **"out of season"** George Adam, "Hors de Saison," *Les Lettres françaises*, October 7, 1944, 7.

76 **"adventure of the mind . . ."** Camus, "Pessimism and Courage," in *Resistance, Rebellion, and Death*, 58, where the date is presented incorrectly (translation modified); *Camus à "Combat,"* November 3, 1944, 309.

76 **"assurance they show"** Camus, *Resistance, Rebellion, and Death*, 59; *Camus à "Combat."*

76 **being attacked in *Action*** It was a new form of obscurantism, a "springboard for an attack on scientific thought, on clear and distinct thought." Its stress on "existence" and the general theme of "concrete situation" were said to evade our specific historical and social situation. Roland Caillois, "Georges Politizer et la critique des mythes," *Action*, October 20, 1944, 5.

76 **"absurd criticisms"** Jean-Paul Sartre, "A More Precise Characterization of Existentialism," in *Selected Prose*, 155.

77 **"point by point"** Ibid., 156.

77 **conciliatory note** He falsely claimed doing both of these in Sartre et al., *Entretiens,* 72.

77 **do just this** See ibid., 71–73.

77 **school of thought** Indeed, *Action*'s review of Beauvoir's *Pyrrhus and Cineas* linked her with both Sartre and Camus. See Gaétan Picon, "Pyrrhus et Cinéas," *Action*, February 2, 1945, 6.

78 **comradeship of the Liberation** In the months afterwards, Beauvoir's first philosophical work was reviewed positively by *Action* and *LLF,* while a Camus lecture was summarized in *Action* without comment. In April 1945, Francis Ponge called attention in *Action* to a "brilliant" article elsewhere by Sartre where "his critique develops step by step with Marxist analysis." F[rancis] P[onge], "Chronique des chroniques et revue des revues," *Action*, April 27, 1945, 8; Sartre's article was in *Confluences.*

78 **"machine against Marxism"** Henri Lefebvre, " 'Existentialisme' et Marxisme," *Action*, June 7, 1945, 8.

79 **"universally known"** Pierre Hervé, "Où amène le 'résistantialisme'?" *Action*, June 29, 1945, 3.

79 **for over a year** Albert Camus, ["The purge is a failure and a disgrace"], in *Between Hell and Reason,* 112–13; *Camus à "Combat,"* August 30, 1945, 594–97.

80 **nuclear weapons** Beauvoir, *Force of Circumstance,* 111.

80 **falling apart** In the fall of 1944, Camus had predicted that the Resistance fraternity would endure for a long time. See McCarthy, *Camus*, 212.

80 **"leader of a school"** Dominique Aury, "Qu'est-ce que l'existentialisme? Bilan d'une offensive," *Les Lettres françaises*, November 24, 1945.

80 **"existentialist offensive"** The first of these consisted of interviews with Sartre, Pierre Emmanuel, and Henri Lefebvre, giving the latter the last word. The second started with Francis Ponge, a Communist and a friend of Sartre's, followed by Beauvoir and Gabriel Marcel. Aury, "Qu'est-ce que l'existentialisme? November 24, 1945, December 1, 1945.

80 **work and dialogue** Sartre, in Sartre et al., *Entretiens,* 73.

80 **"reconciliation raised"** Ibid., 73–74.

80 **totally opposed** René Scherer, "La Querelle de l'existentialisme: ou bien . . . ou bien . . . ," *Les Lettres françaises,* December 21, 1945, 12.

80 **existentialism as a "sickness"** Roger Garaudy, "Jean-Paul Sartre: Un faux prophète," *Les Lettres françaises,* December 28, 1945, 1. See also Garaudy's *Literature of the Graveyard* (New York, 1948).

81 **"through the mud"** Sartre, in Sartre et al., *Entretiens,* 74.

81 **"stubborn" scientism** Jean-Paul Sartre, "Materialism and Revolution," in *Situations*, 255.

81 **had read Marx** He did not make much progress in his reading, even in the 1949 republication of the article in book form. See Aronson, *Jean-Paul Sartre*, 120.

81 **"class consciousness"** Sartre, "Materialism and Revolution," 236.

82 **"received no reply at all"** September 1, 1945, *Camus à "Combat,"* 598.

82 **"modern madness"** Albert Camus, *Notebooks 1942–51* (New York, 1996), 128.

82 **"communication open"** Ibid., 104.

82 **"adversary is right"** Ibid., 105.

82 **"or in dialogue"** Sometime between November 1945 and March 1946; ibid., 124.

82 **"minimum they need"** Ibid., 110.

82 **"witnesses of freedom"** Ibid.; translation modified.

83 **"think in that case"** Ibid.

83 **"without God"** Ibid., 120.

83 **"put to death"** Ibid., 121.

83 **"according to ideas"** Ibid., 113.

83 **"literature of commitment"** Ibid., 122.

83 **"equilibrium" of nature** Ibid., 124.

84 **"not only social"** Ibid., 122.

84 **toward Marxism** Especially in his *Critique of Dialectical Reason.* See Aronson, *Sartre's Second Critique.*

85 **access to power** Control over the military was removed from the Communist Defense Minister; see Wall, *French Communism*, chaps. 2 and 3.

85 **"change its motion"** Camus, *Notebooks 1942–51*, 129.

85 **"burst into our group"** Beauvoir, *Force of Circumstance*, 108.

85 **with each other** Todd, *Albert Camus* (E), 231.

86 **vision for the Left** Arthur Koestler, *The Yogi and the Commissar and Other Essays* (New York, 1946), 193.

86 **"under the sun"** Beauvoir, *Force of Circumstance*, 108–9.

87 **"few nuances"** Ibid., 109–10.

87 **"previously sacrificed"** Ibid., 110.

87 **real-life Bukharin** See Robert C. Tucker and Stephen F. Cohen, eds. *The Great Purge Trial* (New York, 1965) 119–20; and Cohen, *Bukharin and the Bolshevik Revolution* (Oxford, 1980).

87 **lifeless, and ideological** Irving Howe, *Politics and the Novel* (Greenwich, CT, 1967), chap. 8.

88 **face of Stalinism** See Stephen Cohen, "Bukharin's Fate," *Dissent,* Spring 1998; Ronald Aronson *The Dialectics of Disaster* (New York, 1984). 116–17.

88 **been Stalinized** On this see Isaac Deutscher, "The Ex-Communist's Conscience," in *Heretics and Renegades* (London, 1955).

88 **historical value** Camus, *Notebooks 1942–51,* 145–46.

88 **Soviet deportations** Ibid., 146.

88 **"suppress it"** See Lottman, *Albert Camus*, 433, Todd, *Albert Camus* (F),

427–28.

89 **"I'll think about it"** Camus, *Notebooks 1942–51,* 147–48.

89 **"articles for *Combat*"** Ibid., 143.

89 **"Toward Dialogue"** I have used, with modification, the Dwight Macdonald translation of *Neither Victims nor Executioners* (New York, 1960), which first appeared in *Politics,* July–August 1947, and was reprinted frequently. Another translation is available in *Between Hell and Reason.*

89 **"that leads to it"** *Neither Victims nor Executioners*, 9–10; translation modified.

89 **legitimize murder** Ibid., 12.

89 **"millions of men"** Ibid., 16.

90 **"by all nations"** Ibid., 6.

90 **"is not legitimate"** Ibid., 8.

90 **"national framework"** Ibid., 12.

90 **"lies and murder"** Ibid., 18; translation modified.

91 **power and influence** See Wall, *French Communism*, chap. 3; Rioux, *The Fourth Republic*, 112–32.

91 **"shadowy ends"** *Neither Victims nor Executioners*, 21.

91 **"compromise with murder"** Ibid., 21.

92 **"that is, for men"** Ibid., 19.

92 **"closed up and morose"** Simone de Beauvoir, "Conversations with Jean-Paul Sartre," *Adieux,* 267.

92 **"delights of violence"** Jean-Paul Sartre, "Merleau-Ponty," in *Situations*, 175.

92 **"Left-Bank revolutionaries"** McCarthy, *Camus*, 218.

92 **to no avail** This was not the end of the story regarding Camus and Merleau-Ponty. A second conflict involving them took place two years later over what was to become the major public meeting organized by the Rassemblement Démocratique Révolutionnaire, formed with Camus's support by Sartre, David Rousset, and Gérard Rosenthal. This effort to create a non-Communist Left movement in France reached its high point on December 13, 1948, at a meeting featuring Sartre, Camus, André Breton, Richard Wright, and Carlo Lévi. According to one of the organizers, "Merleau-Ponty had been invited but Camus had intervened. He would not attend the meeting if Merleau was present. And since Camus was much more popular, we had to choose him over Merleau" (Cohen-Solal, *Sartre*, 305). Beauvoir does, however, report that the two attended the same meetings in 1947, aimed at forming a non-Communist Left group, until the effort broke up under the pressure of Camus and André Breton to include opposing the death penalty on the list of their causes. Beauvoir, *Force of Circumstance,* 148.

92 **"proper province"** This formulation first appears in *Neither Victims nor Executioners*, 22.

93 **contemporary events** Bridgeland, "Antecedents of the Quarrel Between Sartre and Camus," chap. 2.

93 **"position of victim"** "L'Europe devient de plus en plus pesante . . . La peur est générale. Je viens de prendre position dans un série d'articles, 'Ni victimes ni bourreaux.' J'ai compris combien on pouvait être solitaire dès qu'on tenait un certain langage. . . . On ne peut pas déserter et pourtant la position de victime ne me plaît pas." This passage is cut from the English translation but appears in Todd, *Albert Camus*, 428 (F).

CHAPTER FIVE

95 **"combat, and solidarity"** Sartre, "A More Precise Characterization of Existentialism," 160.

95 **"(myself included)"** Sartre, "My Dear Camus," in *Situations,* 71.

95 **"class solidarity"** Ibid., 73.

95 **"being exemplary"** Ibid., 68.

97 **"concrete case"** Sartre, *What Is Literature?* (New York, 1965), 283–84; translation modified.

97 **"extreme situations"** Ibid., 217.

97 **"oppression forever"** Ibid., 246–47.

98 **"discovering our historicity"** Ibid., 247.

98 **"the working class"** Ibid.

98 **argument for socialism** Aronson, *Jean-Paul Sartre*, 122–53.

98 **"universal idyll"** Or perhaps he had in mind Sartre's distinction between poetry and prose. Camus, *Notebooks 1942–1951,* 171.

98 **"doors or windows"** Sartre, *What Is Literature?* 247.

98 **"conservative nationalism"** Ibid., 248.

98 **"literary craft"** Ibid., 250.

98 **"he's a fascist"** Ibid., 251.

100 **twenty-one lives** Rioux, *The Fourth Republic*, 112–32.

100 **preparing for civil war** Beauvoir, *Force of Circumstance*, 141.

100 **"in the press"** Ibid., 138–39.

101 **human excrement** Simone de Beauvoir, *A Transatlantic Love Affair*, 94.

101 **canceled the series** See Scriven, *Sartre and the Media*, 72–86.

101 **"International Opinion"** Contat and Rybalka, *The Writings of Jean-Paul Sartre*, 1:205.

101 **"battlefield ruins or both"** Jean-Paul Sartre, "First Call to International Opinion," in Contat and Rybalka, *The Writings of Jean-Paul Sartre*, 1:205. The Camus draft reads: "For Europe war means either occupation by Soviet armies or battlefield ruins." *Essais,* 1577.

101 **"social liberation"** Contat and Rybalka, *The Writings of Jean-Paul Sartre*, 1:206. Camus had said that "it is social liberation itself which is retarded by the preparation for war." *Essais,* 1577.

101 **"can be avoided"** Sartre: "La guerre *peut* être évitée." Michel Contat and

Michel Rybalka, *Les Ecrits de Sartre* (Paris, 1970), 206. Camus: "La guerre n'est pas inévitable." *Essais,* 1578.

102 **money (Camus)** Camus, "Nous disons," in *Essais*, 1578–79.

102 **"order" (Sartre)** Sartre, "First Call to International Opinion," 206–7.

102 **"modest and sincere"** Beauvoir, *A Transatlantic Love Affair,* 72; translation modified.

102 **later become** See, for example, ibid., 77.

102 **in good humor** Ibid., 76; translation modified.

102 **"against the wall"** Beauvoir, *Force of Circumstance,* 140.

103 **"by our fear"** Ibid.

103 **hide his black eye** Beauvoir, *A Transatlantic Love Affair,* 143–44.

103 **" 'and still work?' "** Ibid., 140.

103 **"social revolution"** Ibid., 197.

104 **from the CIA** This was widely suspected at the time and has recently been confirmed. See Frances Saunders, *The Cultural Cold War: The CIA and the World of Arts and Letters* (New York, 2000).

104 **to South America** Bair, *Simone de Beauvoir*, 372; Beauvoir, *A Transatlantic Love Affair,* 141.

104 **full human beings** Jean-Paul Sartre, "Avoir faim c'est déjà vouloir être libre," *Caliban,* no. 20, October 1948.

104 **"system of government"** Albert Camus, "Démocratie exercice sur la modestie," *Caliban,* no. 21, November 1948.

105 ***La Gauche*** Albert Camus, "Réflexions sur une démocratie sans catéchisme," *La Gauche,* July 1948.

105 **Hugo did at first** See Jean-Paul Sartre, Pierre Victor, Philippe Gavi, *On a raison de se révolter* (Paris, 1974).

105 **its performances** See for example "C'est Sartre qui a les mains sales," *Les Lettres françaises,* April 8, 1948, 1.

106 **has been rewritten** Afterwards Sartre was at great pains to control the performances of the play. In *Force of Circumstance*, 152, Beauvoir writes that the Party's "internal difficulties were exposed to people who were looking at it from outside with animosity. They gave the play a meaning which it did, in fact, have for them. It was for this reason that Sartre refused several times to let it be acted in other countries."

106 **"what I meant to say"** Contat and Rybalka, *The Writings of Jean-Paul Sartre*, 1:193.

106 **"create a movement"** Beauvoir, *Force of Circumstance,* 176; in the original, these sentences are in italics.

107 **"not support it"** Ibid., 177; again, the original is in italics. This happens to be the period in which Sartre was preparing "Materialism and Revolution" for publication in book form. Interestingly enough, new footnotes indicate that he has been reading Marx. See Aronson, *Jean-Paul Sartre*, 120.

107 **could not accept** Ibid., 167–71.

107 **"from poverty"** Camus, "Première réponse," in *Essais,* 357. In these letters some of the remaining themes of *The Rebel* emerged and with a pronounced leftist tinge. Camus declared himself not to be nonviolent (because violence is inevitable) but only against any "legitimation of violence" (ibid., 355). Refusing to align himself with East or West, he once again stressed the threat of nuclear war as the decisive historical issue, and rejected the "politics of power" because social emancipation was inconceivable amid nuclear rubble (ibid., 1577). He agreed that suppressing war required suppressing capitalism ("I wouldn't mind seeing it"; ibid., 360), but he would not accept either war or the victory of Communism as a means of eliminating capitalism. As far as Marxism was concerned, he accepted "a certain critical aspect" of it and, echoing his conversation about *Dirty Hands* with Sartre, noted that Marx loved men—"real living ones, not those of the second generation" (ibid., 361). Today's Marxists, lost in "the sclerosis of dogma," were guilty of the "rationalist weakness" of preferring theory to reality. They reflected that "long tragedy of contemporary intelligence that can only be summarized by writing the history of European pride." The "divinization of man," "the conquest of totality," and a "messianism without God" inseparable from domination—these were his targets in his work-in-progress.

107 **"future justice"** Ibid., 362.

107 **"killing everything"** Ibid., 363.

107 **"nothing but hot air"** Beauvoir, *Force of Circumstance,* 171.

108 **support for the movement** Cohen-Solal, *Sartre*, 309.

108 **prospect of success** Lottman, *Albert Camus*, 451; see, however, Todd, *Albert Camus* (F), 453–54.

108 **became divisive** For example, Camus the artist now seemed sharply opposed to Sartre the philosopher. See Todd, *Albert Camus* (F), 493.

108 **"reaching a break"** Beauvoir, *Adieux*, 267.

108 **"found disagreeable"** Ibid., 268.

109 **"politics separated us"** Ibid.

109 **weekly lunch** Todd, *Albert Camus* (F), 492.

109 **"frequent but warm"** Ibid.

109 **"much in conversation"** Beauvoir, *Adieux,* 268.

110 ***The Rebel*** Albert Camus, *The Rebel* (New York, 1956) 164–73.

110 **"with their lives"** Albert Camus, *The Just Assassins, Caligula, and Three Other Plays* (New York, 1958), 296.

110 **"of our friendship"** Beauvoir, *Force of Circumstance*, 196.

110 **" 'with one stone' "** Ibid.

110 **"null and void"** Ibid., 269.

110 **"values as a Communist"** Maurice Merleau-Ponty, "The U.S.S.R. and the Camps," in Merleau-Ponty, *Signs* (Evanston, IL, 1964) 268.

111 **"known to us"** Ibid., 269.

111 **" 'will believe them' "** Beauvoir, *Force of Circumstance,* 231–32.

112 **"subsequent development"** Ibid., 233.

112 **"rethink man"** Jean-Paul Sartre, "Faux Savants ou Faux Lièvres," in *Situations, VI* (Paris, 1964), 66.

112 **mentor, left off** Jean-Paul Sartre, "Merleau-Ponty," in *Situations*, especially 174.

112 **"I will fight it"** Jean-Paul Sartre, *The Devil and the Good Lord* (New York, 1960), 148–49.

113 **"collective struggle"** Beauvoir, *Force of Circumstance*, 242.

113 **"Sartre conceived him"** Ibid., 243.

114 **to be a value** According to Beauvoir, the critics misunderstood: "They all made the enormous error of supposing that Goetz, by committing the murder at the end of the last scene, was returning to Evil. In fact, Sartre was once more confronting the vanity of morality with the efficacy of *praxis.*" But Beauvoir was so absorbed in Sartre's problematic that she missed the impact of what happened on stage. Ibid., 242.

114 **"that was required"** Ibid., 261.

114 **"beyond recall"** Ibid., 242.

CHAPTER SIX

116 **"clear-cut choices"** Beauvoir, *Force of Circumstance,* 262.

116 **"what one thinks"** Todd, *Albert Camus* (E), 300.

116 **"man in revolt"** See Donald Lazere, *The Unique Creation of Albert Camus* (New Haven, 1973), 139, commenting on the weaknesses of Bower's translation.

116 **established by revolution** Camus, *Essais,* 1747.

116 **"experience to the idea"** Albert Camus, "Remarque sur la Révolte," in *Essais,* 1689.

117 **Camus's footsteps** See, for example, Bernard-Henry Lévy, *Barbarism with a Human Face* (New York, 1980), and, in the series under Lévy's editorship, Claudie and Jacques Broyelle, *Les Illusions retrouvées: Sartre a toujours raison contre Camus* (Paris, 1982).

118 **political spectrum** Furet mentions Camus approvingly in *The Passing of an Illusion* (547, n. 31).

118 **received his due** See Catherine Camus's introduction to *The First Man* (New York, 1996). This is also the tone, in a more aggressive register, of Todd's *Camus,* and U.S. reviews have followed suit. See Tony Judt, "The Stranger," *New Republic,* February 16, 1996, 25.

118 **defeated, side** See Gerassi, *Jean-Paul Sartre*, 33–35, 180–83.

118 **of the Cold War** The question contains an ambiguity: the war is over but one side has won, the other lost. If we are free from the Cold War's deforming pressures, isn't it because one side was right, the other wrong? For "Cold War

vindicationists"—see Allen Hunter, Introduction, in *Rethinking the Cold War* (Philadelphia, 1998)—Camus was correct, and thus *Man in Revolt* is gilded by a retrospective wisdom and prescience. Tony Judt makes just this case in *The Burden of Responsibility.* But this approach makes two leaps from fact to value that are not self-evident but, rather, need to be demonstrated—first, that the West won *because* it was better, and second, that Camus's argument and the stance underlying it was itself morally as well as intellectually correct. As Judt demonstrates in *The Burden of Responsibility* as well as in *Past Imperfect,* today's champions of the West are far from performing the careful analysis required to demonstrate these conclusions, and might be better seen as latter-day Manichaeans settling old scores. See Aronson, "Communism's Posthumous Trial."

118 ***creates* values** In his first brief essay, "Remarque sur la Révolte" (in *Essais,* 1682–97), published in 1945, Camus mentioned *Being and Nothingness* twice. There Camus gave the impression of an open, exploratory intellectual process. But this vanished from the revision that became chapter one of *Man in Revolt.* The 1945 essay was alive and provocative, proposing and exploring new and politically rich ways of seeing reality, unencumbered by the deductive heaviness weighing on *Man in Revolt.* In the essay, Camus genuinely examined the differences between revolt and revolution. The question had not yet been settled, and the rest of reality had not yet been reorganized around his political, moral, and philosophical opposition of the two. We can see the book's preoccupations imposed upon Camus's earlier ideas by a sentence inserted in a section of the earlier article and near the beginning of the chapter "Historical Rebellion." The original sentence was: "While even the collective history of a movement of revolt is always that of a commitment without a factual solution, of an obscure protest that is committed neither to system nor to reasons, revolution is an attempt to model the act on an idea, to fashion the world within a theoretical framework." *Essais,* 1689. Judgment was not yet final, oppositions were not yet fixed. To these ideas of the mid-1940s, Camus now adds an undemonstrated premise underlying *Man in Revolt:* "That is why rebellion kills men while revolution destroys both men and principles." Camus, *The Rebel*, 106; translation modified.

118 **"therefore we are"** Ibid., 22.

118 ***The Plague*** Camus, *Notebooks 1942–1951,* 91–94.

119 **"logic of nihilism"** Camus, *The Rebel,* 98.

119 **"heart of the ephemeral"** Ibid., 10.

119 **"what we are"** Ibid., 252.

120 **but its apologists** See Eric Werner, *De la violence au totalitarisme* (Paris, 1972), 109.

120 **Sartre still was** Ian Birchall argues that Camus is taking aim at Marxism as distinct from Communism, but his otherwise outstanding summary of the Sartre-Camus conflict takes one early remark from Camus about the dangers of

anti-Communism and ignores Camus's later systematic hostility toward Communism—in order to distinguish, as Camus did not, between Communism and Marxism. I believe that I have shown just the opposite in chapter four. See Birchall, "Camus contre Sartre."

120 **Russians invaded** Beauvoir, *Force of Circumstance,* 231–32.

120 **on many levels** The "Stalinist vulgate" motivated thousands of Party intellectuals and was itself an amalgam of fact, logic, faith, and feeling. See Morin, *Autocritique,* 53–60.

121 **"armed camps"** Camus, *The Rebel*, 226.

121 **"reign of justice"** Ibid., 56.

121 **overthrow God** Ibid., 60.

121 **"murderers into judges"** Ibid., 3.

121 **again as large** According to Gil Elliot, *Twentieth Century Book of the Dead* (New York, 1972), by 1972 the figure was 100 million in total; according to Stéphane Courtois's introduction to *The Black Book of Communism* (Cambridge, MA, 1999) this is the number killed by Communism alone. See my discussion of the controversy over the numbers in Aronson, "Communism's Posthumous Trial."

122 **"it is justified"** Camus, *The Rebel,* 3.

122 **"taste for the superhuman"** Ibid., 4.

123 **"annex all creation"** Ibid., 103.

123 **"advocates of Nietzsche"** Ibid., 76.

123 **"is always right"** Ibid., 137.

123 **"completely alien"** Ibid., 193.

123 **final three chapters** It is also visible in a randomly chosen chapter, "Nihilism and History," in the following topic sentences taken from a little more than four pages: "Human insurrection, in its exalted and tragic forms, is only, and can only be, a prolonged protest against death, a violent accusation against the universal death penalty" (*The Rebel,* 100). "Essentially, then, we are dealing with a perceptual demand for unity" (101). "Therefore, if the rebel blasphemes, it is in the hope of finding a new god" (ibid.). "It is not the nobility of rebellion that illuminates the world today, but nihilism" (102). "Progress, from the time of Sade up to the present day, has consisted in gradually enlarging the stronghold where, according to his own rules, man without God brutally wields power" (ibid.). "To kill God and to build a Church are the constant and contradictory purpose of rebellion" (ibid.). "The nineteenth century, which is the century of rebellion, thus merges into the twentieth, the century of justice and ethics, in which everyone indulges in self-recrimination" (ibid.). "Nihilism, which, in the very midst of rebellion, smothers the force of creation, only adds that one is justified in using every means at one's disposal" (101–2).

123 **eccentric quality** Because of these various weaknesses, many Camus scholars, in retrospect, came to see *Man in Revolt* as Camus's worst book. See McCarthy,

Camus, 248; Todd is uncomfortable with it as well—see his discussion, *Albert Camus* (E), 300–306.

123 **totalitarian societies** Paul Berman, for example, takes Camus's diagnosis of Western civilization as the starting point for his discussion of the sinister appeal of contemporary terrorism. He calls for a "liberal American interventionism" against what he describes as these latest forms of totalitarianism. See his *Terror and Liberalism* (New York, 2003).

124 **and fully Western** For a discussion of these tendencies in Marxism, see Ronald Aronson, *After Marxism* (New York, 1995), 87–123.

124 **trends to come** The postmodernists never wholly embraced Camus as their predecessor, no doubt because of his central metaphysical concern with absurdity and revolt, and his penchant for sweeping judgments and reductive analyses—which differentiates *Man in Revolt* from far less ambitious, more descriptive, and currently more fashionable books like Adorno and Horkheimer's *Dialectic of Enlightenment.* But in many ways *Man in Revolt* was a model "genealogy" describing the appearance of intrinsic contradictions of the modern spirit, and Camus's vision of self-limiting revolt is a prescient articulation of a post-Marxist and postmodern radical politics.

124 **for social justice** See Ronald Aronson, *After Marxism*, 181–257. See also Broyelle and Werner, *Les Illusions retrouvées*, as well as Jeffrey C. Isaac, *Arendt, Camus, and Modern Rebellion* (New Haven, 1992); and the best exposition of Camus's politics, David Sprintzen, *Camus, a Critical Examination* (Philadelphia, 1988).

124 **" . . . is relative"** Camus, *The Rebel,* 284.

124 **settle everything** Werner, *De la violence au totalitarisme*, 51.

124 **"and of risk"** Camus, *The Rebel,* 289.

124 **"committed on principle"** Ibid., 286.

124 **"which codify it"** Ibid., 292.

125 **"form of violence"** Ibid.

126 **three separate texts** I have in mind *Anti-Semite and Jew, Truth and Existence* (Chicago, 1992), and *Notebooks for an Ethics* (Chicago, 1992).

126 **"rule or insanity"** Camus, *The Rebel,* 249.

128 **book on the Martin case** Jean-Paul Sartre, *L'Affaire Henri Martin* (Paris, 1953).

128 **"*Communists and Peace*"** Sartre, "Merleau-Ponty," 198; translation modified.

128 **104 deputies** Jean-Paul Sartre, *The Communists and Peace* (London, 1969), 38.

128 **"a few faces"** Ibid.

128 **"voted in vain"** Ibid., 40.

129 **"have given it"** Ibid., 44.

129 **"due to him"** Ibid., 46; translation modified.

129 **"manifestation of violence"** Ibid., 48.

129 **"brawl into murder"** Ibid.

129 **"original violence"** Ibid.

130 **"oppressed condition"** Ibid., 49.

130 **"own excesses"** Ibid.

CHAPTER SEVEN

132 **"contemporary world"** Camus, *The Rebel,* 87–88.

132 **Camus and Sartre** Sartre, *What Is Literature?* 175–92, especially 185, n.1.

132 **"into the crowd"** André Breton, "The Second Surrealist Manifesto," in *Manifestoes of Surrealism* (Ann Arbor, 1969); translation modified.

133 **"conservatism and conformism"** André Breton, "Sucre jaune," *Arts,* October 12, 1951, 1.

133 **"view on Lautréamont"** Camus, "Révolte et conformisme," in *Essais,* 731.

133 **"not the case"** Ibid., 732.

133 **"would be there"** Camus, "Révolte et servitude," in *Essais,* 754.

133 **"thing itself"** Breton, "Dialogue entre Albert [*sic*] Breton et Aimé Patri à propos de '*l'Homme Révolté*' d'Albert Camus," *Arts,* November 16, 1952, 3; quoted in Mark Polizzotti, *The Revolution of the Mind: The Life of André Breton* (New York, 1995), 576.

134 **sapped his energy** See Todd, *Albert Camus* (E), 306.

134 **"scornful" and "immodest")** François Di Dio, "Voilà le temps de l'innocence," *Le Soleil Noir: Positions,* no. 1 (February 1952).

134 **used toward him** Lottman, *Albert Camus*, 525.

134 **"remarkable study"** See ibid., 526.

134 **"than an article"** Pierre Lebar, "Revue des revues," *L'Observateur,* April 24, 1952.

134 **"free Left"** Camus, "Révolte et servitude," 749. After showing his irritation that *La Nouvelle Critique* had only now reviewed his book "after having meditated for seven months," Camus transparently used the occasion to refute Hervé point for point without mentioning Lebar by name. This ill-tempered performance was made even more disturbing by coeditor Roger Stéphane's placating reply to Camus. *L'Observateur,* June 5, 1952, 18.

135 **"more people"** Camus, "Entretien sur la révolte," in *Essais,* 738.

135 **"the dilemma"** Beauvoir, *Force of Circumstance,* 264.

135 **writers' summaries** See Lottman, *Albert Camus*, 500.

136 **bristled easily** Beauvoir, *Force of Circumstance,* 260.

136 **least be "polite"** Marie-Pierre Ulloa, *Francis Jeanson: Un intellectuel en dissidence de la Résistance à la guerre d'Algérie* (Paris, 2001), 105.

136 **one reviewer** Claude Mauriac, *La Table Ronde,* no. 48 (December 1951), 98–109.

136 **had to have known about** Jeanson had published a very measured criticism of Camus in "Pirandello et Camus à travers *Henri IV* et *Caligula,*" *Les Temps modernes*, November 1950. Ulloa takes this as the decisive demonstration that

Sartre could not have been "innocent" in handing the job to Jeanson (*Francis Jeanson,* 105).

137 **"much in conversation"** Beauvoir, *Adieux,* 268.

137 **"say to him"** Beauvoir, *Force of Circumstance,* 259.

137 **"my conversion"** Sartre, "Merleau-Ponty," 198; translation modified.

138 **after his death** On this issue, see Ronald Aronson, "Sartre's Last Words," introduction to Jean-Paul Sartre and Benny Lévy, *Hope Now* (Chicago, 1996).

138 **"quite willing"** Beauvoir, *Adieux,* 268.

138 **were married** Interview with Francis Jeanson, Claouey, France, July 23–25, 2001.

138 **"mind's vocation"** Francis Jeanson, "Albert Camus ou le mensonge de l'absurde," *Revue Dominicaine,* no. 53 (February 1947), 107. Other articles appeared in *La France Intérieure* in January and February and in the Bordeaux daily newspaper *Sud-Ouest* in May. See Ulloa, *Francis Jeanson,* 104–5.

139 **"to will it"** Ibid.

139 **"than the Marxists"** Francis Jeanson, "Somebody called Sartre," in *Sartre and the Problem of Morality* (Bloomington, 1980), 235. Jeanson's itinerary is described by Ulloa, *Francis Jeanson.*

139 **French workers** Francis Jeanson, "Définition du prolétariat?" *Esprit,* July–August 1951, 20.

139 **"difficult to do"** Beauvoir, *Adieux*, 269

140 **against itself** William L. McBride, "The Polemic in the Pages of *Les Temps modernes* (1952) concerning Francis Jeanson's Review of Camus' *The Rebel*," in *Sartre and Existentialism*, vol. 8: *Sartre's French Contemporaries and Enduring Influences* (Hamden, CT, 1997).

140 **"ineffectual attitudes"** Camus, *The Rebel*, 136.

140 **"diverse forms"** Francis Jeanson, "Albert Camus ou l'âme révoltée," *Les Temps modernes,* May 1952, 2071. This and subsequent translations are by Adrian von den Hoven.

140 **"sure of itself"** Ibid., 2072.

140 **"Red Cross morality"** Ibid.

140 **"history and economics"** Ibid.

141 **"infrastructures"** Ibid.

141 **"professions of faith"** Camus, "Révolte et servitude," 754. This and subsequent translations are by Adrian van den Hoven.

141 **"revolutionary ideologies"** Ibid., 2078–9.

141 **"rebellious Slave"** Ibid., 2084–85.

141 **"perfect society"** Ibid., 2085.

141 **"collective agony"** Ibid., 2086.

143 **author's position** Camus, "Révolte et servitude," 754.

143 **editorial interference** See Roger Quilliot's comment, *Essais,* 1719.

143 **"reality and history?"** Ibid., 758.

143 **or malevolence** Ibid., 762.
144 **"lied to them"** Ibid., 760–61.
144 **"to my face"** Ibid., 756.
145 **"I was wrong"** Ibid., 761–62.
145 **"direction of history"** Ibid., 772.
146 **"implicit dogma"** Ibid., 764–65.
146 **"Caesarian socialism"** Ibid., 765.
146 **"concentration camps"** Ibid., 767.
146 **"of the matter"** Ibid., 768.
146 **"it entails"** Ibid.
146 **"Communist state"** Ibid., 770.
147 **"about Stalinism"** Ibid., 771.
147 **"end it today . . ."** Jean-Paul Sartre, "Reply to Albert Camus," in *Situations*, 71; this and subsequent translation modifications are by Adrian van den Hoven.
148 **"when necessary"** Ibid., 71–72.
149 **"between you"** Ibid., 79.
149 **"wounded vanity"** Ibid., 71.
149 **"your Thermidor"** Ibid., 72; translation modified.
149 **"pedestal with you"** Ibid., 73; translation modified.
149 **"jury weep"** Ibid., 74.
150 **"Chief Prosecutor"** Ibid., 77–78, translation modified.
150 **"how frivolous"** Ibid., 81, translation modified.
150 **"praise you"** Ibid., 86–87.
151 **"thus tyrants"** Ibid., 66.
151 **"few of them"** Ibid., 90.
152 **"live them"** Ibid., 91.
152 **"class solidarity"** Ibid., 97.
152 **"classical tradition"** Ibid., 95.
152 **"condemn, Sisyphus"** Ibid., 91.
152 **"(myself included)"** Ibid., 95; translation modified.
153 **"struggle of man"** Ibid., 98; translation modified.
153 **"in Billancourt"** Ibid.
153 **"accessible to all"** Ibid., 99.
153 **"afraid to change"** Ibid., 101.
153 **"oppressed masses"** Ibid., 100.
153 **"against history"** Ibid.
153 **"became a mirage"** Ibid., 101; translation modified.
154 **"be forgotten"** Ibid., 105; translation modified.

CHAPTER EIGHT

155 **"the other stupid"** Todd, *Albert Camus* (E), 311; translation modified.

156 **"concerns all of us"** R[oger] S[téphane], "Le Débat Sartre-Camus," *L'Observateur*, September 4, 1952, 19.

156 **common enemies** Lottman, Albert Camus, 532.

156 **political ideology** "Une Polémique entre MM. Albert Camus et Jean-Paul Sartre," *Le Monde,* September 13, 1952.

156 **"essential hope"** "Le Différend Camus-Sartre," *Combat,* September 18, 1952, section A.

156 **"dealing with life"** Ibid.

156 **"petty nastiness"** Pierre de Boisdeffre, *Le Monde,* September 24, 1952; Bernard Frank, "Un Redressment littéraire," *L'Observateur,* September 25, 1952, 18.

156 **"He's too little"** Quoted in Todd, *Albert Camus* (E), 312.

157 **first place** Ibid.

157 **little luck** Ibid.

157 **around and marched out** Dionys Mascolo and Renée Gallimard, quoted by Lottman, *Albert Camus*, 533.

157 **"too closely"** Todd, *Albert Camus* (E), 311; translation modified.

158 **"Good luck to them!"** The entire quotation appears in Todd, *Albert Camus* (F), 573–74.

158 **"mind, is disloyal"** Albert Camus, *Carnets III: mars 1951—decembre 1959* (Paris, 1989), 63.

158 **"less pleasant"** Sartre, "Interview at Seventy," 63; translation modified.

159 **"slow in coming"** Camus, *Carnets III,* 30.

159 **never shake *that*** Was this true only insofar as Camus was on the receiving end, allowing him, for example, to foolishly anticipate a positive review of *Man in Revolt* in spite of its challenge to Sartre? Was he one of those people who, professing loyalty, above all demanded it from others while failing to show it themselves? This aspect of friendship was severely tested during the Algerian War as more and more of his Algerian friends concluded that France had to withdraw completely. See for example, Daniel, *Le Temps qui reste,* 75, 95.

159 **their disagreement** Interview with Camus's friend from *Combat,* Jean-Bloch Michel, quoted in Lottman, *Albert Camus*, 534.

159 **love story** Todd, *Albert Camus* (E), 312.

160 **"speak about it"** Ibid., 313; translation modified.

160 **"for martyrdom"** Camus, *Carnets III,* 62.

160 **"look seedy"** Ibid.

160 **"pharisees of justice"** Ibid., 63.

160 **"pieces of silver"** Ibid., 64.

160 **"road of many"** Lottman, *Albert Camus*, 538.

160 **which he prized** According to Lottman he kept them "carefully wrapped in a large package." Ibid.

161 **"and neutralized"** The correspondence occurred in November 1952. Quoted in Todd, *Albert Camus* (E), 314.

161 **"that magazine"** Albert Camus, "Défense de la liberté," in *Essais,* 777, translated in Lottman, *Albert Camus*, 541; translation modified.

161 **soften it** Jean Grenier to Albert Camus, December 26, 1952, "Correspondance Albert Camus–Jean Grenier," in *Oeuvres complètes d'Albert Camus*, vol. 9 (Paris, 1983) 354–57; Camus and Grenier, *Correspondence, 1932–1960,* 157–58.

162 **"mystification"** Albert Camus, "Défense de *L'Homme révolté,*" in *Essais,* 1708–9; this and subsequent translations are by Adrian van den Hoven.

162 **"in this world"** Ibid., 1708.

162 **"with policemen"** Ibid.

162 **I believed on trial** Ibid., 1705.

162 **"lived experience"** Ibid., 1709.

162 **leads to servitude** Ibid., 1710.

162 **"literary society"** Ibid.

162 **"and resist it"** Ibid., 1711.

163 **"degrade it"** Ibid., 1714.

163 **"enough for me"** Ibid.

163 **disagreement with Sartre** Almost fifty years later Francis Jeanson read Camus's "Défense de *L'Homme révolté*" for the first time. He considered it much clearer and more direct than *Man in Revolt* but containing the same tendency for Camus to elevate himself above the world. Interview with Francis Jeanson.

163 **"without flinching"** Camus, *Carnets III,* 102.

164 **"calf of realism"** Sartre, "Albert Camus," 110.

164 **"at this moment?"** Ibid.,109; translation modified.

165 **"what he thought"** Todd, *Albert Camus* (E), 415.

165 **last good friend** Jean-Paul Sartre, "Self-Portrait at Seventy," in *Life/Situations,* 63–64.

165 **separate ways** Todd, *Albert Camus* (E), 415–16.

166 **united as a class** See Aronson, *Jean-Paul Sartre*, 218–25. It is worth noting that Sartre's embrace of Communism was criticized by non-Party Marxists Claude Lefort and Ernst Mandel.

166 **Henri Martin** Sartre's contribution was published in "Le cas exemplaire d'Henri Martin," January 17, 1952, *Les Lettres françaises,* 2.

166 **commonplaces** Elsa Triolet, "Le Grand Jeu," *Les Lettres françaises,* June 14, 1951, 7.

166 **"protect peace"** Claude Morgan, "Les intellectuels devant leurs responsabilités," *Les Lettres françaises,* September 18, 1952, 4.

166 **"last summer"** Georges Sadoul, "Respectueuse? . . . Ou irrespectueuse?" *Les Lettres françaises,* October 8, 1952, 9.

167 **attack on them** At their moment of reconciliation at Vienna, Dominique Desanti could not help saying that *Dirty Hands* had wounded her personally. See her book *Les Staliniens* (Paris, 1975), 250.

167 **"cause of peace"** Contat and Rybalka, *The Writings of Jean-Paul Sartre*, 1:191.

167 **"and names"** Excerpted in ibid., 271; translation modified.

167 **"stuff on us again"** "Intervention de M. Jean-Paul Sartre," December 12, 1951, in ibid., 272.

168 **"world's peoples"** Ibid.

168 **"reconciliation at home"** Ibid.

168 **freely and openly** See ibid., 270–79.

168 **"Le Figaro"** Ibid., 273.

169 **"on gallows"** Camus, *Carnets III,* 70.

169 **"efficiency"** Quoted in Todd, *Albert Camus* (E), 314.

169 **"war of extermination"** Sartre, "Mad Beasts," in *Selected Prose,* 208; translation modified.

169 **"your own bomb"** Ibid., 210.

169 **"Berlin tragedy"** Albert Camus, "Berlin-Est, 17 juin 1953," in *Essais*, 1772.

170 **"pro-Western agitator"** Ibid., 1771–72.

171 **"wherever it occurs"** Contat and Rybalka, *The Writings of Jean-Paul Sartre*, 1:285.

171 **"socialist leaders"** Sartre, "Merleau-Ponty," 293–94.

171 **slight hope** In this analysis of his political evolution toward the Communists, written in 1961 after Merleau-Ponty's death, Sartre shows how his own ideas developed from those of his colleague. The theme in question was developed by Merleau-Ponty in the 1950 editorial on the Soviet camps done in his and Sartre's name as editors of *Les Temps modernes.* See Sartre, "Merleau-Ponty," 265–66.

172 **"most of its orders?"** Sartre, *The Communists and Peace,* 123.

172 **"I follow them"** Sartre, "Merleau-Ponty," 268–69.

172 **"reign of the human"** Ibid., 269; translation modified.

173 **"weight in the world"** Jean-Paul Sartre, *Kean*, in *The Devil and the Good Lord and Two Other Plays* (New York, 1960), 189.

173 **"real acts"** Ibid.; translation modified.

174 **"feel for them"** Camus, *Carnets III,* 85.

174 **"and to progressives"** Ibid., 90.

174 **climate of the time** Ibid., 95.

174 **"enough for me"** Ibid., 101–2.

174 **"to be insulting"** Ibid., 102.

175 **"to the future"** Camus, "L'Artiste et son temps," in *Essais,* 804.

175 **"now on, creation"** Camus, *Carnets III,* 103.

CHAPTER NINE

176 **Maria Casarès** Todd, *Albert Camus* (E), 318.

176 **make a difference** See Todd, *Albert Camus* (F), 584–94.

177 **"how to write"** Albert Camus, letter of August 7, 1954, quoted in *Essais,* 1491.

177 **as "vegetating"** Todd, *Albert Camus* (F), 592.

177 **return to writing** "Lettre à Gillibert," in Albert Camus, *Théâtre, Récits, Nouvelles* (Paris, 1974), xxxvi.
177 **"blotting paper"** To Jeanne Polge, Todd, *Albert Camus* (E), 321.
177 **Soviet life** Contat and Rybalka, *The Writings of Jean-Paul Sartre*, 1:302.
177 **"pushing it"** Sartre, *The Communists and Peace,* 170; translation modified.
178 **"My Dear Camus"** And as he was first described by Jeanson's play on words in his title "Albert Camus ou l'âme révolté," referring to Hegel's "beautiful soul" being revolted by the present. See chapter 7 above.
178 **toward Camus** Camus, *The Rebel,* 298–99.
178 **"in the back"** *Carnets, III,* 111.
178 **"all over again"** Ibid., 113.
179 **"way one breathes"** Camus, *Carnets III,* 146–47; quoted in Todd, *Albert Camus* (E), 323; translation modified.
179 **"Judge-penitents"** Camus, *Carnets III,* 147.
179 ***The Mandarins*** Beauvoir, *The Prime of Life,* 267.
180 **"resemble us at all"** Simone de Beauvoir, *The Mandarins* (New York, 1991), 586.
180 **"fanaticism in work"** Beauvoir, *Force of Circumstance,* 269.
181 **"beginning to diverge"** Ibid., 268–69.
181 **partisans insist** Todd describes it as a "fierce exercise in the denigration of Camus." *Albert Camus* (E), 323.
181 **better place** See Terry Keefe, *Simone de Beauvoir: A Study of Her Fiction* (New York, 1982), 181–99.
181 **like Algren** Bair, *Simone de Beauvoir,* 428.
182 **"insulting repudiations"?** Beauvoir, *The Mandarins,* 428.
182 **Sartre-Camus break** When Henri's book is published, the young woman he later marries, Nadine, criticizes him in Jeanson's language: "The whole right is covering you with flowers; it's embarrassing." Ibid., 416. Paula dismisses his style as "tediously classical." Ibid., 523. And Henri, sounding like Sartre criticizing Camus, talks about how delighted conservatives were about the Soviet work camps: "The Right used the camps to discredit the Communists, as if it was completely justified in doing so. As soon as you talk about exploitation, unemployment, famine, they answer you with 'and how about the slave labor camps.' If they didn't exist, they would have invented them." Ibid., 494. At least three other phrases are lifted from statements by Jeanson, Sartre, and Camus; see 416, 428, and 490.
182 **"slime on my back"** Todd, *Albert Camus* (E), 323.
182 **"with a sewer"** Ibid., 325.
183 **"ideas of morality"** *Sartre by Himself*, 78.
183 **"through his work"** Ibid., 88.
183 **"write anymore"** Lottman, *Albert Camus*, 571.
184 **"congenital impossibility"** Camus, *Carnets III,* 150.

184 **totalitarian methods** Ibid.

184 ***L'Observateur*** It started with what Camus regarded as that journal's misuse of a letter he had sent in support of editor Roger Stéphane, who had been jailed for publishing material deemed harmful to the war effort in Indochina. In addition, *L'Observateur* had criticized Camus, former editor of the austere *Combat,* for succumbing to the new commercial style of journalism of *L'Express* and its fashionable editor, whom Servain-Schreiber had recruited from *Elle.*

184 **"pitted me against Sartre"** Albert Camus, "Le Vrai débat," in *Essais,* 1760.

184 **"carried out"** Ibid.

184 **"passion for freedom"** Ibid., 1760–61.

185 **"resemble them"** Ibid., 1760.

185 **three years earlier** J.-M. Domenach, "Camus-Sartre Debate: Rebellion vs. Revolution," *Nation,* March 7, 1953, 202–3.

185 **"gates of cemeteries"** Quoted in Camus, *Essais,* 1710.

185 **"problem of our movement"** Albert Camus, "Réponse à Domenach," in *Essais,* 1753.

185 **"so is Domenach"** Ibid., 1752.

186 **"I will die"** Ibid., 1740.

186 **"principles of Islam"** Alistair Horne, *A Savage War of Peace* (New York, 1977), 95.

187 **"today's tragedy"** Albert Camus, "Terrorisme et répression," *L'Express,* July 9, 1955, 4.

187 **"northern cities"** Ibid.

187 **"in humiliation"** Ibid.

187 ***"colonized people"*** Albert Camus, "L'Avenir algérien," in *Essais,* 1873.

187 **"their personality"** Albert Camus, "Misère de la Kabylie," in *Essais,* 903–38.

188 **lead to a solution** Albert Camus, "L'Absente," in *Essais,* 969–70.

188 **brought together** Albert Camus, "La Table ronde," in *Essais,* 971–72.

188 **lead to dialogue** Albert Camus, "Premier novembre," in *Essais,* 981–82.

189 **"common soil"** Albert Camus, "Appeal for a Civilian Truce," in *Resistance, Rebellion, and Death,* 133.

189 **"Algerian tragedy"** Ibid., 134.

189 **"foreign ambitions"** Ibid., 140.

189 **"xenophobic madness"** Ibid., 135.

189 **"before reality"** Ibid., 141.

189 **"suffer terror"** Ibid., 142.

190 **their slogans** "M. Albert Camus lance un appel pour une trève en Algérie," *Le Monde,* January 24, 1956, 4

190 **three-fourths Arab** "Le meeting du Comité des intellectuels contre la poursuite de la guerre," *Le Monde,* January 29, 1956, 4.

190 **from the FLN** The meeting is described by James D. Le Sueur, *Uncivil War: Intellectuals and Identity Politics during the Decolonization of Algeria* (Philadelphia, 2001), 36–44.

191 **civilian truce** "Camus's rhetoric was never so hollow as when he called for pity for civilians. This was a war of populations against each other." Beauvoir, *Force of Circumstance,* 341.

191 **"innocent victims"** Jean-Paul Sartre "Colonialisme est un système," *Situations, IV* (Paris, 1964), 27.

191 **"subhuman of the Algerian"** Ibid., 43.

191 **"themselves by force"** Ibid., 44.

191 **"colonist is a colonist"** Cohen-Solal, *Sartre*, 369.

191 **"solution by force"** Sartre, "Colonialisme est un système," 47.

191 **"tender heart"** Ibid., 40.

191 **"colonial system"** Ibid., 48.

191 **"reformist mystification"** Ibid., 47.

191 **"daily struggle"** Ibid., 46.

191 **first be suppressed** Ibid., 40, 47.

191 **"help it die"** Ibid., 47.

191 **"colonial tyranny"** Ibid., 48.

192 **"fullest expression"** Albert Camus, *The Fall* (New York, 1957), v.

192 **"*racial* superiority"** Sartre, "Reply to Albert Camus," 79.

193 **"Tower of Babel"** Camus, *The Fall,* 4.

193 **"hides eczema"** Ibid., 5–6. For this line of analysis, and for many of the specific references, I am indebted to the groundbreaking work of André Abbou, "Les Structures superficielles du discours dans *La Chute* [*The Fall*]," *La Revue des lettres modernes,* 1970 no. 4; and Warren Tucker, "*La Chute*: Voie du salut terrestre," *French Review* 43, no.5 (April 1970).

193 **"before the court"** Camus, *The Fall*, 17.

193 **"how frivolous"** Sartre, "Reply to Albert Camus," 81.

193 **"well as I could"** Camus, *The Fall,* 87

193 **"could you be"** Sartre, "Reply to Albert Camus," 80.

193 **"in a way"** Camus, *The Fall,* 8–9.

193 **"being exemplary"** Sartre, "Reply to Albert Camus," 91.

193 **"an exemplar"** Camus, *The Fall,* 146.

193 **"culture has gaps?"** Ibid., 128.

194 **"superman"** Ibid., 27–28.

194 **"heart of hearts"** Ibid., 29.

194 **"by our friends!"** Ibid., 31.

195 **"line of vehicles"** Ibid., 53.

195 **"my embarrassment"** Ibid.

195 **"suddenly ceased"** Ibid., 70.

195 **"owe me this one"** Todd, *Albert Camus* (F), 637.

196 **"condemn, Sisyphus"** Sartre, "Reply to Albert Camus," 90–91; translation modified.

196 **"if you will"** Camus, *The Fall,* 54.

196 **"up to facts"** Ibid.

196 **"picture of myself"** Ibid., 54–55.

196 **"strike and conquer"** Ibid., 55.

196 **"on his knees"** Ibid., 56.

196 **"for judgment"** Ibid., 78.

196 **"moralizing and judging"** Ibid., 134.

196 **"on my shoulders"** Ibid., 137.

196 **"that it promises"** Todd, *Albert Camus* (E), 342; Camus, *Théâtre, Récits, Nouvelles,* 2035.

197 **"what I'm saying"** *The Fall,* 119.

197 **fighting evil** Gaétan Picon, *Mercure de France,* July 1956, 688–93.

197 **"deal of curiosity"** Beauvoir, *Force of Circumstance,* 349.

197 **"judge-penitent"** Camus, *The Fall,* 8.

197 **"issue of existentialism"** Albert Camus, Interview with Dominique Aury, *New York Times Book Review,* February 24, 1957, 36. Quoted in Lazere's *The Unique Creation of Albert Camus,* 189.

198 **"saw action"** Camus, *The Fall,* 121.

198 **"word, romantic"** Ibid., 122.

198 **"all the same"** Ibid., 125.

199 **"advocate of slavery"** Ibid., 131–32.

199 **"and my power"** Ibid., 132.

199 **"a few risks"** Ibid.

199 **"never in grace"** Ibid., 135.

199 **"comes along"** Ibid., 136.

199 **"you know that?"** Ibid., 14; translation modified.

200 **cowardice, and hypocrisy** Camus's most recent activities had been on behalf of a civilian truce in Algeria—does the novel also express a pied-noir's guilt about colonialism, or about not being able to do enough to end it? In *Albert Camus of Europe and Africa*, O'Brien speculates about Camus's guilt without analysis of the text, and the speculation is taken as fact by Edward Said in *Culture and Imperialism* (New York, 1993). On the other side, Tony Judt asserts, similarly without inspecting the text, that *The Fall* reflects Camus's guilt for not speaking out earlier against Communism on "all the occasions when he had something to say but didn't say it, or else said it in a muted and socially acceptable form for the sake of personal sensibilities and political loyalties." Judt, *The Burden of Responsibility*, 114.

201 **hidden himself** Todd, *Albert Camus* (E), 343; see Todd, *Albert Camus* (F), 638, 818 n. 9.

201 **Camus's books** Sartre, "Albert Camus," 109.

201 **"same tone"** Ibid., 101.

201 **"one better"** Camus, *The Fall,* 130.

201 **in Budapest** He was still angry with *France Observateur* for publishing Naville's attack. See Contat and Rybalka, *The Writings of Jean-Paul Sartre*, 1:222.

202 **"Soviet bureaucracy"** Translated in ibid., 1:334.

202 **"lying and sclerosis"** Ibid.

202 **"lead to socialism"** Jean-Paul Sartre, *The Spectre of Stalin* (London, 1969), 6.

202 **"define the end"** Ibid., 87.

202 **"our strength"** Ibid., 46.

202 **"intervention inevitable"** Ibid., 47.

203 **"among the young"** Ibid., 27.

203 **"or not at all"** Ibid., 61.

203 **until he died** This is eloquently conveyed by Gerassi, *Jean-Paul Sartre*, 30–37.

205 **"their criminals"** Jean-Paul Sartre, *The Condemned of Altona* (New York, 1963), 141.

205 **"was my destiny"** Ibid., 145.

CHAPTER TEN

208 **died in 1961** Sartre, "Merleau-Ponty," 318–20.

208 **"your friend"** Beauvoir, *The Mandarins*, 512.

209 **6,000 to 20,000** John Talbott, *The War without a Name: France in Algeria, 1954–1962* (New York, 1980), 48.

209 **on civilians** See Talbott, *The War without a Name*, 81–87; and Horne, *A Savage War of Peace*, 183–87.

209 **word *independence*** Danièle Joly, *The French Communist Party and the Algerian War* (London, 1991), 48.

209 **realistic course** Raymond Aron, *La Tragédie algérienne* (Paris, 1957).

210 **"on non-Muslims"** Albert Camus, "Entretien," in Jean Daniel, *Le Temps qui reste: Essai d'autobiographie professionelle* (Paris, 1973), 257. The book was republished in 1984, as cited earlier, without Daniel's three concluding interviews with Malraux, Sartre, and Camus.

210 **"crushing it"** Jean-Paul Sartre, "Vous êtes formidables," in *Situations, V* (Paris, 1964), 67.

210 **degree of autonomy** Albert Camus, "Lettre à *Encounter,*" in *Essais,* 1878–79.

210 **with Sartre** Albert Memmi, "Intervention," in Jeanyves Guérin (ed.), *Camus et la Politique* (Paris, 1986), 194–95.

211 **"one of them"** Albert Memmi, *The Colonizer and the Colonized* (Boston, 1965), 39.

211 **"remain silent"** Ibid., 43.

211 **"paralyzes him"** Albert Memmi, "Camus ou le colonisateur de bonne volonté," *La Nef,* December 1957, 95.

211 **"of his own people"** Ibid.

211 **about Algeria** Lottman, *Albert Camus*, 639.

211 **"peace and equality"** Camus, *Essais,* 1882; for a report of the event, see Lottman, *Albert Camus*, 647–49.

211 **"before justice"** Camus, *Essais,* 1882.

211 ***Le Monde*** Albert Camus, "Lettre au *Monde*," in *Essais*, 1882–83. See Todd, *Albert Camus* (E), 378–79; and Lottman, *Albert Camus*, 648–49.

211 **"knowing about it"** Ibid.

212 **"slave galley"** Albert Camus, "Create Dangerously," in *Resistance, Rebellion, and Death,* 250; translation modified.

212 **"genius is over"** Ibid., 251; translation modified.

212 **"and systematically"** Jean-Paul Sartre, "A Victory," introduction to Henri Alleg, *The Question* (New York, 1958), 13.

212 **"victim or executioner"** Ibid., 14–15.

212 **Vians' party** This was confirmed by his 1961 preface to Fanon's book. See below, 222.

213 **Alleg's text** See Contat and Rybalka, *The Writings of Jean-Paul Sartre*, 1:345–46.

213 **complicity in sabotage** Sartre, "Nous sommes tous des assassins," in *Situations, V*, 68–71.

213 **"bloodshed at present"** Albert Camus, Preface to *Algerian Reports*, in *Resistance, Rebellion, and Death*, 118.

213 **"European children"** Ibid., 116.

213 **"slaughter and mutilate"** Ibid.

213 **"weakened country"** Ibid., 118.

213 **"European expansion"** Ibid., 120; translation modified.

214 **"this world"** Ibid., 113–14.

214 **"Algerian nation"** Albert Camus, "Algeria 1958," in *Resistance, Rebellion, and Death*, 145.

214 **"situation and poverty"** Aron, *La Tragédie algérienne*,109.

214 **"Algerian French"** Camus, "Algeria 1958," 148, quoted by Aron, *La Tragédie algérienne*, 108.

214 **"colonialism is over"** Ibid., 148.

214 **"Arabs of Algeria"** Ibid., 147.

214 **never faced** In *The Company of Critics* (New York 1988), Michael Walzer stresses the positive side of Camus's membership in the pied-noir community, and contrasts it with the "detachment" of Sartre's and Beauvoir's more abstract intellectuality. Yet there were times when a more abstract and universalist logic—"critical distance" rather than "critical connection"—might have helped

Camus to be realistic about the long-range needs of his community. In this sense, the danger of bad faith runs in both directions.

214 **"his silence"** Camus, "Algeria 1958," 153.

214 **"includes my family"** Camus, Preface to *Algerian Reports*, 113.

214 **"their race"** Ibid., 113; translation modified.

215 **"aggravating the terror"** Camus, "Les Déclarations de Stockholm," in *Essais,* 1882.

216 **leading the attack** Sartre, *Situations, V,* 89–144.

216 **seemed to ease** See Todd, *Albert Camus* (E), 402–11.

216 **"love and happiness"** Beauvoir, *Force of Circumstance*, 484.

216 **"he conclude"** Sartre, "Albert Camus," 111.

216 **"loved" *Camus*** Ibid.

217 **since the quarrel** Ibid, 109.

217 **"calf of realism"** Ibid., 109–10.

217 **"always through it"** Ibid., 109.

217 **"imprison Voltaire"** Cohen-Solal, *Sartre*, 415.

218 **from the natives** Memmi, *The Colonizer and the Colonized*, 13.

219 **threatening presences** See O'Brien, *Albert Camus of Europe and Africa.*

219 **"resistance to oppression"** "Discours du 10 décembre 1957," in *Essais,* 1072. Quoted in David Schalk, *War and the Ivory Tower: Algeria and Vietnam* (New York, 1991), 61–62.

220 **system of apartheid** Horne, *A Savage War of Peace*, 485–86.

220 **"in a corner"** Mouloud Feraoun, quoted in Horne, *A Savage War of Peace*, 430.

220 **to ward off** Horne, *A Savage War of Peace*, 486.

220 **shot dead** The story is told by Le Sueur, *Uncivil War*, 55–56, 83–84.

221 **"defend them"** Jean-Paul Sartre, Preface to Frantz Fanon, *The Wretched of the Earth* (New York, 1965), 11.

221 **"fall to pieces"** Ibid., 13.

222 **"put to the fuse"** Ibid., 17

222 **"under his foot"** Ibid., 18–19.

222 **"institutions of peace"** Ibid., 19.

222 **"higher quality"** Ibid., 20.

222 **"rooted out"** Ibid., 21.

223 **"doubt, executioners"** Ibid.

223 **Arab-hunting** The French word is *ratonnades,* literally "rat-hunts" and based on the pejorative pied-noir slang for natives in Algeria, *ratons*; the original English translation says "nigger-hunts."

223 **"Muslims alive"** Ibid., 23.

223 **"their power"** Ibid., 18.

223 **anti-colonial brutalities** At Benny Lévy's prodding Sartre commented on this

essay in his final interviews; see Sartre and Lévy, *Hope Now*, 91–94; several of his points are summarized above.

223 **Frantz Fanon** Sartre and Lévy, *Hope Now*, 91–94.

224 **"context of scarcity"** Jean-Paul Sartre, *Critique of Dialectical Reason* (London, 1976), 132.

224 **unforced cooperation** See Aronson, *Jean-Paul Sartre*, 243–86, and *Sartre's Second Critique*.

224 **"acting politically"** Sartre, Entretien inédit du 13 janvier 1958, in Daniel, *Le Temps qui reste*, 251. Sartre did not, however, continue to advocate pursuing liberation by any means necessary. Beginning in the 1960s he laid out a series of guidelines for revolutionary violence; these included turning to it as a last resort, limiting it to what is absolutely necessary, and making sure that it comes from the oppressed themselves. Thomas C. Anderson, *Sartre's Two Ethics: From Authenticity to Integral Humanity* (Chicago, 1993), 125–28. As Anderson perceptively points out, missing from these limitations is any distinction between targets of violence, whether noncombatants and civilians on the one hand or members of the regime or its military and police on the other. While Sartre later rejected political assassinations proposed by a would-be revolutionary vanguard while approving of the violence that wells up from the masses, he accepted the terrorism directed at Israeli athletes at the Munich Olympics of 1972. As Ronald Santoni shows, Sartre never resolved these tensions. *Sartre on Violence: Curiously Ambivalent* (University Park, PA, 2003). This complex and subtle study appeared as this book was in press. Paradoxically, however, the later Sartre can be credited as a force influencing the post-1968 French New Leftists to keep terrorism at a minimum compared with their counterparts in Germany, Italy, and the United States. His personal example of indulging in verbal but not physical violence, his presence as a Far-Left mentor of young activists, and his sponsorship of radical publications were among the factors that helped to restrain them. See Michael Scriven's insightful *Jean-Paul Sartre: Politics and Culture in Postwar France* (London, 1999), 63–79.

EPILOGUE

226 **"that to him"** Todd, Albert Camus (E), 415.

227 **Vietnam and Algeria** Ibid., 416, quoting from Jean-Paul Sartre, "A Plea for Intellectuals," in *From Existentialism to Marxism* (London, 1974), 252–53.

227 **"remain your friend"** Maurice Merleau-Ponty, *Parcours II* (Paris, 2000), 169.

227 **his "ultrabolshevism"** Maurice Merleau-Ponty, *Adventures of the Dialectic* (Evanston, 1973).

228 **"while before"** Beauvoir, *Force of Circumstance*, 259–60.

229 **"what a jerk!"** Gerassi, *Jean-Paul Sartre*, 185; translation modified.

229 **"Jeanson's article"** Sartre, "Self-Portrait at Seventy," 63.

229 **"friend I had"** Ibid., 64.

229 **"quite harshly"** Beauvoir, *Adieux,* 269.

229 **"Algerian War"** Ibid.

229 **didn't steal it** Jean Cau, *Croquis de mémoire* (Paris, 1985), 96.

229 **new directions** See, for example, Jean-Paul Sartre, "Kennedy and West Virginia," and Robert V. Stone and Elizabeth A. Bowman, "Sartre's Morality and History: A First Look at the Notes for the Unpublished 1965 Cornell Lectures," both in Ronald Aronson and Adrian van den Hoven, eds., *Sartre Alive* (Detroit, 1991).

229 **hell on earth?** See Aronson, *Sartre's Second Critique,* 150–83.

230 **"built on hatred"** Albert Camus, "Sur les Îles de Jean Grenier," in *Essais,* 1160. However, in his biography of Camus, McCarthy describes the tensions between the jealous teacher and his celebrated pupil and suggests that this foreword must have been galling to Grenier.

230 **"force of circumstances"** Sartre, "Reply to Albert Camus," 101; translation modified.

230 **ambiguous and delightful** See Aronson, *Jean-Paul Sartre,* 295–302.

231 **his own voice** See Aronson, "Sartre's Last Words?" Introduction to Sartre and Lévy, *Hope Now.*

231 ***erreurs de Sartre*** One of the chief compilers has been Bernard-Henry Lévy, in *Le Siècle de Sartre: Enquête philosophique* (Paris, 2000), 469–502. For a detailed discussion of the phenomenon see Michel Rybalka, *Bulletin d'information du Groupe d'Etudes Sartriennes,* no. 14 (2000), 79–128.

231 **nearly every turn** These descriptions by Lévy are quoted in Daniel Singer's review, "Sartre's Roads to Freedom," *Nation,* June 5, 2000. Lévy's *Le Siècle de Sartre* is, nevertheless, a searching appreciation of Sartre, which engages with his strengths and weaknesses and, among other things, contains one of the best appreciations of the Camus-Sartre relationship (408–24). Lévy's "rehabilitation" of Sartre tries to rescue the good, early Sartre from the bad, later one. For a discussion of Lévy in the context of the Sartre revival in France, see Elizabeth A. Bowman, "Thanks to B-HL, France Rediscovers Her Hated Sartre," *Sartre Studies International* 8, no. 2 (2003).

232 **over twenty years** Sartre's first political break was in the 1940s with his onetime friend Aron, who was on the editorial board of *Les Temps modernes* briefly, and then joined *Combat* as editorialist as Camus's role and influence were waning. Then he went on to pro-Western and anti-Communist articles for *Le Figaro.* At the same time he retained a lifelong interest in his old friend's philosophy, devoting two books to Sartre, both of which were unanswered. Now the old enemies greeted each other: "Bonjour, mon petit camarade," said Aron as they shook hands. Sartre died a few months later, and Aron spoke about his former schoolmate with considerable knowledge and, despite his strong criticisms, great appreciation. Reflecting on this later, Aron made clear that there had been no

reconciliation, that he still found Sartre's politics abhorrent, that their greeting had meant nothing special because it was the expression their generation of Ecole Normale Supérieure students had always used, and that he continued to disagree with Sartre's thought. But he unashamedly admired Sartre's intellectual power. It was also clear as Aron spoke and wrote that Sartre, although aiming constant hostile epithets at him, had been very much in his life and on his mind. See Raymond Aron, *Memoirs: Fifty Years of Political Reflection* (New York, 1990), 446–58.

232 **"must be saved"** Michel-Antoine Burnier, *L'Adieu à Sartre* (Paris, 2000), 111.

232 ***Black Book of Communism*** See Aronson, "Communism's Posthumous Trial."

232 **scorn for Sartre** In the words of the author of the English foreword, their goal is to "effectively shut the door on Utopia." Martin Malia, foreword to *The Black Book of Communism* (Cambridge, MA, 1999), xx. On p. xvii, Malia praises Camus, criticizing Sartre on the same page and on xv. See also Tony Judt, *Past Imperfect: French Intellectuals, 1944–1956*, and Judt, *The Burden of Responsibility*.

POSTSCRIPT

235 **a trip to France** Lottman says that Camus's purpose was to sum up his current attitude toward his "Saint-Germain-des-Prés friends, or [to give] dramatic form to the popular image of that group" (*Albert Camus*, 433). Todd sees the play as "an effort at self-criticism and letting off steam," as well as a parody of both Camus and Sartre and of the "heavy-mindedness of some of Sartre's crowd" (*Albert Camus* [E], 235). But neither addresses how directly and frequently Camus refers to Sartre.

237 **"life was ridiculous"** Janet Flanner, *Paris Journal, 1944–1965* (New York, 1965), 14.

237 **"a disgust for humanity"** Ibid., 49.

239 **as late as mid-summer** The notes do not deepen or clarify what Camus has already written. Some seem concerned with staging, others talk about M. Vigne adopting a Laplander and justifying this, still others are about other matters.

239 **absurdity and heroism** The play on absurdity calls attention to Camus as much as to Sartre, as Lottman and Todd indicate. If M. Néant ends up by sounding very Sartrean, his opening words on absurdity at first make it difficult to decide whether Camus is spoofing himself or his friend. We have heard something like this several times before in our story. In *The Fall,* Clamence goes from seeming to be a Camus-character to seeming to be a Sartre-character. In the story "The Renegade," it is difficult to discern exactly who Camus has in mind, someone like himself or someone like Sartre, with his character of the "progressive" European whose tongue is cut out by North African natives. We now see that "L'Impromptu des philosophes" was the first occasion where a Camus-character

and a Sartre-character seem, momentarily at least, to be blended. What does this device mean? In his "Defense of *Man in Revolt*" we have seen Camus suggest an answer: in putting the "progressive Left" on trial he was "at the same time putting what I believed on trial." In other words, his most controversial book was not only a critical exploration of others' attitudes, but of his own as well. His various criticisms and portrayals of Sartre might then, at the end of our journey, be seen as ways of understanding and criticizing himself. Obviously this question calls for further exploration.

239 **a commedia dell'arte** See Camus, *Carnets III,* 95, 110, 152.

239 **little intellectual depth** Camus was certainly capable of performing a philosophical critique, as he demonstrated in a letter to *La Nef* published in January 1946. An article about *Caligula* in that magazine had just claimed that the entire play was "only an illustration of Sartre's existentialist principles." He replied that he was "beginning to be slightly (very slightly) impatient about the continual confusion" identifying him with existentialism. His letter included the following:

> One doesn't accept existentialist philosophy because one says that the world is absurd. From this point of view 80 percent of Métro passengers, if I were to believe the conversations I hear there, are existentialists. Truly, I can't believe it. Existentialism is a complete philosophy, a vision of the world, which presupposes a metaphysics and an ethics. Although I perceive the historical importance of this movement, I don't have enough confidence in reason to enter into a system. This is so true that Sartre's manifesto, in the first issue of *Les Temps modernes,* seems unacceptable to me. ("Lettre à Monsieur le Directeur de *La Nef,*" in Camus, *Théâtre, Récits, Nouvelles,* 1745–46)

index